THEORY IN MARKETING

Theory in
MARKETING

EDITED BY

REAVIS COX
Professor of Marketing

WROE ALDERSON
Professor of Marketing

STANLEY J. SHAPIRO
Assistant Professor of Marketing

All of
Wharton School of Finance and Commerce,
University of Pennsylvania

PREPARED UNDER THE SPONSORSHIP OF THE

AMERICAN MARKETING ASSOCIATION

Second Series · 1964
RICHARD D. IRWIN, INC.
HOMEWOOD, ILLINOIS

First Printing, June, 1964
Second Printing, June, 1965
Third Printing, March, 1970

Library of Congress Catalog Card No. 64–21023

PRINTED IN THE UNITED STATES OF AMERICA

ACKNOWLEDGMENTS

THE SUCCESS of any volume of originally commissioned essays and the speed with which such a volume is published depend in large part upon the cooperation received from the participating authors. The editors consider themselves especially fortunate in this respect as all of the contributors to *Theory in Marketing: Second Series* submitted quality manuscripts within a reasonable period of time. Since the volume was originally considered as a platform from which those with something to say about marketing theory might speak, the various contributions are presented much as they were first submitted. However, the relatively few suggestions made by the editors were invariably received, if not always accepted, in the same spirit of helpful criticism in which they were intended. Also, the many ancillary tasks required of those who contribute to a book of essays were carried out by our contributors with precision, dispatch, and good cheer.

The contributions made in one form or another by other individuals also deserve recognition. Dean Willis Winn of the Wharton School used funds made available by the Ford Foundation to provide the editors with the necessary secretarial assistance. First drafts of many of the manuscripts in this volume were distributed to those present at the Marketing Theory Seminar held at the University of Colorado in August of 1963. Members of this seminar made a number of perceptive comments on the material they reviewed and many of their suggestions were subsequently incorporated into various manuscripts. Past marketing theory seminars can also be assumed to have had some influence on the intellectual content of the volume since many of the contributors have attended these annual programs since their inception in 1952. The two Chairmen of the American Marketing Association Publication Committee during the period that the book was in preparation—Professor Charles N. Davisson of the University of Michigan and Professor Edwin Lewis of the University of Minnesota—played an essential role in obtaining Association sponsorship. Mr. Richard Wendel, a Teaching Fellow at the Wharton School, provided valuable research assistance.

Finally, the editors would like to acknowledge the very real contribution made by Molly Horowitz, Eva Reiff, and Dolores Moss. These very diligent secretaries willingly and ably performed the necessary typing and clerical chores. Their flawless efforts are all the more noteworthy since this publication was only one of the many projects in which they were involved at the time.

THE EDITORS

PHILADELPHIA
MAY, 1964

CONTRIBUTORS

WROE ALDERSON is Professor of Marketing at the Wharton School of Finance and Commerce and Director of its Management Science Center. He studied at the George Washington University, the University of Pennsylvania, and the Massachusetts Institute of Technology. He is past president of the American Marketing Association, founder of the management consulting firm of Alderson Associates, and a member of the Operations Research Society of America and The Institute of Management Science. His publications include *Marketing Behavior and Executive Action;* the first edition of *Theory in Marketing* with Reavis Cox, published in 1950; *Marketing and the Computer* with Stanley J. Shapiro; and *Planning and Problem Solving in Marketing* with Paul Green.

HENRY B. ARTHUR is George M. Moffett Professor of Agriculture and Business at the Harvard Graduate School of Business Administration. Prior to his appointment at Harvard, Professor Arthur was an officer of Swift and Company for twenty years, holding the title of Economist. He received a Bachelors and an Honorary L.L.D. Degree from Union College and his Ph.D. in Economics from Harvard. He has been employed by the Federal Government in various research and consulting capacities over the years. His particular interest in markets and prices includes work he has done at Harvard, as well as in government and industry.

LEO V. ASPINWALL is Professor Emeritus of the University of Colorado, having headed the Marketing and Real Estate Division from 1934 to 1961. He served in the Bureau of Business Research of the University of Colorado from 1927 to 1934. Professor Aspinwall received his A.B. degree at the University of South Dakota and his M.B.A. degree at the University of Colorado. He has also served as Consultant and Technical Advisor with Alderson and Sessions in Philadelphia.

F. E. BALDERSTON was awarded a Ph.D. in Economics from Princeton University in 1953. He is a member of the University of California (Berkeley) faculty as a Professor of Business Administration and chairman of the Center for Research in Management Science. His central field of interest is marketing, and his research activity includes a study of lumber manufacture and distribution in Sweden, work in computer simulation, and research on multiple-branch organizations. Publications include *Simulation of Market Processes* (University of California, Berkeley); "Simulation Study and Management Decision Making" (Da-Gse Lecture Series, Athens, Greece); "The Evolution of Management Science" (Lecture Series No. 2, Center of Economic Research, Athens, Greece); and "Models of Multiple Branch Organizations" (*California Management Review,* Spring, 1962). He is presently on leave from the University in order to serve as Commissioner of Savings and Loans for the State of California.

SEYMOUR BARANOFF is Professor of Marketing at Pace College, teaches Marketing Theory in the Graduate Program at the City College of New York, and is currently Editor of the Marketing Series of the Pitman Publishing Corporation. He is Educational Director for the National Sales Promotion Executives Association and a Member of the Board of that organization's New York Chapter. Dr. Baranoff received his B.A. degree at Brooklyn College and his M.S. and Ph.D. degrees at New York University. He has been a consultant to a variety of retail organizations, contributed articles to professional and trade retail publications, and conducted basic research studies in retailing in cooperation with the Pace College Executive Research Conference and the Marketing Science Institute.

WILLIAM J. BAUMOL is Professor of Economics at Princeton University, having taken his Ph.D. at the London School of Economics. Currently associated with *Mathematica*, he has had a number of years experience with the consulting firm of Alderson Associates. Among his publications are *Economic Dynamics; Economic Processes and Policies; Business Behavior, Value and Growth;* and *Economic Theory and Operations Analysis.*

DONALD F. BLANKERTZ is presently Professor of Marketing, Vice Dean of the Wharton School for the Graduate Division, and Director of the Graduate Division of the Wharton School, University of Pennsylvania. He received his A.B., M.B.A., and Ph.D. degrees from the University of Michigan. Dr. Blankertz was one of the contributors to the first edition of *Theory in Marketing*. His writings also include *Marketing Cooperatives* (1940); *Profitable Retail Advertising* (coauthor); *Cases and Problems in Marketing Research* (with R. Ferber and H. Wales); as well as numerous articles that appeared in professional journals. His activities include business experience, service on The War Production Board and Headquarters, Army Air Force, and marketing research consulting. Dr. Blankertz is a member of the American Marketing Association and is listed in *Who's Who in America.*

PERRY BLISS is Professor of Marketing and Business Organization, and Chairman of the Marketing Department of the School of Business Administration of State University of New York at Buffalo. He received his B.A., M.B.A., and Ph.D. degrees at the University of Buffalo. Dr. Bliss is a Member of the National Board of Directors of the American Marketing Association, and has served as a Member of the Board of Editors of the *Journal of Marketing.* His most recent writings include *Marketing and the Behavioral Sciences: Selected Readings* and an article on "Business and the Consumer" published in *Business Topics.*

RALPH F. BREYER received his B.S. in Economics, M.A., and Ph.D. from the University of Pennsylvania, where he is Professor of Marketing in the Wharton School of Finance and Commerce. His major publications are *Commodity Marketing; The Marketing Institution; Consumer Plant and Equipment* (with Reavis Cox); *Bulk and Package Handling Costs; Quantitative Systemic Analysis and Control: Channel and Channel Group Costing.*

GERALD A. P. CARROTHERS is Chairman of the Department of City Planning of the University of Pennsylvania. He holds degrees in Architecture, in City Planning, and in Economics and Regional Planning. Dr. Carrothers has taught at the Universities of Manitoba and Toronto and has been a member of the research staff at M.I.T. He has been editor of the *Papers and Proceedings of the Regional Science Association* and was associated with Walter Isard in writing portions of *Methods of Regional Analysis*. Dr. Carrothers is also the author of several articles and monographs in his fields of interest.

RALPH CASSADY, JR., is Professor of Marketing and Director of the Bureau of Business and Economic Research at the University of California, Los Angeles. He received an American Marketing Association National Award in 1952 for "significant contribution to the advancement of science in marketing." He was elected to Hall of Fame in Distribution by the Boston Conference on Distribution in 1954. He is a member of the FAO Panel of Experts on World Fishery Problems and is listed in *Who's Who in America*. His publications include numerous articles in business, legal, and economic journals, as well as monographs and books. Among the latter are *The Nature of Competition in Gasoline Distribution at the Retail Level* (1951); *Price Making and Price Behavior in the Petroleum Industry* (1954); and *Competition and Price Making in Food Retailing* (1962).

C. WEST CHURCHMAN received his Ph.D. degree from the University of Pennsylvania, and taught philosophy at the University of Pennsylvania and at Wayne State. During the war, he was head of the mathematical section at Frankford Arsenal. In 1951, he went to Case Institute of Technology to start the Operations Research Group there. He now teaches at the University of California. In 1962–63, he was director of research at System Development Corporation and president of The Institute of Management Sciences. His published works include *The Theory of Experimental Inference; Prediction and Optimal Decision; Introduction to Operations Research* (coauthor), and other articles and books on philosophy and management science.

REAVIS COX, a past President of the American Marketing Association, is a member of the faculty of the Wharton School of Finance and Commerce at the University of Pennsylvania. He holds the A.B. degree from the University of Texas, Austin, and received his Ph.D. in Economics from Columbia University. Dr. Cox engaged in newspaper work in various parts of the United States between 1921 and 1931. He entered college teaching at Columbia in 1931, from where he transferred to the Wharton School in 1935. He is since 1938 Professor of Marketing. Dr. Cox has written or collaborated in writing many articles, reviews, and books concerned with various aspects of marketing. He is presently at work on a general study of distribution costs, a series of studies of the marketing of building materials, and a study of the structure of retailing in Europe. He is a consultant to various associations, corporations, and Government agencies.

RALPH L. DAY is Professor of Marketing at The Pennsylvania State University. He has served as Associate Professor of Marketing Administration at the University of Texas and as Visiting Assistant Professor in the Graduate School of Industrial Administration at the Carnegie Institute of Technology. Dr. Day also has a number of years' experience in industrial marketing and retailing, and consulting experience in industrial economics and marketing research. He is author of *Marketing in Action: A Dynamic Business Decision Game* and a number of professional articles.

PAUL E. GREEN is currently Associate Professor of Marketing at the Wharton School of Finance and Commerce, University of Pennsylvania, and an Associate Director of the School's Management Science Center. He received both his M.A. and Ph.D. at the University of Pennsylvania. Prior to joining the Wharton School's faculty in 1962, he spent 12 years in industry with such firms as the DuPont Company, Lukens Steel Company, and the Sun Oil Company. His current interests include the use of quantitative techniques in marketing planning and decision making.

MICHAEL H. HALBERT is Technical Director of the Marketing Science Institute, and was formerly a member of the advertising research staff at Du-Pont. He is a graduate of the University of Pennsylvania and has published a number of articles on marketing research and consumer behavior. He is associated with ORSA, The Institute of Management Sciences, and the American Marketing Association.

WALTER ISARD is Professor of Economics, and Chairman, Department of Regional Science of the University of Pennsylvania. He received his B.A. degree at Temple University and his M.A. and Ph.D. degrees at Harvard University. He has previously served as Consultant to T.V.A., Resources for the Future, Inc., Ford Foundation, and as Associate Professor of Regional Economics and Director, Section of Urban and Regional Studies, Massachusetts Institute of Technology. He is the author of ten books and reports and some eighty articles in his fields of interest.

ALFRED A. KUEHN is Associate Professor at the Graduate School of Administration, Carnegie Institute of Technology, and a consultant to a number of major advertisers. His research has centered about the analysis of consumer brand shifting and the related influences of marketing variables. Dr. Kuehn is coeditor of *Quantitative Techniques in Marketing Analysis* (Irwin, 1962) and has published a variety of articles on advertising budgeting, merchandising strategy, business games, and the use of heuristic programming in the solution of marketing problems.

LAWRENCE C. LOCKLEY is Chairman of the Department of Marketing of the School of Business Administration of the University of Santa Clara. He received a B.A. and M.A. degree from the University of California and an A.M. and Ph.D. degree from Harvard University. Dr. Lockley formerly taught at the Schools of Business of Columbia University, the University of Southern California, and New York University. He served as Chief of Census of Service Industries of the 1935 Census of Business, and as Manager of the Central Marketing Research Division of E. I. Du Pont de Nemours & Co. Among his recent publications are a *Monthly Economic Letter* and a report for the NICB entitled *Use of Motivation Research in Marketing*. He is co-author of *Cases in Marketing; Readings in Marketing; Advertising Agency Compensation; Marketing by Manufacturers;* and *Use of Consumer and Opinion Research.*

RICHARD M. MARTIN is Professor of Philosophy at New York University and one of the most prominent of philosophical logicians. He has previously taught at Princeton University, the University of Chicago, Bryn Mawr College, the University of Pennsylvania, and the University of Texas. The author of *Truth and Denotation; The Notion of Analytic Truth;* and *Toward a Systematic Pragmatics,* and a contributor to several volumes of essays, he has published numerous papers in various philosophical journals. He has had research fellowships or grants from the John Simon Guggenheim Memorial Foundation, the Fund for the Advancement of Education, the American Council of Learned Societies, and the National Science Foundation. A Guest Professor at the Universität Bonn in 1960 and 1961, he has given lectures at many universities in both the United States and in Europe. He is a member of the Editorial Board of *The Monist* and has served as a member of the Executive Committee and the Council of the Association for Symbolic Logic.

EDMUND D. McGARRY is Professor of Marketing and Economics Emeritus at the University of Buffalo. He received his A.B. from West Virginia University, his M.B.A. from Harvard University, and his Ph.D. degree from Columbia University. He was a Fulbright Senior Lecturer at the University of Edinburgh in 1955–56, a Visiting Professor of Marketing at the University of Arizona in 1958–59 and at the Instituto Post-Universitario per lo Studio dell' Organizzazione Aziendale in Turin, Italy, in 1961. His more recent writings include a chapter entitled "Some Functions of Marketing Reconsidered" in the first edition of *Theory in Marketing*, and several articles published in *The Journal of Business* and the *Journal of Marketing*.

REV. WILLIAM C. McINNES, S.J., is Associate Dean of the College of Business Administration at Boston College. He studied at Boston College, Brown, and M.I.T. and received his Ph.D. in Business Administration from New York University in 1954. He is a member of the American Marketing Association, the Academy of Management, and Beta Gamma Sigma. He also serves as a Director of the Ethics in Business seminars at Boston College.

WILLIAM S. PETERS was one of the contributors to the original edition of *Theory in Marketing*. He received his M.B.A. and Ph.D. degrees from the University of Pennsylvania. He is currently Professor of General Business at the Arizona State University in Tempe, Arizona. He has written on stock control and tourist surveys in the *Journal of Marketing*, on urban demography (*Social Forces*), and on the statistical analysis of regional consumption and trade patterns, published in the *Proceedings of the Regional Science Association*.

OTTO POLLAK is Professor of Sociology at the University of Pennsylvania, where he also serves as Director of a graduate training program on the Sociology of Intervention Systems under the auspices of the National Institute of Mental Health. In the past, he served as Social Science Consultant to the Jewish Board of Guardians of New York (1949–1956). Afterwards, he served as Research Consultant to Family Service of Philadelphia (1957–1962). His major publications are: *Social Adjustment in Old Age* (1948); *Criminality of Women* (1950); *Social Science and Psycho Therapy for Children* (with collaboration from the staff of Jewish Board of Guardians) (1952); *Integrating Sociological and Psychoanalytic Concepts* (1956).

WILLIAM J. REGAN received his Ph.D. degree in business from Stanford University in 1958. He is presently an Associate Professor at San Francisco State College, where he teaches Marketing subjects, Foundations of Business, and Public Relations, and where he serves as Coordinator of the Graduate Program. Several years of employment in retail merchandising and a summer fellowship with the J.C. Penney Co. in New York provided practical insight for this article. He has published a number of other articles and is an Assistant Editor of "Marketing Articles in Review" for the *Journal of Marketing*.

STANLEY J. SHAPIRO is an Assistant Professor of Marketing at the Wharton School of the University of Pennsylvania. He received an A.B. degree from Harvard College and earned his M.B.A. and Ph.D. at the University of Pennsylvania. He has coedited with Wroe Alderson *Marketing and the Computer* and is the author of an article entitled "Comparative Marketing and Economic Development: Some Unresolved Issues" to be included in the forthcoming volume on *Science in Marketing*, edited by George Schwartz. Dr. Shapiro has done research in the areas of marketing history, metropolitan information systems, and livestock marketing.

HANS B. THORELLI is Professor of Business Administration at the Graduate School of Business of the University of Chicago, where he came from Marketing Services Division of General Electric. He received his L.L.B., M. Soc. Sc., and Ph.D. (in Political Science) degrees from the University of Stockholm. His publications include *The Federal Antitrust Policy—Origination of an American Tradition;* and (as senior author) *International Operations Simulation, With Comments on Design and Use of Management Games;* as well as numerous articles on marketing, business policy, and organization theory.

HENRY WHITESIDE, who received his M.S. and B.S. from Washington University, St. Louis, is presently Principal of Webb School for Boys in Bell Buckle, Tennessee. Until recently, he was Lecturer in Marketing at the University of California, Los Angeles, and Managing Editor of the *California Management Review*. He is a former Vice-President and Research Director of J. Walter Thompson, Chicago, and prior to that, he was employed by Gardner Advertising Company, St. Louis.

TABLE OF CONTENTS

IV. MARKETING THEORY AND MARKETING MANAGEMENT

INDEX

INTRODUCTION

Reavis Cox

THE APPEARANCE of a second volume of essays concerned with theory in marketing offers a welcome opportunity to see how far and in what directions we have moved since the first volume appeared in 1950. Of course students have been developing theories of marketing for a much longer period. Perhaps the most influential single contribution thus far made—Shaw's first statement of the functional approach to marketing—dates back half a century. But the conscious effort to establish a sophisticated theory or set of theories as a joint effort of students in the field is about twenty years old. What have we achieved in that time?

The Development of Falsifiable Hypotheses

A number of essays in the present volume suggest that we are beginning to make some progress toward that *sine qua non* of effective theory —the formulation of falsifiable hypotheses. This is a supremely important development in these days when faith runs high in science as the device *par excellence* for acquiring reliable knowledge. The scientific method has been well defined as the method of tested, and therefore testable, hypotheses; and testable in this context means falsifiable by comparison with empirical evidence. The method never has proved any statement about the objective world to be true. It has proved that some very important statements are false. If we can reduce our ideas about marketing to propositions that are testable in this way, we shall have taken a long step toward creating a science of marketing.

The primary importance of Lockley's article in the present volume seems to me to lie in the fact that at least some of the "principles" he states are falsifiable by appeal to empirical evidence. Whether his "principle of drift," his "principle of diminishing sales effort," and so on, will pass the test of comparison with what we can measure, classify, and count is less important for the development of theory than the fact that we can subject them to the test. If they are false, we probably can prove them to be so by looking at some well-chosen examples. So, they can either be disposed of quickly or accepted as at least probable with a higher degree of confidence than one could otherwise feel.

1

Another example is cited by Regan when he discusses Hollander's test of McNair's "wheel of retailing" as a device by which the historical development of retailing can be described and explained. Hollander collects evidence from a wide variety of places and sources. While not statistical, it is persuasive in its conclusion that the "wheel" concept is not universally applicable. In contrast, we cannot be sure whether Regan's own concept of the historical development of retailing is either testable by reference to the available evidence or valid if it can be so tested. Regan identifies three stages through which he believes retailing has passed historically—these he calls simplex trading, multiplex trading, and omniplex trading. Unfortunately, his definition of these stages lacks precision and so will be difficult to quantify and expose to statistical tests. The diagrammatic analyses he offers, however, have much to be said for them as ways of breaking an extremely complicated problem down into pieces that can be subjected to effective analysis.

Shapiro's report on his test of the Alderson survival theorem as applied to a nonprofit organization illustrates both the importance and the difficulty of setting up falsifiable hypotheses and comparing them with the observable world. The result at which he arrives is not so much a refutation of the theorem as an indication that it is not really falsifiable. The meaning of "survive" in this context turns out to be highly uncertain, and the motivations of the decision makers are shown to be very hard to identify, let alone to observe and to measure. The organization Shapiro tested obviously went through a succession of severe crises, in the course of which it experienced a thorough reorganization and sweeping changes of function, policy, and personnel. Yet, Shapiro reports some difficulty in determining whether this behavior system survived at all and, if so, in what senses. Correspondingly, he finds it troublesome to say in what respect the system died or became extinct. Also, he was unable to determine as a matter of observation the extent to which survival in any of its several possible senses served as an objective or goal influencing the day-to-day calculations of the organization's officers and directors.

We must conclude that in its original relatively crude formulation the survival theorem does not stand the test of empirical checks. Alderson finds himself faced with the necessity either of abandoning the concept he has developed or of refining it in such a way as to preserve the truth it contains and to render the idea subject to effective testing. Which of these alternatives will prevail in the end remains to be determined.

Borrowing from Other Social Sciences

These essays make it abundantly clear that marketing theory is still closely attached to other social sciences. The attachment, however, is not an altogether comfortable one. In particular, many marketing men are not too happy at finding themselves classified as engaging in applied economics. Many of them feel that this classification is too restrictive, especially when economics itself is defined in the extremely rigorous but narrow fashion many economic theorists seem to prefer. Students of marketing know that many of the phenomena with which they have to deal belong at least as much in sociology, or psychology, or political science as they do in economics.

Some of those who are restive under the bonds that tie marketing theory to economics object not so much to being called economists as to the inadequacies they find in established economic theory. Arthur's article is a case in point. His central concern is with agricultural controls and their effects upon the structure and function of markets. He receives less help in his analysis than he thinks he should receive from general economic theory. Its concepts, procedures, and doctrines are too narrow to serve his purposes. He finds economists too much absorbed in trying to meet the tests of logical rigor appropriate to mathematics and too little interested in trying to describe, explain, and forecast what happens in the real world.

One way of dealing with this matter is for marketing students themselves to propose revisions in the established doctrines of economics. In substance this is what Blankertz does. He maintains that the conventional distinction between suburban and urban expenditure patterns, a distinction employed by many students of economics and social affairs, can lead to some erroneous judgments. If his analysis is correct, there is little or nothing in suburban living per se that makes the patterns of expenditure of families at given levels of income significantly different from those to be found in city living. The major factors controlling family expenditure, he believes, are family income and family size. Differences in aggregate expenditure patterns as between city and suburbs are to be accounted for primarily by differences in the distribution of families by size of income and by number of members. The significance of what he says seems to be that we often can explain differences in expenditure patterns among groups of consumers by reference to differences in the patterns of family income and family size without bringing in vaguely formulated variables such as "suburban" and "urban." Blankertz can thus be said not so much to reject the idea that in this context marketing is a branch of economics as to insist that the tools of analysis borrowed from economics be corrected, sharpened, and clarified.

Although there is much merit in what these critics of economics have to say, attention also must be paid to what Baumol offers in defense of economics. In substance he warns students of marketing not to write off economic theory too hastily and too completely, since there is still life in the old textbook model of the firm. More importantly, he reminds us that economic theory is itself not static. Economists also develop new ideas from time to time. If we are to dismiss economic concepts as irrelevant to marketing we must dismiss these concepts as they are today, not as they were in Alfred Marshall's prime or even as they were in the days when economics was what John Maynard Keynes, not yet honored by a title, said it was. Baumol obligingly demonstrates what he means by showing how established models can be modified to take into account observed phenomena that these models do not explain in their simpler forms.

Conspicuous among the ways in which efforts are made to develop marketing theory by borrowing from other fields is the frequent combination and joint application of ideas drawn from two or more disciplines. Alderson's article provides an excellent example of this approach. He uses in combination ecology, a concept borrowed essentially from biology with overtones of anthropology and sociology, and equilibrium, a concept developed in physics. As is usual with him, in discussing the applicability to marketing of such terms as "survival," "adaptation," "web," and "niche," and in considering the various kinds of equilibrium observable in marketing (and sought by those who participate in marketing), he throws out many flashes of insight and imagination that will stimulate thoughtful analysis by others.

The borrowing we do is not from the older disciplines alone. Students of marketing, and in particular those younger people who bring with them a better training in mathematics and statistical techniques than is ordinarily within the competence of their elders, are employing decision theory, information theory, operations research, mathematical models, and related instruments in their efforts to analyze marketing problems. Examples in the volume may be found in the articles by Green, Kuehn and Day, whose background is essentially in statistics, and in the article by Isard and Carrothers, two men prominent among the developers of regional science.

At least two of the articles show clearly, however, that we have not reached the bottom of the well in sociology, psychology, or political science. McInnes, it is true, suggests that we may already have borrowed too much from other disciplines; but Pollak and Thorelli find some new insights for us in their fields. Pollak draws upon a combination of psychoanalysis and sociology to point out some limitations in the concept of "rationality" as applied to consumer buying. His observations raise new and difficult problems for decision theory as applied to what the consumer does.

Thorelli, approaching the subject from the viewpoint of a political scientist, also has things to say that any would-be theorist in marketing must heed. By emphasizing "the breach between Euclidean economics and everyday decision making in the marketplace," he reinforces the doubts of marketing students concerning the applicability of conventional economics to their problems. As if we did not have enough to trouble us already, he also introduces into marketing the concept of political ecology as an addendum to the concepts of biological, anthropological, and sociological ecology about which much has already been heard.

Commenting upon what is involved in facilitating the economic growth of underdeveloped countries, Thorelli gives us another insight that is particularly important for marketing men. What he says in effect is that the problem of economic development is in considerable part one of changing attitudes rather than one of providing money, equipment, and technical skills. Being engaged currently in an effort to make some comparative studies of the structures of retailing in various countries, I am particularly sensitive to this point. After looking at many statements about the relationships of the number of shops to the number of people or families, the proportion of total retail trade taken by chain stores, the strength of consumer cooperatives, the relative importance of supermarkets and shopping centers, and other objective measures of "structure," I remain convinced that one of the most significant differences between European and American retailing lies in the attitudes of those active in retailing. Although there are conspicuous exceptions, there is reason to believe, for example, that retailers have been, and to a considerable extent still are, much less aggressive competitors in Europe than in the United States. European retailers seem to be relatively unconcerned with growth, as contrasted with security and stability, and considerably more inclined to act as distributors for producers rather than as suppliers for consumers.

My judgment as to the existence and importance of differences in attitude between European and American retailers is admittedly impressionistic. It has been derived from interviews with a narrowly limited number of people who were selected because they were believed to be well informed. A field survey designed to satisfy all the recognized rules for collecting data and drawing inferences from such data might or might not support these impressions. If their existence is verified, these differences in attitude must somehow be brought into the theoretical formulations we are trying to establish.

Thorelli also deals with an unsettled point of fundamental importance when he makes the statement that marketing science is normative. By this he means that marketing science is concerned with evaluating the relative merits of alternative actions. To some students of marketing, his statement will seem to be excessively narrow. It is closely related to the familiar confusion of technology with science that lies at the base of many debates as to whether science is even possible in marketing. Thorelli's position probably is valid if we think of marketing science as being, in an old-fashioned phrase, scientific management applied to the work of marketing executives in business. If we think rather of the problems of the academic scholar, whose basic interest lies in observations, descriptions, measures, and explanations as contributions to knowledge valued for their own sake, then we must have some doubts whether marketing theory or marketing science is really normative.

Some Dangers in Borrowing

The element of analogy is very important in many of the efforts made by students of marketing to borrow from other sciences. By definition, analogies are never perfect. We need not be too surprised, therefore, if they break down now and then as we try to use them in enriching our science.

Ideas, concepts, and procedures borrowed from other disciplines may cause still further difficulties. For example, turn again to the problems raised by Alderson's survival theorem. The concept of the struggle to survive in an environment too niggardly to support all those who are born into it comes, of course, from the theory of evolution. As we have taken the concept over, however, we have changed it in a very fundamental way by shifting our emphasis from the species to the individual. Students of marketing, and especially those who devote much of their working effort to consulting with particular enterprises, are basically concerned with the survival of the individual. This is true even when we concentrate our attention upon what Alderson has called an organized behavior system. In practice, the organized behavior system tends to look very much like what the economists have commonly designated a firm or an enterprise. Certainly those students of marketing retained to advise business managers are concerned with the survival of the individual firm in the narrowest definition of the term.

In the ordinary doctrine of evolution, however, nature is visualized as being utterly indifferent to the fate of individuals. Insofar as it can be considered to have any concerns at all, nature finds them in the fate of the species. Under its rules the important unit is the species, and a species "survives" as long as it can preempt a niche that will support a few individuals in successive generations. Which particular individuals survive and how long they survive are matters of no importance. Individual dinosaurs lived very short lives as geological time goes, but the species dinosaur flourished for many millennia. This persistence is a great success in evolutionary terms. In the end the dinosaur failed not because particular individuals died but because the entire species disappeared from the catalogs of living forms.

Clearly then, if we are going to use a concept of evolution to explain what goes on in the minds of managers of marketing, we need to modify the biological concept drastically. In particular, we must differentiate very sharply between the struggle to survive of, say, the species "country general store" and the struggle to survive of John Q. Doe, operator of a specific store at a specific crossroads. Perhaps the doctrine of evolution as an explanation of what happens is simply a variant of Adam Smith's doctrine of the invisible hand in that survival is a by-product of what individuals do as they seek to achieve their particular goals rather than the specific goal toward which they supposedly direct the energies of the enterprise. Shapiro failed to find that those managing the hog producers marketing organization in Ontario devoted much attention to survival as a goal. There was no evidence that the individuals concerned, whether or not they gave much thought to their own survival in some economic or political role, had any interest in or concern over the survival of the species of organization to which their particular buying group belonged.

Perhaps what we are dealing with here is just another aspect of the confusion between science as a set of rules or procedures to guide the individual and science as a generalized description or explanation. Science, like nature but unlike engineering or technology, is not concerned with individuals. It seeks to create not a large file of case reports but a small number of formulas, each as simple as possible, that summarize what one can say about an entire population after observing a large number of individuals. In the process of generalization we inevitably suppress much of what is known about individuals. We learn some important things about the forest but very little about the trees. In contrast, it is usually a specific tree upon which consultants and managerial scientists focus their attention.

Mathematics and Marketing Theory

In view of all the interest it has attracted, mathematics receives surprisingly little use in these pages. Time alone will tell whether this circumstance reflects primarily the limitations of the mathematical approach to marketing or the limitations of the students of marketing. Those who belong as I do to the older generation of marketing students will admit freely that their mathematical preparation for current ways of dealing with business and economic problems is far from adequate. Fortunately we have reason to hope that students better equipped to deal with mathematical formulations will emerge from the doctoral programs in ever increasing numbers as the years go by. We also should have available better and better data against which to test the validity of principles enunciated by mathematical and other theorists.

It is worth noticing that mathematical approaches to marketing will be greatly improved by the development of strong marketing theories. Each mathematical model makes a number of assumptions as to the nature of the relationships among the variables with which it is concerned. Such relationships can be derived from the observation of what John Q. Stewart has called "empirical regularities." We shall be happier with them, however, when they are supported not only by observation but also by theory. That is, we shall feel better when one can say that the relationships are not accidental but are subject to a rational explanation.

Peters considers one matter that troubles many of those who work with statistical decision making. As he points out, decision making under uncertainty has received much attention of late. The discussion usually involves the use of subjective probabilities as one element in the procedure proposed. We often simply assume that the decider can arrive at such

probabilities and state them in a precise quantitative form. Peters shows
that the assumption is at least partially justified by the results of much
work done on the problem of how these probabilities are in fact arrived at
by consumers. No doubt similar studies can be made of how such probabilities are arrived at by business managers who have decisions to make.
What Peters has to say is of interest, it may be noted, not only for what
it tells us concerning the development and improvement of theories about
decision making, but also because it illustrates graphically an important
circumstance of our times. This is the bewildering speed with which a
new idea can develop into a massive literature. The number of people who
are ready to seize upon any promising suggestion and add to it their own
extensions and elaborations is very great. It does not take long for a fruitful suggestion to spawn a literature overwhelming in its magnitude, bewildering in its diversity, and often esoteric as to content. How the student
of marketing can keep abreast of the flood is an unsolved problem.
It may be mildly comforting to know that he will find the same situation
in every field of human knowledge; but he still will be appalled by the
magnitude of the challenge.

Kuehn and Day provide an example of how the concept of probability
can be used in efforts to solve problems of marketing. They demonstrate
quite clearly that consumers who seem to behave capriciously or irra-
tionally when measured in terms of "exact" categories become understandable when measured in terms of probabilities. This is a very useful
conclusion but raises some difficulties when put alongside the paper by
Peters. Evidently Peters, Kuehn, and Day are talking about different
things when they use the term "probability." There has been much controversy among philosophers, psychologists, mathematicians, scientists,
statisticians, and others, as to the nature of probability—whether it is at
base logical, mathematical, statistical, objective, subjective, psychological,
personal, and so on. We may safely assume that most students and practitioners of marketing know very little about the difficult literature in
which this controversy is embodied. They nevertheless suffer from confu-
sions that arise because those who write about the use of probability
models in marketing do not always make clear what kinds of probability
they have in mind and what consequences flow from their selecting one
as against other possible concepts in their analyses.

Progress in Establishing an Independent Discipline

It would be most encouraging if the essays in this symposium showed
beyond serious doubt that students of marketing are making substantial
progress toward setting up a systematic and disciplined theory of their
own to supplement and possibly to supplant the offerings of related disciplines. Unfortunately, the essays do not demonstrate this fact. As Halbert tells us bluntly, "Marketing has no theory that is defensible on the
grounds of its logical consistency, philosophic adequacy, or experimental

foundation." To a degree, we are lending as well as borrowing, although some doubt exists as to how eagerly our offerings are being accepted by those in the more firmly established disciplines. For example, Blankertz in his "law of uniformity" is really trying to refine and improve upon some of the correlations conventional economists have made between consumption patterns and other measurable or observable variables. Whether they will accept the gift remains to be seen.

Cassady's work with price warfare also should be of interest to a great many economists. His immediate purpose seems to be not so much to work out better (that is, more realistic) price theories as to provide better observations than we have had in the past of what really goes on in one sector of the marketplace. His report should be helpful to economists who want to make their theories conform more closely to the empirical evidence. Cassady tells us that in some circumstances—circumstances it may or may not be helpful to designate as oligopoly or imperfect competition —direct price competition takes the form of a war triggered by the failure of the prevailing price structure to reflect closely the economic situations in which the competitors find themselves. The war ends in a truce or equilibrium that holds until demand or supply conditions change enough to require another drastic adjustment. Whereupon a new war is likely to break out. Meanwhile, minor, day-to-day adjustments can be made by so-called nonprice forms of competition.

If this argument is true, perhaps one can conclude also that even in a fully competitive market a continuous small but direct adjustment of prices is not the normal response of competitors to changes in the forces of supply and demand. Perhaps small adjustments are made more commonly in nonprice forms, which are really disguised or indirect price changes. Only drastic adjustments in supply and demand may need for their resolution overt changes in price leading to the outbreak and settlement of a price war.

McInnes, following up his suggestion that we should borrow less rather than more from other disciplines, proposes in effect that we start with our own concepts, use them to analyze own our problems, and work out our own mathematics and logic to deal with them. As his starting point he takes the concept of the market and defines marketing as an actualization of market potentials. It is this actualization that generates exchanges. Generalizing from some observations of market phenomena, McInnes offers a model of the marketing system as he sees it. There is no doubt that what he does is useful as a guide to philosophical explanations of what marketing is, what it does, and why it exists. Whether this approach can be used to formulate hypotheses that will be testable by quantitative empirical research has not yet been demonstrated. McInnes himself is hopeful.

Whiteside suggests that we need to improve our concepts of the entities with which we are dealing in our study of marketing if we hope to achieve substantial results in our analyses. This thought can be helpful in dealing with Regan's effort to describe the historical development of retailing and to predict what lies ahead as regards the structure of retailing and the nature of the retail institutions it comprises. Perhaps the appearance of a new retail form emphasizing direct price competition is itself a sort of price war that breaks out when the forces governing the supply of and demand for retail services (as distinct from the supply of and demand for the goods retailers sell) change drastically. In between times, adjustments to smaller changes in the structure of supply and demand can be made by nonprice modification of the amenities and services offered to customers, with or without changes in formal prices.

Lockley's idea that vendors as they compete with one another are continually trying to upset the existing equilibrium in their favor also needs to be brought into this analysis. It can be argued that when they modify the products or services they offer to the public, competitors want to throw the market slightly out of balance, but not by enough to start a war because of the retaliations such actions invite.

The Vitality of Old Ideas about Marketing

There is some danger that the older approaches to marketing will be buried under an avalanche of literature authored by those developing new approaches. This may happen not because the newer approaches are really better but rather because they attract the attention of ambitious students, and by their nature lend themselves to endless proliferation. This danger is particularly acute when a new approach restricts itself to abstract analysis based upon assumed data. Like exercises in pure mathematics or pure logic, structures derived from such procedures invite repeated additions by other logicians who change the assumptions and extend the analysis. They also lend themselves to continuous refinement in minute detail as critics spot and work to eliminate flaws in a predecessor's reasoning. Some scholars find this type of approach particularly appealing because they do not have to test their conclusions against empirical evidence.

It is therefore encouraging to find strong evidences of vitality in some of the oldest ideas students of marketing carry about in their kit of analytical tools. A good example is McGarry's discussion of the merchandising function. Shaw's early "classic," to which we have already referred, introduced an idea that will not die. He maintained that the best way to study marketing is to organize what marketing does under some "functional" classification. McGarry shows us that the ore in this vein is far from exhausted. We may agree or disagree with the particular formulations McGarry makes, but we cannot get away from the impression that he is dealing with substance, not empty logic.

Breyer also works with one of the oldest concepts in the literature of marketing—that of the channel of distribution. He was one of the earliest developers of the concept of the channel and long ago applied it to the analysis of marketing problems. What he writes here can therefore be thought of as his latest addition to almost a lifetime of study using this basic approach.

The channel problem is clearly one of the major managerial problems in marketing. Virtually every basic textbook in marketing talks about it. Describing precisely what the channel structure is at any time, explaining why it came into existence, and predicting what it is going to become— these are intellectual problems that challenge the most able analyst. Yet the concept of the channel remains vague and uncertain in much of the use made of it. This concept must be clarified and refined if it is to serve as a solid base for a theory of marketing, for the collection of statistics designed to test hypotheses formulated in such a theory, or for the devising of principles to be followed in the management of channels. This is the task Breyer has set himself. How far he has moved may be judged by comparing what he says with what used to be said when it was thought that the subject had been pretty well covered if one differentiated between "direct" and "indirect" channels and referred to the process of making channels more direct as "integration."

Balderston's article offers another sophisticated example of the development of the channel concept and its use in the study of marketing. He also gives a good illustration of how model building supported by a variety of mathematical techniques can be applied to marketing problems. Balderston himself emphasizes the importance of channel analysis as a device that will help managers choose among alternative policies. It is also clear, however, that the sort of work he and his associates are doing can become extremely useful to pure theorists who have no immediate interest in showing managements how to optimize the returns they receive from their operations.

The Self-conscious Marketing Theorist

Of considerable interest, and perhaps significant in some important way, is the fact that despite the progress students have made, they continue to be self-conscious about how to create a marketing theory and what they will have once they have created it. Consider, for example, the article by Bliss in this symposium. Undoubtedly outside observers will find it extremely interesting that marketing theorists continue to worry about what they mean by "knowing" and what it is possible for them to "know" under any definition of the term.

The constrast between students of marketing and physicists in this regard is striking. Most physicists leave to the philosophers and particularly to the philosophers and historians of science such problems as what does man really "know" about the physical world as the result of the physicists' endeavors, how does man know that he knows, what are the limitations on his knowledge, and so on through the long list of metaphysical problems appropriate to the cogitations of philosophers. In their own work the physicists seem to go along confidently accumulating what they assume to be knowledge and developing their discipline by formulating mathematical equations and inequalities. They do not bother very much with what the philosophers say about their work. Perhaps the time has come when marketing men also should cease to worry about these philosophical problems; come up with whatever judgments, observations, or conclusions they can devise; and let others fret about the significance of their work.

That we in marketing are not ready to resolve the problem by ignoring it is indicated by the presence among the authors in this symposium of a professional philosopher and a professional logician. Churchman takes a new look at a problem we have already considered: Are theory and science to be treated as aspects of understanding and explaining or as aspects of management? He expresses himself as being dissatisfied with the distinction between science and technology or engineering. Instead he proposes that theory be considered a mode of management and that managers be classified into opportunists, planners, and idealists. Perhaps there can be found here a clue to the best answer to this troublesome problem.

Martin has some penetrating things to say about the logical difficulties marketing theory must solve if it is to achieve perfection in its statements. Much of what marketing men have written is characterized by looseness of expression, vagueness of idea, and uncertainty of analysis. Marketing theory obviously has a long way to go before it achieves anything that can be thought of as even approximating perfection.

It should be helpful to those who are students of marketing rather than philosophers, either amateur or professional, to have writers such as Churchman and Martin lift a corner of the curtain and give us a glimpse of the great debates going on among the philosphers themselves as to the nature of language, logic, and theory. It is consoling if not encouraging to realize that the problems we have in marketing are only a particular variety of a much larger type of problem characterizing virtually all of human knowledge.

Since life is short and most of us have difficulty in encompassing even the field of marketing, we are likely to be somewhat hesitant about wandering off into the vast expanses of philosophy. Consequently, one may well ask how a student of marketing is to learn enough about mathematics and logic to use them effectively in his studies. The easy answer is a variant of the familiar advice as to what to do when you need to have a field surveyed but do not yourself know how to survey it: "Hire a surveyor." Perhaps we shall have to hire philosophers and logicians to work with us. A side effect of our endeavors may be the development of a new staff job, that of the advisory philosopher. We shall still have to decide, however, when a surveyor is needed, who is a competent surveyor, when his results are good, and how to use these results.

If we decided in the end that we do need an advisory philosopher for marketing, Halbert demonstrates by his article in this symposium that he will be a formidable contender for the job. He sees theory as being needed for at least two purposes that are different but not, it is to be hoped, mutually exclusive. One is to help business executives think about marketing in ways that will make it more manageable. The other is to help students who look at marketing as observers rather than as participants make what they see less confusing and more understandable. Halbert points out clearly where we stand in our search for such a theory, what help we are receiving from other disciplines, and what we still need to do.

Where We Stand

Insofar as the material appearing in this volume is a fair sample of the work being done throughout the profession, we can come to some conclusions. Unquestionably the level of sophistication of this volume is much higher than that of the first volume. The persistence of efforts to obtain respectable and defensible theories in marketing provides continuing evidence of the richness of this area of human behavior and experience as a field for study. Nevertheless, our discipline is still characterized by the presence of much uncertainty and confusion. We are far from having formulated a body of theory as impressive as that achieved by the theoretical economists and, even more importantly, by the theoretical physicists. Not settled as yet is the question of whether we seek a theory for operating managers, for their staff associates and advisers, or for the academicians. Perhaps we seek all three but need to define them as three different jobs to be done.

A final, more personal comment needs to be made. If there is any one individual who deserves the credit for stimulating, encouraging, and goading us into struggling as best we can with the formidable problems the various authors touch upon, it is Wroe Alderson. As a coeditor of this volume, he will no doubt object to being singled out in this way for attention and praise. However, nothing is more striking about this volume of essays than the frequency with which his name comes up as the source of some idea or the stimulator of the work that led to some idea. Not only in his own writings and in the specific articles he has encouraged others to write, but also in his general support of theory as a field of study and in his organization of a long series of seminars concerned with the subject, he has unquestionably been the dominant force keeping us to the task of working out an effective body of theory. Those who have had the privilege of being stimulated by what he has done in this area can only hope that there lie before him a great many more years during which he will continue to drive us into doing what we all know needs to be done but would be tempted to evade in his absence.

I. The Design of Marketing Theory

1. THE REQUIREMENTS FOR THEORY IN MARKETING*

Michael H. Halbert

IN ANY examination of the organized behavior system we called civilizations, we can observe some people devoted to reflection on the nature and operation of various activities of such systems. These people are often distinguished from those more active in the conduct of affairs by calling the first group, thinkers, and the second group, doers. It is abundantly clear, however, that in many areas of human activity, developments occur without any serious attempt to be reflective about their origins, their current activities, and their possible future. The greatest periods of culture growth have not necessarily coincided with the periods of greatest reflection. If we look at the current state of marketing activity and marketing thought, two apparently incongruous pictures appear. In the world as a whole and in the United States particularly, marketing is flourishing. It is growing and changing more quickly than perhaps any other institution of the society and rapidly increasing its impact on the total economic system. As an activity, then, marketing is both dynamic and progressive.

But when we look at the development and the present state of marketing theory the picture is just the reverse. From the point of view of the aid that theory can furnish to the practitioner, marketing has very little to offer. From the viewpoint of the established sciences, marketing has no theory that is defensible on the grounds of its logical consistency, philosophic adequacy, or experimental foundation. Why is it that we have and can have a marketing practice that is highly successful without an equally successful development of marketing theory? Before we can develop the requirements for theory in marketing we must look at the way the grounds differ for developing a practice as opposed to developing a theory adequate to explain that practice.

In every culture studied by anthropologists or historians, some form

---

* This chapter is based on part of the material to be published in a book entitled *The Theoretical Basis for Marketing Science,* developed by the Marketing Science Institute. It is reproduced with the permission of the Institute.

of exchange has existed. That exchange should develop is predetermined by two factors that are to be found in any organized human society—specialization and motivation. Not only are productive skills an objective of specialization within a culture, so also is specialization in resources and specialization in wants and desires. When specialization is coupled with motivation, exchange naturally occurs. Anything so vital a part of a society tends to be come institutionalized, acculturated, and ritualized. This is borne out by anthropological studies in which every culture examined shows some ritualistic aspects associated with the problems and practices of exchange. In fact, in early societies most of the exchange structure was integrated with the religious and other ritualistic aspects of the system. There is also good reason to believe that exchange of goods between tribes had its origin in a practice designed as a symbolic guarantee that the tribes were at peace reather than as a method of trading surpluses for mutual satisfaction and use. As man increased his ability to produce more finely differentiated means for the satisfaction of his wants and desires, the importance of the exchange function in culture increased until at the present time we have in many parts of the world cultures that could be described as marketing societies rather than as agricultural or manufacturing societies.

But to do a thing well it is not necessary to have an adequate theory of how it is done. Many people eat well without being nutritionists; men learned to see long before they learned the theory of optics; women had babies before they had obstetricians. The two necessary conditions for the development of a theory are the need for it (either for practical reasons or for intellectual satisfaction) and the availability of the techniques to develop the theory. The practice of marketing has attracted many able, competent, and highly motivated men who serve as marketing executives and marketing managers. These men realize that their marketing activities are growing more and more difficult as the complexity of the marketing environment increases and as the commitment to marketing alternatives becomes more binding for longer periods of time and involves larger and larger proportions of the total corporate assets. Thus, each of these men begins to develop marketing theory for himself.

In general the marketing executive or manager does not call it marketing theory. While he is concerned with gaining a practical understanding of how his system works, this concern is manifested in finding rules of thumb and immediate guides to action; his "theory" is implicit rather than explicit. His motivation is intensely practical and directed towards the performance of an almost impossible task. He needs ways of thinking about this task that tend to make it manageable and that enable him to relate his experience in past situations to his current problems. It is this kind of theory development that supports the notion that experience is the best teacher. Yet to learn from experience one must have a framework of concepts within which to interpret past events; otherwise experience cannot be relevant and nothing can be learned from it.

At the same time that the pressure for more adequate theory in marketing develops from the people who operate the marketing system, a parallel pressure for the development of theory is generated by the force of intellectual curiosity. Every large segment of human activity has been subjected to an attempt to organize it on the part of people with theoretical interests. The extent to which this attempt is successful usually depends upon the availability of appropriate analytic and conceptual techniques, upon the total amount of manpower and intelligence devoted to the effort, and upon the cooperation of the operating system being studied. In the current case for marketing theory it appears that the conditions are more favorable than they have ever been in the past for the emergence of a more definitive science in marketing. More and more, intellectually curious people are studying the business system and the marketing part of that system. More and more, they are given adequate opportunities, adequate cooperation, and adequate support.

The purpose of the theorizer is to understand the phenomenon he investigates. Since understanding is a communicative process, especially so in science, the theorist would like to develop concepts about which he can talk in such a way that a great deal can be explained with a few concepts and that the confusing world of appearances can be reduced to an orderly world of understandable relationships among definable entities. Thus, the conventional theorist is motivated more by his dislike of confusion than by his desire to improve the operation of the system while the practical operating marketing man is motivated by his need for improved practice rather than by his intellectual desire to order his world. But each needs the other, and it often turns out that the theorist is an intensely practical, down-to-earth researcher, while the pragmatically oriented practitioner is concerned with concepts, theories, definitions, and relationships as much as his more theoretical counterpart. The theoretician needs data from operating systems. He needs a laboratory from the real world to experiment in, to check his hypotheses, and to validate his theories.

The main concern of this essay, then, is with the requirements for theory in marketing. This task presupposes some description of what is meant by theory (in marketing or other disciplines) and a statement of where marketing theory currently stands. Accordingly, one finds discussed in the remaining sections of this essay—

1. The meaning of theory as used in this chapter, including the place of observation and measurement in theory.
2. The contributions which marketing and other fields (e.g., business, law, economics, the behavorial and methodological sciences) have made to what currently exists as marketing theory.

3. The requirements which continued developments in marketing theory will have to meet.

The Meaning of Theory

Like all abstractions, the word "theory" has been used in many different ways, in many different contexts, at times so broadly so as to include almost all descriptive statements about a class of phenomena, and at other times so narrowly as to exclude everything but a series of terms and their relationships that satisfy certain logical requirements. We shall want to take a somewhat middle position here and say that at the very least a theoretical statement within the domain or framework of marketing must do more than merely describe the phenomena being observed. Even here, though, we must be careful, for to describe implies to have observed, and to have observed implies a choice as to which aspects of the marketing world should be chosen for observations.

Also implied in any description are choices of what the measurements or classifications used in the descriptions were. All of these are decisions which are based ultimately on a theory or a set of theories that explain what it is important to observe and report about marketing phenomena. Thus, the process of observation or recording or description cannot be divorced from the process of theory construction.

Perhaps more important to our present viewpoint, however, is the notion that we cannot accent the somewhat arbitrary, slightly naive descriptions of scientific method that lay out a sequence including observation, the construction of hypotheses, and theory development, as though theory were the end product of this process rather than an integral and necessary part of each phase of it. This is all by way of emphasizing the distinction between implicit and explicit theory.

Even in the simple recording of a sale of any company's product, there is implicit not only a theory that describes what a sale is, who the parties to the sale are, and what the price is, but the much more pervasive background theory that tells us why it is worth using up company resources to record the sale at all. If it should be recorded, then *how* it should be recorded implies what future operations are to be performed on the data, and this in turn implies knowing the information requirements for managerial decisions and, ultimately, policy decisions. The often heard complaint of analysts or executives that "the data weren't recorded in a way that makes such and such an analysis or decision possible" is an illustration of the awkward results of being implicit instead of explicit about the requirements of the information. Therefore, we shall constrain our discussion of theory at this point to explicit theory.

It is in this sense that a theory must be more than just a recording of observations or the results of an analysis performed upon such data; it must also be more than just a set of definitions and logical operations that can be performed on the definitions. There must be the complete statement of the operational or "semantic" relations between the terms in the definitions and the behaviors in the real world to which the definitions refer.

One of the most common definitions of theory is an explanation of a set of phenomena. But explanation involves people (data don't explain themselves). Why would anyone *want* to explain a set of phenomena? Why, to *use* the explanation, of course—to use it in making decisions, perhaps for the most basic of research needs, perhaps for the most pressing of practical reasons. A theory, then, must include an explanation of its own uses; that is, how one can make decisions with it. Thus (ideally) a theory exists for a set of phenomena when all of the possible decisions to be made involving those phenomena can be explained. These explanations must fit all possible individuals who make these decisions, and the fitting must be satisfactory to the theorist involved.

The inclusion of "must be satisfactory to the theorist" leads to rather interesting consequences. The emphasis on the relation of theory to decision making implies that people are a part of any theory and that the purpose of the development of theory is not to explain and to understand the physical world as separated and apart from human interests and human endeavor, but rather that any adequate notion of theory must include the behavior of people who are operating on the class of phenomena about which the theory is constructed. Thus, if one wishes to find out about the theory of metals, one observes people behaving with metals and asks them to explain the decisions they are making. Those people who can explain most adequately have the best theories of metals, and one usually expects to find them in scientific research laboratories. Following the same line of reasoning, if one wishes to find out about theories of marketing, one observes people making decisions about marketing phenomena, be they buyers or sellers, executives or manufacturers, business or government policy makers. Here we run into what at first looks like an anomaly, for we do not always find the most adequate explanations of the decisions made about marketing in our universities and academic circles.

The more adequately developed the theory of an area is, the more likely we are to find a professional, academic class concerned with this theory. In mathematics, astronomy, chemistry, physics, etc., we expect to find (and do find) the most adequate explanations for the decisions made about these areas in our better universities; yet in most of the business disciplines and in many of the social and behavorial disciplines it is at least as likely that adequate explanations for decision making will be found among the better practitioners (and the more thoughtful and reflective ones) as it is that they will be found in universities or in academic research areas.

This is by no means a criticism of academia; it rather reflects the state of theory development in these areas. If marketing is to develop and proceed as a science in future years, we can confidently expect the development and presence of marketing theory in the university circles to increase very rapidly and to take its expected and respected place among the other scientific disciplines in academic circles. That this is not yet the case merely provides us with a challenge for the future. The interest exists; the practice of marketing goes on and provides the resources wherewith to develop a theory.

The Present State of Marketing Theory

The current state of marketing theory reflects not only the contributions of marketing practitioners and theorists but borrowings from other disciplines as well, e.g., (*a*) business, law, and economics; (*b*) the social and behavorial sciences; and (*c*) the formal or methodological sciences. Marketing, however, has no recognized central theoretical basis such as exists for many other disciplines, notably the physical sciences and, in some cases, the behavorial sciences. This lack of a conceptual foundation for marketing can be seen most clearly in an analysis of the course materials in the marketing curricula of the graduate schools of business in this country. In a survey recently completed by the Marketing Science Institute it is worthwhile noting that out of the 158 curricula surveyed, in which 140 references are used, only 31 of the references can be classified as dealing with marketing theory to any significant degree. This does not reflect a lack of interest in theory on the part of academicians, but rather a lack of available material for the teaching of marketing theory— material that meets the academic and scientific requirements for such an undertaking.

Such a condition is not surprising in light of the point of view developed in the first section of this chapter. Since marketing has been considered by our culture primarily as an art or technique rather than as a science, most of the formal content that current marketing *has* collected has been derived from other areas rather than being original with marketing.

If we are to examine the rest of organized science for the current basis of marketing theory, in which particular directions shall we search? This depends, of course, on the object of the search. Science is a complicated activity, and there are many different ways of classifying its total content. The classification scheme used here is in terms of the different levels of generality of the material.

Content. The *content* material of a science consists of the observations, measurements, and descriptions of the phenomena studied. These are usually called facts or data to distinguish them from theories, although this distinction is not as clear as one might think.

Techniques. The second kind of borrowing that marketing can expect from other areas is the borrowing of *techniques.* Broadly speaking these are the ways of generating the content material just described. Techniques include both the process of measurement and analysis. Moreover, many techniques arising in other fields must be modified and adapted before they are suited to marketing. The questionnaire from psychology and public opinion polls has had extensive development by market researchers, and is more useful than when it was first borrowed. Conversely, many of the early difficulties with motivation research were due to the attempt to use the techniques of clinical psychology without modification or adaptation to the requirements of marketing.

Concepts. The third class of material that comprises a science consists of the concepts, theories, and generalized ideas that form the abstract but essential element which distinguishes a science from an art or practice. Content is concerned with "what"; technique is concerned with "how"; concept is concerned with "why." The borrowing of concepts from another science is extremely dangerous, but can be extremely productive. The literature of marketing, of the other business disciplines, of the social and behavioral sciences, and of the management and methodological sciences was examined to see what it offered in terms of relevant content, technique, and concept. Table 1 puts in perspective the kinds of material we can expect to borrow from the various fields of study.

TABLE 1

CONTRIBUTIONS OF VARIOUS SCIENCES AND DISCIPLINES TO
A SCIENCE OF MARKETING *

Science or Discipline Area	Type of Contribution		
	Content	Technique	Concept
Marketing	Major	minor	
Business disciplines	Major	minor	
Behavioral sciences	minor	Major	minor
Methodological sciences		minor	Major

* The entries in the table are to suggest the relative importance of the current potential of each scientific area for the content, the techniques, or the concepts of an emerging science of marketing.

While marketing theory, as currently constituted, does include the concepts of such noted scholars as Alderson, Converse, and Aspinwall, it can be noted from Table 1 that the major contribution of marketing as a discipline to marketing as a science has been in the area of content. We shall wish to examine next the contributions which other fields of study have made (and appear likely to make in the future) to theory in marketing.

The Business Disciplines, Law and Economics

The business disciplines are the first group to be reviewed for potential contributions to marketing theory. It is no surprise that their literature, as well as that of marketing, consists mostly of content and not technique or concept. The relevant books, articles, and speeches are mostly concerned with the operation of various aspects of the business system and not with the theoretical aspects of that operation. Taken as a group, business disciplines supply guidelines on how to recognize a problem when it exists, and what kinds of data are useful in helping to solve the problem. In many cases, the writings also supply a recommended solution. In law and in economics things are a bit different. Both of these areas have a long history, and each has developed its philosophers and theoreticians.

Most of the other areas of business, however, are in no better state than marketing with respect to having a basic conceptual or theoretical framework. If we may distinguish between a discipline and a science on the grounds that a discipline has techniques and a science has theories, then we must go further and say that techniques supply answers to questions and theories supply criteria by which answers are to be judged.

For example, in the area of real estate management there is an extensive literature on how to locate a suburban shopping area and on the evaluation of specific urban sites for specific types of business enterprises. These prescriptions, however, are developed from an analysis of experience and a history of similar situations on which data are available. Few of the writers claim that their advice is deduced from general theories of real estate; rather, it is induced from a careful analysis of experience. There is much practical value in borrowing the techniques and content of the business disciplines, but since these disciplines are themselves lacking established theoretical bases it is not surprising that looking for marketing *theory* in an area that has little enough of its own is unfruitful.

There is a well-developed body of literature concerning the philosophy of law, but its theoretical content is related more to sociology and political science than it is to marketing. Those writings in law which deal with the aspect of legal impingement on marketing do so in general with a rather superficial bow to the notion that the function of law is to enforce the will of society on the recalcitrant few. Thus, there is seen in antitrust discussion some confusion as to what the will of society is. The interpretation of some cases suggests that it is to protect consumers from the evil effects of monopoly power. Other cases and their interpretation suggest that it is to protect some business enterprises from their more successful competitors.

Perhaps the most fundamental idea from legal philosophy that has applicability to marketing theory is that in a society where men are motivated by their own diverse desires, the function of law is to provide a structure that permits maximum attainment of individual desires with minimum infringement on another's ability to attain his desires.

Economics has a longer history than most of the other business disciplines and has a well-developed body of economic theory. Much of this theory has found its way into marketing, and concepts of price elasticity, of market equilibrium, and of economies of scale are familiar to most marketers. The concept of economic man has been of great value to marketing but has also had some unfortunate consequences. But many of the most pressing problems in marketing develop from exactly those aspects of the system that economic theory has chosen to ignore.

This choice on the part of economists was quite conscious and deliberate, for if they did not make these simplifying assumptions, they could not have developed the great wealth of material that has been so useful to date. Economic man is assumed to have full and complete information about the decision under consideration. In classical economics when the problem of price equilibrium is being considered, it is assumed that all customers and all suppliers know the location of all products, and that the information about price, quality, quantity, and availability is instantaneously available and completely correct. Thus, the entire area of negotiation which is so vital to marketing is assumed out of the picture by the economist's emphasis on a single point of equilibrium.

Perhaps the central theoretical concept of economics has been that of rationality. Economic theory holds that people behave in their decision making as though they were trying to achieve the most of some value, often called utility and often measured in money. In his definition of "economic man" the late von Neumann was careful to point out that he had no reason to believe that people behave according to the assumptions that he was making, but that these assumptions were necessary in order to develop the theory advanced in the *Theory of Games and Economic Behavior*.[1] The concept of rationality so central to economic theory appears on examination to be a very difficult concept indeed. If we define rationality as behavior designed to maximize utility and then define utility as that which behavior tends to maximize, we are not very far ahead. It can easily be shown that for any behavior there is a set of values such that the behavior is rational (maximizing) for those values.

If we pursue this argument to claim that values as well as behavior need to be rational, we are led into the impossible morass of attempting to distinguish rational values from irrational values. The present state of value theory barely enables us to investigate the problem of consistency of values let alone to establish their rationality. The only useful definition of rationality seems to be "your behavior is rational to me if I can explain it." This definition of rationality is a measure of my ability to explain and really tells me nothing about your behavior.

The Social and Behavioral Sciences

The concept of rational and nonrational behavior leads us naturally to a consideration of the social and behavioral sciences as a source for marketing theory. If the economists have done marketing a disservice by overemphasizing the rational and economic motives of human behavior, the social scientists and, in particular, the psychologists have attempted to

---

[1] John von Neumann and Oskar Morgenstern, *Theory of Games and Economic Behavior* (2d ed.; Princeton, N.J.: Princeton University, 1947).

swing the pendulum to the opposite extreme by emphasizing irrational and psychodynamic motivations. It is true that a housewife shopping in a supermarket is not solely motivated by the dollars-and-cents consideration and does not have a small computer in her head. It is also true that her marketing behavior cannot be explained adequately by considering only the state of her psyche, the social pressures on her from friends, and the sex symbolism of the various package designs.

Although the "economic man" (or woman) described for us by the classical economists forms only a part of any adequate marketing description of real people, it is an essential part. The complex and perhaps confusing picture of the customer drawn for us by the behavioral sciences seems more like the kind of human beings we meet every day than does the rather pallid utility maximizer of the economists. There is more to behavioral science (and even to psychology) than Freudian psychodynamic personality theory, however, and the overall picture drawn from anthropology, political science, demography, and linguistics, etc., as well as from psychology is extremely useful. Their major contribution is more the opening up of a whole new area of exploration than the contribution of any specific set of techniques or directly usable ideas.

The behavioral sciences permit, and in fact require, that marketing science take explicit account of the human and social aspects of individuals and of groups engaged in marketing behavior. No longer is the housewife/consumer or the vice president of marketing allowed the refuge of "human nature." If we are to develop an adequate science of marketing we must investigate the people and the social groups that perform the marketing actions with the same scientific care and conceptual honesty with which other scientists investigate the phenomena of interest to them. What the behavioral sciences in total offer is a method of approach and a set of techniques that enable us to design and implement that investigation. These sciences have developed a whole group of techniques that are admirably suited for use in the development of marketing theory. This is not so much because these techniques are useful for measuring marketing behavior per se, but rather that the behavioral sciences have had to deal with the problem of measuring and analyzing systems which to a large extent they cannot control.

The history of successful measurement and experimentation in the physical sciences rests largely on the development of laboratory techniques and the ability to manipulate the environment and the objects of study in very closely controlled and easily repeatable situations. With the social sciences it is almost the reverse. There has been a great deal of laboratory experimentation in psychology, but even in that science and particularly as one moves to personality theory and to clinical psychology, the laboratory becomes less appropriate and the actual world of human behavior is the arena in which the methods of science must be applied in order to develop appropriate data and to test suggested hypotheses. Many of the other social sciences have very little laboratory work behind them, such as sociology, anthropology, linguistics, and political science. Each of these disciplines has some recourse to the laboratory, and so also does marketing.

But each of these disciplines has faced squarely the problem of making measurements and testing hypotheses in the on-going world in which very few of the variables can be controlled, and the particular objects under study, i.e., human beings, have memories and cannot be put through the same procedure twice since they will remember their earlier experiences. They cannot be told to act as if they were trying to maximize their monetary return. Even in the laboratory, values are not so easily manipulated. Since marketing and marketing research are concerned with these same kind of phenomena, it is not surprising that the techniques of social survey research have been so thoroughly borrowed and amalgamated into marketing that now there is as much developmental work in this area being done by market researchers as there is by opinion research specialists.

There are two further specific conceptual notions from the behavorial sciences that should be incorporated into marketing theory. The first of these has to do with the notion of values as they affect human behavior and especially as they influence the decision-making process. In most of the formal work in statistics and decision theory, values are taken as inputs to the decision-making process. The major notion of decision theory is that the decision maker chooses among alternative courses of action so as to achieve an outcome with the highest value to him, based on the incomplete information that he has at the time of decision making. The extensive and complex developments in decision theory treat primarily the problems that arise because of different kinds and amounts of information and various kinds of available alternatives.

At first glance decision theory appears to be a very satisfactory approach to problems. People certainly do tend to choose those activities which they find rewarding and pleasant, and to avoid those which they find unpleasant and distasteful. Some of the oldest notions in psychology center around this so-called pleasure-pain principle. Yet we frequently see the reverse situation where people tend to like what they do, rather than do only what they like. A taste for avocados must be cultivated, and it is common to be indifferent to chamber music at first and only come to like and appreciate it after several hearings. The extreme proponents of this position claim that the major function and goal of society is to inculcate good taste (values) in the arts, in architecture, food, dress, music, literature, and in ethics and morals. Certainly a person's values are as much conditioned and determined by his behavior as the other way around.

Even if we take the naive position, however, that values are fixed inputs to decision making, we are left with the extremely difficult question of where *do* the values come from and what causes them to change. There is good reason to believe that maturation plays a large part in the develop-

ment and change of values. Our children look forward with eager anticipation to the time when they are old enough to stay up all night whenever
they want to, or to eat as much candy as they want. They refuse to believe their elders when they are told that their values will change, and
by the time they can stay up as late as they want, they will be glad to get
to bed early, and that they will lose their taste for candy or at least
develop tastes for some of the foods they now dislike. The seven ages of
man apply no less to his psyche and his values than they do to his physical
development. Of all the behavioral sciences it is the sociologists and anthropologists who have the longest history of careful attention to this
problem of the generation and modification of value systems.

There are, then, three major ideas or concepts from the social and
behavioral sciences that should be incorporated into the development of
any science of marketing. The first of these is that there is no simple route
to the explanation or understanding of human behavior. The physical and
biological sciences are not adequate to explain the kinds of behavior with
which marketing men are concerned. The economists have provided an
approach to this type of understanding, but it requires the behavioral
sciences to broaden that approach so that the human beings described are
realistic ones, and behave the way the real humans we know behave.

The second important notion of interest to marketers is that our scientific research methods must be turned inwards as well as outwards. We
must study marketing operators and marketing sicentists and their behaviors, assumptions, and attitudes as carefully, as rigorously, and as dis-
passionately as we study any other aspect of the marketing system. It is
always easier, as the history of science has shown, to study *things* rather
than *people* and to study *other* people rather than *ourselves*. But if we
are ever to understand and predict the marketing system and the culture
of which it is a part, we must take the final step and study ourselves. Only
after we know what we do and how we do it can we begin to do it better.

The third contribution from the behavioral sciences lies in their development of concepts and techniques for the study of on-going real systems
involving people in their normal interactive environment. The development of the social sciences in large part is the development of measurement and analytic devices for studying these kinds of systems. While
laboratory research has its place, the current limitations on the development of social theory are the limitations imposed by lack of resources and
lack of available techniques for field research. The same is true in marketing, but there is much that marketing can learn from the successes and
failures of the behavioral scientist in coping with this difficult but crucial
problem.

Method vs. Content in Science

When we turn our attention to the formal methodological sciences to
see what they have to offer of use in marketing theory, we must first un-

derstand the essential difference between the methodological sciences and the content sciences. Any science must have two parts: it must have a philosophy and it must have content. The content refers to the various phenomena to be studied and explained by the particular science. In our case these are clearly the phenomena of marketing. The philosophy of a science refers to the *rules* by which one can *test* statements concerning the phenomena under study. Some sciences are described and named by their content area, such as chemistry, physics, aerodynamics, biology, marketing, etc. Some sciences are described and named by the kind of formalisms with which they deal. Here we have the areas of mathematics, logic, epistemology, theology, etc. To the extent that there is any unified meaning to the notion of "the scientific method" it is derived from these formal sciences rather than from the content sciences.

It is often stated that marketing will never be a science like physics and that unless it is it will not be a "real" science. Remarks of this type indicate confusion between the methodological sciences and the content sciences. Physics is a content science no less than is marketing. It has been able to employ more adequately the techniques of logic and mathematics and it is on *this* ground rather than because physics deals with material objects that it deserves accolade as an exemplary science. This distinction is brought out quite clearly in the following passages:

> As a rule [market researchers] acquire competence in conducting investigations not by mastering principles of scientific inquiry but rather by developing habits of research that are modeled on examples of sound scientific workmanship. Moreover, discussions that are intended to articulate the structure of scientific procedure usually have no direct bearing on the detailed problems with which [marketers] are normally occupied. In consequence broad issues in the logic of science are rarely matters of active concern to practicing [marketers], and most of them devote little serious thought to such "philosophical" questions as the functions a satisfactory theory must perform, how theory is related to the gross objects of familiar experience, and whether the abstract notions of a theory denote things that have some kind of . . . reality.
> Nevertheless, questions of this sort may become pressingly relevant to the work of [market researchers], and may require careful attention from them, when new experimental discoveries or radical innovations in theoretical ideas create puzzles that profoundly challenge entrenched scientific doctrines or habitual models of analysis. . . .[2]

The author, Ernest Nagel, is a recognized philosopher and is here distinguishing between the behavior of content scientists and the behavior of philosophers of science. However, as can be seen by the bracketed inserts in the preceding quotation, the item was quoted as though the parties concerned were market researchers and marketers. The original article, however, had the term "physicists" where we have inserted "market researchers." The author was thus talking about physics and physicists

---

[2] Ernest Nagel, "Review of *Understanding Physics Today*," by W. H. Watson, *Scientific American*, Vol. 209, No. 4 (October, 1963), pp. 145–49.

and not about marketing. The way in which marketing science *should* be like physics is in the detailed, careful, and extensive use of logic, mathematics, and the rest of the *formal* mechanisms of science. This is the same way in which marketing science should be like astronomy, biology, or any other science. Logic is useful for all sciences, and one cannot have a science without it. One *can* have a science without cyclotrons. In our borrowings from the methodological disciplines, we should not look for concepts that are directly relevant to marketing as a content area, but rather those which are relevant to the development of any science.

In summary, current marketing theory has borrowed extensively from the content area of the business disciplines, and the concept and technique area of economic theory (marginalism, opportunity costs, economic rationality). The social and behavioral sciences have provided techniques of measurement and experimentation and concepts useful to the study of people as opposed to things. Finally, it is apparent that we shall have to look increasingly to the methodological sciences to provide concepts and structure in marketing theory.

This brief excursion into the major sources of theory in marketing is but a prelude, however, to a more central question: What are the requirements that theory in marketing should meet? We discuss this question (and the important role that the methodological sciences play in the attempt to answer it) in the concluding section of this essay.

The Requirements of Theory in Marketing

There are many aspects of theory development and testing in marketing for which we shall make increasing demands on the methodological sciences. In this essay, however, we shall discuss only the one notion mentioned earlier—the notion of criteria for the adequacy of theory. The reason for singling out this particular aspect of philosophy for consideration is that much of the confusion in the discussion of possible and proposed theories in marketing (and in business) arises out of a lack of understanding of the *different ways* in which a theory can be inadequate.

These criteria are discussed in logic and philosophy under the names of *syntax, semantics,* and *pragmatics,* although the first two of those terms mean something quite different from their standard common English usage. The discussion treats each in turn. Although our attention is directed to this particular part of the philosophy of science, we should not forget that all of the material that bears on scientific method and adequate theory formulation and testing is of relevance to the design of any science and most especially so to the conscious design of a new science.

One of the earliest concerns of the science of logic has been the exploration of relations among statements. These are called formal properties and depend for their validity on the rules of logic rather than linguistics, semantics, or operational definitions—topics with which we shall deal later. In a formal deductive system there are certain terms or elements called *primitives* which are undefined within that system. It may come as a surprise to some that logic insists on primitives or undefinable terms, yet it was proved in 1931 by the German philosopher and mathematician, Kurt Gödel, that no system can be designed that is completely self-contained; that is, that every term in it can be defined in the language of other terms. This came as a culmination of the fruitless search for a completely defined and probably self-consistent system of arithmetic. After the primitives have been introduced, the next step is to develop postulates and axioms which relate these primitives to each other, thus defining *operators* or terms which serve to interconnect the primitives in the deductive system. For example, in the simple statement "$1 + 1 = 2$" the "1's" would be primitives of the system and the "$+$" and "$=$" would be operators or relational terms.

We are all familiar with the "if . . . then" type of statement such as "if all A is B and all B is C, then all A is C." This is the syllogism, the prototype of all deductive reasoning. A criticism sometimes offered against this type of deduction is that it tells you nothing about the real world; it merely says that *if* certain things are assumed, then certain consequences follow. Admittedly, this type of statement does not tell us anything about the real world. Such statements only tell us things that are logical consequences of what we already know, but this can be a most valuable source of knowledge.

There is a rather famous logical conundrum in which a student is accusing his teacher of wasting his (the student's) time. The student says, "Is what you teach me logical?" To which the teacher replies, "Yes, indeed." The student then says, "Therefore, all of the consequences are contained in that which I already know—the premises." The teacher acknowledges that this is so, and then the student asks, "If there is anything in the consequences that is not contained in the original premises, then the logic is faulty, is it not?" Again the teacher agrees, and the student can now propound the conundrum, "Then everything you teach me is either faulty or that which I already know. Why then should I study with you?"

The fallacy in this particular conundrum is rather obvious; it depends upon the meaning of the term "that which I already know." The conclusion that with only five letters to a license plate I can identify 11,881,376 different automobiles is *contained in* the structure of arithmetic and multiplication but is not *known* to me until I perform the appropriate calculations. In the statement of the conundrum, the student confuses the terms "contained in" and "already known."

Syntactics. Many of the most fruitful theoretical systems in the history of science have been fruitful because of the richness of the conclusions that could be deduced from a very few original postulates and axioms. We shall deal later with the problem of fruitfulness and richness, but here we are concerned with the formal aspect of theory that is called *syntactics*. Syntactics has to do with the legitimacy of the operations that can be performed on the elements that form the theory. Many of the historical paradoxes in logic derive from using the same term in two different ways or from performing operations on a term that are not appropriate.

In marketing one often tries to solve problems by relating the present problem to other similar cases. This is often what is meant by using experience. Let us suppose we can adequately define "similar," so that we can tell when one situation is similar to another. (This problem will be considered when we discuss *semantics*.) The *syntactical* problem of the legitimate statements we can make about "similar" remains. There is a particular difficulty inherent in this approach that can be used to illustrate the syntactical nature of the problem. If situation A is similar to situation B and situation B is similar to situation C, then is situation A similar to situation C? The answer may be of some importance to us, since we want to know whether we can use our experience gathered, say, in test markets for A in assessing the probable outcome of test markets for C. The logician would inquire as to whether the relationship of similarity possessed the property of being transitive.[3] If it is defined so that it does, then we can safely conclude that the situation A is similar to situation C. But the definition of "similarity" that makes it transitive might restrict the term so much that A no longer is similar to B.

There is an even more powerful question that the logician might raise. Is the relationship of similarity in the *equivalence* class of relationships? This is not the place to explore these particular logical notions,[4] but it is clear that A may or may not be similar to C depending on the way we define similarity. This brings us to the major point of the illustration. Most of the use of marketing terms such as "similar situation" are not defined well enough so that these logical questions can be answered. Only as a science becomes mature and develops theoretical statements that have been accepted and used for some time does it attract the attention of methodologists and philosophers who then begin to examine the syntax of the theories and often point up extremely fundamental problems in the statement and manipulation of these theories.

The major function of the logician in this situation is to call our attention to the ambiguity in our definitions and in the use of language. This is a formal ambiguity and not the problem of operational definitions. It is

---

[3] Let R be any relationship that can hold between two elements of a set (a, b, c, . . .). The relationship is written "aRb." This is read, "a bears the relationship R to b." R is transitive if and only if, given aRb and bRc, we can deduce aRc.

[4] A relationship is in the equivalence class if it is transitive, reflexive, and symmetrical. Reflexive means that aRb implies aRa. Symmetrical means that aRb implies bRa.

the distinction between the use of language to describe relations and the use of language to describe real world phenomena. It is clear that the notion of similar is a relational notion, not an empirical one.

The problems of syntax that we have examined here are mostly trivial and rather easily solved, but many of the most serious problems in logic, whose solutions would affect the fabric of all deductive sciences, are syntactical in nature. In the development of marketing science we will need to pay attention to these problems or, in the most literal sense, we will not know what we are talking about.

Semantics. A theory may fulfill all of the syntactical requirements with complete adequacy, and still have serious faults. The statement of the primitive notions, the operators, and the permissible manipulation of the symbols in which the theory is stated may all be complete and logically correct. The difficulties may lie with the way in which the theory is related to the real world. We have said previously that science contains two kinds of statements. Some of these statements are to be tested by an analysis of their syntax, i.e., by formal rules, and some of the statements are to be tested by experimentation, i.e., by observations made in the real world. If we are to use a theory to tell us what observations to make, then we must be clear, precise, and complete in our description of what constitutes a relevant observation and how to interpret such observations so as to test the theory. This area of the philosophy of science is called *semantics.* Unfortunately, this term has a substantially different meaning in the branch of linguistics that deals with the human response to the meaningfulness of symbols. In philosophy the notion of semantics is confined to the relationship between the elements and operators in a formal statement of theory and to operations that can be performed on real phenomena either in terms of manipulation or in terms of observation. Most of the pleas in the literature and in private discussions to define terms better are pleas for more rigorous attention to the semantics of the theory being discussed.

Logicians and general system theorists are prone to develop theories in terms of abstract symbols. Thus, some of the rigorous formulations of probability theory define probability as a number between zero and one that can be manipulated in certain ways (i.e., that possesses certain syntactical properties). Some of the proponents of this definition of probability act as if they are unconcerned with the "meaning" of probability as a measurement device or a predictive device or a descriptive term for real occurrences. Theories of this type are at least explicit about their relative unconcern with the semantic problem. A greater difficulty arises when theories use nouns and verbs from common language. Although the terms are in some cases defined syntactically by the theorist so that his manipulations are permissible, they often do not have clear definitions with reference to observations. In almost all cases, common English (or any other natural language) uses words too loosely for direct carry-over to a scientific usage.[5]

A good example of this is in the use of the term "preference" as it is used in economic utility theory and in consumer analysis. There is much discussion as to whether preferences are transitive or not, i.e., is it logically (syntactically) required that if I prefer lobster to chicken and prefer steak to lobster that I must prefer steak to chicken? Actual investigations of human preferences have revealed that in certain situations preferences are not transitive. In spite of this fact, many theoretical formulations using the concept of preference require that it be transitive. To a logician this is merely a case of using a particular term in two different ways, and if these two separate meanings are kept clearly differentiated, there is nothing but an awkward language problem; there is no logical difficulty. The logical difficulty occurs when the theorist is not specific about which meaning of preference he is using, and thus may try to describe actual consumer data on the basis of a theory that requires (in its formal sense) that preference be a transitive relationship.

As a more basic point in the discussion of the semantic requirements for theory, we can examine the requirements of an operational definition of preference. How do we measure preference? Should a person's preference be defined as the response to a verbal inquiry, or in terms of some actual behavior? If we take either of these positions we must specify the particular form of the verbal inquiry or the particular kind of behavior that we wish to observe. We also must know how to interpret the verbal response or the observation of behavior. If we examine the first possibility and say that we wish to define preference as the response given by a subject to a particularly worded question, we rapidly get into serious difficulty.

Suppose I am asked a particular question and in flippant or recalcitrant mood I answer exactly opposite to my real feelings. Do we wish to accept my response as a measurement of my preferences? If we do, then we need a theory that is useful for prediction even when the responses are from recalcitrant and flip respondents. If we do not, then we need a set of definitions that enables the interviewer to tell when I am being flip and recalcitrant and what to do about it. Since there is so much difficulty in defining preference as a verbal response, it will certainly be no easier to distinguish between a well-intentioned cooperative response and one that is designed to irritate the interviewer. It is this line of reasoning that has occasionally led psychologists to define intelligence as the score achieved on intelligence tests. If one accepts that definition seriously, the predictive power left to the concept of intelligence is the ability

---

[5] For further development of this point, see the discussion of explication in R. Carnap, *Introduction to Semantics* (Cambridge, Mass.: Harvard University Press, 1948).

to predict scores on intelligence tests—not a very happy state of affairs.

If the operational definition of preferences in verbal terms is so unsatisfactory, let us examine the definition of preference in terms of real behavior. If the reseacher wishes to measure my preference for lobster over chicken, and he observes me in a restaurant with a menu on which both lobster and chicken are available, and I choose chicken, is he then justified in saying that I prefer chicken to lobster? Maybe he should observe me in other restaurants at other times. Perhaps I would behave differently if the price for lobster were only half the price for chicken. Perhaps I would behave differently if I were at home rather than in a restaurant. Maybe the person with whom I am dining exerts an influence on my choice. Or perhaps I don't really care, and I pick the item that appears first on the menu. How the researcher handles these questions determines what he *means* by the term "preference." The investigation of preference in its behavioral setting has been one of the most difficult and awkward problems in psychology and in the management sciences.

Certainly a minimum requirement for the measurement of preference seems to be that the preference should be exhibited in more than one situation. If I am given a choice for President of the United States between Roosevelt and Dewey, and if one wishes to measure my preference by my voting behavior, they will have to examine a situation that occurred only once and will never occur again. Is it meaningful therefore to talk about my preference for Roosevelt or Dewey as President? If we say, "Yes, it is," we then have some extremely difficult syntactical problems related to the possibilities in terms of the predictive use of such a measurement. If we say, "No, it isn't," then we must specify how many observations *are* required for an adequate measure of preference. It is in this area of semantics that one can be arbitrary if he wishes, but the meaning of the definition of preference and of theories using it will be greatly affected by the particular result of the arbitrary decision.

Pragmatics. Even if a theory is adequately described in terms of its semantic and syntactic aspects, it still may not be a very good theory. The way in which it fails to be good may be because of a lack of attention to the richness or fruitfulness of the theory in terms of the needs, desires, and problems of the people who may have use for it. The aspect of the analysis of theory concerned with the *use* of theory is called *pragmatics*. We require of our theories that they be rich, fruitful, and useful and apply to important problems as well as that they be formally adequate and definitionally precise.

An investigation of the pragmatic requirements of theory takes us out of the realm of logical formalism and into the more difficult, but perhaps more vigorous, area in which philosophy is concerned with real problems of on-going human systems. If we explore seriously the pragmatic aspects of science, we are led rather directly to a concern with the problem of value. It is not enough for a theory to have a large number of deducible theorems; these theorems should apply to important problems. A theory with but a few deducible theorems that applied to the establishment of universal peace would be considered far more valuable than a theory whose outcome permitted the detailed construction of innumerable TV Westerns. The difficulties of dealing in a philosophically adequate way with the problem of value, though, are far too extensive to be more than indicated in this essay. Probably the central difficulty is the decision as to *whose* values at what time should be the controlling factor. If we adopt the notion that it is always the decision maker's values, then a lawyer should make decisions based on his best interests, not his client's. This approach also makes it difficult to deal with group decision making. It is not always easy to tell whether a theory will be useful and to whom. Many theories have been developed in "pure mathematics" and have later proved to be of high pragmatic value. The intellectual curiosity of one generation is the practical engineering tool of another.

Implications: Marketing Theory and Human Values

When we examine the goal requirements for marketing theory, we can identify at least three groups whose values must be overtly taken into account. These three groups are: the *institutions* engaged in the process of marketing (manufacturers, intermediate sellers, retailers, industrial sales groups, etc.), the *consuming public*, and the *government* policy maker. Even a cursory analysis of the goals for marketing theory and marketing science held by these three groups reveals conflicting as well as cooperative goals. Any major development of marketing science that served the goals of only one group at the expense of either of the other two would pose the same kind of ethical problem that nuclear physicists faced when almost their entire effort was devoted to harnessing the destructive energies of atomic power, rather than to a balanced development including the productive and medical uses of atomic energy.

In fact, one of the most difficult but pressing of all problems facing the development of theory in marketing is the resolution of conflict in goals. This is not only a problem for the eventual science of marketing, it is a problem for all existing sciences and disciplines, and indeed it is a problem for the individual. Every single person has to resolve conflicting demands on his time, on his resources, on his loyalties, on his emotions. That this resolution is not easy nor always satisfactory is shown by the statistics of our mental hospitals and the case records of our psychoanalysts. That it is no less satisfactory on a national and international level is shown by the state of world affairs and of the armaments' race. The problem belongs to all of humanity, to philosophy, to mathematics, to politics, and even to marketing science. The requirements for theory in marketing and the problems engendered in meeting these requirements will surely tax the ingenuity and patience of the most resourceful and dogged of marketing theorists for years to come.

2. AN APPROACH TO MARKETING THEORY

Lawrence C. Lockley

MARKETING serves as the bridge between production and consumption. The common interest of producers, intermediary vendors, and consumers is the hope of an increase in consumption. The first two seek increased scope of activity as a means of achieving stability, growth, and profits. Consumers seek additional consumption as a means of increasing satisfactions. Complications arise when producers and vendors must overcome direct or indirect competition to reach and to increase their outputs or sales, and when the consumer must make choices between alternate offerings in the attempt to maximize his satisfactions. Although the original common interest remains alive, its achievement becomes possible only by the skill with which the several parties concerned overcome the frictions preventing the easy flow of goods and services to the point of consumption.

The consumer can and will find his way through the maze of alternate satisfactions and spend his money for one or another of the consumables offered him. His bases of enjoyment are so subjective that one must assume his choices or selections optimize his opportunities as he sees them at the moment in time when he makes a purchasing decision. In contrast, the vendor whose offering is taken by the consumer differs from the vendor whose offering is rejected. The latter has not achieved his purpose or attained the satisfaction he sought and, indeed, may possibly never do so. The problem of marketing requiring explanation or understanding is the problem of the producer and of the marketing institutions which stand between him and the consumer.

Marketing has been characterized as "an organized behavior system." [1] Several areas of marketing present a sufficiently numerous bundle of decisions and actions to allow organization. Viewed from the standpoint of the consumer, marketing would appear to be a combination of heteroge-

---

[1] Wroe Alderson, *Marketing Behavior and Executive Action* (Homewood: Ill.: Richard D. Irwin, Inc., 1957), p. 193.

neous steps, both simultaneous and successive, arranged in an order which would put the merchandise desired at the disposal of the consumer at a location where and at a time when he happened to want the goods. It must be stressed that the consumer does not think of sales promotional activity, at any range of costs, as contributing to the satisfactions he seeks.

Viewed from the standpoint of the marketing institutions which comprise the channels of distribution for various goods, marketing becomes, as Wroe Alderson once suggested, a complicated sorting process by which large flows of goods or services are broken into smaller streams and set before consumers in such a way that margins may be exacted or earned.[2] Relatively little stress is placed here on sales promotional activities intended to broaden the market. Yet, it is evident that behind this sorting process is a considerable history of sales promotional effort intended both to interest consumers in the product and in the specific brand and to obtain adequate and favorable representation through the appropriate channels of distribution.

Neither the consumer-oriented view nor the vendor-oriented view of marketing is complete. Each assumes a tidy universe applicable to consumer or to vendor, yet each is as influential a force in marketing arrangements as the other. Given consumers with needs and vendors with goods or services to sell, we must suggest a relationship between the two which may be regarded as inherent and not as instituted by either party to the transaction. No more workable hypothesis can be found than the concept of the equilibrium.

Marshall's statement of the nature of the equilibrium will serve as a good starting point:

When demand and supply are in equilibrium, the amount of the commodity which is being produced in a unit of time may be called the *equilibrium-amount,* and the price at which it is being sold may be called the *equilibrium-price.*

Such an equilibrium is *stable;* that is, the price, if displaced a little from it, will tend to return, as a pendulum oscillates about its lowest point; and it will be found to be a characteristic of stable equilibria that in them the demand price is greater than the supply price for amounts just less than the equilibrium amount and *vice versa.* For when the demand price is greater than the supply price, the amount produced tends to increase. Therefore, if the demand price is greater than the supply price for amounts just less than an equilibrium amount; then, if the scale of production is temporarily diminished somewhat below that equilibrium amount, it will tend to return; thus, the equilibrium is stable for displacements in that direction. If the demand price is greater than the supply price for amounts just less than the equilibrium amount, it is sure to be less than the supply price for amounts just greater: and therefore, if the scale of production is somewhat increased beyond the equilibrium position, it will tend to return; and the equilibrium will be stable for displacements in that direction also.

When demand and supply are in stable equilibrium, if any accident should

---

[2] *Ibid.,* p. 229.

move the scale of production from its equilibrium position, there will be instantly brought into play forces tending to push it back to that position; just as, if a stone hanging by a string is displaced from its equilibrium position, the force of gravity will at once tend to bring it back to its equilibrium position. The movements of the scale of production about its position of equilibrium will be of a somewhat similar kind.[3]

The concept of an equilibrium is a universal natural concept. The population of fish and food tend to reach an equilibrium in each stream or body of water. The action of osmosis brings about an equilibrium between separated bodies of liquids. Human populations tend to reach a point of equilibrium in terms of their sources of support. Whatever organization of natural phenomena we consider, we see a tendency for forces ultimately to come to rest in an equilibrium.

Strangely, this same tendency is apparent in the marketplace. Consider the case of staple foods (as will be discussed in more detail later) offered in cans. Some products are promoted by food packers as nationally advertised brands and some offered by wholesalers or retailers as private brands. Many years ago, when canned foods were relatively new in the market, some of the well-advertised brands had a disproportionate share of the market. But as time has passed, there seems to have developed a sort of rough equilibrium in this field, an equilibrium which is only temporarily upset by special promotional efforts.

This same type of equilibrium is present, actually or incipiently, among competitors in many individual consumer markets. Men's shoes, household mechanical appliances, breakfast cereals, soaps and detergents, and bed sheets and blankets illustrate the tendency toward equilibrium. Among dentifrices, for example, the advertising, the point-of-purchase promotional material, the package design, the product formulation, and the channels of distribution have come to be about the same. Share of the market may have reached a point of stability. In the absence of any marked modification of these forces, we may have an excellent illustration of a market equilibrium.

If we start with the belief that markets, under static conditions, tend to reach equilibria, then we may look to the introduction of dynamic factors which disrupt these equilibria as a key to the interpretation of marketing phenomena. Who has an interest in disturbing an equilibrium and in what way would he want to disturb it? An equilibrium develops only when conditions become static—that is, when each competitor seems to have a share of the market which does not grow or shrink, and when consumer purchases appear to maintain a fairly constant distribution among competitors. This fact suggests that the several competitors must want to modify this equilibrium. If a particular vendor can move the demand curve for his particular product to the right, he will have bet-

---

[3] Alfred Marshall, *Principles of Economics* (8th ed.; New York: The Macmillan Co., 1920), pp. 345–46.

tered his position consequentially. Each competitor will strive to have a greater share of the market than he would obtain merely by means of his presence in the market.

Vendors, therefore, will make every effort to upset an equilibrium existing in a market in which they are selling. Just as important is the influence of buyers, who seek to reduce the supply price by searching out alternate sources of satisfaction, by bargaining, by withholding patronage, or by any other device available to them. Whereas vendors would like to move the demand curve to the right, so that the demand price would be more favorable to them, buyers would like to move the supply curve to the right, so that their dollars would fare better in the marketplace.

Among the bystanding parties at interest, it is probably the government alone which would like to preserve the equilibrium of the market. When dynamic factors are introduced by vendors or by buyers, conditions may change considerably and rapidly. The government would prefer a more stable set of conditions so that regulation could be introduced and observed. Through legislation to bring about certain social changes, through the application of fiscal policy and through legislative and regulatory modification, the government introduces dynamics not spontaneous to the marketplace. The concurrent introduction of spontaneously originating dynamic elements makes it difficult to determine the effects of governmental activity. Thus, the government develops interests different from those of vendors and buyers. It tends to consider as desirable the preservation of market equilibria.

The Place of Competition between Vendors in Market Dynamics

Given the range of interests of those concerned with marketing theory, it is important to consider the ways in which vendors may attempt to maximize their marketing opportunities. Because the attempt to market goods and services is in the hands of vendors, it is their decisions, their policies, and their actions which lead to individual success or failure and to efficiency or inefficiency in marketing.

The marketing of goods and services is undertaken in an environment of competition. For present purposes, we may say that competition leads vendors to attempt to obtain a greater share of a market than would normally fall to them merely by virtue of their presence in the market. A slight refinement of terms enables us to think more precisely about the nature of a competitive environment and of the results of such an environment. Let us view the actions of the vendor as *competitve actions*. These can be very specific actions, and, moreover, they can be classified and considered as to their consequences.

When a vendor finds that the market he seeks to penetrate with the goods or services he sells is in equilibrium, he will attempt to upset that equilibrium with one or a series of competitive actions. In general, the stimulation of primary demand (that is, demand for the type or kind of goods or services) grows out of social and technological change. Some efforts to stimulate primary demand can increase demand (where demand for a product is expansible). But the vendor who seeks to upset the equilibrium will do so by attempting to stimulate selective demand.

The competitive actions at the disposal of the vendor are many. He may attempt to improve product design, so that the product yields either more utilities to the consumer, or yields utilities more easily. He may redesign his package, so that the product will be more conspicuous as it awaits the consumer on a shelf or a counter. Alternately, the new design may make the product more accessible, or it may offer a secondary use for the package. The vendor may improve point-of-purchase promotional material or provide sales training for his wholesaler's or retailer's salespeople. He may find more efficient channels of distribution or better ways of utilizing or of training his own sales force. He may be able to obtain from his retail vendors preferential shelf or store location for his goods. He may undertake sampling and couponing extensively enough to increase the speed with which the product flows through his channels of distribution. He may find better advertising appeals or a better combination of advertising media. He may maximize his marketing mix. And finally, he may manipulate price.

These are, in general, possibilities open to the vendor in his attempt to stimulate selective demand. The major problem, always, is the vendor's difficulty in taking one or a combination of these steps in a way which his competitors cannot follow or equal. Indeed, typically, they will imitate, equal, or exceed any competitve actions he may adopt.

The basis for stimulating selective demand is the development of a form of product or marketing differentiation which adds to the utility sought by the consumer. Just as soon as a vendor finds a point of product differentiation which does attract buyers, he has disturbed the equilibrium which existed before he discovered this feature. Let us remember the history of table salt. Many years ago, it was offered in muslin bags, untreated, and usually hardened into large lumps which could not be used in saltshakers or even put on food easily. The salt offered by all vendors was the same. A firm and apparently lasting equilibrium existed until one vendor modified the salt so that its hygroscopic product characteristic was controlled. At the same time, the container was improved—as it could be when the salt was made free running. At once, this brand of salt, improved as it was, became the outstanding favorite of consumers; no food store could afford to be without this brand in its inventory. The previously existing equilibrium was upset. Not until the competitive actions of rivals made it possible for them, too, to offer free-running salt was an equilibrium of sorts reestablished. Again, the first vendor undertook a second competitive action: he introduced a small amount of iodine into his salt and advertised the therapeutic values of this additive. Again, the equilibrium was upset, but this time, it was easy to imitate the first vendor's competitive action. Soon, all leading brands of table salt were available with or without iodine. Since that time, additional competitive actions have been taken. Pouring spouts have been improved, and picnic sizes of salt packages introduced. No subsequent change in product or marketing characteristics, however, has brought about as great a change in the equilibrium as the first one, because no subsequent change has added so much to the utility sought by the consumer.

Canned foods, frozen orange concentrates, men's dress shirts—in fact, every product facing competition—have the same history. A series of product modifications have been the basis for the stimulation of selective demand, and retaliatory competitive actions have brought about a reestablishment of an equilibrium. How long can this process go on? For some products of relatively simple nature, there may be only a limited number of changes which can be brought about. After a few rounds of initial and retaliatory competitive actions, all changes that the then existing state of the arts and human ingenuity can suggest will have been made. Granulated sugar, shoelaces, men's stretch sox, and epsom salts may be suggested as products for which there is very little selective demand by brand, and for which equilibria seem to be relatively stable and enduring.

For more complicated products, it is possible to introduce a flow of product modifications over a considerable period of time. Competitive actions sometimes can be protected from imitation by patents or by secret processes. Certain textile processes, for example, have not been copied because the formula by which the process is performed is not easy to learn by analysis. One of the most popular soft drinks has maintained its competitive advantage for over half a century by means of a carefully guarded formula which no competitor has yet been able to imitate.

Nevertheless, there is a slow cycle inherent in the competition between products in the market. Early in the competition, a period of equilibrium develops. Various competitive actions to upset this equilibrium will be attempted, and the successful competitors will find methods of product or marketing differentiation which will add to the utility sought by the consumer. On the basis of such product or marketing differentiation, selective demand will be stimulated. The equilibrium will be tipped in favor of the vendor most successful in his efforts at differentiation. Other vendors will attempt to find competitive actions which will either give them a preferred position with the consumer or, at the least, nullify the product or marketing differentiation which was the basis of stimulation of selective demand by the first vendor.

Ultimately, new points of differentiation will be imitated or equaled, and still others will be found. Just as rapidly as one vendor succeeds in finding some point of differentiation, his competitors will equal or nullify it. At last, all possible bases of product or marketing differentiation will have been exhausted and the equilibrium once more reestablished. This time, it remains until some change in technology makes possible a further and previously impossible point of product or marketing differentiation. It may be difficult to forecast the length of time the completion of this cycle will require, but it is reasonable to expect that such a cycle will occur ultimately in all competitive situations where no permanent legal protection for product differentiation can be maintained.

The Nature of Marketing Tendencies or Principles

The essential purpose of a theoretical framework is to make possible some basis for forecasting developments. If one tendency appears to demonstrate a degree of uniformity and certainty, then we may be able to find other aspects of the marketing process which will react to this tendency in a reasonably uniform way. Certain principles related to the fact that the tendency toward equilibrium inevitably reasserts itself are discussed in the following paragraphs.

Theories of Market Reaction—The Principle of Drift. Competitive actions that stimulate selective demand for a particular product will induce consumers to buy this product in preference to other products which appear to offer similar utilities. Assume that a potato chip has been packaged and prepared in such a way that it does not become stale on the shelf of the food store. Also, this potato chip has been deep fried in a fat which adds a distinctive and appetizing taste. Those consumers who want to buy potato chips and who like the new flavor are likely to make every effort to purchase this particular brand as soon as they learn about it. They may shop several food stores in the attempt to find the item.

Under such a set of conditions, those food stores which stock the particular brand of potato chip will take maximum advantage of this fact. They are likely to give the product adequate and preferential location and display. They may mention it in their advertisements and call attention to the product with window strippers. They will use whatever methods they can to bring consumers with a demand for this product into their stores. In doing so, retailers will provide strong reinforcing promotion for the product. Conceivably, if the form of product differentiation which adds to the utility sought by the consumer is not matched or offset by the actions of competitors, an equilibrium will not be reached or reestablished until the utility offered by the product is decreased through social or technological change.

Suppose, while selective demand is high for the product which was first differentiated, a competitive vendor introduces an equally efficient package and a range of different flavors. Consumers may now buy crisp potato chips in their choice of appetizing flavors. This combination of competitive actions at once wipes out the substantial advantage previously enjoyed by the first product but may leave both the first and second products enjoying more consumer preference than all the other potato chips on the market.

Even with two brands of potato chips enjoying stimulated selective demand, however, the urgency to "tie in" on the part of the food stores is somewhat diminished. Also, the vendors of other brands of potato chips will be under great pressure to find adequate retaliatory competitive actions. Ultimately, all brands of potato chips would appear in equally good packages, with a wide variety of flavors. Equilibrium would again be established with consumers relatively indifferent as to which brand they purchased.

It is thus reasonable to expect that, over time, available points of differentiation for products will be adopted and countered, so that no one product will long enjoy preeminence. The use as an example of what might ordinarily be regarded as a convenience-goods item must not obscure the fact that this tendency is continually at work among all kinds of products. Before the advent of the automatic washer, conventional washers had reached a point at which both brand preference and product improvement seemed to have been run through all possible changes. When automatic washers were introduced, the first few brands were very well received. At the present time, however, an increasing number of competitive modifications are being adopted by other manufacturers of automatic washers, and the consumer is becoming progressively less interested in individual brands. There is some doubt as to whether brand preference for men's shoes and men's suits is as strong as it once was. Certainly the growth of private brands in the food industry indicates that an equilibrium in this area has tended to be reestablished.

It may, therefore, be said that a tendency discernible enough to be called a theory or a principle of *drift* exists:

> *There will always be a tendency for merchandise to drift down from a "specialty" to a "shopping" to a "convenience" goods classification.*

This is, of course, another way of saying that an equilibrium tends to be reestablished as soon as it is disturbed. But in terms of marketing practices, emphasizing the classification of goods is a more useful way of making the statement.

If this theory explains a uniform tendency, then it becomes a suitable vehicle for prediction. Moreover, it establishes the need for planning a constant program of product modification and for considering in advance the likelihood of product development, package improvement, and other forms of innovation ultimately having to be supplemented by some sort of diversification. The need for product modification and ultimate diversification is foreseeable.

The Principle of Diminishing Sales Effort. There is a further theoretical statement, a corollary of this principle of *drift*, which can be taken into account. It is widely recognized that the sales support given by retailers and by intermediate vendors is related to the volume in which they sell. The rate of stockturn is usually a more eloquent spokesman for retailer or wholesaler support than is the size of the gross margin. Those products for which selective demand can most specifically be stimulated are the ones for which retail and wholesale sales support can most easily be maintained. Just as soon, therefore, as a product is sufficiently differentiated to allow the stimulation of selective demand, it becomes a product which retailers and wholesalers can profitably support. But this favorable situation survives only so long as customers continue to prefer the product.

Just as soon as other products begin to find equalizing characteristics and attract customer interest, the first product loses its customer insistence, and there is a tendency for the reestablishment of an equilibrium. We can, then, offer this generalization:

> *As competition forces a greater supply of more nearly equivalent merchandise onto the market, the sales aggressiveness of individual vendors decreases.*

This statement might be called the principle of *diminishing sales effort*.

This principle can be seen at work in the marketing of canned foods. A good many years ago, the leading—and nationally advertised—brands of canned foods were those brands the quality of which was uniform and high. Less well-known brands were very frequently of poorer quality. It was possible on the basis of clearly superior quality to stimulate selective demand for the leading brands. Obviously, these brands, being easier to sell, had retailer support. Private brands, in contrast, were difficult to sell.

But since many of the private brands were packed by the proprietors of advertised brands, it became economical to process optimum-sized lots under identical conditions of quality and production and to label the can as orders were received. Various of the private brands thus came to be of the same quality as the nationally advertised brands, and consumers ultimately regarded them as equally acceptable. Prevailing attitudes changed slowly because consumers learned gradually over a number of years that the two classes of branded products were of identical quality. However, as this awareness developed and it became increasingly a matter of indifference to consumers which brand they purchased when price was the same, it likewise became less profitable for wholesalers and retailers to push the advertised brands.

Similar applications of this principle can be found in many lines of merchandise. No one brand of men's white dress shirts now has a preponderate share of the market. Aluminum cooking utensils sell under different brands, but there no longer appears to be any marked preference. Indeed, this principle has worked so thoroughly on the market for aluminum cooking vessels that the field of competition has moved in part to utensils made of other metal alloys. Many brands of electric blankets and electric sheets are now available and apparently competing on more or less even terms.

The Principle of Institutional Proliferation. We turn now to another inference from the reinstitution of equilibria in markets in which competitive actions have finally utilized all possible methods of stimulating selective demand. Two concurrent and mutually exclusive trains of thought exist regarding the use of intervening institutions between the manufacturer and the retailer. Vertical integration and shortening the channel of distribution allow the manufacturer a considerable degree of control over the aggressiveness of distributor or wholesaler selling. Household appliances supported by a considerable volume of consumer advertising typically have been marketed through channels of distribution, which were as short as possible. Very often, factory branches or a factory-owned supply corporation will carry the merchandise from the factory door to the retailer.

This very simple and direct method of marketing allows the manufacturer to control the amount and kind of sales pressure which will support his merchandise. The salesmen who sell to the retailer are the employees of the manufacturer. They are able to pressure many retailers into purchasing on credit an optimistically calculated volume of merchandise. Consequently, the manufacturer is able to plan his production, confident that he has firm orders for an amount that will enable him to manufacture in economical lots. As long as the merchandise is sufficiently differentiated to allow the stimulation of selective demand, the retailer will be happy to promote one brand and avoid carrying closely competitive merchandise in his inventory.

The extent of retailer support, however, will depend on the preference of the consumer for the merchandise in question.

As rapidly as other manufacturers are able to equal the points of product differentiation on which selective demand once depended, retailers will lose their enthusiasm in accordance with the principle of *diminishing sales effort.* The cost of maintaining direct factory wholesaling activity then becomes unduly high. Not aggressive sales effort but increased exposure to sale will become the desired objective. The manufacturer will soon seek broader wholesale distribution.

Although the development of trends among wholesalers is less readily apparent than among retailers, it is still possible to generalize on what will happen. We can formulate one more principle:

> As a particular field of merchandise reaches a state of competition where reasonable parity exists among competitive offerings, there will be a tendency for the proliferation of intervening institutions or middlemen to take advantage of the economies of specialization.

This principle has been most fully developed in the marketing of textiles, where a succession of intervening institutions combine processing and marketing. Each agency is able to specialize and thus to effect economies of greater magnitude than his maintained gross margin. Moreover, the standardization of output (e.g., greige goods) makes the stimulation of selective demand highly unlikely.

As middlemen specialize, they may become less conspicuous. Consequently, we may not be as fully aware of developments in wholesaling as we are of developments in manufacturing and retailing. Yet, it is through a change in emphasis on sales effort at the wholesale level that one can be most certain of the restablishment of an equilibrium.

The Principle of Brand Proliferation. Situations arise in which it is difficult for individual vendors to find a basis for stimulating selective demand even though primary demand exists for the type of product under consideration. Vendors may have worked jointly to establish the basis for stimulating primary demand, or the presence of such demand may be due to some change in technology or the social order.

If there is no ready or feasible way of differentiating the products which might satisfy primary demand, the stimulation of selective demand will be difficult or impossible. Could effective methods of differentiating products in this field be found, a very few brands might be expected to offer such additional utility through product differentiation as is required to satisfy existing needs. However, when this concentration on a limited number of successfully differentiated products proves impossible, we should anticipate many vendors seeking entrance into the market.

Much the same result could be expected when competitive actions on the part of rival vendors have equated the several competing brands and canceled out attempts at differentiation. We may, then, formulate what can be called the principle of *brand proliferation:*

> *When selective demand cannot be developed or becomes infeasible to maintain for a product class for which primary demand exists then additional brands may be expected to develop or to be offered by other vendors until an equilibrium is reached.*

The results of this principle have been seen in the marketing of canned foods. When the formerly dominant national brands were matched in quality and acceptance by private brands, a host of additional brands were able to enter the market. Gas ranges for household cooking have followed this pattern in the past. In surveys in which the brand of gas range was asked of householders, the present writer has found several score of different brands in service in single localities. An equilibrium will be established or reestablished—in the absence of any selective demand on the part of purchasers—when each product achieves only that volume of sales which its mere presence in the market attracts.

The Principle of Nonprice Competition. Little has been said as yet about the most universal of competitive actions, price competition. In the absence of product or marketing differentiations affording the basis for an attempt to stimulate selective demand, all vendors are able to resort to manipulating prices. We have seen spectacular instances of the use of price competition. In many years, food retailers have sold granulated sugar for no more gross margin than the extent of the cash discount. The margin on cigarettes has typically been small. When price cutting has whittled retail gross margins down to abnormally low levels, gross margins for the original vendors are also likely to be low.

Although price competition is available to all vendors, it is a constructive sort of competitive action only under limited circumstances. In general, the full development of a market seems to require considerable sales promotional effort—an effort, by the way, which adds appreciably to the social dividend by distributing the standard of living more widely than it might have been distributed were goods offered on a completely nonpromotional basis. The constructive aspects of price reduction appear most clearly when the demand which will be satisfied by a particular product is elastic. Offering such items at a lower price evokes a considerably greater consumer use of the product. If the product is produced under conditions of decreasing cost, there is an additional advantage to price reduction.

Highly elastic demand and decreasing costs of production, however, are factors which merely postpone the ill effects of using price as a competitive tool. Ultimately, competitive actions based on price reductions tend to reduce the vendor's and the retailer's margins to the point at which neither one can afford the costs of sales promotion.

Efforts are made to avoid these ill effects of price competition with the result being very much the same as the result of the enforcement of fair-trade legislation, a step making price competition impossible. Although one can prevent some kinds of competitive actions, it is difficult to keep vigorous rivals from competing. As price competition is decreased, for whatever reason, nonprice competition will be emphasized. Reliance on nonprice competition may produce a more sophisticated or more difficult range of competitive actions—actions possibly requiring sizeable financial resources.

We may, then, adduce the following principle of nonprice competition:

> *For products for which product or marketing differentiation becomes difficult, there will be an increasing tendency toward nonprice competition, and the extent of this nonprice competition will tend to be in proportion to the size or resources of the vendors competing.*

It is easy to point out the evidences of nonprice competition in the field of retailing, where the elaboration of premises, the introduction of nonretailing services, and the offering of generous credit arrangements are frequently encountered. Although opinions differ widely on the subject of institutional advertising among vendors of consumer goods, it is possible to regard this type of advertising as an evidence of nonprice competition at the manfacturers' or processors' level.

Approaches to the Study of Marketing

These several principles indicate an analytic approach to marketing which offers a solution to the question of market development. Originally, the study of marketing was built around an examination of how agricultural products were marketed. In the days when most consumer goods were sold in bulk, this basis of organization was entirely suitable. With the development of an ever greater number of branded consumer items, the central interest of the study of marketing became the promotion and exploitation of the nationally advertised brand. Insofar as the principles previously suggested are concerned, it was inevitable that developments in the market would tend to limit the usefulness of advertised brands and increase reliance on intensiveness of distribution and on retail display. As factors other than brand exploitation and advertising come to be significant in the field of marketing, development of a symmetrical organon of thought requires a new orientation.

One approach to marketing analysis is suggested by the principles adduced in the present chapter. The writer's studies and observations over many years lead to the conclusion that the principles herein formulated are of general validity and application. It is extremely likely that a systematic study of the rise and development of brand exploitation would suggest a number of additional principles. It is equally likely that the previously formulated principles would be useful to the student of marketing who wants to plan the development of marketing programs. One could consider how and to what extent the fulfilment of these principles suggests marketing methods which would maximize the market and the returns from the exploitation of various brands. The major point of uncertainty involves the degree to which these (and other similar) principles could be regarded as tendencies or as *laws* of marketing.

Marketing can be examined from a number of points of view. One can consider marketing in terms of technological progress applied to the production of vendible items. Similarly, it is possible to regard marketing in terms of the movement of populations, first, westward, and second, toward urbanization; or as a very interesting and applied branch of the study of materials handling; or as the method of satisfying sociological and psychological satisfactions. Finally, it is entirely feasible to regard marketing as a phase of the development of government regulation.

Doubtless there are other approaches to the study of marketing. No mention of mathematical model building has been made. It is assumed that the model to be built would be a representation of one or another of the bases of organization mentioned at the opening of this section and that model building would constitute a tool of analysis. Much the same comment can be made concerning the attempt to program marketing developments or systems on a computer. Here, too, it is assumed that the development or system would resemble one of the general approaches suggested and that the use of the computer would constitute a method of analysis rather than a new aspect of marketing.

The field of marketing encompasses the rather brief list of possible points of view from which it was previously stated marketing could be studied and analyzed, along with the use of a historical method which would tend to be inclusive. While it is possible to adopt any one of these viewpoints as basic in organizing marketing as a subject for study and analysis, nevertheless any systematic examination would require consideration of all these aspects of the field. Only then will we be able ultimately to erect an organon of thought of some elegance.

3. A CONCEPTUAL APPROACH TO MARKETING

William McInnes

ALTHOUGH the practice of marketing is as old as civilization itself, efforts to evolve a theory or a science of marketing are relatively new. It is, in fact, only in the present century that the term "marketing" as well as the concepts surrounding that term have received any widespread acceptance.[1] The activity of the marketplace has far outstripped the reflections of the theorists.

While the marketing system has expanded to colossal dimensions, the development of marketing thought—through concepts, hypotheses, theories, or principles—has proceeded at no such rapid pace. The promise of the early conceptual work of pioneers such as Ralph Starr Butler, Arch Shaw, and Louis Weld did give birth in the twenties—"the Golden Decade in the development of marketing thought"—to integration, classification, and some "principles."[2] This was followed in the thirties by a new emphasis on text writing, course elaboration in the universities, and the introduction of consumer considerations. The forties witnessed an offsetting interest in the managerial aspects of marketing and marketing policy. But when the first book to be devoted entirely to marketing theory was about to appear, there was general agreement that even at mid-century "there is a plethora of individual facts and a dearth of conceptual schemes which would relate these facts in meaningful generalizations."[3] There had been some attempts to form generalized theories but these "fail to satisfy students because they do not account for or take into consideration all of the relevant observed facts."[4]

---

[1] For the widest historical treatment of the development of marketing thought, cf. Robert Bartels, *The Development of Marketing Thought*, (Homewood, Ill.: Richard D. Irwin, Inc., 1962), pp. 1–3, 10–12.

[2] *Ibid.*, p. 174.

[3] Edmund D. McGarry, "Some Viewpoints in Marketing," *Journal of Marketing*, Vol. 18 (July, 1953), p. 33.

[4] Wroe Alderson and Reavis Cox, "Towards a Theory of Marketing," *Journal of Marketing*, Vol. 13 (October, 1948), p. 139.

The publication of the first edition of *Theory in Marketing* brought to the dynamic field of marketing fresh concepts borrowed from such disparate areas as physics, psychology, vector analysis, behavior systems, and regional trade.[5] But 12 years later, Bartels, in summing up the progress of 60 years, could still write that although marketing thought has devoted much attention to describing prevailing practices, to classifying activities and institutions, and even to developing some basic generalizations, "relatively little use has been made of theoretical analysis, of concepts from related social sciences, or of experimental hypotheses in the construction of systems of marketing thought." [6] The task, therefore, remained "for someone to present an acceptable integration of marketing that will serve as an introduction upon which more specialized study could be built or as a comprehensive explanation of marketing for both specialist and non-specialist in the field."[7] Apparently, "a box of tools for analyzing the facts and events"—to borrow a phrase from Schumpeter—is still required, and, hence, there is still room for a different conceptual approach to the problem. This essay is one such attempt.

Many concepts in marketing, particularly the more generalized ones, have been brought in from other fields such as economics, psychology, or the physical sciences. Such an approach, extremely popular today, has the advantage of widening perspectives and of fitting the model into more generally known streams of thought or behavior patterns. But a widened perspective has been accompanied by a blurring of focus. Marketing tends to become only applied psychology, or applied economics, analogical biology, or a specialized behavior system. In the search for general principles from which marketing action can be deduced, the specific role and functions of marketing are too easily lost.

An alternative is to start with the most concrete and specific phenomenon observed by both the practical businessman and the theorist. That phenomenon is the market. Most theorists and practitioners would agree that marketing has something to do with "dealing in a market," and while this does not tell very much about marketing, it does at least give focus to the problem. The primary observable phenomenon for any theory of marketing is the hard practical fact of the market itself.

Nor is the acceptance of this fact of the market merely the starting point for businessman or theorist. It is also the ultimate criterion for either action or theory. A businessman is successful only when he succeeds in the market; a theorist has advanced theory only when he says something about the market. Though the theorist or research director may utilize tools from several different disciplines, the basic model must spring from the phenomenon of the market. The market is not only the point of com-

---

[5] Wroe Alderson and Reavis Cox (eds.), *Theory in Marketing* (Homewood, Ill.: Richard D. Irwin, Inc., 1950).
[6] Bartels, *op. cit.*, p. 207.
[7] *Ibid*, p. 182.

munication between practice and theory, it is the ultimate judge of both.

This essay, then, will begin with observations of market phenomena. Next, it will generalize from these observations, isolating the dimensions of the market. Finally, after specifying these dimensions and relating them to the tasks of marketing, it will propose a model of a marketing system.

What Is a Market?

Markets result from the social intercourse of men when the makers and users of economic goods and services seek to satisfy their needs and wants through exchange. But what specifically is a market? To practical businessmen, markets are often considered to be places—Wall Street, Covent Garden, or Pike Street—where an exchange occurs. They are "determinate areas and times for intercourse between buyers and sellers." [8] This inexact notion, arising out of the traffic of traders in the marketplace, may not be scientific, but it does emphasize contact and geographic location as requisites for exchanges. In our modern world of electronic communication, however, it is hard to conceive how the extent of the market is entirely congruent with a determinate geographical area.

The interregional trade theory of E. T. Grether is an application of the geographical concept of markets and marketing.[9] His explanation of the "business activities involved in directing the flow of goods and services from producer to consumer or user" [10] centers around multiple geographical markets. Marketing theory analyzes the behavior of the firm (or the region as a trading unit) as it adjusts its horizontal spatial relationships to industrial, regional, and national groups.

A second conceptual approach is institutional rather than geographical. In this view, leaning heavily on John R. Commons, it is patterns of collective action in control of individual action which make markets, and, hence, theory should center on institutions rather than on individual actions.[11] One of the first writers to apply the institutional approach to marketing was Ralph Breyer.[12] With his natural aptitude for seeking the

---

[8] "Market as a Place of Sale," *Palgrave's Dictionary of Political Economy*, Vol. II, 1923 ed. Marshall defines a market as "a district, small or large, in which there are many buyers and many sellers all so keenly on the alert and so well acquainted with one another's affairs that the price of a commodity is always practically the same for the whole of the district" (*Principles of Political Economy* [3d ed.; London: Macmillan & Co., Ltd., 1895], p. 188). It can be seen on analysis that this definition applies only to the unrealistic condition of perfect competition.

[9] E. T. Grether, "A Theoretical Approach to the Analysis of Marketing," in Cox and Alderson (eds.), *op. cit.*, p. 118.

[10] This is the nominal definition of marketing proposed by the Definitions Committee of the American Marketing Association in 1948. Cf. *Journal of Marketing*, Vol. 13 (October, 1948), p. 209.

[11] Cf. John R. Commons, *The Economics of Collective Action* (New York: The Macmillan Co., 1951), pp. 120–44.

[12] Cf. Ralph Breyer, *The Marketing Institution* (New York: McGraw-Hill Book Co., Inc., 1934).

wholeness and order in marketing phenomena,[13] he saw marketing as
"primarily a physical function made necessary because of the separation
of production and consumption," [14] and the main institutions of the
market to be supply and demand, space, time, and competition. Reavis
Cox's concept of marketing as a combination of flows through organizations which "takes place between entire channels rather than between
individual entities along the channel" is also an institutional approach to
marketing.[15]

With its emphasis on group behavior, the institutionalist approach
broadens the perspective of marketing theory. But it tends to overlook
the individual forces that, collectively, make up institutional behavior; nor
does it explain the relationship between the two. Besides, it highlights
interactions rather than causes, and, hence, it tends to description rather
than analysis. The institutional approach has been perhaps the most adaptable to the importing of tools from other areas, but caution must be
exerted lest in the assimilation process the distinctive characteristics of
market phenomenon be obliterated.

A third stream of marketing thought flows from the headwaters of
economic theory. A market is treated as a process "actuated by the interplay of the actions of the various individuals cooperating under the division of labor." [16] The basic conception is one of equilibrium of supply
and demand under varying conditions of pure or (more recently) imperfect competition.[17] The process of objective exchange valuation becomes

---

[13] Ralph Breyer, letter to Robert Bartels in 1940 (Bartels, *op. cit.*, p. 224).

[14] Bartels, *op. cit.*, p. 184.

[15] Reavis Cox, "Quantity Limits and the Theory of Economic Opportunity," in
Cox and Alderson (eds.), *op. cit.*, p. 240.

[16] Ludwig von Mises, *Human Action* (New Haven: Yale University Press, 1949),
p. 258.

[17] To Adam Smith, the market was synomymous with the power to exchange.
The source of this power he located in the costs of production. Cost of production
created value, and value made a market. The Austrian and marginal utility schools
in later years shifted the discussion of the sources of value to the demand side of the
market. In their opinion, it was utility, and not costs of production, which created
value. Alfred Marshall combined the work of his predecessors and made the market
the consequence of both supply and demand mutually interacting and determining
each other. Marshall's market was like the intersection in an electrical circuit of
alternating current. With Say, he agreed that supply created demand; with the
Austrians, he agreed that demand also acted on supply. Then he combined both.
The forces interacted. One explained the other. But what of the intersection itself?
What of the market? What was that? It remained, like the pointer on a scale, an
abstraction: an indicator but not something real. Chamberlin found this approach a
"complete misfit" (Edward Chamberlin, *The Theory of Monopolistic Competition*
[Cambridge, Mass.: Harvard University Press, 1936], p. 10) for modern conditions
because the theories of value had been formulated independently of institutional
factors. He introduced the elements of elasticity of the demand curve, product differentiation, and selling costs which have an impact on marginal revenue and marginal costs and so affect the valuation process by destroying the automaticity of
equilibrium assumed by earlier writers. However, he did not explore factors other
than value which also tend to break down the automatic working of the exchange
process.

the center of attention for the economists with some (e.g., classical school) focusing on the supply side of the process, and others (e.g., the Austrians) on the demand side. The difficulty that arises from any attempt to make marketing a direct application of economic theory is that the basic premise of valuation limits too closely the multiple dimensions of the market. Such precision aids economic analysis but only at the expense of marketing analysis. Although market facts may be translated into costs and prices, they are not synonymous with either. Economic theory brings to the study of the market a strong central concept—valuation. But this is by no means the only concept for an integrated theory of marketing.

A final approach, especially associated with Edmund D. McGarry, is the functional, a classification of those activities which constitute "the *sine qua non* of marketing, those things without which marketing would not exist." [18] Though there has never been any general agreement on how many tasks make up marketing, the functional approach tries to isolate what is essential to the field and so it has advanced marketing thought.[19] What is lacking, however, is an explicit relation to the market itself as the criterion or what is an essential task and what is not.

All of the above approaches—geographical, institutional, process, and functional—have contributed to the progress of marketing thought. The next step would appear to be to make more explicit the concept of a market and then to relate marketing directly to that concept. An adequate conceptualization, like the geographical approach, should include the physical flow of goods between regions—but it should also include the multiple flows of negotiation, ownership, and information. Like the institutional approach, this integrated concept should touch on collective patterns of behavior and institutions—but it should also investigate the individual forces from which institutions emerge. With the process approach, it should analyze valuation—but it should explore the physical, psychological, and perceptional dimensions assumed in economic theory. With the functional approach, it should be able to classify and segregate the essential tasks from the nonessential—but it should also be able to make more explicit the market criterion for classification. The approach may be widened in scope so that it can borrow the tools of psychology, sociology, mathematics, and economics—but the model should be based on a concept of the market that will preserve its distinctiveness as a marketing theory. In addition, it should be capable of analyzing not only existing situations

---

[18] Edmund D. McGarry, "Some Functions of Marketing Reconsidered," in Cox and Alderson (eds.), *op. cit.*, p. 268.

[19] A tabular presentation of marketing functions proposed by several authors is given in Franklin Ryan, "Functional Elements of Market Distribution," *Harvard Business Review*, Vol. 13 (January, 1935), pp. 208–9. Even though, the classification is twenty-eight years old, the modern listing has not seen many substantial changes. This is probably due to the failure to develop a clear criterion of selection rather than to any historical stagnation of marketing activity.

but also opportunity in the market system. Ideally, it should be general enough to include the marketing mechanism of Russia as well as of the United States.

The Market and Marketing

In a social economy, where the maker of economic goods does not use them and the provider of economic services does not benefit from them, there is a real separation between producers and consumers. But while they are separated, they are also necessarily related. Hence, the separation is accompanied by an interdependence which is very real. As soon as a person (or firm) produces a good or service, he is in the market for a consumer.[20] As soon as a person (or institution) develops the capacity to consume, he is in the market for a producer. There is a mutual, necessary attraction between the parties. Another name for this real, interdependent relationship between producer and consumer is a market. The market is the gap which separates producer and consumer. As the separation of producer and consumer grows greater under an expanding division of labor and increasingly differentiated consumer wants, the relationship becomes no less real but only more complex. Thus, more people, higher incomes, more sophisticated desires mean—almost paradoxically—bigger markets even with increasing separation of consumer and producer. The market is made from two elements: separation and relationship.

In an exchange economy, the relationship of producer and consumer—i.e., the market—is a universal fact. The mere fact of relationship, however, is insufficient to generate an exchange.[21] The existence of a market relation is the foundation for exchange not a substitute for it. Producers of wheat in Kansas City by the very fact of planting wheat become related economically to consumers of bread in Boston. But there is no exchange, even when objective exchange valuation is identical, until several intermediate steps are taken. From a marketing point of view, the market relation is both an obstacle and an opportunity. It is real enough and yet it is not fully realized. It is not actual but rather potential. It has the real elements needed to generate exchange, but these elements are not presently actualized. An analogy may be helpful in illustrating this relation. Hydrogen and oxygen bear a definite and real relation to the compound known as water. When joined together, they form water rather than anything else. But while they both bear a definite and real relation to

---

[20] The modern development of "the marketing concept" is a recognition of this dependence of the manufacturer, financier, banker, retailer, etc., on the market as the vital source of their existence and activity.

[21] A market concept limited to analyzing existing reality would not be particularly useful. A concept, or theory, must be dynamic, not static. It must embrace opportunity as well as present conditions. The basic argument here is that the market must be considered in a wider perspective than any present evidence of exchange. Otherwise, there would appear to be no possibility of explaining development of markets.

water, they remain only potentially water until they are combined, usually with the aid of a catalyst. Similarily, producers and consumers are related by a market, but no exchange occurs until some force or agent brings them into actual contact. This force, making a potential market contact into a real market contact, is what is generally known as marketing.

Marketing is any "motion"[22] or activity that actualizes the potential relation of producer and consumer. The essential task of marketing is, therefore, always related primarily to the market. The work of marketing always begins with the discovery of market potential. Its function is, as Cherington realized over forty years ago, "the establishment of . . . a contact."[23] A concept of marketing in its widest sense, therefore, is *any activity which actualizes the potential market relationship between the makers and users of economic goods and services.* A science of marketing would attempt to analyze and form testable hypotheses about this actualization; the practice of marketing would exploit the actualization process to generate sales.

Dimensions of Market Potential

The concept of marketing given above is wide. This is necessarily so because the market on which it is based is wide, and marketing is coextensive with the market. Hence, it is only when we determine the dimensions of the market that we can determine the corresponding dimensions of the marketing task. Marketing task and market potential are inseparably linked, for marketing makes contact from separation and bridges the gap between producer and consumer. The next step, then, is to try to specify the dimensions of the market, i.e., we must determine the modes of separation between producers and consumers.

The most visible dimension of a market is the *spatial separation* of the parties to an exchange. That is why markets are frequently associated with a specific meeting place. Only when the parties get together in some way can an exchange occur. The greater the physical separation of the parties, the wider the physical dimensions of the market and the greater the potentiality in their relationship; the nearer they come together, the narrower that dimension and the smaller the spatial market potential.

But geographic separation carries as a necessary consequence a time lapse. There must be a time lag between production and consumption of at least the time necessary for the movement of goods through the intervening space. Thus, the second dimension of the market is *separation in time*.

---

[22] This concept was first suggested by Arch Shaw in 1912 (*Some Problems in Market Distribution* [Cambridge, Mass.: Harvard University Press], 1915). While it may appear too abstract, it does have a convenient relationship to market potential and market actualization, particularly to the philosophically inclined theorist.

[23] Paul Cherington, *The Elements of Marketing* (New York: The Macmillan Co., 1920), p. 12.

Every market situation includes a time factor. The greater the time lapse between production and consumption, the greater the time dimension of the market potential; the shorter the time lapse, the smaller the time market potential.

Following closely upon space and time dimensions is the separation of information and persuasion. Customers don't know about supply sources; producers don't know where customers are. There is always a *perceptional separation* between producers and consumers in a market.[24] The fewer consumers who know or are interested in that product, the greater is the market potential.[25] When customers are well informed and highly motivated, the smaller is the remaining market potential. If a large majority of customers know about razor-blade brands and are sold on a particular brand, there is little market potential remaining for other manufacturers of razor blades unless these latter manufacturers can provide new information and new motivation that will switch brand loyalty.

Even when fully informed and motivated makers and users of economic goods are brought together, no exchange is completed—at least in a private property system—until the title of ownership is conveyed. The market relation has an inherent *separation of ownership* that makes up one of its dimensions.

Allied to this separation of ownership in the market structure is the *separation of values* placed upon the product by producer and consumer. The producer measures his sacrifice in terms of costs and competition and sets an offering price. The consumer measures his want satisfaction in terms of utility and ability to pay. The greater the separation of valuation, the greater is the market potential; the closer the valuation, the smaller the market potential. Because of the high price of color TV sets today and the growing desire of customers for such sets, there is a large market potential. Because this potential represents a separation of valuation rather than an agreement on an acceptable price, we conclude that there is a large market potential for color TV, even though there has been little marketing until recent years to exploit that market potential. It is important to remember that the existence of a market is not the same as a

---

[24] The term "perception" is used here to connote both ignorance and inertia; i.e., a lack of knowledge *and* interest. Neither producers nor consumers of economic goods are concerned only with the speculative knowledge of a product. It is only motivated knowledge leading to an exchange that is pertinent.

[25] At first sight, this hypothesis seems to suggest a paradox that the greater the disparity of the relation between makers and users of goods, the greater the market—i.e., that the market for a product is better when consumers and producers don't get together rather than when they do. But it should be remembered that the basis of the relationship between the parties is a connecting link so that no matter how greatly these parties are separated, the very fact that they are producers and consumers involves a necessary mutual interest. It is not stated that a market equals an exchange. But it does suggest that a market is a bigger phenomenon than some marketing people would admit. This implies, of course, that the marketing task is greater—but it also leaves room for admitting the possibility of marketing activity wherever there is a market.

sale. But even without a sale, it cannot be denied that the market somehow exists, and one of its dimensions is valuation. If consumer capacity and willingness to pay and producer capacity and willingness to offer differ greatly, this fact does not obliterate a market. It only makes the separation between the two parties that much wider.

Thus, the basic model of a market consists of a set of real but potential realtionships in five dimensions: space, time, perception, valuation, and ownership. The streams of power structures affecting a market enter through these limits; the actions of behavior systems filter into the market through these dimensions. Underlying social and economic changes on either the producer or consumer side of the market—births, deaths, rising incomes, new plant locations—not only change the market terminals but also affect the market potential. Since market potentiality is measured by the extent of separation of the parties to an exchange in each of these five dimensions, the greater the separation, the greater the market potential. Every underlying change, however, is always specified in the market relation as a change in the degree of separation of space, time, perception, valuation, or ownership. Thus, while the market is not a closed system apart from the real world, it does have its distinctiveness guaranteed by its five dimensions. These dimensions form the basic pattern that makes a market; they are the five dimensions of market potential that confront every marketing agent and determine every marketing institution.

To convert a five-dimensional concept of market potential into a working model requires some tools for measuring its quantitative aspects. The task is not simple, but neither does it appear entirely impossible. There are generally acceptable standards for measuring space potentials (miles, feet, etc.) and time potential (hours, minutes, etc.). The economists have provided the units of money costs and prices to measure values.

To measure in some way the separation of ownership would seem to call for a combination of legal as well as physical units. To measure perceptional separation requires the borrowing of sophisticated tools from psychology and sociology, and at our present stage of knowledge, would yield far from perfect results. But the inadequacy of the tools does not seem to invalidate the basic market model. The search should be for sharper tools rather than for a modification of the model if the market itself is real.

An economist or businessman might well reduce all the measurements of market potential to dollar costs. This would be both convenient and practical. But it should be remembered that such an effort looks at the market institution purely as an economic activity through the narrow medium of dollar costs. It is easy to overlook opportunity when the range of vision is too narrow. A market planner might find a wider perspective by studying markets in terms of spatial and time units before translating these units into economic costs. A social historian might want to evaluate a market in terms of the more original units of space, time, perception, and ownership as well as valuation. The preservation of the five dimensions allows appraisal of a market as a social organization as well as a managerial tool. To consider only costs is to lose something of the multiple dimensional structure that is a market.

Statistical data can provide the raw material for quantification of the model. But it should be kept in mind that statistics are always historical and so can never reveal a completely current situation. Besides, they are often not available in sufficient detail to apply to specific products, especially where branding has developed high product differentiation. Statistical resumés of past sales of a firm provide merely an indicator of market potential. They reveal only that part of the market potential that has been exploited, not the total potential that remains. Yet, it is precisely in this latter area that opportunity exists. Hence, records of sales must be used with caution as indicators of potential, and they should be supplemented with other data for effective measurement.

Sometimes, when an accurate measure of the dimensions of a market potential cannot be attained, it is possible to measure relative changes in any of the dimensions. Although such an operation cannot find absolute values, it can reveal relative rates of change of potential. The rate of increase in transportation facilities, the rate of change of crop output, the relative increase in consumer expectations and intentions to buy, all give some indication of the change in market potentials even while not requiring knowledge of the underlying absolute figures. With increasingly sophisticated mathematical tools, the difficulty resulting from lack of absolute figures is not as great as it used to be.

For some products, market potential is more determinate than for others. Natural resources have a more definite location on the production side of the market than do services. Doctors' fees have, through custom, a more definite valuation potential than does scrap steel. On the consumption side of the market, industrial users are generally easier to locate than users in the consumer market, since many industrial firms cluster together geographically. But in all cases, potentials exist. They represent, simultaneously, both an obstacle and an opportunity for the businessman: an obstacle because they require effort to be overcome; an opportunity because it is through the removal of an obstacle that reward can be earned.

Marketing and Market Potentials

If a market represents a separation—in space, time, perception, valuation, and ownership—between makers and users of economic goods, then some force is required to bridge the gap and realize the opportunity latently existing in the market potential. That force, or activity, we call marketing. And since its one job is to convert market potentials into actual markets, it is convenient to call the process of marketing, *actualization*. By its effort, marketing actualizes what is merely potential in the market relation. It generates—from a preexisting situation—an exchange.

Actualization. The five potentials of space, time, ownership, valuation, and perception are important because they circumscribe the field of marketing. They are the bases from which springs all marketing activity, the opportunities which confront all marketing agents. They reveal the only possibilities of successful marketing action. But though they are important to marketing, they do not represent marketing itself. Marketing is the creative force which reacts on these potentialities as material. Hence, it is necessary to analyze marketing activity, an activity which in its essential and generic meaning is actualization. Marketing *is* actualization—the force which actualizes the potentialities of the market relation. It is the motion which closes the gap caused by the separation of makers and users in a social economy and defined by market potentials. Thus, actualization is a central concept for a science of marketing.

The actualization of the space potential can have its origin only in the space potential existing between producer and consumer. It embraces all those motions needed to bring the product from the geographical point where it is produced to the point where the consumer wants it.

The motions of space actualization may assume different forms which are limited only by the primary principle of directness of route between terminals. A firm may shorten the distance between production and consumption by branch plants using local resources. Shopping centers may move into the centers of populations. Or a firm may find a more direct route from its plant to its consumers. It may move goods by rail instead of water, or by plane instead of truck. Directness, of course, must always be related to the consumption and production terminals of the market. If consumers are shifting, then the most direct route is the one which shifts with them.

Out of space actualization arise three motions which must be performed, though they may be shifted among agencies. They are: assembly, transportation, and dispersion. Goods must be gathered together; they must be shipped; they must be broken down into consumable units. For specific products, the importance of each of these motions varies, but none can be dismissed entirely. In some instances, it is possible to shift the tasks to the consumer himself, but even this cannot be considered as having eliminated the movement. When a shopper carries her groceries home in her own car, she is performing the marketing activity of transportation. The customer who, on the other hand, calls in for one pound of butter to be delivered to her leaves both the transportation and dispersion task to the retailer.

Time actualization is the marketing motion which places the goods a customer wants before him at the moment he wants them. If the consumer is willing to take the product as soon as it comes off the production line, time actualization is of small importance in the marketing picture. But if the producer is compelled to hold the goods for a long period, then actualization of the time potential is very significant.

The primary principle of time actualization is speed. The product should move in the shortest time possible between the consumption and production terminal of the market. But speed also must be considered as a relative quantity. It must be related to the production possibilites and to the desires of the consumer. Time actualization is successful only when it places before the consumer the goods he wants when he wants them. It does not determine that moment but only attempts to meet that deadline when the consumer has determined the moment for himself. If the interval between production and consumption can be shortened, or if the two terminals can be better synchronized, then time actualization will decline, but otherwise the tasks which flow from this actualization must be assumed by someone.

Time actualization is manifested in what can be called the *chronologizing functions*. These chronologizing functions are the activities which close the time gap. They are of three types: financing, risk management, and storage. Financing supports the investment while it is in the channel of distribution; risk management pays for the costs of the uncertainties involved in the time lag; storage provides the means for holding physical quantities of the product until wanted by consumers.

Ownership actualization embraces all the motions of conveying title from producer to consumer. It is extremely important because even though buyers and sellers may be in the same place at the same time, no exchange will take place until title has been transferred. Only when this step is taken is the transaction complete. This phase of actualization is the traffic management of the market relation.

The major manifestations of ownership actualization appear in the negotiating functions of contact and termination. Contactual negotiation embraces finding a market, making a market, and creating a market. Terminating negotiation embraces all those activities which facilitate the transaction and bring it to a full conclusion, e.g., drawing up contracts, keeping records, maintaining standardized procedures. Each of these activities assists in the transfer of title, though they have nothing to do with the physical or temporal distribution of goods. Hence, they are forms of ownership actualization.

Valuation actualization is made up of all those motions necessary to align sellers' bids and buyers' offers. Its range or movement is circumscribed on the one side by the consumer's ability and willingness to offer. The motion itself, when not effected by the equilibrium forces of competition, must be carried out by some marketing agent. It is usually expressed in what is called price policy, either lowering producers' offers or raising buyers' bids in order to bring about the contact which generates an exchange. This may be done by adjusting terms of sales, varying terms of shipment, quoting discounts off list, setting odd prices or price lining. All of these actions stem from the fundamental motion of valuation actualization. Through this actualization, the imperfections which keep automatic pricing from clearing the market are not removed from the market, but transactions can be realized in spite of the imperfections.

Perceptional actualization brings within the perceptional range of consumers the goods that are available for sale. It adjusts the consumer to the product. It is manifested in the activities of disseminating information and of persuasion, the former to overcome the ignorance of the perceptional potential, the latter to overcome the inertia of that potential. Through these activities, users are adjusted to the product. They are given ideas and motives. The ideas may be transmitted through several different types of media; persuasion is carried to the consumer through the use of appeals. Ordinarily, the work of perceptional actualization is carried out by the seller. However, in periods of shortage and in some parts of the industrial market, this task has been successfully shifted to the buyer. What is important to realize is not that this or that agent carries out a marketing task but, even more fundamentally, that the marketing tasks must be carried out by someone. The function is more basic than the institution.

It is by relating the activity of marketing to the corresponding market potentials from which that activity must flow that a list of marketing functions becomes possible. It is of secondary importance, then, as to how long the list is; what matters is that under this conceptual system, a criterion of selection is known.

The existence of producers and consumers provides the raw material for a market relation. As soon as a manufacturer is in business, he is automatically drawn to the market. As soon as a consumer exists, he is in the market for some goods, and every change in his capacity or willingness to consume is reflected in the market in some way. The very existence of these two groups and their mutual interdependence sets up the relationship that is the market.

The potentiality of the market relation, on the other hand, springs not from the appearance of producers and consumers on the scene but from the extent of their separation as specified in five dimensions. The greater the separation of the agents, the greater the potential.

The market, therefore, is a complex phenomenon consisting of both relationship and of potentiality. The former represents a power of attraction; the latter, a power of separation. Nor are these opposing powers equally offsetting. In a dynamic economy, the separations increase more rapidly, and the whole market system of relationships grows very complex and more rigid. A catalyst is needed to effect the actualization of market potentials, an activity not disturbing the basic relationships of the market but adjusting the product to the individual consumer. Under conditions of mass production, it is frequently impossible to adjust to change by retooling or redesigning the product. But this does not necessarily mean the end of exchange itself. There are other means of meeting the individual preferences of as many consumers as possible without substantially remaking the product. This is what is generally referred to as merchandising.[26] It is the catalyst that adapts standardized products to individual consumer preferences. It adds to the product some incidental feature which will make the finished article more attractive to individual buyers. The purpose of this addition is to bring into the market buyers who would otherwise be indifferent to the product, because of some incidental whim or preference. Merchandising in this sense takes five forms: incidental changes in the product itself; package changes; service changes; changes in methods of offering where neither space nor time is the prime consideration; and the offering of a premium with the product. Substantial change of the product would not be marketing but production adaptation and so is not included under merchandising activities. Merchandising is the catalyst of the marketing system necessary to facilitate actualization under conditions of the mass market. It gives the individual in a mass market *what* he wants.

The five marketing tasks, corresponding to the five dimensions of the market and facilitated by the catalyst of merchandising activity, when carried out by some marketing agent, fulfill all the conditions for actualizing a market potential and generating an exchange. It should be noted, however, that though each mode of actualization may be analyzed separately, they present themselves as a total force to the marketing executive. All of them must be carried out by someone before any exchange can take place. The marketing manager must, therefore, consider the total dimensions of space, time, perception, ownership, and valuation as well as weigh the merchandising activities which will maximize sales. Marketing tasks can be taken on or sometimes shifted to others—but they cannot be ignored.

Besides, all phases of marketing actualization are interrelated. The appearance of specialized agencies to handle parts of the actualization may add to the efficiency of the motions, but this also adds to the interdependence of the institutions involved. Faster express service provided by railroads improves the performance of time actualization, but it may add to the problems of price actualization because it costs more. Decentralization of agricultural markets adds to the efficiency of space and time actualization, but it is possible to decentralize only when communication facilities permit a wider dissemination of market news and prices.

---

[26] Merchandising has been defined elsewhere as "the planning involved in marketing the right merchandise or service at the right place, at the right time, in the right quantities, and at the right price" (AMA Definitions Committee, *op cit.*, p. 26). This seems, however, far too broad and, in fact, makes merchandising and marketing synonymous. Here the term is used in a much stricter sense—as indicated in the text—as but one component in the whole marketing structure. Merchandising results, strictly, not from the separation of producers and consumers but from the rigidity that arises from mass markets and inflexible mass-production requirements. It is the response of marketing to the particular difficulties of size rather than of separation. It acts not so much to make a sale as to maximize a sale when the basic conditions for an exchange have been created.

The end result of actualization is a market transaction and the satisfaction of consumer wants. Actualization allows the consumer to know about a product and to obtain it for himself where he wants it, at the price he is willing to pay, in a form suited to his individual preferences. If the motions involved use up a minimum of resources to achieve this goal, then marketing efficiency is at a maximum. Marketing institutions appear and disappear in the market, but behind them are the permanent forces of actualization working on market potentials to close the gap in the market relation.

Significance and Application of the Concept of Actualization

Perhaps the most convenient way to suggest the applications of this concept of market potentials and marketing is to propose some generalized hypotheses that should follow from the original premises. This can be done under four headings: institutions, management activities, the role of marketing in the social economy, and the relation of the concept to further research.

If the concepts of market potential and marketing actualization are valid, market institutions are primarily the effects rather than the causes of marketing functions. The distinct lines of identification between wholesale, retail, and service institutions should be expected to be more blurred in real life than they are in the texts. Institutions, therefore, would be the products of change more than the innovators. The real force of change would result from the underlying social conditions that affect market potentials together with the marketing actualization performed in response to the changes in the market potentials. The institutions should reflect these changes even more than they cause them, and there should be evidence of counterveiling power in market potentials as opposed to producer institutions. The existence of an institution should depend ultimately on the functions it performs in relation to the market potential it faces rather than on any other factor.

This conceptual approach also opens the door to considering the consumer as a marketing agent capable of assuming market functions herself and, therefore, capable by her impact of altering marketing institutions. The functions would still exist; it is only the agent performing them that changes. There still has to be transportation, storage, financing, merchandising, assembly, etc. But these may, and have been, shifted to parties other than producers, wholesalers, or retailers. Marketing theory would suggest to the economist that if he desires to study the implications of such a shift in responsibility, he should include some measure of the cost of the function performed by whatever agent assumes that function. To the sociologist, marketing theory would point out that all five dimensions of marketing actualization must be considered before a complete sociological analysis can be made of either market institutions or marketing functions.

The concept of marketing actualization would, at first glance, frighten a practical businesman. This is not surprising, since theory is not the coin of the marketplace. But it would not be as frightening if the concept were translated into the concrete phrase: if you wish to be successful as a marketing agent, you must first determine when, where, who, and at what price consumers want your product, and then you must arrange to tell people about your product, motivate them to buy it, get it to the right parties where and when they want it and in the way they want it. This phraseology lacks the formality of theoretical speech—but it does make communication possible. And it does preserve in substance the concept itself.

It suggests, too, that a strong marketing orientation is required of a business manager, an orientation which reflects a respect for both market potentials and marketing actualization possibilities. Since a continuing knowledge of market potentials is essential for rational marketing action, some provision in every firm for keeping abreast of the market should be made. The more complex and diffuse the market grows, the greater the need for this function. The more sophisticated and generally available the tools for measuring markets in specific dimensions of time, space, consumer information and motivation, valuation, and ownership become, the greater the precision that can be obtained in determining the location of markets. Statistics can shadow market potentials (though never circumscribe them, for they are data from the past) and suggest a useful way of filling out the skeletons of market dimensions. Sales statistics, however, would have to be used with caution. They would show the strength of past activity but not the full scope of present or future possibility.

Market potentials, however, form in this approach only the raw material for marketing. It is not research information but action based on correct information that can yield results. Marketing orientation in a firm, therefore, would imply a strong line marketing organization with research as a staff function whose effectiveness is always to be measured in terms of the action results it produces. The ability to actualize market potentials is the criterion for judging a marketing organization. Respect for market forces is but one of the qualifications to be expected in a marketing executive. Equally important for actualization are the qualities of force and imagination through which the manager uses that knowledge.

If rational marketing action requires both knowledge of market potential and imagination in responding with marketing action, it seems to follow that marketing can never be completely scientific. Creativity, in fact, would grow increasingly vital where there is a great quantity of knowledge, but little response in action. There could never be a complete resolution of the problem of science versus art in marketing management, only a tension with some attempt at balance. Marketing in the present view is a responsive action to a market situation. It does not by itself create demand nor any of the dimensions of the market. It rather must exploit what it can discover by chance, intuition, or research. No theory, therefore, of such phenomena can be strictly scientific. "The logic of marketing has rested upon variations of a simple mechanistic concept of marketing," complains Bartels.[27] Any such beginning assumption of a mechanistic concept is doomed to failure if markets and marketing are not purely quantitative. This does not, of course, deny the possibility of measurement; it only limits its scope. Measurement must follow the model, not determine it.

The present concept of marketing looks at the market not only as a business activity but also as a social phenomenon. The data may be translated into terms of costs, at least approximately, but this is not always necessary. Some studies, depending on their purpose, might profit more by dealing in original units than in economic costs. Even a marketing manager might find it more helpful, at least initially, to talk in terms of the distances to be covered, the time lapses involved, the legal titles to be conveyed, and the amount of paper work included. Marketing is more than a management tool; it is an element of the social structure.

The implication for future research springs from the fact that the concept, rooted in market phenomena, offers a general framework within which data can be gathered, hypotheses ventured, and measurement refined. Quantification will require many contributions from related sciences—from demography, motion and time studies, economics, mathematics and probability analysis, psychology, law, biology, and sociology. Much interest has, in fact, been aroused in assimilating these tools to solve marketing problems, even to the point of almost obliterating the field of marketing itself. This seems to do a disservice to the progress of marketing thought, which must always be rooted in the market if it is to remain a distinctive area for investigation. Research should be fitted to the problem, not the problem to research.

At the present stage, the above approach offers only a concept. The tasks of hypothesis formulation and verification lie ahead. But one assurance remains: no matter how inadequate or unreal the mental constructs proposed by theorists, one solid, baffling, yet intriguing fact remains to give impetus and direction to all marketing speculation. That fact is the starting point and checkpoint for all theory. That fact is the market.

---

[27]Bartels, *op. cit.*, p. 207.

4. ON ATOMIC SENTENTIAL FORMS AND THEORY CONSTRUCTION

Richard M. Martin

I.

THEORIES are expressed in language. To characterize a theory, therefore, is to unearth the linguistic forms employed. Logical analysis, the "new way of words," is preeminently concerned with linguistic forms but need not therewith neglect the way in which these forms are related to the subject matter being examined. Two areas of logical analysis are therefore distinguished, the *syntactical* and the *semantical*. Syntax, concerned solely with linguistic forms and their interrelations, is to be supplemented with a semantics in which linguistic forms are related to subject matter. Both approaches are needed fundamentally for the complex and multifold purposes of the philosophy and methodology of science. To these, one adds a *pragmatics*, in which the human (or other) user of language is explicitly brought into account.

Some theories are already available, full bloom, as it were, whereas others must be formulated *ex nihilo*. More often, we find theories in embryo or in a presystematic state, and our task is to give them an exact logical format. When we speak of theory construction in marketing, it is presumably this latter situation that is meant. We have a body of doctrine, rather scattered perhaps, not too well formulated, not too clear at many crucial points. We wish to improve this situation—to explore the "logical geography" and interrelations of the fundamental notions of marketing theory, to see explicitly how further notions may be defined in terms of these basic notions, to examine and draw out the consequences of various alternative assumptions and hypotheses, and so on. Of course, such a program is highly ambitious, and we must be content in this essay merely to consider a few pertinent themes.

Strictly speaking, every theory as expressed in a language system contains a logic as a part. Hence, the basic notions of logic are fundamental ingredients in language systems. The logical ingredients include such words or phrases as 'and', 'or', 'if—then', 'if and only if', 'for all', 'for some', and 'is identical with'. Further logical notions are definable

68

in terms of these basic notions. Also, *variables* are employed and taken to range over some clear-cut, well-demarcated domain of objects. Perhaps, 'is a member of', in the sense of class or set membership, should be added to the foregoing list of logical ingredients. But whether class or set theory belongs to logic or to mathematics is not clear. (Given a class or set theory of sufficient power, the usual arithmetic of real numbers may be formulated within it, so that mathematics and class theory are, in a rough sense at least, coextensive.) Further, many scientific theories may be formulated in such a way as not to presuppose a class theory. Thus, class or set theory appears less fundamental than logic, conceived in a narrow sense as not involving the notion of class membership. Mathematics is a luxury for science, but logic is its daily bread.

Over and above the basic logical ingredients, a few additional notions are required to characterize the particular subject matter being examined. These are usually *predicates* and may be abbreviated by what we call *nonlogical* predicate constants. Consider, for example, 'buy' and 'sell' and typical contexts in which they occur. Our task, in part, is to determine the precise logical character of these contexts. There are short and long contexts, the shortest being *atomic*. Longer contexts are built up out of atomic ones by means of 'and', 'or', etc.

Let 'X' and 'Z' be variables ranging over some class of human beings, 'y' a variable ranging over concrete goods in some sense, and 't' a variable ranging over time-stretches.

(1)   'X sells y to Z at t'

then provides, presumably, a fundamental linguistic form for talking about selling. We could introduce 'S' as a nonlogical predicate constant, designating the relation of selling, so that

(2)   'X S y, Z, t'

abbreviates (1).

'S' is then what we call a *quadratic* or *four-place* relation, taking as it does four arguments. Forms (1) or (2) we call *atomic sentential* forms, if 'S' is taken as *primitive* (or undefined). In this event, no attempt is made in the given context to analyze or define it in terms of other (perhaps more basic) predicates. We note also that 'S' is taken in such a way that its first and third arguments are variables for human beings, its second is a variable for concrete goods, and its fourth is a variable for time.

Buying is immediately definable in terms of 'S'. We let

'X B y, Z, t' abbreviate 'Z S y, X, t'.

X buys y from Z at t if and only if Z sells y to X at t.

The foregoing constitutes of course only an extremely simplified, even naive attempt to provide an exact linguistic form for 'sells' and related terms. If legal matters are introduced, many complications arise. Human persons must then be regarded as legal entities, and the goods bought or sold must be regarded not as concrete objects but as legal rights to perform with them certain acts or act-types but not others. Suitable logical analyses of the legal person, of rights and privileges, and of acts must thus presumably be sought. Further complications would arise if we were to look more deeply into various psychological, sociological, or economic factors. In principle, there is no limit here as to what can be put under the logical microscope. In practice, however, certain predicates are selected as sufficiently clear and unambiguous for the purposes at hand.

II.

As a more detailed example of theory construction, let us attempt to formulate logical foundations for a theory of human *acts* or *actions*, or *performance* in general, of which buying, selling, and the like, are special cases. Although much important preliminary work has been done in the analysis of actions, no one it seems has attempted to develop a strict logical theory for such analysis. A few tentative and programmatic steps were taken in the author's *Toward a Systematic Pragmatics*.[1] Let us attempt here to improve these and take a few more. Any first attempts of this kind are, of course, fraught with difficulties. Inevitably, some oversimplification or overelaboration will appear here or there. Ultimately, we are interested in interrelating performance with various notions from syntax, semantics, and even quantitative pragmatics.[2] But this is not an easy task, and only a few tentative suggestions toward such a development can be given at this time.

The distinction between sign-designs and sign-events is a familiar one in logical syntax. A sign-design is an abstract shape or pattern, whereas a sign-event is a specific configuration of ink marks or of audible sounds. An analogous distinction can be introduced between *action-kinds* or *-types* and *action-events*. By an action-kind is meant roughly a specific class of similar actions, such as the lighting of cigarettes, or the submerging of a given object or of given objects in a chemical solution, or the noting that a pointer is opposite such and such a numeral on such and such a dial. Action-kinds have *instances* performed *by* human beings *on* specific objects *at* specific times. These instances we call *action-events*. All action-events of a given kind are of course sufficiently "similar" to each other in certain respects.

---

[1] Richard M. Martin, *Toward a Systematic Pragmatics* (Studies in Logic and the Foundations of Mathematics) (Amsterdam: North-Holland Publishing Co., 1959). See also, Richard M. Martin, *Truth and Denotation* (Chicago: University of Chicago Press, 1958), chaps. I and II. The material in sections II–V of the present essay is borrowed, with the kind permission of the editors, from the author's "Performance, Purpose, and Permission," to appear in *Philosophy of Science*.

[2] See in particular Richard M. Martin, *Intension and Decision* (Englewood Cliffs, N.J.: Prentice-Hall, Inc., 1963).

In an extended treatment, one would presumably wish to take account of both action-events and action-kinds, just as in an extended treatment of syntax and semantics, one would wish to consider both sign-designs and sign-events. As a matter of fact, however, no such extended treatment of syntax and semantics has yet been given. These subjects were first developed with expressions construed exclusively as sign-designs. A similar method ought presumably to be followed in developing a general theory of performance. In this first attempt, we shall probably do well then to take into account primarily action-kinds, although action-events need not as a result be neglected.

(We may observe parenthetically that an action-event is an occurrence of an action-type, just as a sign-event is an occurrence of a sign-design. Likewise, in the philosophy of science, it is conducive to clarity to distinguish between events and event-types. The phrase 'occurrence of an event' is strictly speaking meaningless. Events do not occur; they merely are. The word 'event' involves a temporal dimension as a part of its meaning. The word 'action', however, does not. Nor does the word 'sign'. Hence, we distinguish here between types and occurrences by using an appropriate terminology.)

Some action-kinds, or the expressions designating them, may be said to be *monadic*, some *dyadic*, some *triadic*, and so on. If an action-kind is monadic, we may say that an expression for it is of *degree one;* if dyadic, of *degree two;* etc. And often there is choice as to the degree of an expression for an action-kind. For example, 'lighting a cigarette' may be taken in the monadic sense according to which we say that person X lights a cigarette x at time t. It might also be taken as involving a match, a lighter, etc. In this second dyadic sense, we would say that X performs the lighting *on* the cigarette x *with* the match or lighter y at time t. The specific purpose at hand would presumably dictate which kind of analysis is preferable, the monadic or the dyadic. In the general theory to be suggested, each action-kind considered is to have its degree uniquely specified.

Given an action-kind from everyday life, how best to analyze it or to explicate it, as it were, is not the concern of the general theory. Often, there will be alternative ways, and it will not always be clear that one way is necessarily "better" than another. It might be that these alternative ways will not logically exclude each other. The situation is similar to that often met with in the logical analysis or explication of other notions. For example, the word 'father' may be regarded as a class word on some occasions, but on others it may be better to regard it as a dyadic-relation word. The alternative analyses need not exclude each other, however, and 'father' is in fact correctly used in both ways.

To simplify, let us consider for the present only monadic action-kinds. The general theory to be suggested, however, can easily be extended to action-kinds of higher or even of zero degree as we shall see. A zero-adic (medadic) action-type takes no explicit account of an object of action and is often expressed by intransitive verbs. Swimming, sleeping, bathing, etc., are presumably medadic. Of course, one swims *at* some place, but there is no direct object of one's swimming.

Let 'f', 'f$_1$', 'f$_2$', etc., now be constants, i.e., names, designating distinct monadic action-kinds. In the *general* theory of performance, little more concerning these need be said. In any specific application of the theory of course specific properties of each action-kind should be laid down. For example, if 'f' is the monadic action-kind *the lighting of cigarettes*, then an axiom should be laid down that whenever 'f' is performed on *x* by someone, *x* is in fact a cigarette. (See Section IV below.) *Variables* also will be needed, ranging over action-kinds. Let these be the *italicized* letters '*f*', '*g*', and '*h*', with or without numerical subscripts. (The roman letters 'f', etc., as above, are to be constants.)

In order to accommodate action-kinds and to develop a theory concerning them, a general relation of *performance* is introduced as follows. Let 'Prfm' be a primitive and let it occur significantly in contexts of the form

(1)   'X Prfm f, x, t'.

The first argument-place must be occupied by a variable or name for *persons* (or *users*), the second by a variable or name for *action-kinds*, the third by a variable or name for an *individual,* and the fourth by a variable or name for a *time-stretch.* Form (1) may be read "The person X performs an action of type f on the individual *x* at time *t.*"

Let us assume now that expressions of the form (1) are admitted *within the object-language L*, where *L* is one of the usual logical systems of first order. We assume, in other words, that *L* contains not only the thing-variables '*x*', '*y*', etc., but three new sorts of variables (and perhaps constants) as well, for human beings, for time-stretches, and for action-types. The theory of performance and action-kinds is not a theory about linquistic expressions. Hence, it seems appropriate to develop this theory within an object-language and therewith independent of syntax, semantics, and pragmatics. Then later the theory of performance may be inter-related with these, and various notions connecting performance with semantical or pragmatical notions may be defined.

Note that (1) above is significant only where in place of '*f*' we have a variable or name for a *monadic* action-type. For *dyadic* action-types, we must let 'Prfm' be significant in the context

'X Prfm f, x, y, t',

read "X performs f on *x* with *y* at *t*," with perhaps some other appropriate preposition in place of 'with'. Similarly, provision must be made for action-types of higher degree. As has already been remarked, for the present we will concern ourselves only with monadic action-kinds and hence with 'Prfm' only in contexts of the form (1).

Let us think of 'Prfm' throughout in a very concrete sense involving only the simplest kind of physical action-types, action-types consisting of physical motions or processes. Further, the objects upon which the actions are performed are to be thought of as physical or physicochemical objects. These restrictions are not strictly needed, but they help to facilitate the intuitive model. Later, we shall wish to allow also actions upon other users or persons as well, so that (1) will be significant if in place of 'x' a variable or name for a human being is inserted. But first, let us develop the theory in the simplest way. It can later be extended step by step in various directions as may be needed.

When we say that X Prfm f, x, t, the relevant action-event of the type f is to be thought of as being carried on continuously through the whole of t so that when t ceases, the action-event does also. Perhaps the phrase 'during t' suggests this better than 'at t'. To say that X performs f on x *during* t suggests that X does so continuously. We shall use the phrase 'at t', however, bearing in mind specifically what is intended.

To handle time, we presuppose some simple theory of time-flow, akin perhaps to that of Woodger.[3]

The analysis of action-kinds should be of particular interest for the philosophy and methodology of empirical science, especially perhaps for the analysis of the notion of a scientific *experiment*. Experiments involve actions performed upon specific objects by certain persons at certain times. Curious as it may seem, the notion of an experiment has never received the attention it merits. It is surely one of the most important concepts in the philosophy of science, and there is need for its adequate analysis and explication. Such an explication would involve a theory of actions and performance rather fundamentally.

Note that action-kinds or -types, but not action-events, are admitted as values for variables. The effect of talking about action-events is, however, achieved by formulae of the form (1), i.e., 'X Prfm f, x, t'. Presumably X cannot perform two instances of the same action-kind on the same object at the same time. Nor can two persons perform the same action-event upon the same object at the same time. Nor, indeed, can a person perform the same action-event on two distinct objects at the same or at different times. In fact, an action-event should be regarded as uniquely specified by a sentence of the form (1). Thus, we may even think of action-events as being *virtual ordered quadruples* of a suitable kind.[4] Let

(2)   '$<X, f, x, t>$'

be introduced as short for 'the virtual relation among Y, g, y, and t_1 where $Y = X$, $g = f$, $y = x$, and $t_1 = t$'. Action-events corresponding to

---

[3] Cf. J. H. Woodger, *The Technique of Theory Construction (International Encyclopedia of Unified Science*, Vol. II, No. 5) (Chicago: University of Chicago Press, 1939), pp. 32–33; and *The Axiomatic Method of Biology* (Cambridge, Mass.: Cambridge University Press, 1937), pp. 56 ff.

[4] Martin, *Truth and Denotation*, pp. 49 ff.

given action-kinds may then be designated by expressions of the form (2) with appropriate constants in place of the free variables. It is doubtful that we shall need such expressions in the sequel, the effect of such being achieved well enough in contexts of the form (1).

Monadic action-types are in effect triadic relations, with their domains, middle domains, and converse domains suitably restricted. To say that X performs f on x at t is to say that X stands in a certain triadic relation R to x at t. The theory of monadic action-types is thus in effect a branch of the theory of triadic relations. Hence, one might suppose that action-events could be thought of as triples rather than quadruples. For example

$$(3) \qquad\qquad <X, x, t>$$

might be thought of as an action-event. The objection to this is that any triple of this kind would then be an action-event, without a specification of the action-type. The triple consisting of Theaetetus, a certain chair, and a certain time would then be an action-event, even if the time t is not within Theaetetus' life-span or even if the chair x is a fine Chippendale of the eighteenth century. Further, expressions of the form (3) would require that there be one and only one action-event involving X, x, and t. There might, however, clearly be two or more action-events involving these three, or perhaps none at all. We should wish to be able to differentiate between Theaetetus' *sitting* on the chair x at t and his *making*, say the chair x at t, surely quite different action-events. The notation involving quadruples enables us to bring this out clearly. For distinct f and g,

$$<X, f, x, t>$$

and

$$<X, g, x, t>$$

are distinct action-events, as we should surely wish them to be.

Note that the time parameter 't' is used explicitly throughout. We should certainly like to be able to say that Theaetetus sits on the chair x at one time but not at another. With the time factor explicitly brought out, such statements may easily be made. But note that no *spatial* factors or coordinates are needed nor for that purpose any coordinates for temperature or other physical properties—although, if desired, these could be introduced for special purposes. Why should the time factor then be given so privileged a status? The objects x are regarded here as enduring, physical objects upon which certain actions may be performed during their life-span. A person X may perform an action of a given type upon x at one time during its life-span but not at a later time. The time factor is needed to differentiate explicitly between these. Spatial and other physical factors, on the other hand, are implicitly involved in x itself. In general, it seems, these physical factors need not be mentioned unless the specific context requires it.

III.

Let us now turn to several notions definable on the basis of 'Prfm', which seem not only interesting in themselves but useful as well.

We have assumed that '=' in contexts of the form '$f = g$' is admitted as a logical primitive, and hence that suitable axioms for it are available. We assume further that distinct constants for action-kinds designate distinct action-kinds. Thus '$\sim F = G$' always holds where 'F' and 'G' are distinct constants for action-kinds and '$\sim$' is the sign for negation.

Closely related to identity is what may be called *performative equality*, more specifically, *absolute* performative equality. We say that an action-kind f is *performatively equal* to an action-kind g *in the absolute sense* if and only if for any x everyone who ever performs f on x also performs g on x at the same time and conversely. (The word 'absolute' here is to suggest the universal quantifiers implicitly involved.)

Clearly, identical action-types are performatively equal, but performatively equal action-types need not be identical. Hence, it is important to distinguish performatively equal but not identical action-types. It might well happen that whenever one action-type is performed the other is also, and conversely. But even if this should hold, the system should presumably be rich enough to distinguish these action-types in other ways, i.e., to ascribe to one some property not ascribed to the other. (See Section IV below.) If the system is not rich in this way, identity and performative quality should be regarded as the same.

We may also distinguish various types of *relative* performative equality, relative, i.e., to a given person, to a given object, or to a given kind of object, or to both a given person and a given object or kind of object, etc. First, we may say that f is performatively equal to g *relative to person X* if and only if for all x and t, X Prfm f, x, t if and only if X Prfm g, x, t. Also, we may say that f is performatively equal to g relative to the *object* x if and only if for all X and t, X Prfm f, x, t if and only if X Prfm g, x, t. Also, f is performatively equal to g relative to *both* X and x where for all t, X Prfm f, x, t if and only if X Prfm g, x, t. Similarly, other types of relative performative equality could be introduced.

Suppose, for example, that whenever a person X sits on a four-legged chair, he touches the front legs of the chair with his heels, and conversely. These two action-kinds are then performatively equal relative to X. Similarly, because whenever one stands on a floor x, one is in an upright position and has one's feet on x and vice versa, these two action-types are performatively equal in the absolute sense.

Each of these types of performative equality might be useful for the phenomenological analysis or description of some situation. Although the differences are slight, like the differences between the sexes, these are differences which are useful on certain occasions.

We may say that one action-kind f is a *part* of another g (in one sense), if and only if for all x, X, and t, if X performs g on x at t, he also performs f on x at some temporal part of t (but not necessarily conversely). There are undoubtedly other part-whole relations to distinguish here, but this is the only one that is needed for the present.

To illustrate this notion, let 'g' stand for the action-kind of lighting a cigarette in the usual way and let 'f' stand for the action-kind of drawing in on the cigarette while it is between one's lips. Then clearly f is a part of g, because whenever X lights a cigarette x in this way, he draws in upon it while it is between his lips. (We assume that the cigarette is between his lips for a part at least at the time during which he is lighting it.)

Several *relative* part-whole relations between action-types may also be defined. These may be relative to a given person, to a given object, or to both, and they are analogous to the various notions of relative performative equality. The various relations of performative equality and of part to whole clearly have the appropriate properties of identity and part-whole relations.

An action-type is said to be *null* if and only if it is never performed by anyone on any object. We should not wish to assume that there are null action-types. This is a matter for observation to decide. It might so happen that some action-types are null or it might not. Neither possibility should be excluded.

An action-type would presumably be *universal* if everybody is always performing it on everything. There seems no need to introduce action-types of this kind, however, and in fact, it is quite clear that there are none unless one stretches enormously the ordinary meaning of 'action'.

Let us consider now certain kinds of *sums* and *products* of action-types.

Suppose that X performs an action of the kind h upon x at t if and only if he performs *both* f and g on x at t for all X, x, and t. The action-type h is then a kind of simultaneous product of f and g, more specifically, an *absolute* simultaneous product because of the reference here to all X, x, and t. The complex action-type of writing (composing) while typing, e.g., is presumably the absolute simultaneous product of composing and typing, because whenever X writes while typing a page x at time t, he both composes the page and goes through the mechanical motions of typing, and conversely, for all X and x.

But there is also a notion of simultaneous product *relative* to given X, x, and t. We say that h is the simultaneous product of f and g *relative* to X, x, and t where X performs h on x at t, if and only if he performs both f and g on x at t. Suppose X holds a book x in his hands during t and reads it at the same time. The complex action-type holding and reading relative to that X, x, and t is then the simultaneous product of the action-type holding and of the action-type reading, *relative* to X, x, and t.

Given any two action-types (as confined to the same objects), it seems natural to assume that their absolute simultaneous product exists. It might so happen that this product is *null*, but still, we should wish to regard it as a suitable action-type even if no one ever happened to perform in this fashion. It follows that for any X, x, and t, there is a relative simultaneous product for any two action-types, even if null.

In a similar way, absolute and relative simultaneous *sums* of two action-types may be introduced. It is not clear that such notions would be very useful, however, and, given any two action-types f and g, we need not assume that there is an action-type h as their absolute simultaneous sum or as their relative simultaneous sum.

Other kinds of product are what may be called the *absolute* and *relative successive products* of two action-types. Suppose that for all t, X, and x, X performs h on x during t, if and only if for some t_1 and t_2, X performs f on x at t_1 and g on x at t_2 where t_1 and t_2 are successive, exhaustive temporal parts of t. Clearly, h is then merely the product of f and g performed at successive times.

As in the case of simultaneous sums, it is not clear that we should assume that absolute, and hence relative, successive products always exist: f and g might be quite separate action-types performed on x at successive times. There seems to be little reason to allow action-types always to be combined to form a successive product. Unless a strong reason is forthcoming, let us not unnecessarily overpopulate the realm of action-types.

Some action-kinds exhaust or fill the time in which they occur, so to speak; others do not. The lighting of a cigarette during time t takes up the whole of the time t and cannot take place within half of t, say, or within three quarters of t, or within a time containing t as a proper part. In other words, if X lights a cigarette x during t, he can light x at no proper temporal part of t, nor can he light x during the whole of a time of which t is a proper part. But other action-kinds need *not* fill up the whole of the time in which they occur. If any person X sits on a chair x during time t, he is also sitting on x during every temporal part of t. (All times t are continuous, so to speak, and must contain all parts between any two separate parts.) Action-kinds of the former sort shall be considered *exhaustive* with respect to the time in which they occur, those of the latter sort, *nonexhaustive*. Thus, in general, we may say that f *exhausts* t, or that f is *exhaustive with respect to* t, if and only if for all X, x, and t_1, if X Prfm f, x, t, and t_1 is a proper temporal part of t, then it is not the case that X Prfm f, x, t_1. We say that f is *nonexhaustive* with respect to t, if and only if for all X, x, and t_1, if X Prfm f, x, t, and t_1 is a temporal part of t (not necessarily proper part), then X Prfm f, x, t_1 also.

Corresponding relative notions may be defined here also.

The question arises as to whether all action-kinds are either exhaustive or nonexhaustive.

Let us consider the action-kind *eating*, more particularly, eating a meal x during the time interval t. The ordinary use of the word 'eat' is presumably such that this action-kind is neither exhaustive nor non-exhaustive. If one eats a meal x from 1:00 to 2:00 P.M. on such and such a day, it does not follow that he is eating the whole of x at every temporal part of that interval. (Of course, he might be eating a *part* of the meal x at every temporal part of that time interval.[5] This, however, is a very different matter.) Nonetheless, it would still be appropriate to say that he is eating x during the whole time interval. Thus, there seem to be action-kinds which are neither exhaustive nor nonexhaustive with respect to the times at which they occur. Such action-types may be said to be *interrupted* with respect to the times at which they occur. The corresponding relative notions may also be defined.

Let us reflect now a little more closely upon the part-whole relation between action-types and upon how action-types may be analyzed into parts. First, what are the minimal or atomic parts of an action-type? It seems reasonable to require that action-types be analyzable into parts and that this analysis must stop at some point with *minimal* parts. There seems to be no clear-cut way of carrying out such an analysis unless the time factor is brought in. Minimal action-types are presumably performed during what Woodger calls *moments*, i.e., the shortest time intervals in the given context. More specifically, we might say that an action-type is *absolutely atomic*, if and only if it is nonnull and any time at which it is performed is momentary.

As a matter of fact, however, this definition would not be very useful if there are no action-types satisfying it. One and the same person often performs the same action-type at different speeds, as it were, and different persons most surely do. A more useful notion is therefore that of being an atomic action-type *relative* to a person and a time. An action-type f is atomic *relative to X* and t, if and only if that action-type is performed by X at t and t is momentary.

Suppose X moves a physical object from one place to another at time t, and suppose t consists of three consecutive moments, t_1, t_2, and t_3. It seems reasonable to analyze this action-type into three parts: f_1, f_2, and f_3, where f_1 is atomic relative to X and t_1, f_2 atomic relative to X and t_2, and f_3 atomic relative to X and t_3. The whole action-type consists in moving an object from place A to place B. There are intermediary places A_1 and A_2, such that f_1 is the action-type consisting of moving an object from A to A_1; f_2, A_1 to A_2; and f_3, A_2 to B. The velocity or acceleration, or other such physical properties, need not enter into our considerations here. Strictly, f_1 is the action-type of moving an object from A to A_1 with such and such a velocity or acceleration, etc.

We observe that absolutely atomic action-types performed at t, as well as action-types relative to X and t, are both exhaustive and non-

---

[5] We have not admitted here a part-whole relation between individuals, but in a more extended treatment, it would no doubt be desirable to do so.

exhaustive with respect to t. There are thus action-types which are both exhaustive and nonexhaustive as well as action-types which are neither exhaustive nor nonexhaustive, with respect to the times at which they are performed.

There are surely ways of determining minimal action-types other than that suggested. If we are concerned only with certain specified action-types, which in the given context need not be subdivided, these very action-types may themselves perhaps be regarded as minimal. For example, if the context is a legal one involving, say, action-types concerned with the driving, parking, etc., of motor vehicles, these very action-types may be regarded as minimal, there being no need to subdivide them into parts. Presumably the minimal action-types should be mutually exclusive and would be chosen accordingly. To determine the minimal action-types other than by reference to temporal moments would seem then to involve fundamental reference to some special set of action-types germane to a given legal or other context.

Finally, let us comment upon a few virtual classes of particular interest.

Consider the virtual class of all monadic action-types performed by a person X during his lifetime. This is obviously a very important class, completely characterizing the person X with respect to his monadic action-types. Let us call this class (i.e., the virtual class of all f's, such that there exists at least one x and at least one t, such that X Prfm f, x, t) the *total monadic performative class* of X. Such a class, together with the analogous dyadic one, etc., should clearly be of interest for ethics, if moral responsibility is thought to attach to actual behavior. (Perhaps some restrictions on t here would be desirable, so as to relativize X's actions to selected times.)

Another closely related virtual class is that of all objects upon which X has performed some monadic action-type or other during his life-span. Such a class comprises the total environment of objects upon which X acts, the *total monadic performative environment* of X, as it were.

Consider also the virtual class of all monadic action-types ever performed upon some given object x. Again, such a class completely characterizes x insofar as x is a component or factor in monadic actions. Such a class we might call the *total monadic actional class of x*. In the behavioral sciences, physical objects are of interest not because they possess given physical properties or stand in given physical relations to other physical objects, but because they are termini, so to speak, of action, because people perform certain action-types upon them. The total monadic actional class of x is thus presumably of more importance to the behavioral scientist than is x itself.

Again, the virtual class of persons who ever perform some action or other on a given object is an interesting class in connection with the problem of giving a precise analysis of such notions as 'role' and 'status'. Also of interest is the class of all persons who perform some given action on a given object. The former class is the *total monadic human environment* of the object, so to speak, whereas the latter is the total monadic human environment of the object with respect to the one given action-type.

IV.

Whenever new primitives are introduced, axioms or rules must be laid down to characterize them. The following are suggested somewhat tentatively as rules governing the primitive 'Prfm'.

First, we should wish to assume that there is *at least one nonnull* action-type and that there is *no universal* action-type, i.e., there is no f such that for all X, x, and t, X Prfm f, x, t. We assume also the existence of *at least one absolute simultaneous product* of any two action-types. In many cases, of course, this product will be null. Uniqueness with respect to absolute performative equality readily follows in the sense that if h and h' are both absolute simultaneous products of f and g, then h and h' are performatively equal in the absolute sense. As a result of this law, we have also uniqueness of the absolute simultaneous product with respect to the various kinds of relative performative equality introduced.

The next rule, which may be called the *Rule of Atomic Parts*, states that if X Prfm f, x, t, and t_1 is any momentary part of t, then there is a g such that X Prfm g, x, t_1. As a result of this rule, all action-types actually performed by X at t may in effect be decomposed into action-types performed by X at momentary parts of t. These various action-types may or may not be distinct from each other, but they are atomic relative to X and t_1 and hence (trivially) exhaustive of the time t_1 at which they take place.

We have previously distinguished the pure theory of action-kinds from the applied theory. The pure theory may be regarded as characterized by these four general asssumptions, together with such further ones as might be needed. The pure theory is concerned with properties of all action-kinds but without naming any specific one. For the pure theory, no constants for action-kinds are required, although they may be present. In the applied theory, specific action-kinds are not only named, but suitable properties of such kinds are laid down axiomatically. Among such axioms, there are certain ones which we shall call *Rules of Kind*. Usually, these will be of the form that if X Prfm f, x, t, then x is a member of such and such a virtual class F of objects. To return to the example already given, if f is the monadic action-kind of lighting a cigarette, then F here would be for the virtual class of cigarettes. This Rule of Kind would then make explicit that if X performs f on x at t, then x is a cigarette.

In the applied theory, there might, of course, be other types of axioms laying down properties of specific action-kinds and of how they are interrelated. The specification of such properties and relations is, of course, a part of the analysis of these action-kinds, of their phenomenology, as it were. But in the general theory, with which we are concerned here, no such axioms need be specified. Note that the theory is being sketched in a way that such rules can easily be added. As has already been mentioned, the presence of constants for action-kinds is optional.

As an example of the additional axioms needed in the applied theory, consider the following. Suppose 'A_1', . . , 'A_k' are primitive predicate constants, taking variables or constants for action-types as arguments. Each of these predicate constants stands for a property of action-types: A_1, e.g., might be the set of all action-types involving the human arm in one way or another; A_2, the human foot; A_3, on the other hand, might be a set of certain kinds of verbal actions requiring the use of the mouth, throat, and tongue. Presumably, A_1, etc., will be chosen so as to allow a suitable classification of the action-types to be considered in the given application of the theory. Further axioms would stipulate other properties of or interrelations between or among properties, depending upon the phenomenology of the particular action-types considered. And still further axioms might stipulate that such and such a person or persons have in fact performed such and such action-types on certain objects at particular times.

V.

Closely related to the notions of performance introduced above are some notions which appear essential for certain contemporary sociological theories. No doubt, these notions are useful for marketing theory as well.

In *Toward a General Theory of Action*, edited by Parsons and Shils,[6] we note that sociology is regarded primarily as the systematic study of *social action*. Social action, however, is not mere performance in the sense discussed above. Rather, it is performance oriented to the gaining of certain *ends* or *goals*. Further, any performance takes place in certain "situations" or contexts; it is "normatively regulated" and involves the expenditure of energy or effort on the part of the agent or performer. To paraphrase an example from Parsons and Shils, the behavior of *a man driving his automobile to a store to go shopping* may be analyzed as involving these various factors. To go shopping is the goal or end of the action. The "situation" or context consists of the road and car and the present locale of the man. The man must actually expend energy to perform the given action of driving his car. Further, his behavior is normatively regulated, i.e., his present action is a reasonable or "intelligent" means for achieving the given goal.

Let us look at this a little more closely and consider a suitable new primitive for handling this type of goal-directed behavior. Driving an automobile to a given place we may regard as a dyadic action-type. And, of course, we shall also wish to introduce a time factor, although Parsons

---

[6] Talcott Parsons and Edward A. Shils (eds.), *Toward a General Theory of Action* (Cambridge, Mass.: Harvard University Press, 1951), especially pp. 53 ff.

and Shils fail to do so explicitly. How should the goal, shopping, be handled? Shopping might be treated as a monadic action-type, shopping for an item z. But the goal remains the same, even if there is no item actually bought or even to be bought. Thus, for the present purpose, it seems better to regard shopping as zero-adic.

Let

(1)   'X Prfm f, x, y, t, g'

read then "X performs f on x to y at t *in order to perform g*." This perhaps may be regarded as the fundamental kind of locution for the social theory of action and for the use of that theory in marketing. More extended forms must also be considered, allowing for action-types of all degrees, both as present actions and as anticipated goals.

Precisely what Parsons and Shils mean by "situation" is not too clear. Presumably the situation is wholly determined by the agent X, the objects x and y (y in the example given being a place), the time t, and the goal g. If so, "situations" are adequately handled by expressions of the form (1), and no new variables need be introduced to range over them.

Note that no provision is made in (1) for the "normative" factor regulating action. But this normative factor is presumably a sentence of some language system which itself talks about or is relevant to action-types. The given sentence is presumably accepted as a basis for the given action. In the example cited, one normative principle is perhaps to the effect that whenever one drives his car along such and such a road, he in due time (barring the unforeseen) reaches the given store. This sentence is accepted by person X at the time to a high degree. He bases his present action upon it as well as upon many other relevant sentences. Thus, no specific mention need be made in (1) of the normative principle or principles involved. It seems likely that they can be handled by reference to the notions of acceptance and acceptance as a basis for action.

Parsons and Shils point out that social actions are not "empirically discrete" but take place in clusters or "constellations." These clusters, they tell us, are of three kinds: "social systems," "personalities," and "cultural systems." [7]

The agent X is always a human agent. The objects x, y, etc., in (1), however, may or may not themselves be human agents. The kind of locution needed for the discussion of social systems must allow for this. Social systems involve "interaction" between two or more human agents. Thus, they consist of action-types which human beings perform upon human beings. We need then a locution of the form

(2)   'X Prfm f, Y, t, g'

in place of, or in addition to, (1). A cultural system is then presumably a virtual class of action-types f such that for some $X, Y, t,$ and g, X Prfm

----
[7] *Ibid.*, p. 54.

f, Y, t, g. Other conditions should perhaps be added, but at least this much is needed. Personality systems, on the other hand, are relativized to a given "actor." Thus, a personality system relative to person X is presumably the virtual class of all f such that for some Y, t, and g, X Prfm f, Y, t, g. Here, likewise, some further conditions are no doubt necessary, but this much is essential. Finally, cultural systems are constituted by the "organization of the values, norms, and symbols which guide the choices made by actors and which limit the types of interaction that may occur among actors." [8] As suggested, the "norms" are presumably sentences relevant to actions accepted to a high degree by members of the social group. Perhaps, therefore, this notion may be handled as a suitable virtual class of sentences.

In these few comments, we have tried to do no more than to suggest that the preceding material may be suitably extended to provide a sound logical basis for some notions needed in contemporary social theory. These notions must then be extended to the behavior of social groups. At this point, however, difficult problems emerge which are beyond our present, more modest, concern.

VI.

The theory of marketing is not an autonomous theory. Rather, it presupposes pertinent fragments of theory from various special sciences. Surely, some theory of action or fragment of such—perhaps of the kind suggested above—is needed, if marketing behavior is regarded as a species of human action. To this must be added fragments of legal theory and of various social sciences, as has already been suggested.

The analysis of the logical foundations of science is often of help to the working theoretician. High-powered mathematical techniques and "models" may or may not prove helpful. There is constantly the difficulty of forcing empirical data to fit the (usually simplified) mathematical conditions. The application of logic has no such limitations, being concerned exclusively with linguistic forms. No matter how complicated or intransigent the data, suitable linguistic forms can be found to talk about it clearly. Otherwise, let us be silent. That of which we cannot talk clearly is not yet fit data for science.

The search for proper linguistic forms for the sciences is not easy, and we cannot always be sure when we have found them. Also, forms acceptable to one kind of analysis may not be acceptable to another. Usually, we must rest content with forms "good enough" for some intended purpose, which forms themselves, however, may require further analysis. The search for proper atomic sentential forms is probably the most difficult part of theory construction, and yet the bedrock upon which the whole superstructure of science rests.

---

[8] *Ibid.*, p. 55.

5. HOW WE CAN "KNOW" MORE
ABOUT MARKETING

Perry Bliss

SEVERAL LEVELS of "knowing" should be examined in an inquiry of what it is we can know in marketing. Let us look first at the level of simple inspection and reporting.[1]

It is at this level that science starts, or ends, or both. If initially the inductive method of inquiry is used and empirical generalizations are sought, then bits of reality are reported to be so and so. If, on the other hand, a deductive method of inquiry is used, reasoning starts by making some basic assumptions about the relevant area of reality from which conclusions as to actual events are to be reached. Confirmation is usually obtained by reporting that reality in the relevant area is or is not as predicted (deduced).[2]

In any event, the senses are assumed to be able to report simple direct experience. If an investigator is looking at the price tags in a chain-store supermarket and reports that the price of bread is 25 cents a loaf in an A & P store in Centertown, his findings can be quickly confirmed by any interested party. To question this fact is to go too far afield into ontology or epistemology for present purposes.[3] Hence, if what we wish to know in marketing can be found out by a descriptive reporting of simple contemporary events, there is little we can do but use our sense perception.

However, even in the simple naming of the phenomenon perceived—in this case the price of bread in a chain store—the relevant concepts are

---

[1] An interesting discussion of the initial or "lower" levels of inquiry is given in Karl W. Deutsch, "The Limits of Common Sense," *Psychiatry: Journal for the Study of Interpersonal Processes,* May, 1959, pp. 105–12.

[2] In the process of investigation, the deductive and inductive approaches are so intertwined, it is not rewarding to separate them. They are treated separately here for expository reasons only.

[3] The relation of the knower to the known is discussed in any basic text in philosophy or logic. Also, it is taken without further argument that reality is ordered or patterned and that the order can be known. The view on this point is here essentially that set forth by Paul Meadows, "Models, Systems and Science," *American Sociological Review,* February, 1957, pp. 3–9.

involved ones. This has important implications for theory because concepts are the variables that are linked and placed one with another to build higher levels of inquiry. Even at this initial level of direct inspection, concepts of different orders are mixed. Some help us go beyond the data, beyond the directly perceived, more than others. Bread, for example, is the name given to a perceived cluster of real (existing) characteristics. Bread is taken to be a physical object that stands by itself. The concept of price, on the other hand, refers to a measure or ratio equating bread and money. If we know what the concept "price" implies, the term can be used to measure the value of any and all goods—such, for example, as a similar (or different) loaf of bread at another store up the street.

If we consider not only the price of bread in a single store at one time and place but also the price of the same commodity in other stores in the same area, the concept of a "market" and a market price arises. Sufficient inspection and observation of the price of bread in several locations will reveal that prices for the standard loaf in any community tend to cluster and that a typical or market price can be discovered. If this be so, we have now arrived at the notion of the price level of bread in Centertown. We are dealing not with direct perception or inspection but with the mental manipulation of a collection of prices gained by direct perception or inspection.[4]

Nonetheless, inspection of bread prices and knowledge of a going market price for bread will not disclose, by itself, any information concerning the relationship among, say, TV prices or shoe prices. Bread prices, in themselves, cannot go beyond themselves. A higher level (more general) statement therefore must be developed, one that can go beyond the relationships of prices for bread and take in other market prices. This generalized statement must come from data other than prices per se, if it is to explain general prices.

For example, let us assume one can establish the generalized proposition that in an open- and free-market structure, with self-seeking, mobile consumers, different prices cannot exist for the same item at the same time in the same place. The phenomenon of the relationship among standardized bread prices can then be explained as but one case among many (all) such similar cases, given similar market structure and consumer motivation. This higher-level generalization that only one price can rule in a common competitive market may become "known" by observing a number of market situations and finding that prices for standardized goods behave as was indicated by the study of the price of bread. From

---

[4] Concerning a similar conceptual problem, Leontieff points out that the index of United States output of consumer goods refers to no object familiar to direct observation but to a group of objects collected in an index with their only common property being their use by consumers. Wassily Leontieff, "The Problem of Quantity and Quality in Economics," *Daedalus*, Fall, 1959, pp. 631–32.

this method of building up many empirical commodity price findings, it can be "seen" that a general phenomenon is involved.

On the other hand, an *a priori* assumption could have been the original starting point. That is, if we assume the presence of mobile, self-seeking consumers, the making of standardized offerings by the several sellers, etc., we can infer one price as *necessarily* (deductively) the outcome. In this case, the inspection of actual prices in the marketplace would become the last operation in the chain of investigation and be used to check the correctness of the deduction.

In either event we "know" more about the market now than simple inspection, per se, could supply. We have two levels of knowledge—knowledge derived from the senses and knowledge that lies in the conceptual realm beyond the sense level—as more "generalized knowing."

Any statement, however, to the effect that *necessarily* only one price can prevail in such a market refers to the necessity that lies in the logical relationship among the concepts, not among the "facts." Reality has its own pattern of necessary relationships. Of course, it is the real, or existing, relationships that we are trying to get at by our conceptualization. Nonetheless, the best that can be said about the conclusions of a theory, and all really that is ever said, is that the conclusions drawn are consistent with the facts insofar as they have been observed.

To return for a moment to an earlier point, when one goes beyond the data by means of a higher generalization, as was done to reach the concept of a market price, he not only gains knowledge concerning a single price level but also learns something of the general law of markets. The statement that only one price can prevail in a "competitive" market for the same item permits us to know that if several prices exist for that item, the market is not free. Among the possible barriers are the immobility of consumers, the presence of monopolistic elements, and the lack of sufficient knowledge. Any of these would permit several prices of bread to exist.

The use of a higher generalization such as the model of an open market implies knowledge of its opposite—the notion of a "closed" or imperfect market. In this latter situation, variable behavior of prices can be seen as normal. Furthermore, by means of a generalized construct or market model, intelligent questions can be asked of reality and a rational and schematic pattern of inquiry becomes possible. Without a model of some type, one must rely upon an *ad hoc* empirical approach.

In all that heretofore has been mentioned, there is an implicit assumption of regularities. In our previous illustration, we assumed that our product did not differ in quality from moment to moment or within the market from store to store, and that consumers' tastes would remain somewhat the same over time and from store to store. Without such regularities rational analysis is virtually impossible.

Very little can be known about phenomena that appear and reappear

in a random or chaotic fashion, or about products that rapidly change
form or quality, or about consumers who follow no discernible pattern
in their behavior.[5] Most of the few generalizations that exist in marketing
have to do with areas displaying regularities. The so-called convenience
goods that are bought frequently, such as cigarettes, bread, and newspapers, lend themselves to analysis and to findings that have some hope of
being generalized. It is no accident that studies of brand switiching, shopping habits, etc., have been done in areas with sufficient repetition and
regularity to permit successful manipulation of data. High-fashion goods,
one-of-a-kind buys, and fads that come and go practically overnight repel generalization and theoretical analysis.

We need to uncover large numbers of areas in which uniformities
appear if marketing theory is to flourish. Considerable stability in the
phenomena under investigation is necessary to get any certainty in our
analysis, or even to achieve the empirical generalizations that might form
building blocks to a theory. We cannot "know" much about gadflies
except that they gad; although, presumably, this is something.

So far we have discussed knowing by simple inspection, such as seeing
a product in a store at a price. We have also looked at knowing by
manipulating simple concepts, such as "prices" and "money" and "markets" to arrive at a market price. Let us now take up the possibility of
examining the relationship among several separate conceptual areas and
see how this might be helpful in knowing about marketing. For example,
what is involved "in knowing about" the concept "chain store."

Use of this concept means that marketers have picked out of the
environment, have abstracted from reality as being *generally* significant
for theory, the fact that stores are grouped under one ownership.[6] Not
stores that are two stories high, not stores that are operated by former
salesmen, not stores that are free from debt, but units that are "chained"
are the ones that are isolated and named. But it does little good to define
or name something and then stop short at that point. Reasoning must
move beyond the stage of definition if the concept is to have any analytical power.

For example, it might be deduced as self-evident (contained in the
concept) that a chain store, having more than one unit and more than

---

[5] In speaking of the need for regularity if theory is to advance, Stigler says,
"Until we possess many uniformities, we cannot erect broad analytical systems which
are likely to be illuminating in the areas where uniformities have not yet been
isolated. This is true because it is a variety of uniformities calling for systematization
that gives rise to a useful analytical system; with only a few uniformities, too many
plausible (but vague and confusing) generalizations are at hand." George J. Stigler,
Five Lectures on Economic Problems (New York: The London School of Economics and Political Science, The Macmillan Co., 1950), p. 41.

[6] When we define and conceptualize, we abstract from reality some features of
the environment but not others. It is assumed that the features abstracted are thought
to be important and relevant to the field of knowledge at hand and will be "tied"
to other observations to explain further phenomena.

one location, dilutes the risks inherent in a single location. Or perhaps it will be inferred that chain stores will be able to buy for less because of the economies of large orders. (Two or more stores, other things equal, need more merchandise than one.) If such a statement is made, it links the concept of size with the concept of economies of scale borrowed from economic theory. It is only because we know what is involved in the logic of cost curves that we gain by this linkage. Another conclusion that might be suggested by the notion of a chain store is that such organizations are inimical to the American competitive system, which is thought to require the presence of many small independent units. This conclusion implies, in turn, the use of another conceptual model—the competitive model of economic theory and its welfare implications.

Empirically, it might have been observed that chain stores are patronized, in general, by the middle and lower classes. This observation, if it is to be related to marketing analysis, brings in concepts and thought patterns from sociology and suggests that social classes view certain stores as appropriate to their station in life and other stores as inappropriate. Also, psychology provides insights as the "image" of the store is involved.

It is assumed for present purposes that concepts borrowed from economics and the behavioral sciences are adequately developed in their respective disciplines. The task of the marketing theorist is to integrate these concepts into the analysis of marketing problems. Unfortunately, the interdisciplinary contributions have not always been fully developed. The reformulation and restructuring of what are essentially borrowed concepts may indeed be a formidable task.[7] In any case, concepts such as social class, economies of scale, store image, and so on are really not parts of a well-articulated system of theory. Rather, they are signposts that arrest attention and say: Here is something that needs examination and analysis. They furnish orientation to nearby data. Of course, such orientations are important stepping stones to further inquiry and theorizing.

Nonetheless, in the process of being defined, conceptualized, and set in its marketing environment, the concept of a chain store seems to carry beyond itself. It leads by linkage to other concepts and theoretical systems and to generalizations about reality involving several levels of model building not only in marketing but in related disciplines.[8] This is the level of inquiry at which we are beginning to "know" about marketing.[9] To

---

[7] Alvin W. Gouldner, "Exploration in Applied Social Science," *Social Problems*, January, 1956, pp. 169–81.

[8] Although it is necessary that concepts be related logically if they are to be part of a theory, it is also necessary, if the theory is to be fruitful, that they be related empirically. Thought does not legislate reality; smoke had better be related to fire in the real world if it is to be related meaningfully in the world of thought.

[9] An interesting "polar" classification of levels of knowing is given by Mills, when he says, "A conception is an idea with empirical content. If the idea is too large for the content, you are tending toward the trap of grand theory; if the con-

know what is relevant for marketing theory about a chain store is to "see" it through a kit of conceptual schemes.

Empirical generalizations and lower-level models of limited generality are obviously possible and desirable even without a grand theoretical system in which to integrate them. Events do seem to "hang together" in several areas of the marketplace, and many important things can be said about such events. The empirical fact that people tend to cluster in cities in given patterns of land use can lead to some important generalizations about retail structure. The fact that some buyers and sellers consistently pair off in the channel can lead to statements concerning channel cooperation. The fact that many consumers repeatedly shop at given outlets can lead to notions of patronage motives.

Nonetheless, much that we wish to know in marketing will escape if fragmented and atomistic bits of "sound" empirical knowledge and lower-level concepts are not related by some thread of inference to higher levels and more generalized viewpoints. One of the most important problems presently confronting marketing theory concerns the process by which the micro thinker who disregards the whole to study the specific (this group includes the majority of market researchers) and the macro thinker who dwells on the whole while disregarding what is within the system (this is the position of many who favor the "marketing within the economy" approach) can be brought together. If marketing theory is to be viable, it seems advisable to attempt some middle ground between these extremes.

We observe reality in many ways and in many areas. If we are to theorize successfully, the findings of the several disciplines should be synthesized in areas of interaction. If empirical constancy is found in human behavior in one discipline at a point that overlaps another discipline, surely some generalizations can be uncovered. Such constancies will have to be honored eventually by any investigator who deals with the area.[10] For example, studies have been made on ego-involvement, on personal influence and the role of "influentials," on demand elasticities, and, in our own field, on goods classification systems.[11] Can we predict consumer behavior any better by trying to see the common thread in these areas? In purchases which we believe reveal our tastes and in which we are considerably ego-involved, do we obtain the same types of goods as are

tent swallows the idea, you are tending toward the pitfall of abstracted empiricism." C. Wright Mills, *The Sociological Imagination* (New York: Oxford University Press, 1959), p. 124, see also chaps. ii and iii.

[10] Santo F. Camilleri, "Theory, Probability, and Induction in Social Research," *American Sociological Review*, April, 1962, p. 177.

[11] For a general treatment of these areas, see James A. Bayton, "Motivation, Cognition, Learning—Basic Factors in Consumer Behavior," *The Journal of Marketing*, January, 1958, pp. 282–94; Elihu Katz, "The Two-Step Flow of Communication: An Up-to-Date Report on an Hypothesis," *The Public Opinion Quarterly*, Spring, 1957, pp. 61–78; and Louis P. Bucklin, "Retail Strategy and the Classification of Consumer Goods," *The Journal of Marketing*, January, 1963, pp. 50–55.

acquired with some influential in mind and which, therefore, have relatively inelastic demands and lie to the specialty goods end of the goods classification spectrum? Can these concepts be logically related?

Can we link the studies in social class, reference group theory, and household economic behavior to market segments and subsegments in any conceptual interrelationship? Social class theory rests, at bottom, on groups that share a common way of life and hold a similar set of values. These similarities lead to familiarity with specific classes of products, to shared likings, and to common imagery.[12] When events are perceived through shared concepts, common patronage, broadly speaking, develops. It is this common patronage which generates market segments.

The preceding paragraph discusses concept formation and possible concept linkage. Does marketing theory need also some basic concept clarification? For example, what implications do we attach to the concepts "production" and "marketing"? We speak of "production firms" and "marketing firms." General Motors is a good example of the former and Macy's of the latter. But the economists, and common sense in general, treat them both as business firms seeking profits. And, of course, any sharp separation leads to arguments that producing firms (manufacturers) create value added but retailers and wholesalers (marketing institutions) account for the "cost of distribution."

Would it be of any theoretical advantage to marketing thought if strictly *intrafirm* activity were considered production and *interfirm* activity, marketing?[13] Looked at this way, all firms, retailers, and wholesalers as well as manufacturers, are producing units creating something of value (utility) by virtue of their internal dealings within their own organizations. In their dealings with other organizations or with consumers or the general public, they engage in marketing. General Motors and Macy's are thus on the same conceptual footing. Also, there are marketing functions and activities but not marketing institutions, per se. As a corollary to this, integrated firms carry on logistical rather than marketing activities when they deal with units of their own empires. Such a redefinition of marketing and production may create more problems than it answers. Yet, there is an ambiguity in the present use of the terms that requires logical clarification.

And while we are theorizing about basic marketing concepts, how does the concept of marketing relate to that of distribution? Are these

---

[12] For an interesting approach to consumer taste formation, see Tibor Scitovsky, "On the Principle of Consumer Sovereignty," *American Economic Association: Proceedings*, May, 1962, pp. 262–68; also Herbert E. Krugman and Eugene L. Hartley, "The Learning of Tastes," *The Public Opinion Quarterly*, Winter, 1960, pp. 621–31; and Richard P. Coleman, "The Significance of Social Stratification in Selling," in Martin L. Bell (ed.), *Marketing: A Maturing Discipline*, Proceedings of the American Marketing Association (December, 1960), pp. 171–84.

[13] F. M. Nicosia, "Marketing and Alderson's Functionalism," *The Journal of Business*, October, 1962, p. 411 and footnotes.

concepts synonymous? Can similar inferences be made from them? Assume a static economy in equilibrium (the end product of the logic of the competitive system in the absence of an exogenous force). In such an equilibrium economy, would there be any marketing? The mere repetition of yesterday's activities today and tomorrow—if this be equilibrim—is hardly what is meant by marketing. Why must the force which disturbs the state of equilibrium be exogenous? Is equilibrium prevented by inherent or endogenous forces? Might not marketing be the factor which creates change in the system? Empirical studies of new product introductions, of the "two-step" flow of communication, and the like, might afford new concepts which could be logically related in a statement of the role of marketing in nonequilibrium economies. Equilibrium economies, if such exist, would have a distribution system, not a marketing system. The purpose here is not to suggest a macro theory of marketing but merely to clarify concepts.

All of the above are but suggested areas of analysis. The point to be made, returning to the earlier thoughts of this paper, is that concepts are building blocks for middle-range conceptual patterns. These patterns enable us to understand the system and "know" something more of the marketing process. Of course, there are those who hold that theorizing and model building should be kept to a minimum. Stark empiricists believe that marketing investigation should center around specific problems and that when such problems arise, they should be answered by grasping reality in any manner possible. Attempts to generalize and build theories about marketing per se are either out of place or premature. Although this group is critical of efforts to develop a theory of marketing, the theorist cannot afford to ignore the work of his critics. Empiricists are extremely helpful if they truly pass on connected bits of reality. Such findings can be the raw material for those who are theoretically oriented.

6. A NORMATIVE THEORY OF MARKETING SYSTEMS

Wroe Alderson

MARKETING as a phase of group activity appeared rather late in the history of human culture. Despite some tentative beginnings in village societies, the flowering of trade was coincidental with the rise of cities in the great river valleys of Egypt and Asia. Marketing from the first has been an extremely dynamic culture component, accelerating the differentiation of other activities and the functional specialization of both individuals and groups. Human behavior in the marketplace is an essential aspect of human behavior in general. Marketing theory may eventually be recognized as part of the theoretical framework for a general science of behavior.

Theory in the behavioral field is both descriptive and normative. In an earlier treatment of behavior systems [1] the author proposed several survival theorems as descriptive generalizations concerning the behavior of systems. The intent in this essay is to formulate some normative principles of system behavior which will be consistent with the rational self-interest of those who control a system or participate in its activities. It will then be argued that these principles provide the basis for a normative theory of marketing which is relevant for the decision maker. Some marketing developments will be cited in which the question may well be raised as to whether these basic normative principles are being violated.

The Ecological Framework

Pending the more comprehensive formulation of a general science of human behavior, the available starting points for the marketing theorist include economics and cultural ecology. Economics and ecology are two ways of looking at the relations between living things and the resources which sustain their activities. Marketing as a field of study does not rest comfortably under the label of applied economics. There is an overlap

---

[1] Wroe Alderson, "Survival and Adjustment in Organized Behavior Systems" in Reavis Cox and Wroe Alderson (eds.), *Theory in Marketing* (Homewood, Ill.: Richard D. Irwin, Inc., 1950).

between the tools and concepts of general economics and the analytical needs of the marketing specialist, but far from a perfect fit. The broader framework of ecology holds greater promise for the development of marketing science in both descriptive and normative terms. The term "ecology," borrowed from biology, has been applied to human societies with several distinct shadings of meanings. The sense intended here lies close to that of cultural ecology, a term introduced by the anthropologist, Julian Steward.[2] A crucial aspect of culture, says Steward, is the technology through which the culture-bearing society accomplishes adaptation to its environment. The ecology of human societies is one which recognizes culture change rather than biological evolution as the major instrument of adaptation within the relevant time span.

Marketing specialists are working in an applied segment of what may eventually become a general science of human behavior. Every attempt to market a new product or to distribute an old product more efficiently is actually an effort to modify patterns of behavior. Every active marketing program endeavors to accelerate culture change or to delay it. Marketing is directly concerned with the material culture embodied in exchangeable products. In order to understand exchange, the specialist must also try to understand the changing aspirations of individuals and groups in the culture and to assess the opportunities and constraints arising in the social and physical environment.

The behavioral and cultural approach to marketing processes largely falls outside the scope of economics, at least as defined by some of its most distinguished exponents. Economics as the mathematical logic of scarcity is invaluable for marketers but not sufficient. Its abstract theorems concerning allocation of scarce resources have application to marketing activities although the general economist has usually dealt with applications to production. But the level of taste, the technological functions, and the flows of information which the economist *qua* economist takes for granted are the primary business of a science of marketing. The marketing specialist observes how marketing systems work and recommends ways of making them work better. This functionalist approach must take account of the structure of the behavior systems through which men seek their goals and once again requires a perspective which cannot be derived from economics alone.

Cultural ecology, like animal ecology, is concerned with the adjustment of a population to its environment. Steward regards population per square mile as a fundamental parameter of any ecological setting. Emphasis is placed, however, on group behavior and the technology available to a tribe or a larger society in exploiting its resources. Various conditions

---

2 Julian Steward, *Theory of Culture Change* (Urbana, Ill.: University of Illinois Press, 1955). The same general view, without the term "cultural ecology," is more fully documented by Ralph Linton in such books as *The Tree of Culture*, (New York: Alfred A. Knopf, Inc., 1955).

may exist as to the degree of adjustment between a culture-bearing society or group and its environment. In static equilibrium there is little change in the size of the population, in its aspirations, or in its technology. In a state of disequilibrium, resources are steadily depleted by destructive technologies. Increasing population pressure on the remaining means for sustaining life results in even more reckless exploitation and still more destructive competition. What may be called the habitability of the environment, or its ability to sustain a desired level of living, moves steadily downward. In dynamic equilibrium the technology employed produces both an increasing surplus of consumable goods and advances in the technology itself. The society is encouraged to raise its aspirations and to adopt technologies which will meet its expanding requirements without destroying the long-run habitability of the environment. Contemporary societies, both East and West, hope to maintain the conditions for dynamic ecological equilibrium.

The marketing function plays a vital role in the dynamic process of matching goods and needs and in organizing institutions and processes to serve this ultimate purpose. The ecological perspective offers criteria for marketing performance which transcend the limited measures of economic efficiency. Indeed, marketing ideally connects separate production centers or operating systems in such a way as to optimize the outputs of the whole society. It is concerned with the external relations of individual units or organized behavior systems. These relations involve that peculiar amalgam of competition and cooperation which is so well recognized in ecology and so difficult to accommodate within the framework of received economic theory.

Since marketing is a function of organized behavior systems, and since these systems are the agencies through which a society exploits its environment, marketing theory is necessarily concerned with the structure and nature of organized behavior systems. The internal structure and operation of a system has a vital bearing on such external functions as marketing. Some years ago the author asserted the need for recognizing three levels of equilibrium in organized human activities and relating these levels to each other.[3] First there is market equilibrium, which pertains to the network of external relations among organized behavior systems. Secondly, there is organizational equilibrium, which is a form of internal balance within an individual system. Finally, there is the more embracing concept of ecological equilibrium pertaining to the adjustment between a society and its environment.

The notion of survival is crucial and is relevant at all three levels with distinct but related meanings. At the ecological level there is no doubt about the individual's goal of biological survival. Obviously he also has a personal stake in avoiding a state of disequilibrium in which the whole

---

[3] Wroe Alderson, "Conditions for a Balanced World Economy," *World Economics*, May, 1944.

population could be wiped out. With respect to the behavior system to which he belongs, an individual may survive or fail to survive as a member. Generally he will struggle to retain his status as a participant so long as it promises satisfactions greater than those he would expect as a non-member. Finally the problem of survival for the organized behavior system is of critical importance.

Control of Adaptive Processes

The three-level equilibrium scheme will be reduced to a two-level scheme in searching for the roots of normative theory. This approach looks at the internal state of the system and the adjustment of the system to its external environment and considers the ways in which they affect each other. The proximate environment may be defined as the external domain with which the system is in direct and continuous contact and interaction. Most narrowly defined, the proximate environment for a marketing organization would correspond to the markets in which it buys and sells and competes with other marketing organizations.

A more comprehensive concept might be called the ultimate environment. It would embrace the social and physical environment and any external factors which might appear relevant to the survival and success of the organization and which in turn might be critically affected by the organization's actions.

The internal structure might be examined further with respect to the control of the adaptive processes by which the system is related to its environment. An organized behavior system, such as a business firm, normally behaves as if survival were a goal of the system. The underlying objectives are those of the participants in the system. Their expectations of benefits from the system can only be realized if the system survives. To act so as to perpetuate the system is consistent with the power principle which states that rational man will act in such a way as to promote the power to act. The argument does not hold that the goal of survival takes the place of more immediate objectives such as business profits. Rather, the desire of participants to preserve the system is reflected in modifications of the system's behavior in seeking more specific objectives.

Growth is a closely related goal of an organized behavior system. The desire to grow springs partly from a feeling that survival is threatened at the lower scale of operation. Present participants seek growth to attract other participants whose special competence gives greater assurance of system survival. Growth now becomes mandatory in order to satisfy the expectations of more numerous and more ambitious participants. The behavior system struggles for survival and growth within the ecological web consisting of the whole collection of systems through which the society exploits its environment. It will fail to survive if it cannot attract the cooperation or meet the competition of other systems within the web. It will fail if it does not achieve the internal organizational equilibrium which is essential to effective and continuous adaptation. It will fail most irretrievably if the entire society fails and can no longer survive in its environment. A crucial factor in success or failure is to be found in the nature of the system's control processes.

The foregoing may suggest that a system can adapt without conscious or deliberate intent in pursuing its goals of survival and growth. Adaptation without deliberate control does take place in small organizations with a low level of aspiration and a simple static technology. In more advanced systems successful adaptation involves strategic decisions which can only emanate from an effective control center. Internal balance in a system with many human participants is revealed as an extremely complex state in any attempt to analyze it fully. The expectations of participants are interdependent but not identical, and there are often rival attempts to control the system to serve the interests of rival groups or individuals. Even in a well-ordered system of large magnitude there is the complication of numerous subordinate control centers linked more or less effectively with the central command post. In the present analysis the problem of internal balance will be considered in the simplest terms, dealing with the relations of a central control group to all other participants as a group.

The resulting model of the adaptive system consists at the minimum of four elements. Internally the participants are divided into the control group P_c and the subordinate participants, P_s. The two groups of participants are related to each other through a power structure and a communication structure. Externally there is the proximate environment E_i and some broader domain in which the system might aspire to operate, E_a. At the limit E_a approaches the ultimate environment E_u. The system is related to the environment through its technology and the aspirations of its participants. The control group makes crucial decisions as to the aspiration level translated into operating goals and as to the technology to be employed in achieving the goals of the system.

The power structure in the system determines whether the control group can compel or persuade the subordinate participants to accept and implement the strategic decisions. The communication structure determines whether there will be effective coordination in carrying out the common effort. Most of the impact on the external environment is delivered through the subordinate participants, and most of the information about the environment is fed back through the same subordinates or some specialized investigatory group. There is an obvious parallel to the behavior of the human body. The decision reached in the brain to move a certain object is effected by the hand. Information that the act has been satisfactorily accomplished comes back from the sensory nerves in the finger tips or through a specialized sensory organ, the eye.

A powerful control group may be able to set a level of aspiration which diverges sharply from the level of activity at which the system is currently operating. To choose a level of aspiration is equivalent to defining the relevant environment E_a which is relevant for any program pursuing these aspirations. In marketing terms, the definition of the environment may reflect a decision to reach more consumers, to market selectively only to preferred consumers, or to market goods and services not now in the line. In broader management terms, the environment may be defined to include all who are affected directly or indirectly, whether they are users of the product or not. Rational self-interest requires the broader definition if there is a serious threat to the survival of the system in this broader domain. Questions of survival always arise when the system is viewed in the setting of the ultimate environment. These questions are so fundamental that the control group in every large system is obliged to give some thought to the ultimate ecological sanctions which our society faces today.

It has been said that the control group sets operational goals which are the projection of some level of aspiration. Goals specify the outputs to be obtained or the changes to be wrought in dealing with the environment. The control group has a second strategic decision to make. It must specify the optimal technology for reaching the stated goals. All but the most rudimentary systems have some repertoire of behavior patterns allowing a choice among alternative courses of action. A critical choice is often that between a customary or habitual behavior pattern and a modified pattern which the control group believes will be more effective. In a period of rapid technological changes the control group may exert constant pressure for improved procedures as well as for more ambitious goals.

The Pathology of Systems

The several basic elements will be in precise adjustment if the system is in equilibrium. There are several ways in which such a system can go into a state of disequilibrium. The pathology of systems is somewhat analogous to the pathology of the human body. A system may suffer a slight indisposition which is easily remedied. It can drag along at a fraction of its potential efficiency as if it suffered from a chronic disease. Maladjustment can be so severe that the system seems fated to decline steadily toward final extinction in the manner of a human being with a terminal illness.

Several of the more serious maladies of systems will be described in terms of the system model. The control group may fail to exercise direction or influence over subordinates. The latter persist in customary patterns of behavior or improvise their own adjustments at their points of contact with the environment. Such a system is running out of control, and unless control can be reestablished it will eventually disintegrate as a system. A system may possess considerable momentum as the result of past successes, but without effective control it will lose this thrust through collision with obstacles in the environment.

In another form of maladjustment the control group may be in effective command for the time being but without adequate communication from below to register the aspirations and attitudes of subordinates. A decline of morale may follow, resulting in apathy and inefficiency. In other cases there is covert or overt rebellion. Conflict can result in attrition of the subordinate group through elimination of its leaders and the flight of others. It can force a change of leadership in the control group. A new state of adjustment may be achieved if the new leadership projects goals which are more acceptable to the subordinate groups and a technology which is efficient in achieving these goals.

Finally there is the situation in which control group and subordinate group work together but in apparent disregard of salient features of the environment. Quite often the environmental facts are not actually known or their significance for the operation of the system is not correctly appraised. Sometimes there seems to be a tacit conspiracy among all participants to ignore obvious but unpleasant facts. With a system, as with an individual, there seems to be some inherent bias toward believing those things which are consistent with the way in which participants would like to see the system operate.

A form of maladjustment of special interest for marketing and some other aspects of economic and political behavior is the condition which may be called the extinction mode. Once a system is in this condition, the probability of transition to some other state approaches zero and the degree of maladjustment tends to increase rather than lessen, regardless of any action taken. This type of situation is sometimes described as a vicious circle or, more precisely, as a vicious spiral, since a system caught in such a state seems destined to run down. Some concrete examples will be given of systems in the extinction mode.

Systems in the Extinction Mode

The Swedish economist, Gunnar Myrdal, has been a leading exponent of the self-perpetuating adverse trend. In a study of the race problem in the United States, Myrdal documented the existence of a self-perpetuating trend with respect to the condition of the Negro population over a period of many years.[4] The low social status and poor living conditions of the Negro was taken by many whites as indicative of native inferiority and lack of capacity for progress. This judgment was used to justify the denial of opportunities for education and economic advancement. Illiteracy and lack of income tended to perpetuate a life of squalor and other symbols of low social status. The extinction mode is characterized by such adverse interactions but in an extreme form. The self-perpetuating trend steadily depletes the capabilities of the system and finally threatens its very existence.

---

[4] Gunnar Myrdal, *The American Dilemma* (New York: Harper & Bros., 1944).

A prime example of a system in the extinction mode is found in the southern society based on one-crop agriculture before the Civil War. Slave labor was controlled by the threat of force, and no attempt was made to induce cooperation by taking account of the aspirations of the slaves. The poor whites were partially disfranchised by various devices and did not aspire to match the standard of living of the planter class. Existing largely through subsistence agriculture, the poor whites were secure in their intermediate social status so long as the Negroes remained enslaved.

With a monolithic power structure it was possible for the control group to enforce compliance with its choice of goals and technology. Soil fertility was rapidly depleted in many areas where the slave economy prevailed. There was a progressive concentration of slave labor in the deep South which accelerated the depletion of the shrinking base of fertile soil. While many realized the seriousness of their plight they could see no way out since neither planter nor poor white could face the prospect of emancipation of a huge mass of Negroes who had deliberately been kept in a retarded stage of development.

Southern leaders were still striving in the decade before the Civil War to retain their traditional dominance in the power structure of the country as a whole. Many forces were against them, including population increase and technological advance in the North, the lack of new lands suitable for slave agriculture, and the growth of worldwide opinion demanding an end to slavery. The only solution appeared to be secession which would leave the control group in command at least in its own region. If the South could withdraw from the Union without federal opposition it might carry out its military designs on Mexico, Cuba, and Central America and then return in far greater strength to the task of dominating the North American continent. The act of secession, however, inevitably transformed the long struggle for political power into military conflict. Despite the added strain of war, the control group in the South continued to pursue infeasible goals with an obsolete technology to the point of final exhaustion. This instance has been cited, not for the lack of marketing examples but because it is such a complete and dramatic illustration of a system in the extinction mode.[5]

Numerous marketing examples could be found in the bankruptcy records: the old line grocer who did not believe that the supermarket was here to stay and refused to adopt self-service; the wholesaler who wanted to remain independent while his customers were joining voluntary chains or setting up retailer-owned cooperatives; the manufacturer who would sell only to wholesalers in the face of the steady trend in his industry toward direct distribution. In the cases which will be described briefly here, the firms involved still survive, either because they found a way out

---

[5] The author has derived this interpretation of the Civil War as a power struggle largely from the multivolumed history by Allan Nevins.

of what appeared to be a trapped state or because the process of extinction has not yet run its course.

Some years ago Mead, Johnson & Company sold its baby food, Pablum, only to wholesale druggists even though consumers bought the product mainly in grocery stores rather than drugstores. Retail grocers bought it from wholesale grocers who in turn bought it from wholesale druggists. Since Pablum had to carry two wholesale margins rather than one, it became increasingly difficult for it to compete with other baby food lines sold through the grocery trade. Mead, Johnson also had a line of ethical drug products moving through wholesaler druggists. It felt that it could not engage in an overt and protracted effort to correct the situation on Pablum for fear of the loss it might sustain on its other products. The solution was found in doing something which no one previously had thought possible—namely, to create a nationwide organization of food brokers in a single week's time.

In 1920 a federal court placed the meat-packers known as the Big Five under consent decree and set them on the road to extinction. Since then one of the five has gone out of business; two others have been through one or more incidents with bankruptcy and financial reorganizations; a fourth lost money nearly every year for a long term of years until management undertook a drastic curtailment of its operations; the fifth may have enjoyed some relief from pressure because of the troubles of its competitors, but in recent years has had increasing difficulties of its own. The trapped competitive group created by the consent decree was barred from entering many areas of enterprise, such as grocery retailing, while the grocery chains were entirely free to enter meat-packing. The Big Five could not initiate competitive moves against anyone except each other. Meanwhile they were faced with the competition of newcomers, particularly in cured meats and prepared meat products, the only profitable part of the business. As recently as 1959 the large meat-packers made one more effort to have the consent decree lifted, but it is doubtful whether legal relief would provide a real solution for them at this late date.

About fifteen years ago the author made a study which was financed jointly by the large tire manufacturers who were known as the Big Four. One of these companies seemed to be in strong position because it had the largest share of original equipment business, that is, tires sold to automobile manufacturers for new cars. While the margin on this volume was slim, it was thought that being strong in original equipment was the surest way of getting a substantial portion of the more profitable replacement business.

A decade later this apparent advantage seemed all at once to act as a handicap. Pressed into premature innovation on the tubeless tire, the company experienced a rise in complaints and claims for adjustment. The rise in the adjustment rate seemed particularly sharp to the dealers who handled complaints on original equipment tires as well as on replacement tires. With some loss of dealer confidence in the line the quality of dealer sales effort deteriorated. Some dealers went out of business or switched to other brands of tires. As the dealer base continued to shrink, the ratio of original equipment business rose correspondingly. Thus the adverse conditions which threatened the dealer organization were further aggravated. Outside surveys show a sharp decline in the company's volume of business in replacement tires. Heroic measures would be required for this company to recapture its former position in the tire business, and it is not yet clear whether management will accept the large risks which are inherent in these measures. It is well entrenched in other types of rubber products and might even be well advised, so far as tires are concerned, to accept its extinction as inevitable.

Keeping a System Healthy

One of the writer's colleagues at the University of Pennsylvania continues to be unhappy about the notion of survival as a system goal. Recently he said, "Do you really expect the head of an organization to take a shot of survival every morning along with his orange juice?" One might reply that he would not expect the executive to take a shot of profit maximization either, but the critic's case is somewhat better than that. Profit is a quantitative variable which can be maximized, at least theoretically, by meeting specified conditions for an optimal value. In their attempt to develop a more realistic form of analysis, Herbert Simon and his associates abandon the notion of profit maximization. They assume that the executive will try to satisfice, achieving a profit that equals or exceeds a minimum requirement.

Survival as a goal does not fit neatly into either perspective. The executive can neither optimize nor satisfice with respect to survival since it is not a quantitative variable. A biological organism is either living or dead; it either survives or perishes. If one insisted on assigning numerical values, survival might be given a value of one and failure to survive a value of zero.

The best analogy for the capacity of a system to survive is the health of a biological organism. In either case it is rational to exercise proper care to keep the body or the system healthy. The prime strategy in either case is a strategy of avoidance. The individual tries to avoid infection or other conditions which might cause illness. Through occasional medical examinations he hopes for early detection of what might otherwise become an incurable and ultimately fatal disease. The executive watches for maladjustment in the system and attempts to apply prompt remedies. Above all, he should try to prevent the system from falling into the condition which has been called the extinction mode. At best the issue of survival is fraught with uncertainty just as the person who worries most about his health may still die of cancer. The point is that there are some rational steps for the executive to take if he is concerned about the goal of survival for his organization.

Executive action, prompted by survival motives, is not entirely limited to passive or preventive measures. Although survival cannot be quantified, it may be possible to identify a quantifiable variable which could be called capacity to survive. The obvious parallel would be the vitality of a living organism. Of two live individuals, one might have greater vitality or capacity to stay alive in the face of stress or exposure. The rational individual, however, would scarcely seek to maximize vitality or survival potential. Rather he would hope to maintain a sufficient reserve of survival potential so that the system could meet any conditions with which it is likely to be confronted. The interesting but difficult problem of measuring survival potential is not germane to the present discussion.

Survival in the Wider Perspective

The discussion of survival so far would be consistent with a perspective limited to the interests of the single firm. The executive might preserve the health of the firm so that he would then be able to maximize or satisfice. But the rational executive extends his vision and concern to the healthfulness of the setting in which the firm must operate. In addition to survival of the firm he might consider the survival of his immediate community, the survival of the American economy, the survival of free enterprise, the survival of western culture, or the survival of mankind. As businessman, citizen, or student of affairs he may well be aware of survival issues at all levels. His organization might perish because of a catastrophic event in one of these larger systems. If he directs a very large organization, the survival of a larger system might be significantly affected by his decisions.

J. M. Clark [6] has argued that our modern economy cannot work except through the development of a high sense of responsibility among the executives who direct large enterprises. Competition, in his opinion, imposes limits on business conduct but does not control and determine executive decision as postulated in the theory of pure competition. There is an area of discretion which allows room for values which transcend the immediate welfare of the individual firm. Survival values at the broadest reach are still rooted in rational self-interest. These values are supported by ecological sanctions. Environmental constraints are controlling in the long run with severe penalties attached to their violation.

Many firms encounter ecological sanctions in the immediate environment of the communities in which their plants are located. If the industry is engaged solely in the extraction of raw materials, the habitability of the environment is depleted as mineral deposits or forests are mined out. The nature of the activity may make the environment unsightly and unpleas-

---

[6] J. M. Clark, *Alternative to Serfdom* (New York: Alfred A. Knopf, Inc., 1948).

ant even while it produces income for the resident population. As the process of depletion continues the responsible executive will certainly give some consideration to the stranded population which may be left behind when the natural resource is gone. Some have taken effective steps to stimulate alternative forms of economic activity in their own interest and that of the community. Conservation of resources has received increasing recognition in both public and private policy. The doctrine of conservation is a clear departure from the philosophy of pure and perfect competition in the direction of acknowledging responsibility for maintaining the habitability of the environment.

There are other and subtler ways in which the marketing and management practices of a company can affect the quality of life in its community. It is possible that the conservative attitudes of Philadelphia business in the nineteenth century and its failure to employ aggressive promotion was a factor in the relatively static economy of the city today. Apparently there was a tendency to feel that quality should speak for itself and to cling to traditional definitions of quality. A famous hat company in Philadelphia almost went broke making a high-quality, high-priced hat after mass demand had shifted. A new management finally brought the company to a more prosperous state by realizing that the typical customer was interested in a greater variety of apparel and would prefer two hats for the same money even though of lesser durability.

Many American business executives regard the antitrust laws as essential to the maintenance of free enterprise. Their desire to conform may be reinforced by this belief more than by the rather moderate legal penalties which usually apply. Similarly they accepted an American policy which looked favorably on the development of the common market in Europe even though the exports of some American products might be affected unfavorably. The ultimate sanction today is the prospect of atomic warfare. The threat of atomic missiles is not merely that they would kill millions of people but that they would destroy the habitability of large regions of the earth for centuries to come. This continual threat creates an awareness of ecological sanctions of greater intensity than ever before. The dangers inherent in man's powers to control or modify his environment are seen in the damaging side effects of pesticides, synthetic detergents, and powerful drugs. Whatever the discount to be taken on the public reaction to Rachel Carson's *Silent Spring*, she has called attention to survival issues which cannot be ignored by the responsible executive.

It will be more difficult to find satisfactory solutions for some of these problems than it is to write a persuasive criticism. Modern drugs, for example, are dangerous precisely because they are powerful enough to bring about specified physiological effects in the body. Presumably no one wishes to put a stop to the introduction of new drugs even though some individuals with idiosyncrasies may suffer from them. It would not be advantageous to return to the drugs of thirty years ago which had little potency for either help or harm. The responsible executive is required by both private and public considerations to seek further safeguards without slowing the pace of fundamental progress.

There is some evidence that one or more self-perpetuating adverse trends exist with respect to advertising, although this primary marketing institution is certainly not in the extinction mode. The total volume of advertising steadily increases, but it is not likely that the capacity of consumers to pay attention to advertising increases at the same rate. In fact, the more intensive that advertising becomes the larger may be the number of people who deliberately try to avoid it. Determined advertisers may then step up the pressure in the hope of gaining the same amount of attention as before. A still greater number of people begin to feel that the volume of advertising has exceeded a tolerable level and they attempt to avoid exposure as much as possible.

Consumer surveys in recent years have indicated a decline in the credence given to advertising. The clamor of conflicting claims has become so raucous in some fields (for example, headache remedies) that consumers might suspect that no one is telling the truth. The remedy for consumer sales resistance, according to exponents of the hard sell, is to make even more sweeping claims and engage in more violent attacks on competitive products. The very features of advertising which created skepticism are carried to further extremes, and the adverse effect on believability is compounded.

For advertising to become corrupt and ineffective could be a crippling blow to a free-market economy. This type of economy feeds on innovation, and the sponsor must communicate with consumers to induce acceptance of innovation. The prospective purchaser does not evaluate the new product in isolation but relates it to other products and eventually to his vision of the good life. He really wants help from the advertiser in putting the product in perspective, in picturing it in the setting in which he is expected to use it and enjoy it. But what if the way of life suggested by the advertisement is shoddy and unattractive? Who wants to live in a hypochondriac's world in which the greatest joy is quick relief from headache? Who wants to live in a fool's paradise in which smokers believe that they can indulge in nicotine and yet escape all the hazards of indulgence? Who really wants the dullard's cuisine in which bland and tasteless foods are touted as the gourmet's delight? The consumer cannot believe in the product if the advertiser could not possibly believe in the kind of world he projects as a setting for his product.

Marketing attempts to alter the patterns of contemporary culture and advertising is its primary instrument for this purpose. Some critics charge that advertising is an active agency in the debasement of public taste. It is more likely that advertising has contributed to cultural confusion. Advertising itself is a public art, and as an art it deserves and must expect criticism. The *Saturday Review* has made a beginning in establishing annual awards for advertising. But advertising is not only art but prophecy. Its practitioners set themselves up in the business of dreaming dreams and seeing visions. They must embrace more exalted standards of virtue than being good providers for their families and voting the straight Republican ticket. Like Jeremiah, each man must live with the fearful chance that he may be numbered among the false prophets.

Not only advertising but marketing in general is in the business of making promises. The manufacturer promises the consumer that she will derive superior satisfaction from his product and promises dealers and distributors that they will make money handling it. There will always be some disappointment since these promises must be fulfilled in a world of diverse and uncertain circumstances. But what about promises concerning which there is substantial doubt that they can ever be fulfilled? Look at the down time on appliances which were sold with the implied promise that they were trouble-free, and without adequate provision for repair services. Try purchasing three items from three different departments in your city's leading store and see whether the transaction can be concluded without some error or failure in performance. Remember the glorious vision of carefree driving which came with your new automobile as you sit in a hopeless traffic jam somewhere on an inadequate street and highway system—or as you ponder the statistics showing that traffic accidents are the principal cause of death in the active years from fifteen to thirty.

Nearly everyone is engaged in marketing in the sense of offering goods or his own services in the market and in buying the goods and services of others. Everyone makes promises of performance and payment, and individuals live up to their promises in varying degrees. The promises made as an aspect of mass marketing are different. Here we are promising each other through our industrial leaders a better way of life, the fruits of technology and enterprise, the physical means and instruments for supporting desired patterns of activity. These reciprocal pledges add up to a Promised Land which we know is not quite attainable. We make some allowance for what the economist Frank Knight once called industrial poetry. But if the channels of communication are largely filled with misinformation and deliberate deception, the system cannot survive. The writer does not believe that this is true of marketing messages, but the damage would be done if the majority of consumers suspected that it was true. At a minimum, the marketer must believe in what he is doing if he is to convince anyone else. He, at least, should be prepared to live in the kind of world his efforts seem calculated to produce.

Functionalism: Descriptive and Normative

The writer has characterized his theoretical position as functionalism and has accepted the implied commitment to the total systems approach.[7]

---

[7] Wroe Alderson, *Marketing Behavior and Executive Action* (Homewood, Ill.: Richard D. Irwin, Inc., 1957).

The functionalist in marketing engages in the study of systems with the aim of understanding how they work and how they can be made to work better. As a theorist he devises descriptive generalizations of marketing activities and institutions and finds a useful tool in the systems concept. He discovers a number of organized behavior systems in the world of marketing and finds that this recognition of systems of interacting forces aids him in explaining what is going on. He might note, for example, that systems have a tendency to persist over time, behaving as if they pursued a goal of survival.

This descriptive theory does not imply that systems are necessarily efficient in seeking any goal, including the goal of survival. It recognizes that systems cease to exist despite the efforts of participants to perpetuate them. The theory stresses environmental change and maladjustment which often occurs because of the lag in the adaptive processes of the system. In order to adapt, the control group in the system must be aware of the change which requires adjustment and must make the right choice among possible adaptations. The descriptive theory presents a picture of a number of systems occupying the same or an overlapping environment, all seeking goals including that of survival but with varying degrees of adjustment to their opportunities and their problems. In each system there are decisions to be made about the level of aspiration and the technology employed. The decisions taken will vary with factors in the problem situation and with the characteristics of the decision makers.

The normative theory sketched in this essay deals with the question of how systems should operate to achieve their goals. It emphasizes the goal of survival as the means of relating the problem of adaptation in a given system to the larger systems of which it is a part. It recognizes that freedom of choice exists at each level except for the economic sanctions of the market, the social sanctions imposed by a system on its subsystems or individual participants, and the ecological sanctions inherent in the limitations of the ultimate environment. If a system fails because it violates some of these sanctions, then all of its subsystems must fail. The theory does not make the decision maker in a subsystem responsible for the success of the larger system since its management is not under his control. It does hold him responsible for avoiding actions which threaten the survival of the larger system, since this obligation is a corollary of his role in perpetuating his own system.

Functionalism draws a sharper distinction between descriptive and normative theory than is customary among general economists. Some years ago a leading economist was asked whether he regarded his abstract model of the economy as descriptive or normative. More specifically, he was asked whether he regarded it as presenting an ideal of how the market economy should work or the best available description of how it actually works. He answered without the slightest reservation that the model was obviously both. He was not quite saying that the world we live in is the best of all possible worlds. He was asserting that economic activity is determined by market forces with only slight deviation from the pattern expressed in the model. The model should be taken as the norm, and the aim of policy should be to eliminate these deviations from the norm. Under this view there is very little difference between descriptive theory and normative theory.[8]

Functionalism opens a much wider gap between descriptive theory and normative theory, between things as they are and things as they should be according to criteria of rational conduct. There will always be room for improvement in marketing under the functionalist view of marketing theory. The policy maker at any level will be choosing among alternatives in the face of uncertainty generated by change and complexity. He may take account of ethical and esthetic considerations beyond anything which has been presented here. He may choose an action because it is right according to some social norm and not merely advantageous for his organization. His choice must be made within a set of limitations which rest on the fact that he must work through a system and act on behalf of a system. If he endeavors to promote his rational self-interest through a system, he is obliged to take account of the factors which affect the health of the system and its chances for survival.

The greater divergence between descriptive theory and normative theory asserted here with respect to functionalism is also observed in recent developments in dynamic economics. Samuelson and others have asserted that for any system with a goal of growth there is an optimal growth path over time. It does not follow that the control group in the system will discover this growth path or that it will be able to manage the system effectively in pursuing this path. Martin Shubik [9] has given a formal treatment of games of survival among oligopolistic competitors. He shows that a wide range of choice is available to the players in such a game and the formulation of normative rules for the players is by no means simple. He also stresses the factor of incomplete information in making the outcome indeterminate.

The proposed normative theory of marketing systems may be contrasted with Churchman's approach to a scientific ethics presented in a recent book.[10] He formulates four imperatives which he feels show determinate decisions taken by the executive. The normative theory proposed here is probably most closely related to Churchman's discussion of the prudential imperative. The decision maker is advised to take this action or avoid that action in the pursuit of rational self-interest. The basic difference is the emphasis on sanctions rather than imperatives. Sanc-

---

[8] George J. Stigler, *The Theory of Price* (New York: The Macmillan Co., 1952).

[9] Martin Shubik, *Strategy and Market Structure* (New York: John Wiley & Sons, Inc., 1959).

[10] C. West Churchman, *Prediction and Optimal Decision* (Englewood Cliffs, N.J.: Prentice-Hall, Inc., 1961).

tions limit the scope of action rather than prescribing specific action. In this respect the normative theory is more in the spirit of J. M. Clark than of Churchman. Clark recognizes that the test of the market imposes constraints on competitors but that further constraints are necessary to the adequate functioning of a competitive system.

One of the editors of this book, after reading a draft of this essay, said that it appeared to be an attempt to formulate ethical standards for marketing behavior. The author denies such an intention, but the denial rests on his own special conception of what constitutes an ethical choice. He holds that an ethical problem arises only at the point where the accepted rules no longer serve and the decision maker is faced with the responsibility for weighing values and reaching a judgment in a situation which is not quite the same as any he has faced before. If there is a rule which tells him precisely what to do or a sanction which compels him to do it, he may be confronted with a moral or legal issue but not with an ethical problem.

Churchman as a scientist is inclined to believe that every decision would be completely determined if we knew enough to provide the decision maker with adequate rules. He readily admits that we are far from having such rules today. For the present he is obliged to employ such sweeping principles as his ethical imperative which suggests that we should behave in the way that future generations would wish us to behave. The view presented here is more libertarian, resting on a deep conviction of the reality of choice. It relies on constraints imposed by the market, by organized society, and by the ecological structure of the environment. Within these constraints some area of free choice remains. One would hope that the responsible executive will use this freedom creatively. He is behaving ethically when he makes creative choices on behalf of the organization he directs and the culture to which he belongs. The sanctions discussed in this version of normative theory are presumed to operate through rational self-interest. Hopefully the theory can support some normative judgments about marketing goals as well as marketing means without taking on the momentous task of creating a science of ethics.

7. THE SURVIVAL CONCEPT AND THE NONPROFIT BEHAVIOR SYSTEM

Stanley J. Shapiro

THE NECESSARY characteristics and distinguishing features of a theory or a science of marketing are discussed at greater length in other contributions to this collection of essays. It is sufficient here to note that the present state of our knowledge has made it impossible to move very far in the development of a theory of marketing that would facilitate efforts at description, prediction, and control. Also, the precision in theory-formulation characteristic of the physical sciences is lacking in marketing for reasons which need not be reviewed at this time. For the present, consequently, the editors have concentrated on obtaining a series of theoretical perspectives from individuals who have devoted much time and effort to the study of marketing and related disciplines.

The hope remains, however, that this volume, like its predecessor, will contribute to the development of a theory and perhaps a science of marketing. In addition to making a substantive contribution, the essays are intended to serve as a point of departure for others who wish to become involved in the difficult but challenging problem of theory construction for marketing. One approach that might be taken involves the very careful evaluation of the theoretical formulations provided by the various contributors. The prospective researcher could attempt to design and to execute an experiment which would help verify, modify, or discredit some formulation of special interest to him. This chapter contains a report of one such effort and the results obtained therefrom. Although it is hoped that the research findings will be of some interest, the primary objective of the author has been to illustrate the problems and the possibilities inherent in the method he advocates.

The relevance and analytical usefulness of Alderson's discussion of his survival concept was the subject chosen for examination. Alderson's initial position is restated to acquaint the reader with the conceptual framework brought to the study. Considerable factual information is then provided on the behavior system subjected to detailed scrutiny as part of this investigation. Attention is focused on the activities of the system, the conditions surrounding the development of the survival problem, and the success with which this challenge to the organization was met. Next, certain shortcomings of the survival concept revealed by this case study and the topics on which additional research appears necessary are considered. Finally, Alderson's most recent discussion of survival—a discussion found in this volume—is examined to determine the extent to which previously existing conceptual problems have been resolved and new contributions made.

SURVIVAL AND THE ORGANIZED BEHAVIOR SYSTEM

In his contribution to the original edition of *Theory in Marketing*, Wroe Alderson cited as one of the weaknesses of conventional economic theory an overwhelming concern with problems of market adjustment and a corresponding neglect of survival considerations.[1] This distortion in emphasis, he argued, followed from the orthodox economist's view of the firm as a temporary investment on the part of an entrepreneur willing to withdraw his resources as soon as more profitable opportunities arise. Alderson maintained, in contrast, that a firm is a much more complex entity with all the characteristics of what he called "an organized behavior system." In *Marketing Behavior and Executive Action*, Alderson discusses the behavior system and its characteristics in considerable detail.[2] Since his writings on this subject are readily available, emphasis will be placed at this time on Alderson's thinking as regards the concern of such a system with its continued existence.

Behavior systems have two essential components: a group of individuals who work together because collectively each expects to obtain greater satisfaction than he could by working alone; and a set of instruments and resources used by this group within the specific environment in which it operates. Alderson discusses the structural elements of a system—seriality, parallelism, circularity, centrality, and concurrence—and a number of subsystems which control various aspects of systemic behavior. Although the treatment of these topics is quite extensive, all that

---

[1] Wroe Alderson, "Survival and Adjustment in Organized Behavior Systems," in Reavis Cox and Wroe Alderson (eds.), *Theory in Marketing* (Homewood, Ill.: Richard D. Irwin, Inc., 1950), pp. 65–87.

[2] Wroe Alderson, *Marketing Behavior and Executive Action* (Homewood, Ill.: Richard D. Irwin, Inc., 1957), pp. 29–97. Since this entire section is presented as a partial summary of the two Alderson sources previously cited, only direct quotations will be acknowledged by footnotes.

is relevant for present purposes is his concern with the process of internal and external adjustment.

There is a strong similarity, Alderson maintains, between the efforts of a firm to establish itself in a market and an animal's attempt to find a niche in its environment. In elaborating upon his analogy between animal and business behavior, he describes a setting in which firms are free to seek out new opportunities (or niches) and to prosper by providing desired services. Changes in the external environment, however, confront both animals and behavior systems with problems as well as opportunities. Biologists have attempted to explain why certain organisms successfully adapted to changed conditions while others perished. In a similar fashion, Alderson sets forth three theorems each of which discusses a factor enabling organized behavior systems to endure despite survival challenges:

1. An organized behavior system will tend to survive as long as the footing it occupies endures because of the collective action arising out of the status expectation of its components.
2. An organized behavior system may survive the most aggressive attacks of competitors because it is able to exist at the core of its position even though losing ground at the fringes and, meanwhile, mature its own campaign which may utilize strategies that have been overlooked by competitors.
3. An organized behavior system may survive despite severe functional disturbance resulting from environmental changes if sufficient plasticity remains so that new functions may develop or new methods may be adopted for performing existing functions.[3]

In the accompanying discussion, Alderson proceeds to restate his theorems as three reasons why behavior systems tend to persist over time. First, the members believe they can obtain more in terms of goods and status by working towards the survival of the system than by acting individually or by becoming a member of another system. Also, the system has an established position and a continued capacity to act which can be maintained despite the most vigorous attacks of competitors. Finally, the system has the ability to reshape its behavior patterns if environmental changes make this necessary.

Alderson takes considerable care lest he be misinterpreted and charged with viewing a behavior system as a living organism. He emphasizes that the system as such does not have a set of desires and goals. In reality, it is only a means of expressing and realizing the goals of the individuals associated with the system. The individual acts to promote the survival of the system in order to realize his own values and objectives. Nevertheless, systems operate in some respects as if they had goals of their own. For purposes of developing a theory of marketing, the behavior system appears far superior to the economist's concept of the firm—a bloodless

---

[3] *Ibid.*, pp. 54–58.

abstraction that makes no allowance for the shared hopes and conflicting aspirations of those joined in some common economic endeavor.[4]

THE SURVIVAL CHALLENGE CONFRONTING THE ONTARIO HOG PRODUCER ORGANIZATIONS

The research design required that Alderson's concepts of survival and the organized behavior system be employed in an effort to obtain a better understanding of the actions taken by a marketing agency faced with a threat to its continued existence.[5] A detailed study of the system's response was expected to indicate areas requiring additional research and to point the way toward possible extension of the survival concept. At the same time, it was believed Alderson's conceptual formulation would provide a fruitful way of analyzing the conduct of the behavior system in question—a unique marketing organization faced with social and political as well as economic problems.

The nature and activities of the behavior system studied must now be considered. Canadian producer marketing legislation enables farmers to exercise considerable influence on the sale and distribution of farm products. In Ontario, if two thirds of the producers of an agricultural commodity vote to sell their product collectively, the minority are compelled by law to join in a common sales policy. When producers adapt a program of collective marketing, this program is administered by a number of elected farmer-directors who serve on what is known as a "local," "producer," or "commodity" marketing board.

Operating under the provisions of the Ontario Farm Products Marketing Act, the eleven members of the Ontario Hog Producers Marketing Board established a system requiring the entire Ontario hog crop, worth approximately $100,000,000 a year, to be delivered to local assembly yards. With a few minor exceptions, no other method of marketing hogs is legal. The hog board's sales force then attempted to obtain the highest possible price for the hogs so delivered by telephoning the various packers and "playing off" one prospective purchaser against another. Each day, the sales force labored to establish a favorable base price for hogs. Subsequent efforts were devoted to selling individual lots of hogs at a premium whenever and wherever local conditions made this possible. The

---

[4] Alderson's contribution to this edition of *Theory in Marketing* elaborates upon earlier treatments of the survival concept. His essay, however, was written upon the completion of the study summarized in this chapter. As was previously mentioned, those aspects of Alderson's most recent discussion with some relevance to this study are examined in a concluding section.

[5] Stanley J. Shapiro, "Decision Making, Survival, and the Organized Behavior System—A Case Study of the Ontario Hog Producer Organizations" (Ph.D. dissertation, University of Pennsylvania, 1961). The summary of Hog Producer activities described at this time is based upon the much more extensive treatment contained in the dissertation.

program established by the Ontario Hog Producers Marketing Board is discussed more fully in Exhibit 1.

EXHIBIT 1

THE ONTARIO HOG PRODUCER MARKETING PROGRAM

1. Farmers and truckers delivered all hogs to be marketed to one of the Ontario hog board's assembly yards.
2. Yard managers contacted the Toronto sales office by phone or teletype whenever a large enough number of hogs had been assembled for sale.
3. A hog board sales representative telephoned and solicited bids from those packing plants most likely to be interested in purchasing hogs f.o.b. that assembly yard.
4. The hogs were sold to the firm which would pay the highest price. If two or more processors offered the same top price, the hog board decided which plant would receive the hogs.
5. The assembly-yard manager was informed of the eventual destination of the hogs. He then arranged for delivery to the packing plant of the purchaser.
6. After the hogs were slaughtered, the weight and grade of each animal was recorded. The price had previously been established as "x cents per pound dressed weight" with adjustments being made for differences in grade.
7. Trucking manifests, government grading certificates, and all other pertinent documents were forwarded to the hog board's offices in Toronto.
8. A 40¢-a-hog service charge and any amount due a trucker for delivering the hogs to the assembly yard were deducted. A check and settlement statement was then issued to the producer.
9. The hog board received payment from the various processing plants for the hogs that each had purchased.

The history of producer marketing, the structure and operations of three closely related hog producer organizations with a single board of directors—the Ontario Hog Producers Marketing Board, the Ontario Hog Producers Cooperative, and the Ontario Hog Producers Association—and the past grievances, real or alleged, of hog-raising farmers are relevant considerations but need not be elaborated upon at this time. These factors are all discussed at length in the source document. In summary, the Ontario Hog Producer leadership had labored with evangelical zeal for many years to develop its hog marketing program. Although the problems they had faced were formidable and their progress slow, these farmer-directors believed producers were benefiting from increased bargaining power, improved market information, and skilled salesmanship.

The relative authority of government and producer agencies under the provisions of the Ontario Farm Products Marketing Act is a consideration of more immediate relevance. The most notable feature of this legislation is the very extensive authority granted the Farm Products Marketing Board (FPMB)—the regulatory agency established by the Provincial government to administer the Act. The FPMB may license producers and processors, inspect their books and records, settle disputes between these two groups, and determine all conditions under which the commodity should be marketed. At all times, the FPMB retains the power to add to or to reduce a local board's authority, to review all its actions, and to order changes in any producer marketing program. Although political considerations occasionally limit the freedom of action of the Farm Products Marketing Board, the enabling statute places very few restrictions on the board. Exhibit 2 presents in greater detail the legal framework under which the various Ontario producer marketing programs were established and operated at the time of the study.

The Survival Challenge and the Hog Producer Response

It follows then that the Ontario Hog Producers Marketing Board had developed and was operating its program under authority delegated by the Farm Products Marketing Board. The regulatory authority of the government notwithstanding, however, the hog board opposed FPMB efforts to replace the existing method of telephone selling with a form of electronic Dutch auction. Relations between these two groups first became strained shortly after the larger meat-packing companies complained bitterly to the government about certain aspects of telephone selling. These large processors were especially concerned about a decline in their share of the hog crop which, they alleged, was due to hog producer discrimination in favor of small packing plants.

EXHIBIT 2

THE ONTARIO FARM PRODUCTS MARKETING ACT (1950)

The Ontario Farm Products Marketing Act gives power to investigate trade practices, establish negotiatory committees, and regulate and control marketing, or to establish a marketing agency to regulate marketing, to the

↓

FARM PRODUCTS MARKETING BOARD

(1) which supervises the voting that determines whether producers want to establish or to continue a marketing program;
(2) which exercises complete control over the marketing of the commodity, if producers vote in favor of regulation;
(3) which may appoint and grant some of its authority to a negotiating committee or selling agency and may add to or subtract from the authority previously granted;
(4) which may draft up regulations for and delegate power to any

↓

LOCAL BOARD

which will conduct its business in the manner and under the regulations prescribed by and subject to the review of the Farm Products Marketing Board. The local board will supervise the operations of the

NEGOTIATING AGENCY	or	SELLING AGENCY
which depends upon the general provisions of the statute concerning negotiatory agencies for its authority to determine minimum prices and conditions of sale.		which depends upon the powers granted it by the FPMB to promote, regulate, and control the marketing of the product for successful operation.

The members of the Farm Products Marketing Board and other Department of Agriculture officials were reluctant to become involved in this potentially explosive political issue. They restricted their initial efforts to bringing together all interested parties in the hope that a mutually acceptable method of sale could be developed. As might be expected, the ill feeling and distrust that existed between the hog board and the large packers made it impossible for a satisfactory solution to be reached in this manner.

Government officials then took the position that the extent to which discrimination actually occurred was of secondary importance. They insisted that any marketing board established under government legislation and operating with quasi-monopoly powers must employ a selling method that precluded the possibility of discrimination. Given the above criterion of acceptability, Provincial officials found the existing method of telephone selling unacceptable on two counts. The system encouraged identical bids and thus made arbitrary allocation necessary and discrimination possible; and the dealings between prospective buyers and the sales agency were not matters of public record. The failure of telephone selling to allow each processor to bid on every lot of hogs was also criticized.

The Hog Producers Marketing Board vehemently denied all charges of discrimination and challenged the large meat-packers to substantiate their claims. The percentage of the hog crop slaughtered by the smaller processors had increased, the farmer-directors maintained, because hogs were now being sold to the firm offering the highest price. Previously, it was alleged, the larger firms controlled the distribution of hogs by offering illegal bonus payments to livestock truckers who delivered animals to these packers regardless of the prices being paid elsewhere. The fact that telephone selling did not allow all packers to bid on each lot of hogs was held to be of no consequence. Every processor who would find it economical to purchase animals f.o.b. any given location received an opportunity to bid on all hogs available at that assembly yard.

The Ontario Hog Producers Marketing Board and the Farm Products Marketing Board debated the merits of telephone selling for approximately two and one-half years. At any time during this period, the FPMB could have compelled hog producer compliance by exercising the regulatory powers it possessed under the provisions of the Farm Products Marketing Act. The government in power, however, did not consider it politically desirable to order changes in the hog marketing program, if such drastic action could be avoided. Consequently, every effort was made to convince the hog board that it should voluntarily abandon telephone selling.

After considerable delay and much futile negotiation with an uncompromising hog producer leadership, government officials reluctantly acted to force compliance with their wishes. Policies and procedures designed to destroy the independence of the hog board and to reduce its influence among producers were successfully implemented. Although such action was politically dangerous and aroused considerable ill feeling, the government decided that capitulation or further delay would have been still more harmful. On December 20, 1960, a hog board previously weakened by a series of harsh disciplinary measures was informed that the Farm Products Marketing Board had amended existing regulations in a manner which made the auction selling of hogs mandatory.

Forced to choose between the acceptance of auction selling and the termination of the producer marketing program, the farmer-directors reluctantly agreed to introduce a form of electronic Dutch auction. This was one of the last official actions of the Hog Producer leadership as then constituted. At the annual producer meeting held shortly after that time, a majority of the incumbent directors were not reelected to the Ontario Hog Producers Marketing Board. The resulting changes in personnel— the most substantial in the history of the program—can be explained by two factors. Some incumbent directors had no desire to serve on a producer marketing board with neither independence nor authority and did not stand for reelection. Rather, these men decided to devote their efforts to the establishment of cooperative packing plants. Changes in existing electoral districts ordered by the Farm Products Marketing Board also contributed to the turnover in hog board membership.

During their lengthy dispute with the government, the members of the hog board never modified the course of action they originally adopted. All efforts were devoted to making it politically impractical for the FPMB to reduce the autonomy of the hog producer groups and/or to order changes in the existing method of sale. Some success along these lines was achieved during the first year of the controversy, and the strategy chosen was the only one open to a leadership unwilling to make compromises of any kind. The party in power is dependent on rural votes and it would have been compelled to abandon its attacks on the selling method had the entire farm community supported the hog board's position. For a number of reasons, however, this universal support was not forthcoming. Consequently, it was politically feasible for Provincial officials to discipline the hog board and to compel the adoption of auction selling.

CONCEPTUAL SHORTCOMINGS AND AREAS REQUIRING FURTHER RESEARCH

Upon completion of the study, the investigator realized that he had been only partially successful. The approach used was expected to provide new insights into the behavior of the hog board and to contribute to the further development of the survival concept. Only one of these objectives was achieved. The complicating factor was an assumption erroneously made at the beginning of the study—that any behavior system faced with a survival problem would become survival-oriented. As will subsequently be shown, this did not prove to be true. Consequently, Alderson's discussion was of only limited value in the examination of Hog Producer conduct during the time that behavior system faced a survival challenge. Fortunately, and more relevant to the purposes of this essay, the case study pointed out certain shortcomings of the survival concept as then formulated and revealed numerous problems deserving of further study. In the following paragraphs, the three major conceptual weaknesses revealed by this examination are discussed:

1. *The response of a behavior system to a survival challenge is unpredictable.* Although the Hog Producer organizations were confronted with a survival problem, the nature of their response indicated that the system was never survival-oriented. The Hog Producer leadership repeatedly ignored threats to organizational survival and behaved in a manner that weakened the system's opportunity for continued existence. Such action becomes understandable only when some other factor is considered more important than mere survival. Since systems apparently differ in their reaction to the development of survival problems, additional research intended to discover the determinants of a system's response pattern is clearly in order.

Even if continued existence did not become the primary objective, the development of a survival problem might still be expected to influence the goals of a behavior system and affect the criterion of choice used to rank possible solutions. In the hog producer case, the author believes that the goal of the system, the advancing of producer interests, and its criterion of choice, the maximization of producer gross unit receipts, remained unchanged. The reasons that explain this fact are difficult to determine. Possibly, survival problems have only a limited impact on some behavior systems because the seriousness of the situation is never adequately recognized. Although the existence of a potentially destructive condition is acknowledged, the possibility of disaster is considered too remote to have any effect on goals and the decision-making process.

This inability to recognize the peril the system faced could be due to some combination of internal factors and environmental considerations. Such appears to have been the case when the Hog Producer behavior system was faced with a survival problem. Many directors never believed that a government dependent upon rural support would carry out its threats against the Hog Producer organizations. Because past difficulties had always been overcome, the gravity of any present problem was always underestimated. Finally, men filled with a missionary zeal refused to recognize and to be influenced by the possibility of failure.

Whether or not the system becomes survival-oriented is only one of the factors to be considered. If survival becomes the primary objective of the system, attention should be focused on the process by which previously existing goals are displaced. Is the transition an abrupt one or does the system adopt a number of interim objectives, each less desirable than the last, until every effort is finally devoted to assuring organizational survival? In other words, the speed at which the system's level of aspiration adjusts to the existence of a survival situation and the steps by which such change takes place must be determined.

One should also consider how a behavior system must respond in order to be classified as survival-oriented. The issue is clear when the desire to assure organizational survival replaces all other objectives, and the system acts in a manner that will assure survival. Is the system survival-oriented, however, if its leaders recognize the survival problem and attempt to deal with it without devoting all their efforts to this end? Is the system so motivated, if the leadership risks complete destruction in the hopes of finding a solution that will make adaptation of any kind unnecessary?

The author has restricted the term "survival-oriented" to systems that consider survival of primary importance and would make whatever adaptations are necessary to assure continued existence. One could argue, however, that this is too narrow a definition of the term. The Hog Producer leadership might be viewed as concerned with survival but nevertheless willing to gamble "all or nothing" on finding a solution that requires no change in the objective of the system or its method of operation. Rather than modify the selling method and assure survival, the farmer-directors attempted to force the Provincial government to change its position. Some decision as to whether this type of action makes a system survival-oriented is a necessary prerequisite to research in this area.

2. *Distinguishing between adaptation and disintegration can be a difficult task.* Do bankrupt corporations that have been reorganized or social agencies that merge with other welfare groups survive? The problem is complicated by the fact that a threatened system can "survive" in two very different senses of the term. It could find an "appropriate solution" to its survival problem, one which will enable the system to perform the same functions with undiminished autonomy and with no fears for its continued existence, or it might adapt in a manner consistent with changing circumstances. If the system must adapt, the extent of the change can be measured in terms of its effect on the internal structure, the autonomy of the organization, and the functions that are performed. In contrast, systemic destruction is inevitable when members believe that the system cannot adapt to changed circumstances and still provide more satisfaction than could be obtained by individual action or through membership in another system.

What did the case study reveal as to the fate of the Hog Producer behavior system? Did it successfully, if not voluntarily, adapt to changing circumstances, or did it disintegrate? One's answer to this question depends in large part on how he views the relationship of the Farm Products Marketing Board to the Hog Producer behavior system. The eleven directors of the hog board considered the FPMB an external agency with no authority to interfere directly in the administration of a producer marketing program. The FPMB did intervene, however, and its authority and influence over the program can no longer be questioned. Consequently, the displaced leaders—were they familiar with the terminology used in this study—would cite the changes in the authority, influence, and autonomy of the hog board as evidence that the original behavior system has been destroyed.

The author, however, believes that the existence of a behavior system need not be equated with the continued exercise of power by any single group. Given the nature of the Farm Products Marketing Act, the Provincial government must be considered as always having been a component of the behavior system. Consequently, the dispute over the selling method could also be viewed as an internal struggle for leadership. The marked effect of the dispute on the Hog Producer behavior system cannot be questioned. Nevertheless, a reduction in the power, authority, and independence of the hog board is not in itself proof that the behavior system has been destroyed. In this case, the author considers these changes to be indications of adaptation rather than disintegration.

Under what conditions then would the Hog Producer behavior system be destroyed? The author believes that it would disintegrate only if the Farm Products Marketing Act is repealed or the results of some future plebiscite are unfavorable. In other words, this behavior system will survive as long as some form of compulsory marketing program for hogs operates under the provisions of existing legislation. If a behavior system is to be viewed as something more than the lengthened shadow of those in charge, a change in leadership cannot be considered as evidence of the disintegration of the system. Such a conclusion would be inconsistent with an emphasis on the functions performed by a behavior system rather than on its structure. Consequently, Alderson's reluctance to equate the survival of the system with the continuity of its membership appears to be justified.

3. *Distinguishing system from environment can also pose difficulties.* The organized behavior system is defined as consisting of a group of individuals working together, the set of instruments and resources used by this group, and the environment in which it operates. A behavior system, however, must itself operate within a still broader environment or field of environment, and the definition provided is of limited assistance in assigning elements to one or the other of these environments. The problems concerning the relationship of the Farm Products Marketing Board to the behavior system can now be more clearly defined. Was the FPMB part of the environment in which the group (the hog producer organizations) operated and thus a member of the behavior system, or was it merely a part of the larger environment surrounding the entire system? Conversely, the eleven members of the hog board could be viewed either as the relevant behavior system or as the control group of a larger system. Further development of the behavior system concept may depend in large part on the success achieved in clearly delineating the system most suitable

for studying a given problem from the world in which the system operates.

THE CASE STUDY AND ALDERSON'S NEW TREATMENT OF SURVIVAL

Shortly after the previously summarized study was completed, Alderson chose to discuss survival considerations in the second edition of *Theory in Marketing*. Although Alderson was aware of the results obtained from this application of his thinking, his most recent statement is not a deliberate attempt either to rebut the findings or to deal systematically with those limitations of the survival concept supposedly pointed out. The behavior system in question was judged far too atypical in structure and function to merit such treatment. Rather, his most recent formulation explores a whole new dimension of the relationship of the survival concept to marketing systems.

This research report, however, would be of only historical interest if an attempt were not made to relate Alderson's present thinking to the results of the case study. Consequently, those aspects of Alderson's new treatment of survival that seem pertinent will be discussed in this concluding section. Attention will be focused on the conceptual weaknesses that have been overcome, on the new insights provided by applying his revised formulation, and on certain important problems that remain unresolved. Those aspects of his new dimensions with no immediate relevance to the Hog Producer study will not be considered.

The Relevant Environment

Alderson recognized that the environment to be considered in an investigation of a behavior system differs from case to case and time to time. Depending on the purpose at hand, the proximate environment, the environment of aspiration, or the ultimate environment may be the one meriting study. The difficulty of determining whether the Farm Products Marketing Board belonged to the Ontario Hog Producer behavior system was previously discussed. While the behavior system was defined to include the environment within which a group working together used a set of instruments and resources, there yet remains a larger environment within which each system must operate. To which of these environments did the FPMB belong? Alderson's recent formulation provides additional insight into this problem. Perhaps, the FPMB became a component of the hog producer behavior system only after a change in the leadership's aspiration level had broadened the environment in which the system operated.

Alderson's tripartite classification also points up what his earlier work had only implied—that the environment is a dynamic rather than a static component of a system. Also significant is the apparent change in the definition of a behavior system. If, as Alderson indicates, the environment is something the system consciously defines by its actions, can environment still be considered a part of the system proper?

Increased Emphasis on Human Roles

Alderson's new formulation discusses at greater length the differences in authority, interest, and activity existing between the control group and the subordinate elements of a behavior system. This is true even though his views of subordinates as the implementers of strategic decisions may not always be applicable. Subordinate elements play a somewhat different role in many voluntary associations, nonprofit institutions, and political pressure groups. They do not accept and implement as much as they legitimatize. The control group of such organizations is a force in the larger community only so long as it is accepted and feared as the spokesman of an otherwise passive but nevertheless powerful group. Only rarely will the membership be called upon to demonstrate its loyalty by some overt display such as a boycott or a freedom march. If a control group committed to a given position cannot in fact provide evidence of membership support, its influence will fast decline. For example, the inability of the Hog Producer leadership to gain the unqualified backing of the organization's 40,000 members allowed the Provincial government to impose auction selling. These considerations notwithstanding, Alderson's expanded treatment of the differences in function and, perhaps, interest existing among components of a behavior system is an important contribution.

The Pathology of Systems

Alderson recognizes that internal conflict can lead to the displacement of a control group. His treatment of this topic is consistent with his earlier belief that continuity in membership or function is not essential to the survival of a behavior system. The displacement of a control group may be one indication that an existing behavior system has been destroyed and another established. If examination of changes in leadership and function does not reveal the fate of the system, what will? The difficulties of distinguishing system from environment also become relevant at this point. The change in leadership that occurred in the Hog Producer behavior system can be considered the result of internal systemic maladjustment only if the Farm Products Marketing Board is viewed as a long-time, although previously dormant, member of that system. Otherwise, the eventual displacement of the control group must be considered the result of external pressures rather than of internal upheaval.

Survival Concern and Capacity

Alderson explicitly states that the members of a behavior system faced with a survival problem may tacitly agree not to recognize this unpleasant fact. He also discusses the desirability of being able to measure the sur-

vival potential of organized behavior systems. The results of the Hog
Producer case study seems more consistent with the first of these arguments than with the second. The hog board refused to become survival-
oriented even though the system it controlled was faced with a survival
problem. Unfortunately, recognition of a range of possible reactions to a
survival threat provides little insight into why some but not all systems
choose to ignore unpleasant realities. Reasons why the hog board may not
have become survival-oriented were previously advanced.

The ability to measure survival capacity would be desirable insofar as
this capacity is independent of the nature of the survival threat. If there
is more than one kind of survival problem, no single measure of survival
capacity could be developed. In any case, the difficulty of distinguishing
systems that have survived through adaptation from those which have
disintegrated appears to be a more important conceptual limitation.

The Extinction Mode

The concept of the extinction mode provides a useful perspective for
viewing the actions of the hog board. Examining the situation after the
fact, one could conclude that the Hog Producer behavior system was pursuing an extinction mode. The leadership was unwilling to yield to the
wishes of the agency which had granted and could take away its authority. To the author at least, a striking parallel exists between the conduct
of the hog board and that of the pre–Civil War southern leadership attempting to adhere to an untenable position against superior odds.

At the same time, however, it should be realized that extinction modes
may be easier to recognize after the fact. Their development may be the
inevitable result of a strategy of some merit. As Schelling has indicated,
the weaker party to a dispute should often act in a way that gives its opponent the last opportunity to avoid conflict.[6] For example, it may be desirable to occupy a position from which one cannot voluntarily retreat
and then to act so as to make an opponent's efforts to dislodge you mutually damaging. "If one driver speeds up so that he can not stop and the
other realizes it, the second driver has to yield. . . . If one carries explo-
sives visibly on his person in a manner that makes destruction obviously
inevitable for himself and any assailant, he may deter assault much more
than if he retained any control." [7]

The Hog Producer leadership employed tactics of the type Schelling
discusses. By declaring its unalterable opposition to auction selling, the
hog board allowed the FPMB to determine whether the method of sale
would become a subject of public controversy. Although such a strategy
appeared sound at the time, it did not succeed. Government officials decided that more was to be lost by conceding to the hog board than by

---

[6] Thomas C. Schelling, *The Strategy of Conflict* (Cambridge, Mass.: Harvard
University Press, 1960), p. 22.

[7] *Ibid.*, p. 37.

disciplining it. In retrospect, the Hog Producer control group appears to have locked the system into an extinction mode. But what if the Provincial government had capitulated or the northern states had allowed the South to leave the Union in peace? Could both systems still be classified as having adopted an extinction mode?

Conceptual Problems Left Unresolved

Because he was primarily concerned with other aspects of the survival concept, Alderson does not deal with the shortcomings revealed by the Hog Producer case study. For example, the recognition of three possible environments notwithstanding, identification of the behavior system most appropriate for a given study remains a difficult task. Although the concept of a hierarchy of systems or of "systems within systems" has its merit, it nevertheless complicates the tasks of isolation, identification, and enumeration. Similarly, determining the fate of a behavior system confronted with a survival problem has not become any easier. The missing guidelines for distinguishing between major and successful adaptation and systemic disintegration are not provided. Until observers are able to agree as to the fate of a challenged system, the analytical usefulness of the survival concept will be seriously impaired. Finally, only partial progress is made in predicting or measuring systemic response to a survival challenge. How and why any given system reacts as it does still remains a problem requiring for its solution additional research into the nature of behavior systems and survival problems.

Alderson's Approach to Normative Theory

Alderson's discussion of normative considerations is unique in that he intentionally avoids providing a prescription for action. He views the system as pursuing its goals within a framework of economic, social, and ecological sanctions. Also, the decision maker must, as part of his efforts to perpetuate his own system, avoid actions which threaten the survival of all larger, more encompassing systems. Sanctions limit the sphere of choice but they do not prescribe a specific course of action. This is desirable, Alderson concludes, since it allows the decision maker the freedom to act creatively and ethically.

This discussion of "the normative" is somewhat disturbing primarily because of the unique manner in which Alderson employs that term. Traditionally, normative models outline the "ideal," the "one best method," the way things "should" be. Alderson makes it quite clear that he has something else in mind when he discusses normative considerations. Little attention is given to problems of determining which of two given forms of systemic behavior is the "better" or the way things "should" be. Are the farmers of Ontario better off now than they would have been had producer marketing legislation never been introduced? Unfortunately, all other things could not be held equal and only the method of marketing farm products varied. To those searching for the "best" method of marketing hogs or any other commodity, Alderson provides nothing to substitute for the inadequate tools of economic analysis.

A Valuable Concept All the Same

Certain limitations of the survival concept as originally presented and then subsequently modified by Alderson have been discussed. The author, however, does not believe that the results of his investigation have weakened that concept as an analytical tool. The atypical nature, especially the failure to become survival-oriented, of the behavior system examined must be kept in mind at all times. Also, only one aspect of Alderson's new discussion—the material relevant to the earlier attempt to employ the concept —was reviewed in this concluding section. At no time were the merits and usefulness of the concept given as much attention as its alleged limitations. For all these reasons and past frustrations notwithstanding, the author shares Alderson's view that the survival concept will yet prove to be a theoretical concept of considerable conceptual and analytical value.

8. POLITICAL SCIENCE AND MARKETING[1]

Hans B. Thorelli

POLITICS in a free society is the system which tries to make certain that the goods and services produced by the government reflect reasonably well the preferences of the population. Similarly, marketing in a free society is the system which tries to make certain that the goods and services produced by private enterprise reflect reasonably well the preferences of the population. In many respects, these functions are strikingly parallel, and, indeed, they tend increasingly to overlap in an era when the distinctions between private and public seem to become increasingly blurred. Governments in many countries invade domains once reserved for private enterprise. In some nations, trade associations and government-sanctioned cartels actually take on missions which many would once have considered governmental. New institutional forms and policies for cooperation between government and private enterprise in such areas as commodity marketing and defense purchasing and the various joint ventures being undertaken in export marketing and economic development contribute further to interrelating the study of marketing and that of government.

Marketing is a policy science, as are political science and economics. Policy sciences are normative, not in the sense of being inherently biased by one set of values or another, but rather in that they invariably postulate the existence of *some* kind of value structure in terms of which the relative merits of alternative actions may be gauged. These sciences are not limited to studying the process of policy formation in public and

---

[1] Students of marketing interested in salient background readings in political science are referred to David Easton, *The Political System—An Inquiry into the State of Political Science* (New York: Alfred A. Knopf, Inc., 1953); James C. Charlesworth (ed.), *The Limits of Behavioralism in Political Science* (Philadelphia: The American Academy of Political and Social Scence, 1962); Dwight Waldo, *Political Science in the United States of America—A Trend Report* (Paris: UNESCO, 1956); and Robert A. Dahl, "Business and Politics: A Critical Appraisal of Political Science," in Robert A. Dahl, Mason Haire, and Paul F. Lazarsfeld, *Social Science Research on Business: Product and Potential* (New York: Columbia University Press, 1959).

private institutions. They are also concerned with specifying decision rules for managerial action. Marketing may seem "more" normative to some than, say, economics. We do not think that such a distinction is valid, but why others might make it is understandable. Marketing has accepted the extant diversity of goals and values among the parties in the marketplace as given (hence the lack of tightness in most marketing literature), while economics by and large has settled for profit maximization as the all-pervasive goal and price as the all-pervasive policy consideration for both parties to a transaction. Political science as a policy science is in an even more rudimentary stage than marketing. Witness, for example, the inability of political scientists to state by what means democracy might be made viable in newly emerging nations. Note also their internal and surely futile quarrels as to whether a socialist or totalitarian government is a prerequisite for the economic development of such nations. Time may well be ripe for a joint attack by representatives of several policy sciences on a problem such as that last mentioned.

We shall not here enter the endless discussion of whether marketing is, or can ever hope to be, a science in the sense we think of physics as a science, or whether it should more properly be labeled an applied discipline analogous to, for example, architecture in the "natural" sciences. Suffice it to say that marketing and political theory both suffer from a superabundance of unproven (and frequently unprovable) generalizations. This fact has led the more "realistic" representatives in both disciplines to focus their attention on institutional problems which are often of a trivial nature. Less fearful of avoiding reality, economists have taken almost the opposite route in recent years. Institutionalism and "political economy" are no longer fashionable. Instead, the microeconomic theory of decision making of (not *in*) the firm has been developed to esoteric perfection on the basis of highly schematic notions about the nature of objectives and policy. The resulting breach between Euclidean economics and every day decision making in the marketplace has provided the hunting ground for marketing as a discipline. Right now, it may indeed be said that marketing is too important to leave to the economists. Marketing cannot return to the fold until economics embraces notions of diversified goal structures and diversified market policies (with regard to product quality, promotional effort, service, and other variables beyond price and volume), and takes into greater account the impact of institutional arrangements. Meanwhile, more progress in the area of theory about the firm may emerge from marketing and political science than from economics.

It is also in marketing's nature as a policy science that it should be interested in power systems.[2] Pioneering efforts have been made by Alder-

---

[2] The concept of "power" is inordinately vague; "influence" and "authority" are not much better. The underlying reality of differential ability to make decisions which "stick" is undeniable.

son,[3] Ridgway,[4] and others, but much remains to be done especially in the area which may be labeled the *government of markets*. We are interested in the determinants and the impact of power relationships and in the way that decision-making power is exercised within as well as between firms, households, and other units which constitute the elements of market systems. One might hypothesize, for example, that the style of leadership exercised by the dominant firm in a given market system is similar to the style of leadership exercised by management *inside* that firm.

The Political Ecology of Marketing

A vital area of marketing and political science intersection is that of the social, political, economic, and legal framework within which marketing operations take place. We may perhaps coin a phrase for this study of the interaction of marketing and its macro-environment—the political ecology of marketing. The literature in this area is voluminous. It is epitomized in this country by a great number of textbooks commonly entitled "government and business" as well as by a number of more penetrating studies, notably of antitrust policy and of government regulation of agricultural marketing.[5] By and large, studies of interaction between political science and marketing have thus far centered in this field. Nevertheless, this interaction has not been very closely examined. Most of the literature is characterized by a heavy public policy orientation and a consequent underemphasis of the partially different perspectives with which the same problems are viewed by private policy makers in the marketing arena. One would hope that future writings would supplement the respectable work of the past in two additional respects. Greater emphasis on theory and the formulation of testable hypotheses is needed. Much more effort must also be devoted to tackling the admittedly formidable problems involved in gauging and—ultimately—predicting the effects of governmental action on private policy and behavior. This effort would be in the best spirit of the great tradition of political economy.

A rather neglected aspect of the political ecology of marketing is that which might be labeled "comparative government and business relations." Such comparative studies have a high yield potential from the viewpoint of theory as well as of public and private policy making. However, it must be emphasized that truly *comparative* analysis is required, not a mere

---

[3] Wroe Alderson, *Marketing Behavior and Executive Action* (Homewood Ill.: Richard D. Irwin, Inc., 1957).

[4] Valentine F. Ridgway, "Administration of Manufacturer-Dealer Systems," *Administrative Science Quarterly*, Vol. 1 (March, 1957), pp. 464–83. Cf. F. E. Balderston, "Comunication Networks in Intermediate Markets," *Management Science*, Vol. 4 (January, 1958), p. 154–71.

[5] Cf. e.g., Marshall E. Dimock, *Business and Government* (3d ed.; New York: Holt, Rinehart & Winston, 1957); Hans B. Thorelli, *The Federal Antitrust Policy— Organization of an American Tradition* (Baltimore: Johns Hopkins Press, 1955); and Theodore W. Schultz, *The Economic Organization of Agriculture* (New York: McGraw-Hill Book Co., Inc., 1953).

assemblage of descriptive data from various nations. Much of the literature masquerading under the label "comparative economic systems" is deficient in this regard.[6] Questions beckoning researchers include: What taxonomy of political and socioeconomic systems is relevant from the viewpoint of marketing? What linkages exist between political, social, and economic systems and marketing systems? What are the salient differences and similarities with regard to marketing in free-enterprise countries and in the Soviet Union? What public policies are associated with the various types of marketing systems?

Although ecological comparison may be international, a comparative approach may also be employed within a given culture to study the effects of major environmental change. The emergence of free-trade areas and common markets represents a special challenge. The efforts under way at the Marketing Science Institute and elsewhere to investigate systematically the impact on marketing behavior of the European Economic Community seem especially significant at the time of writing.

Governmental policy constitutes an important part of the *ambiente* of marketing, whether the policy concerns trade promotion (e.g., trade fairs), regulating entry (e.g., license requirements in certain trades), maintaining competition (e.g., the core of United States antitrust laws), or direct regulation of private enterprise marketing policies (e.g., price control, output restrictions in agriculture). Insofar as political science has evidenced interest in the ecology of marketing, it has generally confined itself to analysis of public policy. This is an arbitrary, self-imposed limitation. Privately conceived arrangements may have similar purposes and effects, and private government need not be greatly different from public. Such differences, as may be relevant—e.g., as regards the degree to which public authority may be invoked for enforcement purposes—invite comparative analysis. An especially interesting area is that of intersection between public and private arrangements to restrain competition.[7] One wonders what would happen to the barbershop cartels which plague most of our metropolitan centers if public licensing and "inspection" laws were repealed.

International Marketing Operations

Never unimportant in the development of modern civilization, international business operations are now more significant than ever. As the philosophy of customer orientation gains wider foothold, marketing con-

---

[6] An effort to apply a truly comparative framework in antitrust study is illustrated by Hans B. Thorelli, "Antitrust in Europe: National Policies after 1945," *University of Chicago Law Review*, Vol. 26 (Winter, 1959), pp. 222–36. A much more comprehensive comparative antitrust study is being conducted by Professor Corwin D. Edwards; it will be published under the auspices of Brookings Institution.

[7] Cf. e.g., the provocative argument of Walter Adams and Horace M. Gray, *Monopoly in America—The Government as Promoter* (New York: The Macmillan Co., 1955).

siderations will increasingly govern the entrepreneurial decision as to what mode of operation (distribution through local importers, captive sales organization, licensing of local manufacturers, production by self-owned subsidiary, etc.) might properly be adopted by the multinational corporation in the various territories to which it is committed. This prediction gains further credence from the fact that marketing, more than any other part of a business, is directly exposed to the local operating environment. The problem of selecting among local *modus operandi* cannot be solved merely—sometimes not even primarily—on the basis of estimates of comparative costs and market potentials. The evaluation of what may be termed political risks (and opportunities) is—and in the absence of world government will remain—of cardinal importance.

Perceptive observers have emphasized the essential internationality of economic interests and the fact that in many respects modern business is indeed more clearly cosmopolitan or even more global in nature than most governmentally sponsored international (or supranational) organizations, not excluding the United Nations.[8] Presumably, most large multinational firms would like to think in terms of "one world"—a global market free from suboptimization influences generated by the existence of well over a hundred national trading jurisdictions. As it is, overall goals and their achievement are conditioned in large part by the particularistic policies of governments. The evaluation of local political conditions must take into account a broad range of factors, running all the way from the risk of expropriation to the possibilities of special incentives obtained from general legislation or from *ad hoc* direct negotiation with public authorities. The impact of and trends of change in local measures discriminating against foreign enterprise (trade barriers,[9] special taxation, profit remittance restrictions, differential enforcement of licensing and inspection laws and credit restrictions, etc.) may be of crucial significance. So may be the availability (or nonavailability) of support from the country of origin of the multinational firm (e.g., in the form of credit guarantees, insurance against loss, diplomatic representations against untoward actions abroad). Effective surveillance of the climate of public opinion and of changes in confidence in existing governments may spell the difference between success or failure in international operations. Lack of confidence in government may, for instance, result in conditions of extreme inflation or deflation affecting the fortunes of the firm far more than changes in market potential due to competition, new styles of life, and other endogenous market factors.

---

[8] Cf. Corwin D. Edwards, "The Internationality of Economic Interests," *University of Pennsylvania Law Review*, Vol. 3 (December, 1962), pp. 183–93; and Walton H. Hamilton, *The Politics of Industry* (New York: Alfred A. Knopf, Inc., 1957).

[9] Thus far, political scientists have been interested only in historically oriented study of policy formation affecting international trade. Cf. Elmer E. Schattschneider, *Politics, Pressures and the Tariff—A Study of Free Private Enterprise in Pressure Politics* (New York: Prentice-Hall, Inc., 1935).

Political scientists and marketing men may cooperate in the development of methodology as well as in the practice of evaluating risks and opportunities originating in political conditions and developments.

Government participation in international business ventures is also worthy of the joint attention of marketing and political science students. In modern history such participation has distinguished precedents dating as far back as the joint-stock companies pioneering American and East Indian trade in the sixteenth and seventeenth centuries. We are presently experiencing a burst of new developments in this field, with a broad range of different types of joint arrangements being brought into play. The governmental link in these arrangements sometimes emanates from the country of origin of the joint venture (as in the case of British Petroleum), but increasingly we will see it represented by public authority domiciled in the overseas market. In a different sphere we encounter that interesting hybrid of public and private cartel, the international commodity agreement.

A special set of problems likely to become quite urgent in the near future concerns the trade relations between free-enterprise and Communist nations. Competing exporters in the former countries are facing monopsonistic buyers in the latter. The Soviet Union has embarked on an export campaign in petroleum and certain other industries which at times seems to have no other purpose but to upset the normal functioning of world markets and/or to use economic weapons to tie certain nations politically to the Communist bloc. It seems likely that special institutional arrangements will have to be developed to tackle the complex issues of East-West trade—again creating an area of obvious mutual concern to political scientists and marketing men.

The internal organization of multinational corporations offers further food for interdisciplinary thought. Questions such as whether the structuring approach should emphasize product, purpose, territory, or function and whether domestic and "foreign" operations should be separated or integrated are analogous to issues encountered in public administration and in national-local government relations. Some of the most fruitful interchange between marketing and political science may well take place under the spreading wings of organization theory.

Marketing and Economic Development

Politics and economics are inextricably intertwined. Nowhere is the validity of this axiom of public affairs more readily apparent than in the underdeveloped nations. Yet, many economists—including some members of the profession who specialize in developmental economics—deal with the problem of materialist advancement in these countries as if these problems could be viewed apart from the political system. Political scientists often are guilty of adopting a correspondingly narrow perspective. There is also a widespread tendency for social scientists as well as for local political leaders and international technical assistance administrators to assume that socialist or totalitarian government is the only form appropriate for accelerated economic development in the transitional countries. Their attitude is especially remarkable since no real proof exists for this position either in past experience or in economic, social, or political logic. Actually, the kind of government and policies most conducive to economic progress in various phases of development and in different environments is still a largely underdeveloped province of social science.

What we *do* know by this time, on the basis of strong qualitative evidence, is that the following two propositions are true. First, *economic development under a system of free government is possible only where there exists some freedom of choice in consumption and enough variety of consumer goods and services to make choice meaningful*. Only under dictatorships of one coloration or another or in free societies in wartime and similar general emergencies is it possible to achieve such development while paying little or no heed to current consumer welfare. Regrettably, infrastructure and heavy industry have been given attention all out of proportion to their significance in the transformation of underdeveloped countries. If Colin Clark's taxonomy of primary, secondary, and tertiary industries was intended to indicate a sequence of developmental effort, the order of priorities might rather be inverted.[10] At least, a pronounced change in emphasis towards the development of consumer markets and a distribution system worthy of the name would seem eminently desirable.

Secondly, *economic development is largely a question of attitudes, not of money or equipment, nor even of education in particular skills*. The relevant attitudes, for better or worse, seem generally to be those usually associated with the Protestant ethic. Even though studies, such as those by David McClelland and his associates,[11] have failed to convince some people, the multibillion-dollar lesson provided by our foreign-aid program should persuade most reasonable men of the validity of our second proposition.

Let us add now a third proposition, less tested but probably no less valid than the other two: *No vehicle is more powerful than contemporary marketing philosophy in changing attitudes in a manner conducive to improving standards of living in a democratic society*. Existing distribution structures in the transitional nations constitute a roadblock to, not a channel for, economic development. Much worse is the fact that business is not at all customer-oriented. Rather, it is almost exclusively production- or finance-oriented. Entrepreneurial attitudes focus on low volume and high margin. The citizen-consumer has not yet really seen the connection between the three-stage sequence of effort, savings, and

---

[10] Colin Clark, *The Conditions of Economic Progress* (3d ed.; New York: The Macmillan Co., 1957).

[11] David C. McClelland, *The Achieving Society* (Princeton, N.J.: Van Nostrand Co., Inc., 1961).

higher standards of living, a causal chain which marketing-oriented management (especially that of progressive merchandising firms) can demonstrate more simply and efficiently than any other force.

Many underdeveloped nations, including the major part of Latin America, suffer from what may best be described as a village mentality. This mentality is similar to that of the medieval guild system in Europe. Unfortunately, however, the "freeze" of the local culture set in at a much lower level of socioeconomic development in the countries with which we are now concerned. After such societies undergo the ordeal of initial adjustment to the introduction of marketing-oriented consumer industries and channels of distribution, a transformation of attitudes resulting in the *acceptance of change* and *social mobility* can be expected. To achieve economic progress in free but underdeveloped societies, we must keep opportunity percolating and make change a way of life—even more so than in the industrially advanced societies. If this is to be done, marketing-minded private enterprise—*not* antediluvian versions of capitalism such as those encountered in the Levant—must be moved to the very forefront in development planning rather than relegated to a corner.

In the long run, the major effort must be made by nationals of the underdeveloped countries. Nevertheless, examples can be set, know-how provided, and an entreprenurial climate favorable to competition and marketing stimulated by subsidiaries of European and American enterprise. Many policies attempting to strike a reasonable bridge between the partly concomitant and partly inconsistent goals of such firms and the governments of underdeveloped nations have been tried. These measures have failed more often than they have succeeded. The area of governmental policies which will reduce the political risks taken by the foreign entrepreneur and at the same time safeguard the interests of developing countries is indeed deserving of further investigation.

We have pointed in this section to the direct linkage between polity, economic development, and marketing in societies preferring democracy to dictatorship as the agent of economic progress. In so doing we have indicated another major field worthy of the joint attention of political science and marketing.

Industrial and Intracorporate Marketing

Industrial marketing as well as intracorporate marketing differ from other forms of marketing not so much because of the uniqueness of the products and services involved but rather because they frequently involve complex decision-making procedures in large organizations. Some readers still remember the days when the study of decision making in such organizations flowered a good deal brighter in public administration than in business administration, and when it was rather ridiculous to think of "organization theory" as a semiautonomous discipline. To the extent that public administration regains the initiative in the study of complex decision-making processes, marketing will stand to benefit from interaction with this branch of political science.

Public Policy Forecasting, Public Opinion, and Marketing Research

Some day, the realization will dawn upon both lawyers and political scientists that the acid test of scientific research is whether it increases our ability to predict causal relationships.[12] In the meantime, historicism for its own sake, as it were, holds its heavy hand over research in both of these professions. Yet, public and private decision makers are in crying need of what may be termed public policy forecasting. In the area of forecasting, economists have done their homework much better. Although only a few pioneering attempts have been made to forecast public policy in relation to marketing, a glorious future for this joint offshoot of marketing, political science, and law can be predicted.[13]

At one time, political science pioneered the field of public opinion of which marketing research constitutes such a prominent subset. In the last fifteen years or so, however, political science has largely let go of public opinion as a field of research endeavor. It has seemingly taken the view that "we will deal with the facts of public opinion on matters of interest to us, but only when those facts are served up on a platter and the methodology of collecting them has been perfected by somebody else." At the present time, then, marketing may derive new impulses in opinion research primarily from sociology, psychology, and statistics—as indeed marketing research itself is now beginning to enrich the behavioral sciences.

Government as Organizer of Markets

In the "behavior systems" view of marketing—a view which we have mentioned as closely related to political science—one of the organizations involved is frequently considered to be exercising a lead function and a coordinating influence. This phenomenon is often empirically observable. With the sizeable growth in recent decades and in most countries of the public sector of the economy, both in absolute terms and relative to GNP, the government itself has become by far the most important single marketer of goods and services. This extension of governmental activity has not been based on any real or alleged superiority of public bodies as marketing agencies. On the contrary, government agencies are notoriously deficient as regards customer orientation. In the distribution of government services and in regard to the relations of governmental agencies to

---

[12] A handful of lawyers and political scientists are already aware of this fact.
[13] Cf. e.g., Hans B. Thorelli, "Government and Marketing—Will Fusion or Fission Be the Fashion?", *Antitrust Bulletin*, Vol. 7 (May–June, 1962), pp. 453–66; and *Proceedings* of the American Marketing Association Convention, December, 1961, pp. 70–80.

their clientele generally, there is indeed crying need for large-scale technical assistance from marketing to public administration.

The government's role as organizer of markets is not confined to the area of the economy where it appears as the sole or major distributor of services. In other large sectors it assumes the lead function of market systems by virtue of legislation or by exercising the power of a huge buyer. Regulatory legislation gives commissions and other public bodies in this country the final say about such vital marketing parameters as price, quality, and service in a number of public utility industries. Typically, public agencies in other nations exercise regulatory powers over an even broader range of industries. In the field of agriculture, governments everywhere organize markets on the basis of direct legislation, frequently involving large-scale purchasing to support producer prices and the pegging of consumer prices at a low level.

In the long run, however, government's most subtle and yet pervasive influence on behavior systems active in the market may well be where it appears as a large-scale buyer in its own right. United States government stockpiling policies are of crucial significance in a number of global commodity markets for strategic materials. (Some would say this is true for nonstrategic materials as well.) Governments everywhere—national as well as local—are large buyers of equipment and supplies. They influence the marketing practices of firms ranging all the way from manufacturers of electrical generating equipment with global operations to local bakeries. Nowhere is the long arm of the government felt as keenly as in the defense markets, where it is frequently the sole buyer. Here a given contract may spell life and death for individual companies and entire communities. The specifying and regulating influence extends all the way from the main contractor to the hundreds or thousands of subcontractors. Major transformations of market structures and behavior may also be expected from changes in governmental purchasing practice, e.g., the trend away from competitive bidding on an equal opportunity basis toward the "chosen instrument" type of procurement. Here is indeed a challenging field for political science as well as marketing.

Marketing and the Public Interest

A key concept of political theory is that of the public interest. The rationale of democratic government is that it serves this interest. Much of the discussion as to the precise meaning of "serving the public interest" has been rather fruitless and metaphysical. Characteristically enough, however, we seem unable to dispense with such inquiries.[14] The most promising interpretation is probably that which views the public interest as

---

14 Representative recent publications include Glendon A. Schubert, *The Public Interest—A Critique of the Theory of a Political Concept* (Glencoe: The Free Press of Glencoe, 1961); and Carl J. Friedrich (ed.), *The Public Interest* (New York: Atherton Press, 1962).

essentially a synthetic product resulting from the confrontation of the many special interests pursued by various groups in a free society. The essence of government, then, is the continuous search for the dynamic equilibrium configuration of special interests and the implementation of policies consistent with this equilibrium.

For some purposes it may be instructive in a similar vein to think of the modern corporation as a community of interest groups (consumers, stockholders, employees, etc.). The task of management is to ensure the survival and growth of the enterprise, principally by gaining the co-operation of the various groups while maintaining a workable balance between their conflicting interests. This pluralist view of the corporation logically implies that this institution, like the government, also exists to serve the public interest. Such a view, of course, is also the quintessence of the theory of the firm under competitive conditions in economics, although that theory is based on the profit maximization postulate. The pluralist view of the corporation represents a supplementary avenue of inquiry which holds some promise in the growing effort to understand better the internal decision-making processes of large firms. Some evidence to support this notion is already at hand.[15]

A vexing complex of problems related to the interpretation of the public interest centers on the ethical constraints to action. Machiavelli represents an extreme viewpoint of an earlier age in this area, but he is only one example of the standing concern of political theory with matters of ethics in public management. A familiar current issue is that of "conflict of interest" in positions of public trust. Business is struggling with analogous issues. It is not altogether clear that whatever is profitable is ethical, or vice versa. Since the firm's marketing activities are its principal area of contact with its operating environment, problems of business ethics are to a great extent problems of marketing management. Thus, we are concerned with the study of people's notions about such issues as "fair" competition, deceptive advertising, "kickbacks," and gifts to purchasing agents and subliminal persuasion.

This field invites serious research by students of marketing and political science alike. Questions of ethics cannot be dismissed simply by a reference to conscience (although conscience surely is relevant). To a large

---

[15] Cf. R. M. Alt, "The Internal Organization of the Firm and Price Formation: An Illustrative Case," *Quarterly Journal of Economics*, Vol. 63 (February, 1949), pp. 92–110; and William R. Dill, *An Analysis of Task Environment and Personal Autonomy in Top Management Organizations* (mimeographed Ph.D. dissertation, Carnegie Institute of Technology, 1956), *passim*. (For an abbreviated version of Dean Dill's thesis see his article, "Environment as an Influence on Managerial Autonomy," *Administrative Science Quarterly*, Vol. 2 [March, 1958], pp. 409–43.)

An apparently less promising adaptation of a central concept of political science to problems of economics and marketing is the notion of "consumer sovereignty." For a good summary discussion, see Jerome Rothenberg, "Consumer's Sovereignty Revisited and the Hospitality of Freedom of Choice," *American Economic Review*, Vol. 52 (May, 1962), pp. 269–83.

extent, ethical standards are culturally and historically conditioned. For example: what is considered "fair-trade" pricing in some countries is reprehensible resale price control in others; what is acclaimed as "giving the consumer a break" in one culture is branded "unfair" or "disloyal" price cutting in another. Popular notions to the contrary, ethics is indeed an area that *can* be researched. Studies dealing with the prevalence, history, and effects of norms need not be "normative" to any greater degree than studies of consumer attitudes or of any other area of social science research.

The focus of this essay has been on subject matter rather than methodology. This emphasis was intentional; the problems of methodology are common to *all* the social sciences (or even science in general) to a far greater degree than the problems of subject matter. A discussion restricted essentially to marketing and political science in the sphere of methodology would be rather artificial. Clearly, there is a broad range of subject matter of common concern to these two disciplines, even though the disciplines have developed largely without contact with each other. In sum, the plea for bridge-building and interdisciplinary research seems more warranted than usual.

II. Marketing Agencies and Marketing Channels

9. THE STAGES OF RETAIL DEVELOPMENT

William J. Regan

INCREASING attention has been devoted to macro studies of retailing in recent years with the studies themselves emphasizing two different approaches. One involves attempts to identify causal factors in the emergence of major store types. The other is characterized by a historical survey of significant events in retail development.

The hypothesis supporting this article is that a unifying field theory to relate the wide divergencies of structure and function in retailing is a most pressing need. Until satisfactory conservation laws between past and future states are validated, the dynamic theories developed for marketing or retailing will have limited predictive value. Nevertheless, static theory which visualizes relationships can be developed, and, together with past experience and insight, help to show probable designs of the future. After the most promising hypothesis yet advanced to explain retail development is reviewed, a tentative structural theory for retailing will be suggested.

"The Wheel of Retailing"

Professor Malcolm P. McNair introduced "the wheel of retailing" concept to help explain the dynamics of institutional change in the distribution sector of a competitive high-level economy.[1] In this hypothesis, the wheel is seen as always revolving. A new cycle begins because of the innovation associated with a John Wanamaker, a George Hartford, a Frank Woolworth, a W. T. Grant, a General Wood, a Michael Cullen, or a Eugene Ferkauf. Such innovators enter the market ". . . in bad odor, ridiculed, scorned, condemned as 'illegitimate.' "[2] From low-status,

---

[1] Malcolm P. McNair, "Significant Trends and Developments in the Postwar Period," in A. B. Smith (ed.), *Competitive Distribution in a Free High-Level Economy and Its Implications for the University* (Pittsburgh: University of Pittsburgh Press, 1957), p. 17.

[2] *Ibid.*

low-margin, and low-price beginnings, the successful mature not only with relatively high status, high costs, and high prices, but also with a top-heavy vulnerability ". . . to the next revolution of the wheel, to the next fellow who has a bright idea and who starts his business on a low-cost basis, slipping in under the umbrella that the old-line institutions have hoisted." [3]

Professor Reavis Cox would place the wheel concept in a larger context: "We are moving on, so that when the wheel completes its turn we do not find ourselves precisely back where we came from. . . . We not only have to adjust to innovation, maturity, and new innovation but also to a continuing progress in one or another direction." [4]

Application of the hypothesis to empirical data suggests that it is not universally valid but that it ". . . does seem to describe a fairly common pattern in industrialized expanding economies." [5] Professor Stanley C. Hollander discovered that the following examples of retailing behavior did not conform to the wheel pattern:

1. The introduction of supermarkets in underdeveloped countries largely at the top of the social and price scales.
2. Vigorous price competition among Japanese department stores during the first three decades of this century.
3. The record of price-cutting by traditional, well established British merchants in the 1880's and 1890's.
4. Introduction of automatic merchandising as a high-cost, high-margin, high-convenience type of retailing in the United States.
5. The establishment in the United States of department-store branches and planned shopping centers as exclusive-type institutions in prestige locations.[6]

Other students have applied Schumpeter's concepts of innovation to retailing and identified the successive emergences of major store types as "the big disturbances" or the "dynamic leavening" which disrupt familiar patterns of repetitive competition and enforce adaptation to more progressive patterns.[7]

Although these approaches to explaining retail development are useful, to examine change after it has occurred is not enough. The objective should be a unifying concept that has predictive value. Perhaps a look into the structural and functional components of retailing itself may suggest a different approach to identifying a more comprehensive theory for retailing.

[3] *Ibid.*, p. 18.

[4] Reavis Cox, "Discussion," *Ibid.*, p. 57.

[5] Stanley C. Hollander, "The Wheel of Retailing," *Journal of Marketing*, Vol. 25 (July, 1960), p. 41.

[6] *Ibid.*, pp. 40–41.

[7] Joseph A. Schumpeter, *Capitalism, Socialism, and Democracy* (New York: Harper & Bros., 1950); Peter F. Drucker, *The New Society* (New York: Harper & Bros., 1950), p. 29; Perry Bliss, "Schumpeter, the 'Big' Disturbance and Retailing," *Social Forces*, Vol. 29 (October, 1960), pp. 72–76; and M. S. Moyer, "The Roots of Large-Scale Retailing," *Journal of Marketing*, Vol. 26 (October, 1962), pp. 55–59.

In the following sections, attempts are made (1) to classify the major services of retail value-added and to identify the important characteristics of the retail organizational structure, (2) to associate these services with goods so as to identify the major qualitative and alternative combinations of goods and services that can be offered by any retailer, (3) to classify the various stages of retail development, and (4) to test the construct by applying it to the historical value-added emphases of several major store types.

Composition of Retail Value-Added

The various forms of retail service or value-added may be classified under one of five major service headings depending on whether they provide (1) assortment range, depth, and quality (including minor processing or adapting); (2) character of store environment (referring to the relative impressiveness of store architecture, fittings, and general layout); (3) time or place accessibility; (4) communication and promotional techniques to attract patronage (advertising, trading stamps, display); or (5) merchandise transfer services to facilitate exchange of title and physical possession of goods (sales assistance, credit, delivery, returned-goods privileges).

All retailing activities which add value directly to the merchandise will fit into the preceding classification. This includes the historical ". . . bit of theatre to relieve the tedium of isolated lives and a monotonous diet" [8] which today has been institutionalized under promotional techniques. It also includes what have been variously called "authenticating the goods" [9] and "psychological transformation" [10]—phrases suggesting those activities which contribute to the creation of possession utility.

A single store's merchandising strategy is seen in its balance or mix of these items far better than in a summation of the expenses which add up to its gross margin. Despite their nonaggregative character, these elements represent from the consumers' standpoint the total value added by the retailing structure.

Retail managements seek to differentiate their enterprises by varying these input factors of retail value to please the desired consumer segments in their trading areas. The emphases used will vary according to management's understanding of prevailing market conduct as framed within the existing market structure. More specifically, management's operating policies are based on its interpretation of competitive dynamics and unfulfilled patronage opportunities in relation to the market structure of its trading area.

---

[8] Gerald Carson, *Country Stores in Early New England,* Catherine Fennelly (ed.), Village Booklet Series (Meriden, Conn.: Meriden Gravure Co., 1955), p. 14.

[9] *Observer,* July 29, 1962, quoting Stanley Marcus of Neiman-Marcus, Dallas, Texas.

[10] Paul Avril, *Théorie Sommaire de la Distribution des Biens de Consommation* (Paris: Compagnie Française d'Organisation, 1961).

Characteristics of organizational structure which in combination determine the nature of competition include: (1) the extent and character of store concentration; (2) the present and prospective number, age and groupings, economic levels, and other demographic data of effective consumers; (3) the extent to which retail services are considered homogeneous by consumers; (4) the relative freedom of entry into the particular trade; (5) the amount of innovation in the trade and the technology that is available and potentially applicable; (6) the frequency and range of price changes or special sales; (7) the presence of excess trade capacity; (8) the number or rate of failures and mergers; (9) the number, location, and competitive vigor of sources of supply; and (10) the extent of vertical and horizontal integration by suppliers and competitive retailers.

Retail-store managements face different complexes of conditions and objectives. Each must identify the appropriate elements of value-added to enhance its particular competitive position. Accurate appraisal of the relative importance of the various structural elements is therefore necessary.

The Retail-Service Choices

Each retail-store management somehow diagnoses the composite character of store conduct in the market it proposes to serve and decides upon one of the following combinations:

1. Relatively low merchandise costs with relatively low, average, or relatively high retail-service costs.
2. Average mechandise costs with relatively low, average, or relatively high retail-service costs.
3. Relatively high merchandise costs with relatively low, average, or relatively high retail-service costs.
4. Some combination of low, average, and high merchandise costs with some combination of low, average, and high retail-service costs.

Merchandise costs as well as retail-service costs are categorically simplified to three levels: relatively high, average, and relatively low. The relativity expressed is for each product or groups of products sold by suppliers to retailers and for the height of operating expenses incurred by each type of retail outlet. For example, there are men's shirts with relatively low, average, and relatively high invoice costs from the supplier. Similarly, there are operating expense totals for men's apparel stores which can be grouped as relatively low, average, and relatively high for this type store. These operating expenses reflect performance of all services classified above.

For the purpose of this concept, costs are assumed to bear a reasonably close relationship to the intrinsic value of both commodity and retail service. It should be recognized also that retail stores may sell services that are directly sought, such as insurance, travel assistance, funeral arrangements, etc. Such services will be treated the same as physical commodities. In both cases, the retail service is appended to the primary purchase, and customers buy both.

In the historical development of retailing, several discernible stages in the alignment of these merchandise and retail-service variables can be identified. The terms "unilateral," "bilateral," and "multilateral" could perhaps be used to identify these stages. Because they have been over-worked, however, another classification is suggested. The root word involved is "plex" (from plexus), which in its generalized dictionary sense means a network or "an intricately interwoven combination of elements or parts in a cohering structure." With appropriate prefixes, the various stages may be designated (1) simplex trading, (2) multiplex trading, and (3) omniplex trading. Each of these stages represents increasing complexity from the standpoint of retail execution.

Stage I: Simplex Trading. In modern money-using economies, larger amounts of retail service traditionally have accompanied relatively higher-priced goods. The income structure and value orientation prevailing in a particular society would logically be expected to determine the predominant qualitative level for both commodities and retail services. When there are dominant upper- and lower-income groups, the pairings of goods and retail service should emphasize two levels, one relatively high, the other relatively low. The emergence of a large middle class should lead to business orienting itself to serve this class through "average" or "reasonably satisfactory" goods and retail services. New stores may originate at any of the levels. Abercrombie & Fitch, Neiman-Marcus, I. Magnin, Tiffany's, and other relatively high-level combiners of goods and retail services show that a successful entry can be made and a position maintained at a prestige level of merchandise and service.

Based on the assumption that customers preferred retail service roughly equivalent to the quality of their product selections, retail managements have structured their service systems approximately in line with what the economic stratum they served could bear. Diagram 1 shows this relationship with the usual pairings of relatively high-cost merchandise with relatively high-cost service, average merchandise cost with average-cost service, and relatively low-cost merchandise with relatively low-cost service. Most smaller retail stores operate at one of these levels. When stores carry merchandise or offer services appropriate to more than one level, they have moved beyond simplex trading into the multiplex stage.

This predisposition to trading even may have originated in bartering attempts to negotiate equal value commodity exchanges in pre-money economies. To be sure, there were probably matchings of relatively high-cost merchandise with relatively low-cost service, and vice versa. But in the main, it is assumed that an approximate equivalency was regarded as normal in the beginnings of most retail trades.

At every level in this simplex trading stage, retailing presents its simplest challenge in that markets are segmented economically and services stratified according to the central expectations of customers at each level. The pairs of goods and services in Diagram 1 illustrate a relativistic equilibrium condition towards which the retail structure would tend were it not for the intruding designs of innovistic competition.

Stage II: Multiplex Trading. As population, disposable income, sales volume, and profit have increased over the years, store managements sought new markets in order that volume and profit potentials might also increase. Given the desire to expand sales volume in a store emphasizing

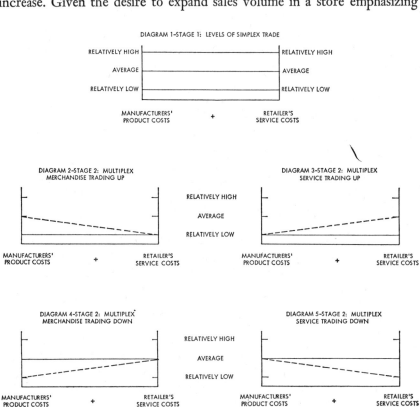

DIAGRAM 1-STAGE 1: LEVELS OF SIMPLEX TRADE

DIAGRAM 2-STAGE 2: MULTIPLEX MERCHANDISE TRADING UP

DIAGRAM 3-STAGE 2: MULTIPLEX SERVICE TRADING UP

DIAGRAM 4-STAGE 2: MULTIPLEX MERCHANDISE TRADING DOWN

DIAGRAM 5-STAGE 2: MULTIPLEX SERVICE TRADING DOWN

average merchandise costs and average retail-service costs (a simplex level), management can easily broaden its merchandise assortment upwards or downwards or in both directions at once. Indeed, in today's competitive environment, it is difficult not to do so. The multiplex stage of retail-store development covers all merchandise and retail-service combinations beyond one-level simplex trading and short of the ultimate in omniplex trading. Many combinations are possible, and all probably exist in today's widely heterogeneous markets.

There are three possible vertical movements which provide the dynamism for advancing from one stage to another. They are (1) trading up, (2) trading down, and (3) trading up and down simultaneously. Perhaps it should be stated at this point that all of these movements must be fully achieved before the omniplex trading stage is reached. Omniplex trading is visualized as a futuristic possibility in which individual stores might be able to match effectively any of the commodity levels with any of the retail-service levels.

There are two basic ways to attract new customers by trading up. Diagram 2 shows one possible response of a store operating at relatively low levels of both merchandise and retail-service costs. Management can raise the qualitative level of the merchandise assortment carried while maintaining the former level of retail service. Diagram 3 illustrates another response—raising the qualitative level of retail services while maintaining the former merchandise assortment. Of these two opposite methods of trading up, the easiest in the short run is to raise the levels of the merchandise carried while holding relatively constant the retail services. Often, however, the new customers attracted by the new merchandise expect and prefer services different from the old clientele. When management perceives this expectation, it usually experiments with and increases the costs associated with store environment, communication and promotion, time or place accessibility, and transfer services.

Diagrams 4 and 5 show the alternative merchandise and retail-service combinations that a merchant matching average-cost goods and services can use to trade down. As in trading up, it is easier in the short run to broaden the merchandise assortment than to change the character of retail service. Trading down has been attempted mainly by those stores operating at a relatively high level, as they broaden assortments to engage the middle-income market. For a number of obscure reasons, full-service, highest-status stores have resisted the compromises necessary in trading down. To date, none of the major store types has achieved greatness through trading down from relatively high levels.

Diagrams 6 and 7 show the more complicated cases of a single retailer attempting simultaneously to trade up and down from a former position of matching average-cost goods and services. Many department stores and departmentalized specialty stores illustrate this crossplex or seesaw stage as they seek patronage from nearly all economic groups in society.

In the contemporary multiplex stage of retail development, two or more market segments are straddled in that merchandise serving differing socioeconomic levels is carried. Because of inherent difficulties in modifying the service mix, little differentiation or inadequate differentiation of retail service is made in the short run. When increasing attention is brought to bear on this problem, hybrid service patterns frequently result. They are compromises that completely satisfy neither the old nor the new market stratum. Diagram 8 depicts the short-run inflexibility of retail service in trading up and trading down stages wherein a retail store broadens its merchandise assortment both well above and well below the middle.

The retail-service variability encountered in trading up and trading down is the retail counterpart to manufacturers' product differentiation. It can be real or illusory, but customers respond to retail-service differentiation just as they respond to product differentiation. Merchants trading down need to reduce their retail value-added by systematizing their services wherever possible, and by simplifying store environment, accessibility, promotion, and transfer services. Merchants trading up must usually change the character of all retail-service inputs. Merchants trading

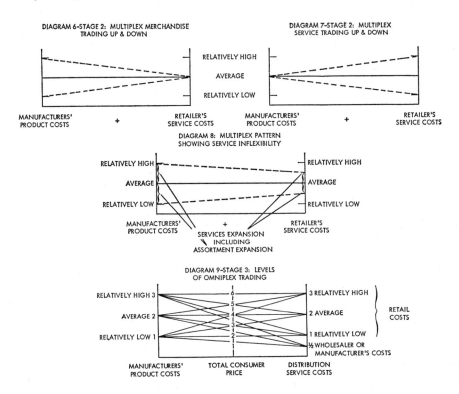

in both directions at once obviously have complicated problems in each of the retail value-added areas.

Stage III: Omniplex Trade. In a completely flexible retail situation, customers would be able to choose any of the possible combinations. In addition, Diagram 9 shows another combination, that of low, average, or high merchandise costs associated with the manufacturer's or wholesaler's distribution cost. This has always been the most avidly sought and difficult combination for the average customer to negotiate and has generally been reserved for the knowledgeable, well-positioned, influential, and well-to-do. The $a + b$ type nomograph in Diagram 9 shows total customer price for any combination of product and service desired. An equal-cost arrangement between product and service has been assumed, but the nomograph device could be applied to situations in which merchandise costs accounted for two thirds or more or one third or less of the total retail price.

Omniplex trading will require that both equipment and personnel operating in complex systems be utilized in a manner enabling store management to differentiate clearly among the several qualitative levels of retail service. One can foresee multichannel systems of retail service in a single store and customers choosing freely, item by item, the particular combination of merchandise and service which is desired. No single store today is organized to offer all combinations of goods and services to its customers. In the aggregate sense, however, each of the combinations that has been illustrated is available at some point in the distribution process.

To maximize satisfactions in the assembly of one's standard of living today requires a large acquisition cost in time, expense, and effort. Under conditions anticipated by omniplex trading, this cost would be minimized. In the following sections attention will be paid to those value-added emphases of several major store types which have contributed to the importance of each.

The Department-Store Emphasis

The department store early dominated the retailing scene in metropolitan centers by exploiting the attraction of luxurious facilities and generous merchandise transfer services. The prevalence around the turn of the century of horse-drawn carriages, spittoons, unpaved roads, dust, and flies made protective glass showcases imperative, and impressive store environments profitable.

Generous merchandise transfer services such as free delivery and unlimited returned-goods privileges were attractive because the rule of *caveat emptor* had prevailed widely until that time and was still practiced in many of the smaller stores. At an early date, nearly the full gamut of retail-service amenities was employed as the primary enterprise differentiating technique of department stores. Check cashing, interpreters and store guides, parcel checkrooms, reading and writing rooms, a free tearoom, a baby nursery, a silence room, and many other niceties were available in 1902 at Marshall Field & Company's Chicago store.[11]

Assortment characteristics and promotional techniques were also emphasized as the department-store group competitively traded up to a retail gross margin in 1929 of 33.4% of retail value, as compared to 22.2% in 1889, 25.6% in 1899, and 29.3% in 1909.[12] Given extended positions in all of the input variables, the traditional department stores have been hard

---

[11] Robert W. Twyman, *History of Marshall Field & Company, 1852–1906* (Philadelphia: University of Pennsylvania Press, 1952), p. 123.

[12] Harold Barger, *Distribution's Place in the American Economy since 1869*, A Study by the National Bureau of Economic Research (Princeton, N.J.: Princeton University Press, 1955), p. 81.

pressed ever since to maintain their competitive positions in the face of persistently rising wages, shorter working hours, and a deterioration in the centripetal attraction of metropolitan centers.

Of all store types, department stores have best used store environment to differentiate retail value-added. This was accomplished through the use of "bargain basements," "thrift floors," and elegant salons with fixtures varying from the severely utilitarian to the extremely ornate. By surrounding merchandise with properly impressionistic settings, merchants impute differential value to quite similar goods. In doing so, they are following the product differentiation technique of manufacturers. In addition, by adapting assortments, promoting differentially, and modifying the transfer services appropriately, department-store executives have been able to attract patronage from widely different socioeconomic groups. Diagram 10 shows the present-day position of the department store. Well advanced into the multiplex stage, department stores as a group come closest to omniplex trading. Considerably more differentiation is needed, however, before this stage can be reached. The largest hurdle is to associate effectively the seesaw combinations of relatively high-cost merchandise with average and low-cost retail services and relatively low-cost merchandise with average and high-cost retail services.

The dotted lines indicate department-store attempts at seesaw merchandising. These combinations represent efforts by retailers to segment markets through the use of special sales and private-brand merchandise. More effective seesaw combinations will be negotiated when department stores direct each element of retail value-added in a manner that allows a differentiated contribution to each exchange.

The Mail-Order House Emphasis

Whereas department stores appealed to urban dwellers, the early mail-order houses aimed their assortments at the more populous but less concentrated rural markets. To gain the patronage of suspicious rural citizens, early catalogs repetitively emphasized dollar savings, merchandise value, and necessarily generous returned-goods privileges. Introduction of the parcel-post system in 1913 greatly strengthened the mail-order house position by putting the federal government squarely behind mail-order accessibility. The gross margin of mail-order houses slowly climbed from 24.4% of retail value in 1889 to 26.8% by 1929.[13]

Foreseeing the increasing urbanization and role of the automobile, Sears began adding department-store operations to its mail-order business in 1925. Location accessibility continued to be the emphasized merchandising criterion, as these stores were located away from the increasingly congested downtown centers and frequently on the perimeter of cities. Parking facilities and location convenience thus offset relatively narrow

---

[13] *Ibid.*

merchandise assortments, utilitarian store environments, stringent transfer services, and modest promotional service emphases.

Only as their location supremacy gradually eroded in the post–World War II period, did these minimum-service stores begin to trade up by placing greater emphasis on the other variables. Today, the large combi-

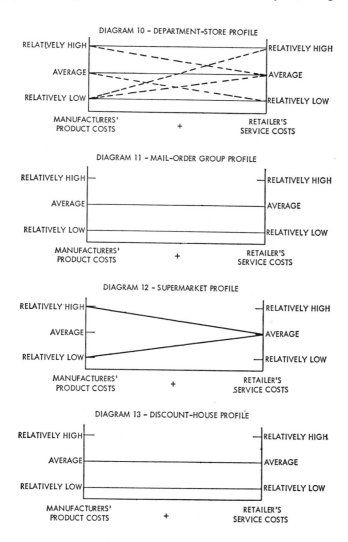

DIAGRAM 10 - DEPARTMENT-STORE PROFILE

DIAGRAM 11 - MAIL-ORDER GROUP PROFILE

DIAGRAM 12 - SUPERMARKET PROFILE

DIAGRAM 13 - DISCOUNT-HOUSE PROFILE

nation mail-order and retail houses have widened the quality of their merchandise assortments, improved the impressiveness of their store environments, become competitive in promotional techniques, and instituted various transfer services, notably diverse credit plans and free round-the-clock telephone ordering. As Diagram 11 indicates, this major store type, formerly operating only at the relatively low end of the simplex trading stage, clearly has moved into the multiplex stage by adding to the middle levels of merchandise and retail service through trading-up movements.

The Supermarket Emphasis

Early growth of the supermarket was predicated largely upon minimizing the retail value-added variables in the 1930's when most customers were primarily desirous of low prices. During this period, supermarkets sold basic staples. They stocked about 1,000 items, which were housed in strictly utilitarian store environments.[14] The low rent locations, although apparently essential, were relatively inconvenient. Promotional and transfer services were kept to a minimum. Even parking facilities were not generally provided in the beginning.[15]

Supermarkets have since responded to competitive pressures and increased their value-added components in each of the input areas. Assortments have widened and deepened not only in foods but also in many nonfood lines. Store environments have been dramatically modernized at substantial cost. Several supermarkets are within easy reach of most metropolitan families. The vigor with which supermarkets have used various promotional tactics to attract and hold patrons has no doubt exceeded that of any other store type.

Perhaps the least appreciated supermarket input is that of transfer services. Supermarkets have been active in replacing labor-intensive services with impersonal systems, equipment, or facilities that often do the job as well or better than relatively expensive hired help. Note, for example, how complete self-service, store directories, and convenient parking have been substituted for personal selling, information counters, and delivery service. Check cashing to a large extent obviates the need for credit.

Largely because of their ability to satisfy customers with transfer services that do not extensively use hired personnel, supermarket managements have been able to trade up in other input variables. This is possible because productivity per employee has continued to rise and margins have been reduced from 22½% in 1934 to 18% on the sales dollar in 1955.[16] More recent trade reports indicate that supermarket gross margins have climbed recently to an average of 20%.[17]

Supermarkets have broadened their merchandise assortments considerably but have yet to differentiate significantly the retail service they offer. Indeed, there has been no need to do so. The remarkable similarity of supermarket value-added infers that customers are highly satisfied. Is

---

[14] John A. Logan, "Progress in Food Distribution," A Statement to the Consumers Study Subcommittee of the Committee on Agriculture, House of Representatives (Washington, D.C.: National Association of Food Chains, May 8, 1957), p. 24.

[15] *Ibid*, p. 25.

[16] *Ibid.*, p. 15.

[17] "Not Much More Room to Grow," *Business Week,* June 4, 1960, p. 45.

there a positive relationship between this satisfaction and the active participation by customers in the supermarket exchange process? Is there a substantial body of customers who might welcome less involvement in acquiring their groceries? If it were profitable, for instance, for supermarkets to offer credit and delivery for a 5% additional fee, supermarkets could be said to have reached the seesaw level of multiplex trade. As shown in Diagram 12, supermarkets as a group remain in the multiplex stage, administering a well-accepted and standardized retail-service mix to customers from all socioeconomic levels.

The Discount-House Emphasis

Largely a post–World War II phenomenon, the open- and closed-door departmentalized discount house started from humble beginnings. Assortment range, depth, and quality were more expedient than planned; store environment was haphazard in low-rent warehouses, obsolete factory buildings, or makeshift cubbyholes; location convenience was tolerable only because of the automobile; promotional costs were frequently limited to word of mouth and direct mail; transfer costs, excepting returned-goods privileges, were minimized.

The restricted membership gambit of "closed-door" discount houses served multiple purposes. By limiting membership to homogeneous groupings, such as government or union employees, and charging token membership fees, an otherwise unobtainable loyalty was engineered. By not selling to the "general public," resale-price-maintenance laws were circumvented more easily. By maintaining a list of members, communication costs were minimized and promotion effectiveness enhanced.

After achieving substantial measures of success, discount houses began trading in the only direction left—up. Assortments have filled out, and better-known manufacturers' lines are now commonly available. Store environments have improved, more conventional promotion is appearing, and transfer services found necessary for some items have been installed for all. Like the other store types discussed herein, the discount house was started by matching average and relatively low-cost merchandise with relatively low-cost retail service. If assortments continue to broaden and retail services increase, it is possible that discount-house development will lead to a merger with the department-store type. Diagram 13 shows the present multiplex trade position of discount stores.

Obstacles and Opportunities in
Retail-Service Differentiation

In associating multiple retail services with multiple products, retailers face an enormous number of possible service-product combinations. This condition by itself compels careful definition and administration of service policies. The growth of individual store size and chain-store ownership groups, as well as the increased size and complexity of markets being served, emphasize the need for administering retail services. Organizational economies of scale, union influence, and the great proliferation in new products are other pressures forcing retail managements to define, to develop, and to maintain service positions consistent with the profile of enterprise differentiation that each wishes to achieve.

Given that most large retailers today must carry diverse merchandise assortments and serve diverse customer characteristics, new patronage is still earned by those innovations that please. Innovations may be of a cost-cutting nature (self-service, a chain form of organization) or of a cost-adding nature (credit, pleasant environment). Successful innovations have been introduced at all trade levels, and much more research is needed on why such innovations have been accepted.

Although it is increasingly clear that retail stores occupy an important position in a community's social structure, the contributions of the behavioral sciences on this subject have not yet been synthesized into marketing economics. If retail stores must integrate a major economic function (physical distribution of goods) with a major social function (individual identification with the larger group) through the market mechanism, how should they do it? How can goods and retail services intended to satisfy at the same time both the objective economic wants of a store's clientele and their subjective social values best be provided? To what extent are these two wants complementary? To what extent do they conflict?

It is likely that the traditional fears of manufacturers concerning "perverse price-quality" relationships are based upon the importance of psychological associations between their products and customers. Manufacturers can see these effects upon their own products easier than retailers because they are concerned with far fewer items and can attend to them more intensively. Perhaps a portion of the interest of manufacturers in "orderly distribution" can be traced to their implicit recognition of the multifarious roles that material objects play in the social, economic, and political lives of people. In the face of a veritable retail revolution, manufacturers, along with the federal government, have assumed the role of stabilizer.

The retail market is the institution which this society uses to rationalize the heterogeneous impact of the many influences of all participating value systems. Emerging from this rationalization is an ever-changing economic order with priorities and sanctions that help structure our social reality. Given this dependent relationship, the "perverse-price-quality" associations of goods and services could confuse as many of those who are predominantly social strivers as it does of those who are mainly economizers. For example, might not persons or families with obsessions for material possessions and limited income prefer relatively high-quality goods with relatively low retail value-added? Or conversely, might not persons or families with strong social class strivings prefer relatively low-quality goods (when unbranded or "inscrutable") if the relatively high retail value-added better served their status-system needs? Of course, each individual's responses vary from market to market, from time to time, and from product to product. Suffice it to say that when the mass market rises to the middle-income group, the complications of retail management grow in some exponential manner.

The Customer Is Still King

Retail stores still exist to serve their customers. Reflecting the significant changes in the last few decades, both stores and customers have been "trading up." The increased complexity in their relationships is the desirable and inevitable result of consistently rising productivity. What customers want remains important, and retailing success will continue to be based upon management's sensitivity and responsiveness to such wants.

Low prices are attractive to those customers who wish to maximize their scales of living. Despite this drive to maximize material standards of living, customers have also remained sensitive to the contributions of style to these standards. The mass distributors who enter the market by trading down from conventional norms provide an opportunity for consumers to raise their standards of living by enlarging their scales of consumption. At the other extreme, prestige high-level retailers contribute importantly to standards of living by improving the styles of those standards.

Customers desire both *material goods* and *services* that satisfy the problems and aspirations of their lives. These goods and services come from all levels and sources. Customers have been likened to "pollinizing agents" in the market in that what they find and like in one store they seek in others.[18] This observation supports the belief that store managements will continue to administer retail services, but innovistic competition will force them to increase and differentiate the retail service choices available to customers in the omniplex direction herein discussed.

---

[18] William J. Regan, "Full Cycle for Self-Service?", *Journal of Marketing*, Vol. 25 (April, 1961), p. 16.

10. RETAILING AS AN OPERATING SYSTEM*

Seymour Baranoff

WHAT IS "retailing"? At first blush, this question seems to be fairly non-sensical. But, as with Socrates, one continues to ask the question—to search and to listen to replies. Most answers are of the simple type—"you go to the store and buy goods." The more sophisticated rely upon such terms as "complex," "interrelated," "dynamic," "people," and "government." It should be noted that despite all the discussion, no well-accepted, agreed-upon model of retailing exists as of this moment.

Yet, retailers perform every day in the real world. They act as if they know why and how the system works. But, as with other activities, (1) we can and often "do" without really knowing how and why, and (2) what is done is done imperfectly. Human progress is based upon know-ing; upon conquering ignorance; upon acting efficiently; upon building a "store of knowledge" upon which to progress even further.

But—what is "retailing"? First, it is necessary to make clear that we are referring to "organized" group behavior. Therefore, occasional exchange and/or barter—such as infrequently occurs in simple economic societies—is not within the context of the meaning of retailing. Second, the "organ-ized" group referred to consists of those engaged in retailing—retailers, wholesalers, and manufacturers. Third, retailing existed whenever and wherever cities existed—Greece, Rome, and other ancient countries. Fourth, it existed whenever and wherever there was an abundance and

---

* This chapter is part of a larger research study (Pace College Executive Research Conference, Research Project Number 2, *Change in Retailing*) designed to define and predict change in retailing. Other parts of the research study (1) established hypoth-eses about specific changes in the internal operations of the retailing system; (2) attempted to define and explain the causal relationship between the external en-vironment and the internal system; and (3) established criteria of predictability about the retailing system based upon a total "Theory of Vulnerability." The pres-ent essay provides a theoretical framework for viewing the function, structure, and dynamics of the retailing system. It was considered essential in order to grasp the full meaning of the evolutionary changes which have taken place and to answer ques-tions about current and future retailing operations.

specialization of labor. Fifth, consumers in ancient cities purchased goods in "open markets," from importers (now designated as wholesalers), and manufacturers (craftsmen). Consumers and all existing types of marketing agencies are thus part of the structure of retailing.

What purpose or function does this structure serve? Retailing serves the function of aiding people to match, conveniently, their wants with available goods and services. A key "concept" is the word "conveniently." It has many shades of meaning and will be explained elsewhere. One may argue that matching wants with goods and services is also the function of marketing. But, this does not negate the idea that it is also the function of retailing. Rather, this would have to be so particularly insofar as retailing is a subsystem of marketing.

A model of retailing is set forth in the following paragraphs, in an attempt to (1) define the function of retailing, (2) identify the system, (3) explain how it works, (4) explain why it works the way it does, and (5) indicate the role of the environment as a stimulator-restrainer. The reader's understanding of the material will be enhanced if the following factors are kept in mind:

1. The functionalist approach is used in this chapter. "Functionalism is that approach to science which begins by identifying some system of action, and then tries to determine how and why it works as it does. Functionalism stresses the whole system and undertakes to interpret the parts in terms of how they serve the system." [1] Further, the operating system will change and contains a dynamic quality. Also, ". . . the functionalist believes that function basically determines structure in group behavior, rather than the reverse." [2] The existence and importance of structure, however, are recognized.

2. "The present view is that marketing would not exist as a separate field of study except to promote practical objectives, and that any theory that will provide a useful perspective for this field is necessarily pragmatic or functionalist." [3] The explanation advanced is considered practical (usable) in line with reality and experience, and likely to lead to useful predictions within reasonable limits.

3. "An organized behavior system is a group taken in conjunction with the environment in which it moves and has its being. The system may be regarded as including the instruments and resources utilized in its operations." [4]

THE RETAILING SYSTEM

A system incorporates group behavior along with instruments and resources taken in conjunction with the environment. Explicitly, the group

---

[1] Wroe Alderson, *Marketing Behavior and Executive Action* (Homewood, Ill.: Richard D. Irwin, Inc., 1957), p. 16. Many of the theoretical constructs and thoughts dealing with "functionalism," "theory," and "system" in the next several paragraphs are based upon Wroe Alderson and Don Martindale, *The Nature and Types of Sociological Theory* (Boston: Houghton Mifflin Co., 1960).

[2] Alderson, *op. cit.*, p. 17.

[3] *Ibid.*, p. 24.

[4] *Ibid.*, p. 25.

engaged in retailing includes retailers, some wholesalers, and a number of manufacturers. Instruments are those aids necessary to accomplish a specific task. Resources are the "backup" stores of goods, including money, knowledge, education, and the like. Resources are differentiated from environmental resources in that the latter are "unmined." Environment would include a society's culture, government activity, philosophy, religion, and so forth—factors outside the system which might influence its operation.

The system, internally, includes group behavior, instruments, and resources. A system also requires inputs and outputs. The inputs of the retailing system are consumers' wants and goods and services; the output is wants matched with goods and services—hereafter called "matched parallelism."

Before the complicated and complex retailing system of the present day is considered, let us ponder a simpler system. Consider a man alone on an island. The "group" is the individual; his instruments are his hands; his resources are minimum; and his environment is all about him. How does he progress? How does he change? First, his advances are based upon his perception, his understanding, his thinking processes, and his instincts. Second, he advances as instruments—fishing equipment, some sort of shelter, and so forth—are developed and used. Third, he changes with changes in his environment. While being restricted by his environment, he adapts to it. The environment can be changed sometimes relatively easily; at other times only with a great deal of effort such as is required to irrigate deserts. The culture, philosophy, religion, and government of a society change over time and have important effects upon business in general, including retailing. Changes in retailing take place in exactly the same way—via changes in group behavior, instruments, and resources and/or the environment—though the pattern is more complex.

The retailing process involves the *continuous* flow of consumer wants and goods into the system (from different directions); the perception of said inputs by the retailing group; activities by retailers designed to match the two inputs; and "matched parallelism," the output, which now becomes part of the environment (as Figure 1 indicates). The environment influences each part, and the flow is continuous.

The difficult part to understand is that the term "consumer wants" really means the want for goods *structured within a framework of "convenience."* It is fallacious to speak in terms of consumers' wants in terms of goods without thinking, simultaneously, in terms of "convenience." Again, the concept of totality exists. The so-called retailing cliché, so often repeated—and perhaps so little understood and practiced—"the right merchandise at the right price, at the right place, etc.," is most apt. But convenience is more. It also includes wanting to be "lazy," to be leisurely, to be thrilled, and so forth. More will be said about convenience later, under "The Instruments and Resources of Retailing" in a subsequent section.

Group Behavior and the Retailing System

Changes in any of the following major factors relating to group behavior will affect the process and structure of retailing.

1. *Perception.* An individual or group of individuals within the larger matrix will act and/or react based upon how he (they) perceives activities and/or the environment. Reacting to competitive pressures is one illustration.

2. *Goals.* A change in goals requires a change in action. An obvious illustration is in terms of immediate versus long-term goals. Goals change, too, with the life cycle of the organization, the age of the owner or group, the acceptance of the individual and/or group, and so forth.

FIGURE 1

VISUALIZATION OF THE RETAILING SYSTEM AS A CONTINUOUS PROCESS

MODEL OF THE RETAILING SYSTEM

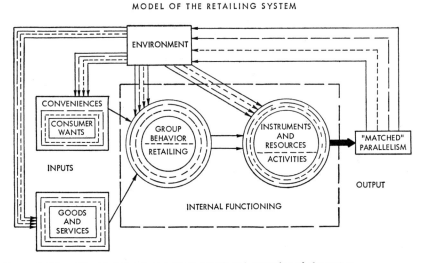

NOTES: 1. The solid and dotted lines indicate growth and expansion of the system.
2. The lines emanating from "matched parallelism" are designed to show (a) continuity and (b) that the satisfactions now become part of the environment.
3. The environment influences the inputs *and* internal functioning.

3. *Power.* Change will be dictated by power and the desire to maintain and enhance power. Status plays an important role within the concept of power. Whenever the power of an institution is threatened, changes take place. For example, when the power and status of department stores were threatened, department-store managers reacted. The current turbulence is the result of such change.

4. *Knowledge and Education.* Changes will occur as the amount of information available to retailers increases. Investments in college, com-

pany, and trade training programs are now commonplace. Without advances in marketing research, electronic data processing, and the behavioral sciences and statistics, elaborate organizational structures would not have developed and there would be no qualified people to promote. One executive put it rather succinctly recently. He said, "I can walk around our store today and point to at least 20 youngsters who can take over the running of our store tomorrow and probably do a better job." This organization has one of the finest training programs in marketing. In contrast, A. T. Stewart's organization took about 50 years to build but collapsed less than six years after his death. He had no training program.

5. *Flexibility.* The amount of flexibility of a group—whether it can act rapidly or is held back by indecision, bureaucracy, or tradition—determines, in large measure, the future of the organization or group. A good example is the general store. Some few adapted over time; the majority did not. Another illustration, portending the future, is the reaction to the opportunities for overseas expansion. How flexible are current organizations? Can they adapt?

6. *Organization and Control.* Oftentimes the nature, direction, and extent of change is dependent upon the type of organization and the amount of control exercised. A "loose" organization is usually weak and ineffective; action is sporadic and slow. There is a correlation between weak organization and poor control. An excellent illustration is the progress and changes made by grocery chains, over time, as contrasted with the seemingly limited progress of wholesaler and retailer-sponsored cooperatives.

The Place of Competition in the Retailing System

One may silently ask, "What about competition? You have not yet discussed this important factor." The reason competition has not been mentioned is that it is not found in every culture or society. It was absent among the Incas, Polish peasants, some Indian tribes, and supposedly, it is not characteristic of retailing in Russia.[5] The judgment as to whether or not competition is good is not at issue here.

One's thinking is clarified if two states are distinguished: (1) whether or not competition exists and (2) the degree of competition. Whether or not competition exists—and, consequently, is perceived and acted upon by those doing retailing—depends, fundamentally, upon the philosophy and attitude of the society. Based upon ecological studies, one might conclude that competition always exists.[6] Perhaps so. Nevertheless, a significant difference between competition as it exists in the United States and

---

[5] George W. Robbins, "Notions about the Origins of Trading," *Journal of Marketing*, January, 1947, pp. 228–36.

[6] G. Hardin, "The Competitive Exclusion Principle," *Science* (U.S.), Vol. 131, No. 3409 (April, 1960), pp. 1292–97. Bernard C. Patten, "Competitive Exclusion," *Science* (U.S.), Vol. 134, No. 3490 (November, 1961), pp. 1599–1601.

competition as it exists, let us say, in India is apparent. The difference appears to result from the philosophy and attitude characteristic of the culture. Bombay, India, a city with a population of about 5,000,000, has no department store, and only a limited number of what we call "specialty stores" exist. The sources of the current attitude are political (the supposed "heavy hand" of England)—and religious (an emphasis on austerity and contentment). For these reasons then, competition is herein viewed as being part of the environment, external to the operation of the retailing system per se. Competition is perceived, and a determination is made within the framework of goals, power, status, survival, and growth. Action—or inaction—then results.

The Instruments and Resources of Retailing

Just as the previously mentioned Robinson Crusoe fashions tools to help him fish, plant, or harvest, so too are tools available to retailers. Just as the islander uses available resources or "backup" stores of goods, so do those engaged in retailing. These instruments and resources are used in the process of matching the inputs—consumer wants—with specific goods. The instruments and resources used are the most efficient mechanisms presently available to facilitate this matching. No implication is made that they need prevail in the future. If anything, one can almost guarantee that they will change.

Some of these instruments, resources, and activities are:

1. *Anticipation—Selection.* One major activity in retailing is to correlate anticipation of consumers' wants with goods selection. Among the available tools would be a variety of record-keeping forms and techniques, market research, samples, the transportation system, and warehouses. The relevant resources include finances, personnel, and education.

2. *Information—The Giving-Receiving Process.* People who want goods and services must have information. We shall not concern ourselves at this time with such factors as the technical definition of information, feedback, and noise or with how information can most effectively be transmitted. Certain factors, however, are pertinent: (1) The process involves a two-way flow—information-giving and information-receiving. (2) People must make decisions about such factors as the generic product class, the specific product, and the market area and particular store at which they will purchase. Viewed in this fashion, manufacturers' advertising is part of the retailing process. Advertising, sales promotion, personal selling, and all that is included in the reader's understanding of these terms are the tools employed. Important to keep in mind here are the many important decisions that must be frequently made. Some of the resources would be media, knowledge, personnel, experience, and finances.

3. *Convenience.* Perhaps the greatest electronic data processing device thus far created has been the human brain, for it has the task of "mixing" many variables and making decisions. Inherent in the concept

of "convenience" is the need to combine a multitude of information with cultural pressures and personal selfishness of the nature discussed by Adam Smith. The individual must weigh the totality that is "convenience," thus allowing for price, closeness, ease of obtaining merchandise, "post" factors, human ego, and other relevant factors.

It is rather fruitless and misleading to say that people want things at the lowest price possible with a minimum of effort. Unfortunately, prices have been emphasized because price data could be gathered with relative ease. The importance of other influences has been minimized, and many businessmen still act on the premise that price alone is important. The point at the moment is *not* that other reasons for purchasing do not exist, but that these retailers *perceive* the role of price as *the* overriding factor. This fact is demonstrated by the often repeated complaint of the downtown retailer: "Those stupid people—they travel twenty miles to the shopping center. My price for this item is lower than what they pay for it out there."

This is not to be interpreted to mean that price is irrelevant or insignificant. Rather, price must be thought of as *one* important consideration operating in conjunction with others. The interesting question is why do retailers act as if they were unaware of this rather simple proposition, despite the abundance of evidence supporting it? For example, in very fine Fifth Avenue stores prices are expected to be higher. Also, a range of prices exists even for such staple items as milk (3–5 cents) or a pack of cigarettes. With regard to the pack of cigarettes, one pays 35 cents for the pack in the vending machine in most large buildings in New York. If one were to go downstairs, step out of the building, and walk less than 100 feet, he would pay 27 cents—a savings of 8 cents or about 23%! Yet, why do so many patronize machines? Are consumers irrational? Retailers may not be aware of what goes on; some may not want to recognize the phenomenon; or it may be a lack of understanding on their part. But consumers are not irrational when the other dimensions of convenience are considered.

"Convenience" must be re-perceived to include the many factors which, previously, stood alone—price, store, and so forth. Further, more thought must be given to what is termed "effort." It is recommended that the word "satisfied" be added; that the more fruitful term is "satisfied effort." Why does one woman travel 15 miles to a beauty parlor when there are a number of such shops within a five-block radius of her house? Why, indeed, when this same woman would prefer to have her hair done in her own home. Obviously, the answer lies in the goods and services available, the amount of information on hand, and the various dimensions of convenience. What, then, are the tools which afford "convenience"?

a) *Price.* What the consumer pays is a cost, for it represents such factors as past labors, anxieties, and risks. What he obtains is "satisfied effort."

To this extent price affords a convenience. The offsetting costs are both physical and psychological. Prices are often considered in terms of how much one earns per hour, per week, or per month. People talk about "knowing the value. of money" or "not knowing the value of money" when referring to the spending habits of youngsters. Finally, one hears, "I can't go out in this dress" or "This isn't apropriate for the occasion," and so forth. All of these considerations respresent real costs to the individual.

Pricing, then, is a tool of convenience insofar as it satisfies efforts.

b) Store. What purposes are served by stores which make them so important? What built-in convenience do they serve? How do they serve the fulfillment of "satisfied effort"?

Broadly viewed, stores are "close" to customers. This is a convenience when compared with production sites. It is a fairly vulnerable advantage, however, when one considers the closeness of the telephone and the mails. The fact that techniques to take full advantage of other means are presently inefficient does not negate the possibility that significant technological breakthroughs could make stores obsolete.

Another major advantage of stores is "concentrated variety." Variety here is interpreted to mean different products, brand names, and sizes. Concentrated, of course, means in one place. The "everything under one roof" idea and the increase in amounts spent by individuals in supermarkets are evidence of the importance of this convenience. It is in harmony with the concept of "satisfied effort" insofar as the customer is momentarily satisfied for the *total* effort spent.

Stores also offer "information." The amount of information received (and not received) plays an important part in determining the degree of satisfaction obtained for the effort expended. There is a positive correlation between the amount of information given to customers and prices charged.

When retailing is examined, there is the tendency to think only of retail stores. But one cannot dismiss the retailing done by mail-order house and other direct-mail solicitors, the expansion of telephone selling, house-to-house canvassing, and direct-from-the-manufacturer purchasing. No evidence exists from which a definitive statement as to changes, over time, in the amounts people buy from various outlets can be made. Census data certainly are inadequate for this purpose.

c) Others. Thus far, the "usual" services have not been mentioned. A complete listing of such services would be of no real value. Some of the more important ones are parking facilities, returns and allowances, credit, and delivery. These services are tools which, along with prices and stores, have the cumulative effect of affording "satisfying effort." The resources are fairly much the same as were previously mentioned—finances, personnel, education and knowledge, and experience.

"Matched Parallelism"—The Output of Retailing

What derives from all of this intricate searching, information-giving, and selection process is an imperfect matching of wants with items which satisfy these wants.[7] It is doubtful that perfect matching will ever be possible. The real question is whether or not the degree of imperfection can be significantly diminished. Two major bottlenecks are our lack of knowledge about consumers' wants and our communications system.

The result, "matched parallelism," now becomes part of the environment which influences the input into the system as well as the factors within the system itself. As indicated in the model, the process is *continuous* and many of the changes take place in imperceptible fashion. At some point, the slow, steady changes assume significant proportions. Worthy of consideration in this respect is the following statement:

The psychological principle most relevant . . . concerns *levels of aspiration*. Success in achieving a level of aspiration, or goal, usually results in the setting of a higher level of aspiration, a new goal. . . . But if an over-simplified rule is to be applied to buying behavior . . . it would be more correct to say, "the more people acquire, the more they want to acquire," than to say, "the more people have, the less they want." [8]

SUMMARY OF THE APPROACH TO RETAILING THEORY

This essay was intended to indicate the nature of the retailing system, its function, and how and why it works. The function of the system is to produce "matched parallelism"—to correlate the many wants with those available goods and services which will satisfy these wants. Inputs in the forms of wants and goods and services are fed into the system. These, in turn, are perceived by those doing retailing. Perception leads to activity and the development of tools. The system is a dynamic, continuous process—ever changing, ever expanding. The reasons why the system works the way it does are many. They have to do with a high level of production, an inability to get things directly, specialization of labor, levels of aspiration, "convenience," adaptation to environment, urbanization, and technology.

---

[7] It would be more correct, technically, to speak in terms of "lack" rather than "wants."

[8] Irving Morrissett, "Psychological Surveys in Business Forecasting," in Rensis Lipert and Samuel P. Hayes, Jr., *Some Applications of Behavioral Research* (Paris: UNESCO, 1957), pp 293–94.

11. SOME OBSERVATIONS ON "STRUCTURAL" FORMATION AND THE GROWTH OF MARKETING CHANNELS*

Ralph F. Breyer

EMBEDDED everywhere in the enormous complex of activities and agreements that characterize the marketing institution is an elemental piece of structure, the so-called marketing channel. In the broadest sense of the term, not only *trading* concerns engaged primarily in selling and buying—producers, wholesalers, retailers, brokers, selling agents, commission houses, etc.—but also *nontrading* concerns engaged principally in other types of marketing activity—commercial banks, transportation and storage companies, insurance companies, and so on—are found in a marketing channel. In this essay, we are concerned only with the trading channel, which consists of various sequences of the former group of "concerns." This channel is, of course, a system, and we shall often refer to it as such. For purposes of this essay, it is sufficient merely to define the term "system" in a broad sense:

> "A system is a set of objects together with relationships between the objects and between their attributes."

Being composed of both human beings and machines, the channel is what is often termed a "man-machine" system. This essay is an attempt to answer the following two questions: When does a channel come into existence? What are the more useful indices of overall channel growth? Standing alone, the observations on channel structure presented in this

---

* This essay is part of a study of marketing channels being conducted under a grant of Ford Foundation research funds made available to the author by the Wharton School.

article should help somewhat in the development of more precise concepts than can be used in the study of marketing channel phenomenon.[1]

To qualify as a channel in this essay, the vertical sequence of trading concerns must bridge the *entire* gap between production and the consumer.[2] The vertical positions of the trading concerns are referred to as "levels"—the producer level, the broker level, the wholesaler level, etc. Any vertical section short of the entire length of the channel is termed a "segment"—producer-to-wholesaler, or wholesaler-to-retailer, or producer-to-wholesaler-to-retailer, and so on. Upon occasion, we shall refer to "type" channels, "enterprise" channels, and "business-unit" (often shortened to "unit") channels. The first is a channel identified solely by *types* of concerns, such as manufacturers, brokers, wholesalers, and retailers; the second, by specific independent *ownerships,* termed enterprises. The business-unit channel is defined in terms of each separately named and/or spatially separated *operating unit* of a trading concern (or enterprise). Thus, two trading businesses under *one* ownership, even though located at the same place, would each constitute a "business unit" in a channel if they operated under different trade names. A branch warehouse located at some point other than the headquarters of the parent trading concern would also constitute a separate business unit.[3]

The need for the "business-unit" concept is most obvious in a completely integrated trading channel. Although such a channel is composed of but one enterprise and would be represented as a $P\text{--}C$ channel, the goods may actually be "moved"[4] from the producer's plant to one of its wholesale warehouses and then to one of its retail stores and finally to the consumer. Obviously, in structural terms, the $P\text{--}C$ designation is entirely inadequate, as it does not show those business units owned by the producer that are operated at the wholesale and retail levels. In terms of business units, the channel is a $P\text{--}W_p\text{--}R_p\text{--}C$ channel, the subscripts indicating ownership by the producer in this case. Where only partial structural integration exists, as, for example, a warehouse owned by a retailer that received all shipments from producers, the enterprise channel con-

---

[1] This monograph summarizes one part of a broader study of marketing channels which has not yet been completed. In the context of the entire study, the material presented here should take on more meaning and value.

[2] This phrase sounds somewhat "clumsy." If we changed it to "production and consumption," it would literally mean that marketing is carried on right up to the actual time and place of consuming the goods, which is, of course, rarely true. On the other hand, "producer and consumer" fails to indicate specifically that marketing starts *after* production is completed. However, when speaking of channel structure, we are generally dealing with trading *concerns* and shall hereafter use the phrase "producer and consumer" in a sense synonymous with "production and consumer."

[3] Even though this branch house did no selling but merely received, stored, and shipped the goods, it would still be considered part of the *trading* channel, because it is an integral part of a *trading* concern.

[4] The term "moved" is employed here as a synonym of "marketed" and is *not* restricted to physical movement of the merchandise.

cept should be expressed by P–R–C, but structurally, the channel should be represented by P–W_R–R–C. Although, strictly speaking, a channel so structured is a hybrid containing enterprise and business-unit elements, it will be termed a "business-unit channel" as long as it contains at least one business unit. The term "trading concern" or "concern" can refer to a nonintegrated ownership such as P in the channel immediately above, or to the concern R which also owns the warehouse W_R, or to the business unit W_R itself, or to all collectively, depending upon the context.

For the time being, we shall ignore the "type" channel and assume that the enterprise and business-unit channel happen to be identical. Therefore, we will deal with them as one channel. Usually, we shall use the P–W–R–C channel (producer to wholesaler to retailer to consumer) for illustrative purposes.

A trading channel is formed when trading relations making possible the passage of title and/or possession (usually both) of goods from the producer to the ultimate consumer is consummated by the component trading concerns of the system. Let us assume that producer P_1 franchises or agrees to permit a wholesaler, W_1, to handle his product, and W_1, in turn, franchises or agrees to permit a retailer, R_1, to retail this same product. A trading channel exists once the terms of the franchises or agreements spanning the whole gap from producer to consumer are concluded between concerns assumed to possess the necessary marketing capabilities. Theoretically, not a single unit of the product(s) may be actually marketed by this specific sequence of trading concerns. Nevertheless, in a practical and important sense a channel was formed, since the capacity to "move" the product(s) was brought into being by establishing the requisite trading relations between competent concerns. Except for certain industrial goods, such explicit agreements between the retailer and the *consumer* at the terminal segment of a channel are rare.

Let us now assume that a dealer, R_1, receives an order from an industrial consumer for an industrial product manufactured by P_1; a product R_1 has never handled before. Knowing that he cannot deal directly with P_1, R_1 contracts to buy the product from a wholesale distributor, W_1, who also has not handled this product before. W_1 then contracts to purchase it from P_1. As soon as these contracts (orders) are consummated, including the contract (order) between R_1 and the consumer, a trading channel has been formed even though the parties had never traded with one another before and a set of trading relations was not explicitly agreed upon. In this case, the channel system was initiated by the closing of contracts containing firm orders to buy cetrain amounts of specific goods. This is true even though the product may not actually move through the channel and no passage of title may occur for six months, because the product must be manufactured to order. Although there is no explicit agreement upon trading relations, the establishment of such relations is implicit in the act of entering into sales-purchase contracts.[5]

The two illustrations provided involve channel formation, because the *intent* is that goods shall move. In the example given in the prior paragraph, suppose that the parties had already established trading relations and were trading in *other* goods under these "agreements." Could we say then that the trading channel for the *new* product already exists? If the *new* product does not require any changes in those trading-relation agreements, we would say "yes." If it does require such alterations, the answer is "no." In any case, one must recognize that although explicitly established trading relations may cover a group of products, a separate and distinct channel exists for each product that actually flows down this particular sequence of trading concerns. In this sense, a new channel is formed *productwise* when a new product moves through an established sequence.[6] A channel is formed, of course, wherever a single product or group of products moves through a new combination of trading concerns. This is true even where the goods are merely consigned or leased at various stages of the channel.

Individual Channel Formation

Individual channels usually exist as components of a channel group. Such a group is characterized by a network of trading interconnections which link the trading concerns or units of the group. A single new trading-relation agreement is sufficient to establish at least one new channel in such a channel group. To avoid getting bogged down at this stage with the intricacies of channel groups, we shall first take up the *single* channel. A single channel is one that has but one trading concern or trading unit at each level. At times, we shall talk of this channel as if it were "isolated" or "free-standing" rather than one of the constituent channels of a channel group. The "isolated" single channel is defined as one with trading concerns or units that trade *only* with one another. Having finished with the single channel, we will then move on to the channel *group* (network), treated as a given, integrated, "structured" system of which the single channel is a mere subsystem. To qualify as a channel *group*, at least one trading concern or trading unit must have established trading relations with a minimum of two other trading concerns or units operating on the same level. (Whether we should include the consumer, who is, of course, a part of the channel, in these formulations is optional. For some industrial products it may be worthwhile or even imperative. In this

---

[5] At times, the goods may be consigned to a trading unit or leased to a consumer. In such cases, sale-purchase contracts of the product per se may never materialize (i.e., lease without purchase option) or are delayed (i.e., consignment sale or lease with purchase option). Here, explicit agreement on trading relations is almost always required.

[6] A further discussion of this situation is found in the following section.

essay, unless otherwise stated, the consumer is excluded from the channel in all subsequent discussions.)

One can maintain that a channel exists when and only so long as goods actually flow. It appears more useful, however, to view a channel system as being formed as soon as new trading relations are established and as continuing to exist so long as these trading relations hold.[7] The actual flow of a product through a channel is almost always intermittent. This is true even for large groups of products that are highly seasonal. If we insisted upon an actual flow of goods, we should, strictly speaking, have to accept the view that the channel is dissolved during even brief periods of a few days when no product(s) move through all or part of the channel and, conversely, a new channel is born on each resumption of the flow. Or, less strictly interpreted, such a requirement would compel us to stipulate the maximum time interval of the intermittency permitted before the channel would be classified as having dissolved. This would perforce be a rather arbitrary decision. On the other hand, we must consider the situation where agreements on trading relations continue in force but no goods have "moved" through the channel for an abnormally long period of time. In such case, we might term this a "passive channel system" in contrast to an "active channel system" where intermittency in goods flow is "reasonable" or "normal." When one of the trading concerns of a channel stops handling the product(s), such action, of course, dissolves the channel.

The formation and dissolution of marketing channel systems is a ubiquitous phenomenon which we shall examine first under the assumption that we have a reasonably large, fixed pattern of trading concern, that is, a large fixed number of producers, of wholesalers, and of retailers available for a P–W–R–C channel structure. We can discern at once at least three different situations. In a highly flexible situation, the trading concerns can and readily do switch their sources of supply or their outlets with minimum inconvenience and cost. If one resource or outlet is readily substituted, such action destroys one channel and creates a second. If a resource or outlet is added or dropped without substitution, there is a net gain (or loss) of one channel. A very considerable part of all consumer-goods marketing, especially that of low unit value, constant demand items, is characterized by flexible trading relations with changes in suppliers and outlets comparatively frequent and widespread.

In contrast to the situation just discussed above is one where more or less continuing trading relations prevail over a considerable period of time. Such stability may be due to true, in contrast to pseudo, franchise arrangements and exclusive distribution agreements. If such arrangements do not embrace the entire channel, they still leave much flexibilty for channel formation or dissolution in the remaining segments. But where

---

[7] Here, the term "channel system" refers to a single channel, either "isolated" or a constituent of a channel group.

such agreements exist, the qualifications of both outlet and supplier are carefully examined in advance; fairly detailed stipulations are usually set forth in a written agreement; and substantial commitments respecting selling methods, advertising, service, merchandising help, etc., are made. These tend to cement the relationship more firmly so that dissolution of the channel by abrogation of the agreement is less easily accomplished, and channel formation is generally a slower process. In any case, many such contracts require thirty to ninety days' notice of an intention to cancel.

Finally, only a qualified flexibility respecting channel formation and dissolution exists in the fully integrated channel where production, wholesaling, and retailing units are all owned by one concern.[8] Such complete integration involves a very considerable investment. A large organization must be developed, and great control exercised through out the length of the channel. Consequently, the substitution of an outside, independently owned, trading concern for one of the owner's own units is much less likely. In this case, as well as where only part of the channel is integrated, the enterprise channel, contrary to our prior stipulation, does differ from the business-unit channel. There is some degree of flexibility in adding or dropping certain of the *business units* owned by any one concern, and such action *could* result in the formation and dissolution of *business-unit* channels. However, since changes in the business-unit channel require considerable investment (or, conversely, the liquidation of a sizeable investment with some possibility of loss), the degree of flexibility in an integrated channel will be rather low, unless the owning agency is supported by considerable financial resources. Where only certain segments of the channel are integrated, the other segments are free of the constraints previously mentioned.

It should be emphasized here that "flexibility" has been used to refer primarily to the ease with which channels are formed and dissolved. Although it is usually the case, such of the channels that exist where conditions are highly flexible may not be of shorter life than those established under less flexible conditions.

For a marketing channel to exist, there generally must be at some time a flow of goods from producer to consumer. "Goods" may mean just one product or several products taken together. In its ultimate sense, the channel concept should be centered on the *single* product. Where several different products flow through the same set of trading concerns, there are an equal number of separate channels productwise. Also, each new product that is introduced creates a new channel productwise, even though no new trading relations are explicitly established. Similarly, the dropping of one product dissolves at least one channel productwise. This

---

[8] If the producer's plant can, or does, not supply all the goods handled by its wholesale and retail units, then so far as these goods are concerned, the channel is not fully integrated and hence considerable flexibility may exist.

view of a channel is justified by the following factors: consumers and traders buy *individual* products; different products may possess markedly different marketing characteristics (selling, merchandising, servicing, pricing, costs, etc.); and individual product identification by such factors as brand or trademark constitutes the nucleus for a unique pattern of competitive effort, even though there will be many other aspects of competition between products.

We have previously assumed that the trading-concern population is fixed in size and pattern. In reality, however, some trading concerns are always going out of business and others entering. With the advent of one new trading concern—manufacturer, wholesaler, or retailer in our *P–W–R–C* structure—at least one and almost always a considerable number of new channels are formed. Conversely, one or more channels are destroyed as each concern exits. Thus, new concerns and new products are great channel multipliers, with the number of channels increasing much faster than the number of firms or products.

Let us now turn to the "type" channel and contrast it with the enterprise and business-unit channels previously considered. As soon as a new *type* of trading concern enters a given marketing sector, at least one and perhaps several new "type" channels are created. The proliferation of new "type" channels resulting from the development of a new type of marketing agency is, however, much more limited than the increase in enterprise and unit channels that occurs when new trading concern or trading unit makes its appearance. "Type" channels may range from broad to narrow depending upon the "type" classification under which the trading concerns are grouped. The *P–W–R–C* channel is obviously very broad as *all* of the varying kinds of pertinent producers are included in *P*, all wholesalers in *W*, all retailers in *R*, and all consumers in *C*. On the other hand, a *multiple-line* manufacturer to a *full-line, full-service* wholesaler to a *limited-line, limited-service* dealer to the consumer would be a much narrower "type" channel. "Types" could be based on the distinctive product or product group handled—an *automobile* manufacturer, a *grocery* wholesaler, a *lumber* dealer—but since we generally have a certain product or product group in mind when analyzing channels, such classification comes into the picture automatically. Even so, where product mix problems at various levels in the channel are important, the "product" classification is inadequate because such mixes may vary widely within any one such classification.[9]

"Type" channel systems are hardy and often compete sharply with one another. In this struggle, some wax, others wane, and the "type" channels which fall in either category may vary from one sector of mar-

[9] "Sorting" concepts, originally developed by Wroe Alderson, are very important in this connection. See Wroe Alderson, *Marketing Behavior and Executive Action* (Homewood, Ill.: Richard D. Irwin, Inc., 1957), chap. vii, "Matching and Sorting— The Logic of Exchange."

keting to another. But it is rather seldom that the "type" channel, especially those based on the broader "type" classifications, go out of existence altogether. Also, the formation of a new "type" channel is a rather infrequent occurrence. Such changes of "type" channels are of much greater consequence than the formation and dissolution of enterprise and business-unit channels, because of the direct effect on a large train of individual trading concerns.

Measures of Overall Growth for the Individual Channel

Perhaps the best measure of overall growth or decline of a marketing channel (or channel group) could be developed from some kind of sophisticated input-output analysis. Such an analysis is a complex and time-consuming undertaking. What we need at the moment is a more readily computed measure of overall growth. The two best measures appear to be (a) the physical units of product "moved" through the channel and (b) the dollar spread of the channel for a given time period. Both are at best approximate and are none too satisfactory measures. The physical unit measures the "put-through" of the channel system, as that term is generally used in engineering. Such a measure has the advantage of eliminating price fluctuations. But where the channel handles several products with varying characteristics, it may be impossible to devise a single unit of measure. Moreover, such a measure would not take into account material changes from year to year in the total "service delivered" [10] by the channel for its customer, the consumer. These services, for example, include such factors as product warranties, consumer credit extension, lessening of "outs" at the retail level (which may well require producer and/or wholesaler cooperation), etc.[11]

The dollar spread of the channel should reflect such "service" changes. It would be computed by subtracting from the *retail* dollar volume of the channel—a figure which is the same as the total sales of the retailer R_1—the production costs of the producer P_1 plus the net profits of the producer allocable to production in contrast to marketing. This subtrahend is here termed "production takeout." The allocation of net profit to production would admittedly be quite arbitrary. Perhaps the best method would be to allocate it in the ratio which direct production costs bore

---

[10] The phrase "service delivered" constitutes *all* of the marketing services performed in getting the goods from producer to consumer. It includes that done by the *non*trading agencies, even though they are not part of the *trading* channel. The justification for this interpretation is that it is the *trading* channel (or more accurately, the individual *trading* concerns that compose it) that authorizes and pays for such "nontrading" marketing work.

[11] Variations of service extended by the trading concerns to one another are not relevant, as these merely involve alterations in allocation of such services among the traders. It is true that such reallocations may bring about lower cost, but this is not at the moment a pertinent issue.

to direct marketing costs. This would avoid the difficult task of apportioning overhead between production and marketing. To cancel out the effects of price changes, appropriate deflators would have to be used.

Let us assume retail dollar volume could not be obtained directly, a condition which is much more likely to prevail when channel groups rather than single, isolated channels are studied. One might then derive the retail dollar volume figure by using producer dollar sales volume with wholesaler and retailer margins expressed as percentages of the producer sales dollar; or, if more convenient, by using the wholesaler dollar sales volume and the retailer margin expressed as a percentage of it. Having established the dollar spread figure for the channel, one can compute both absolute and relative growth of the channel. Should relative growth alone be desired, the retail dollar volume alone could be used with the assumption that the percentage which the "production takeout" bore to the retail dollar volume remained the same from year to year.[12]

In all of these computations of channel growth, adjustments would have to be made for any differences in inventories at each level of the channel at the beginning and at the end of the period.

Channel Group Formation

Only one factor justifies the attention given to the single, *isolated* channel, a phenomenon almost nonexistent in practice. Knowledge of such a channel is helpful in understanding certain "structural" features of those multiple-channel networks of marketing which were previously termed channel-group systems. Single channels do, of course, exist in practice but as components of a channel group. In fact, we can view a channel group as being made up of a collection of individual channels. These single channels, however, are not isolated because each one of their trading concerns has trade dealings with two or more concerns within the given channel group, and often with outside concerns as well. If channel members deal solely with other trading concerns *within* the given channel group, that channel group is then an "isolated" one. Such "isolated" channel groups exist, and some are very important. The channel group that handles the domestic distribution (and this study is confined to domestic marketing) of the automobiles of one domestic manufacturer is, for example, an isolated one, although with the advent of foreign-made cars this situation is rapidly disappearing.

The channel group is obviously more than a mere collection of individual channels. It is in the nature of a network, the structural configurations of which are well known. The formation of the single, isolated channel is structurally defined in the sense that as soon as the requisite trading relations between the full complement of trading concerns spanning the

---

[12] In fact, if "production takeout" percentage and all margin percentages downstream remained the same, one could use the producer dollar volume or wholesaler dollar volume figure alone for the computation of *relative* growth (or decline).

gap from producer to consumer has been consummated, the channel is formed. By definition, no trading concerns or units may be added or subtracted. But for the channel *group* there is no such definite and fixed point marking the completion of its formation. The channel group configurations that merit analysis are generally the resultant of the interplay of the interests of the various trading concerns embraced by the group. Hence, we would generally "set up" a channel group for study by establishing the interests of one or another trading concern or the common interest of a group of trading concerns as the central focus of the study, such as the interest of a particular producer, or wholesaler, or retailer, or of a certain group of producers making a certain product, or of a group of producers, wholesalers, and retailers all of whom are members of a joint product certification program. The identification of this central focus of interest serves to map the pertinent channel group. The primary interest of a sizeable producer is to establish that network of channels [13] for the marketing of his product(s) which will most effectively exploit the ultimate potential markets and at the same time promise him maximum long-run profits.[14] But for almost any product, qualitative, quantitative, and geographic changes in market-demand patterns, product innovations, entrepreneurial innovations (new types of trading concerns), etc., continually occur. This causes a constant flux in the channel composition of the group as it responds to such alterations.

A producer who seeks 100% distribution makes practically no effort to shape his channel-group structure. Instead, he tries to "pump" his product(s) through whatever channels he can with the hope that nearly all potential ones will finally take on the product(s). The configuration of such a channel group will be highly sensitive to changes in such factors as market conditions and competitive tactics. With the possible exception of some staple manufactured products, such channel groups will exhibit a relatively high degree of instability. Agricultural staples are marketed through highly unstable channel groups. The same holds true for manufactured products sold through agents at some stage in their flow down the channels of the group. If the channel group is a *P–B–W–R–C* one, and *B* represents brokers, then the channel configuration will probably be very unstable, as the producers make successive offerings and brokers sell now to certain wholesalers, now to others. A channel is formed every time a wholesaler buys for the first time. When wholesalers who previously purchased refuse to buy, a channel is dissolved if the period of intermittency of purchase is "unreasonably" long.

Very often, however, producers of branded and vigorously promoted items will select the channel group that handles their product(s) with

---

[13] See, however, the second following paragraph.

[14] Assuming, for simplicity's sake, that this is his only objective, which is rarely true.

great care and exercise some degree of control over the different trading concerns. Broad gauge marketing policies, objectives, and plans are developed, and an attempt is made to fashion the channel group accordingly. Such "engineered" channel groups are found especially where selective or exclusive distribution policies are followed. In such instances, the formation of the channel group is a comparatively well thought-out and carefully applied process. In this process, however, emphasis is not usually centered as much on *channel* formation as on the individual trading concerns or units to be included. This is true because the trading concern or trading unit is the primary "activating" unit and possesses a closely knit specialized organization with central direction and control. Also, each such concern or unit generally constitutes a common center used by a large number of individual constituent channels of the given channel group. Moreover, as will be made clear in a subsequent paragraph, a trading concern or unit is at times only *directly* interested in its *immediate* sources of supply and its *immediate* customers. If the producer decides to add or drop such an individual concern, then *ipso facto* at least one and usually several channels are respectively formed or dissolved. Of course, there are times when unauthorized trading concerns get hold of the producer's product(s), in which case the channel so formed might be termed a "bastard channel." In varying degrees and at varying times, wholesalers and retailers also attempt *full-span* "engineering" of their channel group.

Measures of Overall Growth for the Channel Group

As was true for the single, isolated channel, the most useful measures of overall growth of the channel group are the number of physical units of product(s) put through the channel group and the dollar spread for the channel group. Adaptations and cautions similar to those expressed for the single, isolated channel are also relevant. The application of either of these measures to the channel group is generally more complicated than their application to the single, isolated channel. Usually, a number of the trading concerns in such a group will also be dealing with outside trading concerns. Such dealings must be excluded from the computations, because only those goods which "moved" through channels, all of whose trading concerns are a part of the group, can be considered in measuring that channel group's put-through. Consequently, the nonisolated channel-group measurement of growth would require considerable product coding and many separate records. Even in an isolated channel group, where none of the trading concerns deal with concerns outside the group, if the retail dollar volume figures required for computing dollar channel spread by the use of relative margins is to be derived, such margins would need to be properly weighted. In any case, the considerable differences in growth or decline generally present in the various parts of the channel group would be lost in the *overall* measure for the group. Hence, a great deal of "subgroup" or "subsystem" analysis would be required.[15]

The number of consumers served by the channel group, the types of consumers served, the geographical area of the consumer market, the number of products handled, the number of trading concerns in the group, and the number of constituent channels in the group have but limited usefulness as measures of overall channel-group growth.[16] Contrary to appearances, it is not easy to use the number of products handled as a measure of growth. All parts of the channel group may not handle each and every product, and the number of items not universally carried may fluctuate from time to time.

The number of individual constituent channels and the number of trading concerns and/or trading units are two possible measures of growth that would not apply to the single channel. However, both have very little usefulness, as they give ambiguous measures of channel-group growth. For instance, an increase in the number of constituent channels might be caused by the following factors: an increase in the interconnections between the same number of trading concerns handling the same products; an increase in the number of products handled by all or part of the channel group; or an increase in trading concerns or units. Also, growth in the number of trading concerns or units in a channel group may or may not mean an increase in the volume handled or an increased number of constituent channels.

To measure the growth of the individual constituent channels of a channel group would seldom be worthwhile. It would always be more difficult than measuring the growth of single, isolated channels. Products are not easily traced through the many channel routes that tie into *each* trading concern or trading unit. Moreover, a specific trading concern, especially in the nonintegrated channel group, usually has little direct interest in the growth or decline of each specific channel of which it is a part. Its attention is rarely focused beyond its immediate supplier upstream and its immediate outlet downstream. As stated before, however, the measurement of growth by subgroups of channels of a channel group, based on "type" of channel, product(s) handled, geographic areas, etc., might well be worthwhile.[17]

A complicating factor in all cases are the changes that occur over time in the composition of the channel group. Some trading concerns drop out

---

[15] See, for example, Reavis Cox and Charles S. Goodman, "Marketing of Housebuilding Materials," *Journal of Marketing*, July, 1956, pp. 36–61. In this original study, the authors develop seven measures of work done in each marketing "flow."

[16] The author developed a method for establishing such costs for channels and channel groups in his study "Quantitative Systemic Analysis and Control: Study No. 1—Channel and Channel Group Costing," 1949, although his purpose at the time was not the use of such costs for measuring growth.

[17] Here, the channel group is a "mixed" one in that it contains more than one type of channel, such as a channel group with both P–W–R–C and P–R–C types.

and others come into the group. Consequently, the year-to-year measures of growth or decline are not made with reference to an identical channel-group structure. Even where the set of trading concerns remains the same, the pattern of the interconnections between them, i.e., the individual constituent channel pattern, may be altered. This is especially true for those groups where freedom and ease in changing connections are not restricted by selective or exclusive distribution arrangements.

Integrated and Mixed Channel Groups

The formation of fully integrated channel groups is, of course, completely controlled by the single ownership. Although the constituent business units may have limited freedom in determining with whom they will deal, all changes in the structure are dictated by the owner. The channel structure pattern of such a group is comparatively stable. The same measures of growth would apply to it as apply to nonintegrated groups and could probably be computed with less difficulty, because the records kept by the owner would cover the entire channel group. Much the same can be said for the integrated portions of partially integrated channel groups.

Finally, a channel group, unlike the one used for illustrative purposes, may be composed of two or more types of channels. Such a group has already been termed "mixed." A channel group with a mixed structure will be more adaptable to the requirements of varying marketing situations. In addition, it is generally known that some of the most severe competition in marketing occurs between the various types of channel groups. Much the same situation with respect to formation and growth exists for the "mixed" and the "simple" (one-type) channel group.

12. DESIGN OF MARKETING CHANNELS

F. E. Balderston

MARKETING channels are institutional configurations for directing and supporting the flows, from production to use, of things of value. We discover a marketing channel by tracing what happens (or thinking about what can happen) to one or more units of one or more items en route from one or more origins to one or more destinations at one or more points in time. Marketing effort is important in general—and marketing channels exist in particular—because actuality refuses to meet the classical conditions laid down for effective economic organization.

Marketing channels are social systems—in Alderson's words, "organized behavior systems" [1]—which have technological, economic, sociological, and psychological features. When we speak of the *design* of marketing channels, this implies conscious choice of a pattern with foreknowledge of the results the pattern will deliver. Not much is yet known about how to undertake the task of designing comprehensively *any* complex system of social phenomena. Thus, ideas for the design of marketing channels are still fragmentary, and we will be able to make only limited statements; by the same token, of course, marketing scholars, concentrating on this problem, may inferentially contribute to much broader problems of pure and applied social theory.

We will comment on five issues in this essay on marketing channel design:

1. *How does one discover* the existence of a marketing channel?
2. *Why have channels?* That is, what are the functional requirements and operating features of the "natural" systems which grow up?
3. *For whose benefit* do we consider the channel to operate? That is, considering the issue of conscious evaluation, whose criterion do we employ —that of a "leading" firm; all firms participating; all households directly served; or "society"?

---

[1] Wroe Alderson, *Marketing Behavior and Executive Action* (Homewood, Ill.: Richard D. Irwin, Inc., 1957).

4. What are some critical design components for which analysis presently exists?

5. What can now be done to set up and evaluate marketing channel models even where our analytic knowledge is as yet incomplete?

Marketing Channels as "Natural" Systems

Marketing scholars, over the last fifty years, have put prodigious effort into the development of concepts for identifying leading features of marketing channels and into detailed observations on channel behavior. One must go to Breyer for the essential contributions on two elements of a theory: (1) the recognition of institutional forces leading to norms of orderly behavior [2] and (2) the structural configurations, the resource-absorbing work of marketing channels and the problem of comparing costs of alternative channel arrangements for a given commodity flow.[3] We return at a later point to a discussion of the first of these, but the second involves the question of grouping the sequences of marketing activity, which in its turn depends on the nature of a fundamental adjustment process.

Various scholars have pointed to the presence of—and have suggested ways of thinking about—a central adjustment process which accommodates to one another a heterogeneous supply array and a heterogeneous (but differently distributed) array of demands.[4]

The Detection and Measurement of "Natural" Channel Systems. We will discuss four distinct elements of the adjustment process with a view, first, to providing a means of *detecting* marketing channels and then of explaining what they accomplish. First, there are sorting transformations which are required to bring items of an initially heterogeneous array into internally homogeneous classes. The class definition, in turn, may be in one or more dimensions. The question arises as to how each dimension is to be measured (whether by the absolute presence or absence of a defined attribute, or by the place of each unit within an ordinal ranking, or by the size of the unit in a cardinal measure). Also at stake is the question of sequence in which these tests of dimensionality are to be made. If each of n dimensions is independent of the rest, then n tests can be applied in any arbitrary order. If not, the multidimensionality of the items needs to be treated in a manner such that one dimension dominates others and must be treated first.

---

[2] Ralph F. Breyer, *The Marketing Institution* (New York: McGraw-Hill Book Co., Inc., 1934).

[3] Ralph F. Breyer, *Quantitative Systemic Analysis and Control: Study No. 1— Channel and Channel Group Costing* (Philadelphia, Pa.: R. F. Breyer, 1948).

[4] F. E. Clark and C. P. Clark, *Principles of Marketing* (3d ed.; New York: The Macmillan Co., 1942); R. S. Vaile, E. T. Grether, and Reavis Cox, *Marketing in the American Economy* (New York: The Ronald Press Co., 1952); especially chaps. v, vi, and vii; Alderson, *op. cit.*; and D. A. Revzan, *Wholesaling in Marketing Organization* (New York: John Wiley & Sons, Inc., 1961), especially chap. i.

Second, once homogeneity within sorting class is achieved, the process must bring about transformations of lot-size.

Third, transformations in time are required (this is "the inventory problem").

Fourth, transformations in space may be necessary.

Two distinct questions can be asked concerning each of the dimensions according to which the array might be sorted: (1) how far need the analysis go in the *extent* of each feature of the assortment? and (2) how "fine" does the measure need to be within any small interval of this measure of the assortment?

As an example of the first of these issues, let us consider the possible dimension of "commodity type," where there is a series of such types to be considered in the analysis of a marketing channel. One does not need to consider the possibility that *every* commodity produced in the economy will be attracted into the natural mode of operation of a channel system, as some commodities will be fundamentally irrelevant to the organization of the marketing channel that is under study. However, to use an example from field studies of the lumber trade, "softwood plywood" can be classified as a commodity different from "softwood lumber." One must be prepared to ask questions concerning the likelihood that these two commodity types will appear together in the sorting operations of business entities at various stages.

Another example of the question of the "fineness" of the dimensional measure can also be taken from this discussion of the lumber market. Within the generalized commodity type, "softwood lumber," there are numerous individual species which may be produced by a given sawmill or which can be drawn from different manufacturing sources into wholesale and retail assortments. For some purposes it is sufficient to examine "softwood lumber" regardless of species, but for others it may be necessary to label separately such species as Douglas fir, California redwood, western hemlock, or sugar pine.

Most descriptions of marketing channel configurations rest squarely upon a *prior* commodity classification in which the commodity dimensions are of fixed length and fineness. It is easy to see why scholars have chosen this approach rather than developing a *theory* of the emergence of the system of behavior. Such a theory would involve the simultaneous choice of the originating supply array (and its dimensional properties), of the final consumption array (and its dimensional properties), and of the intermediate adjustment process (with marketing tasks undertaken at a degree of complexity which would depend on the characteristics of the originating and absorbing distributions). In principle, one could empirically detect a marketing channel by tracing the forward movement of the samples of commodities in the originating array, somehow defined, or work backward by starting with samples from the ending array and finding their origins.[5] A third possibility involves investigating the flow properties of the channel system by studying a sample of the commodity handlings that occur during the course of the adjustment process, but until we know how to identify this process more effectively, we cannot specify the population from which such empirical samplings would be drawn.

The detection of marketing channels must now proceed more modestly than would be implied by the above, through fixing of at least some of the following elements:

1. The initial commodity array and the "final" array;
2. The definitions of the sets of business entities (manufacturers, wholesalers with stocks, etc.) involved in necessary activities;
3. The specification of the *sequences* in which the various sets of entities will be linked together;
4. The specification of the *activities* which will be examined.

Suppose that all four of these features are fixed. Then we still have the problem of understanding how effort may be allocated, as the following example demonstrates. (See Table 1.)

Consider the channel arrangements for commodity x, in which

S_1 is the set of originating suppliers;
S_2 is a set of "intermediary" entities;
S_3 is the set of "final" entities;
F_1 is a functional activity, some total amount of which must be undertaken somewhere in the channel system;
F_2 is a second functional activity; and
F_3 is a third functional activity.

TABLE 1

ACTIVITY COEFFICIENTS, IF THE ELEMENTARY FUNCTIONAL ACTIVITY j IS WHOLLY PERFORMED BY ENTITIES IN SET i

	F_1	F_2	F_3
S_1	r_{11}	r_{12}	r_{13}
S_2	r_{21}	r_{22}	r_{23}
S_3	r_{31}	r_{32}	r_{33}

In Table 2 we define *all* alternative channel sequences through which the above functional requirements could be met.

Given this framework, it is possible to state the problem of minimum cost or maximum revenue allocation of functional effort. Each activity (channel alternative) A_i has associated with it an unknown *level* of operation x_i and a net revenue per unit c_i. This net revenue coefficient would

---

[5] A gargantuan job of measurement of the individual flows of marketing effort, done by tracing backward from the point of final absorption, is reported by Reavis Cox and Charles S. Goodman in "Marketing of Housebuilding Materials," *Journal of Marketing* (July, 1956), pp. 36–61.

TABLE 2

DEFINITIONS OF CHANNEL ALTERNATIVES

	A_1	A_2	A_3	A_4	A_5	A_6	A_7
S_1	$F_1F_2F_3$	0	0	F_1F_2	F_1F_3	F_2F_3	F_1F_3
S_2	0	$F_1F_2F_3$	0	F_3	F_2	F_1	0
S_3	0	0	$F_1F_2F_3$	0	0	0	F_3

	A_8	A_9	A_{10}	A_{11}	A_{12}	A_{13}	A_{14}
S_1	F_2F_3	F_2F_3	0	0	0	F_3	F_2
S_2	0	0	F_1F_2	F_1F_3	F_2F_3	F_1F_2	F_1F_3
S_3	F_2	F_1	F_3	F_2	F_1	0	0

	A_{15}	A_{16}	A_{17}	A_{18}	A_{19}	A_{20}	A_{21}
S_1	F_1	F_3	F_2	F_1	0	0	0
S_2	F_2F_3	0	0	0	F_3	F_2	F_1
S_3	0	F_1F_2	F_1F_3	F_2F_3	F_1F_2	F_1F_3	F_2F_3

	A_{22}	A_{23}	A_{24}	A_{25}	A_{26}	A_{27}
S_1	F_1	F_1	F_2	F_2	F_3	F_3
S_2	F_2	F_3	F_1	F_3	F_1	F_2
S_3	F_3	F_2	F_3	F_1	F_2	F_1

be derived by taking the gross margin per unit and subtracting the unit variable costs of performing the required functional activities in the manner indicated by the activity definition. The sets S_1, S_2, S_3 have given functional capacities E_1, E_2, E_3, respectively.[6] Each activity assignment (some combination of the F's in Table 2) has a unit requirement, a_{ij}, against each of the capacities. Thus, we can say in matrix notation, the problem is to find:

$$\text{Max } V = cX$$
$$\text{Subject to } Ax \leqq E$$
$$\text{and } x \geqq 0 .$$

This linear programming formulation is clumsy and could be simplified for easier solution, but it demonstrates the basic structure of the problem of marketing theory more clearly than would a compressed statement of the optimization problem. This formulation shows that the assignment of functional efforts to particular levels in the channel system requires consideration of many combinatorial alternatives and of the costs associated with each one. Thus, the problem is inherently messy.

Scales of Operation at Critical Points in the Channel. A vital issue, not tackled in the above linear programming formulation, is the choice of a scale at which each of these transformations will be undertaken.

---

[6] If it is desired to break out separately the capacity requirements and technical coefficients for each functional activity, then for each set of participants, there could be *three* resource limits instead of one, and three *rows* of activity coefficients pertaining to each activity alternative.

For any one of the transformations considered individually, this depends upon the density distributions of the supply array and the intended demand array, and also upon the cost function for the transformation to be undertaken. The crudeness or fineness of the transformation may in turn be a matter of choice, and the degree of refinement may determine certain parameters of the cost function.

We are supposing the presence of a single basic adjustment process with the four elements previously mentioned, so that one of the issues to be determined is whether the technologies of these four subprocesses are independent and distinct or—what is more likely in most cases— whether they are interdependent, with the result that the choice of scale becomes a compromise among appropriate scales for the individual transformations.

In the "natural" system, each marketing agency—even if it is concerned only with a single commodity—may undertake many or few functional activities, each one of which may deserve treatment as a contribution to the adjustment between the supply array and the demand array for the commodity. Similarly, each activity may involve one or more of the kinds of transformation already mentioned.

These remarks bring us back to Breyer's concern with structural configurations. Put most briefly, the issue arises as to the number of stages needed in a sequence of agencies to treat these adjustment problems between the initial supply and the eventual demand arrays. The natural system is a continual contest regarding the number of stages and the allocation of efforts between one stage and another, precisely because of the large number of possible combinations of choices. The number of possibilities is so large that chaos could rule—no systematic and orderly behavior would emerge. Yet, we do find orderliness and finely coordinated behavior, and we need to know why and how it comes about and how it may be modified when new conditions arise.

Centralized and Decentralized Transaction Making. One of the most complex problems of overall channel design, if the designer were in a position to determine the entire structure of intermediary operations, would be to choose an appropriate degree of market centralization. Institutional studies of various central cash markets for agricultural products have shown these markets can become critically important both from the standpoint of logistics—the movement, handling, and storage of commodities—and from that of information assembly, transaction making, and the creation of price signals which can be used both by the central-market participants and by those entities which choose not to involve themselves directly.

In order to analyze the alternatives, the channel designer needs to be able to compare the logistic efficiency of centralized and decentralized arrangements, and he must also be able to estimate the information-handling and computational burdens of the centralized and the decentralized schemes.

It is no accident that this issue resembles that of comparing the characteristics of centralized and decentralized national economics: many of the formal analytic problems are the same. Thus the theoretical work carried out in the latter area is relevant.[7] Empirical investigation of the information-processing features of centralized exchange markets is, however, very difficult to undertake. One effort in this direction has been reported tentatively and is continuing.[8]

In addition to the logistic and the informational features of centralized and decentralized markets, important problems of evoking the allegiance and the cooperative behavior of participating firms are encountered in making the market work effectively. Even if efficient logistics and information-handling would be achieved by a centralized market, once established, there are interesting questions as to whether a path of institutional development exists which will permit the formation of such a market. Some attempts to establish central-clearing schemes have been failures—and in one such case known to this author, the resistance of wholesaling firms wedded to the decentralized pattern was a factor of some importance. In the presence of such institutional forces, the channel designer faces very great difficulties of predicting what it will take to evoke the needed response by potential participants in the market system.

Central markets are often quasi-public facilities and fall under extensive regulation—as, for example, SEC regulation of the securities exchanges. Marketing theory should consider whether these regulatory bodies have a theory of what they are doing, and why.

Criteria of Channel Effectiveness

The linear programming formulation presented above asserted that the objective was to *maximize total net revenues* to all members of the sets S_1, S_2, and S_3, subject to the capacity constraints. The question of dividing the pie among the sets, and among the members of each set, was not considered.

In another and differently restricted model of communication networks, the focus was upon the determination of that number of whole-

---

[7] K. J. Arrow and L. Hurwicz, "Decentralization and Computation in Resource Allocations," R. W. Pfouts (ed.), *Essays in Economics and Econometrics* (Chapel Hill, N.C.: University of North Carolina Press, 1960); L. Hurwicz, "Optimality and Informational Efficiency in Resource Allocation," K. J. Arrow, S. Karlin, and P. Suppes (eds.), *Mathematical Methods in the Social Sciences* (Stanford, Calif.: Stanford University Press, 1960); T. Marschak, "Centralization and Decentralization in Economic Organizations," *Econometrics*, Vol. 27 (July, 1959), pp. 399–430; and G. Debreu, *Theory of Value, an Axiomatic Analysis of Economic Equilibrium* (New York: John Wiley & Sons, Inc., 1959).

[8] P. L. Schmidbauer, "An Estimation of the Quantity of Decision-Making Required by a Market," Working Paper No. 31, Center for Research in Management Science (Berkeley, Calif.: Center for Research in Management Science, July, 1961).

sale intermediaries which would minimize the margin charged to the sets of manufacturers and retailers viewed as users of the intermediate market.[9] Since commodity flow through the channel was treated as given in this approach, the effective criterion was that of *minimizing cost to the channel's users*.

Neither of these approaches to the definition of a criterion, however, deals with a most significant underlying question: how much marketing service, and of what kinds, is it desirable for the channel system to deliver to the ultimate users of the products it handles, and how do the quantities and qualities of such service affect the amount of commodity output which will pass through the channel?

When it is couched in these terms, the criterion of channel effectiveness encompasses, but only with respect to the channel system that is under examination, many of the questions that have been discussed much more broadly under the heading of the productivity of distribution. Cox and Goodman addressed themselves to the measurement of the total amount of each functional activity performed in order to effect delivery, to a sample site, of the major items in the bill of materials for a typical single-family house. They then sought to make a judgmental evaluation of the potential improvement of channel effectiveness which might be made in each of these dimensions of functional activity, taken separately.[10]

Marketing efficiency, in relation to cost, was the implicit criterion underlying this approach, but the authors did not seek to translate the separate measures of marketing work into either a "benefit" or a "cost" criterion. Further, while they obtained extremely detailed estimates of the amounts of functional activity undertaken in a marketing channel, their investigation could not encompass the comparison of the present system with other ways of combining marketing activities or of altering the scale of operations at some points in the channel.

The vexing question of the criterion is resolved rather easily, in principle, when attention is shifted from the global problem of channel design —including the specification of desired relations among all the entities involved—to the microproblem facing the individual firm, which is that of choosing a (possibly complex) distribution system to benefit its own operations, given some assumptions about the manner in which the "rest of the world" will function.

Not unnaturally, it is this perspective which dominates most of the literature of operations research in application to marketing problems. Frequently, the assumed criterion is that simplest of intellectual constructs, profit maximization. But there is no reason in principle why this analysis for the firm could not use a variant of utility maximization (to encompass other goals besides profits), or even a complex of goal statements to re-

[9] F. E. Balderston, "Communication Networks in Intermediate Markets," *Management Science* (January, 1958), pp. 156–71.
[10] Cox and Goodman, *op. cit.*

flect a series of priorities and objectives which may not be capable of reduction to a single index measure. The important point is that, so long as the firm under analysis can be considered a single, unitary entity, the *source* of a criterion measure is simpler to define, and the character of the criterion is in principle more definite, than can be the case if channel designs must be evaluated subject to the combined judgment of the firms involved, or of "society."

Channel Design for the Individual Firm

The individual firm faces the channel problem in three ways, which differ from the preceding efforts at "global" analysis of an entire marketing channel as a system. First, the goals or objectives of one firm, no matter how far one chooses to complicate these beyond the assumed goal of simple profit maximization, are nevertheless simpler to identify, and simpler to apply in the evaluation of alternatives, than is the channel criterion problem when designing channels. Second, if the firm operates, or can operate, as a multiestablishment enterprise, some of the channel alternatives need evaluation in light of the relative efficiency of market participation and internal administrative controls. This is also a critical problem for the "global" channel designer, as the assignment of functional activities to different *loci* of operations often implies choices between one pattern of administrative efficiencies (or inefficiencies) and another—but the analysis of these problems in the case of the single firm is simpler conceptually.

The third difference between the single-firm channel problem and that of the "global" channel design is, however, a complicating rather than a simplifying difference. As was shown in a preceding section, models of a marketing channel system are generated by (1) identifying commodities or commodity groups to study and then (2) examining the various issues which arise in assigning functional activities to the participating entities. The single firm, however, is not necessarily restricted to participation in a single channel system. It may—to make matters most difficult of all— use the same facilities and manpower, at one or more establishments, to participate simultaneously in several marketing channels. While Breyer raised the question of how to define large systems involving several interdependent channels, the preceding review of design problems should be sufficient to indicate that even for the single channel the problems of analysis are as yet far from being solved.[11] The analysis of the single firm which is (or may consider becoming) involved in several channel systems will be considered briefly below, but for the most part we will confine attention to the elements of channel design for the firm that is involved only in a single channel system.

A series of problem areas, each of which is only a part of the problem

---

[11] Breyer, *Quantitative Systemic. . . op. cit.*

of system design facing the firm, are reviewed in the following paragraphs. First, several approaches to problems of logistics and location are examined. A few other kinds of issue are then considered—chiefly, sales-solicitation alternatives and a brief note on two problems of pricing which have channel design implications. Finally, we discuss briefly the problem of putting together the pieces of the puzzle in large-scale models which may enable the firm to discern simultaneously most of the important implications of channel design.

Logistics

A. *Separated markets.* In one of the influential early articles on the application of linear programming to business problems, Henderson and Schlaifer discussed, among other things, the possibility of using the transportation-model linear program to determine what pattern of shipments a firm might most profitably make from *m* origins, under its control, to *n* distinct and mutually independent markets.[12] While the minimizing of total shipment costs was the main focus of attention, the authors did point out that additional market constraints could easily be built into the problem, to reflect either an estimated upper limit of the amount that market *j* could absorb or a *minimum* delivery amount which the firm might set as a matter of marketing strategy. The *source* of such maximum or minimum limiting constraints was not specified: they could be supplied by management judgment, by an analysis of trend in the historical pattern of shipments to each market, or by an attempt at analysis of the strategic interaction between the firm and its competitors in each market. The point, however, is that wherever these limits are known, they can be added to the model which optimizes shipping costs. This kind of constraint may be an important building block in the complex production-distribution models which are considered in our subsequent discussion of large-scale moels.

In quite another context, the present author has considered problems of branch representation in each of a number of mutually independent submarkets.[13] Here also, policy constraints on minimum branch volume and environmental constraints on the maximum the local market can absorb can be included easily in the model.

B. *Warehouse location and operation.* Bowman and Stewart examined the question of where to locate warehouses and how big to make each one of them to service local markets effectively, by examining the aggregate cost effects of a number of marginal considerations.[14] Choosing a "typical" geographical distribution of customer requirements, they first

---

[12] A. Henderson and R. Schlaifer, "Mathematical Programming—Better Information for Better Decision-Making," *Harvard Business Review*, Vol. 32 (May–June, 1954), pp. 73–100.

[13] F. E. Balderston, "Models of Multiple-Branch Organizations," *California Management Review*, Volume 4 (Spring, 1962), pp. 40–57.

[14] R. Bowman and E. Stewart, "A Model for Scale of Operations," *Journal of Marketing*, Vol. 20 (January, 1956), pp. 242–54.

developed a branch-warehouse model, then fitted branch warehouses and a plant warehouse into the total marketing area. In an unpublished paper, Andresen and Lutz developed a macro approach to essentially the same problem.[15]

Besides such cost parameters as the carlot cost per mile and the LCL cost per mile, which must enter into such models as these, it is necessary to specify in some way the costs of storage and handling as a function of warehouse volume. As one example of potentially radical change in such cost functions, Meserole points out that high-speed data processing is modifying warehouse management by making possible the arbitrary assignment of goods to warehouse locations on a frequency-of-visit basis.[16] In the same sources, Magee discusses approximate cost functions for a physical distribution network.[17]

Despite enormous progress in the rigorous analysis of inventory systems, of which the most comprehensive treatment is that of Hadley and Whitin, there remain some critically interesting substantive problems for which optimizing rules are not yet well formulated.[18] At present, we cannot simply plug in a solution method for the general case of the n-commodity, m-stage inventory system, and thus dispose of the inventory management issue by means of one powerful optimizing rule.

C. *Logistic networks.* The firm may wish to consider as channel alternatives the possible sequences of commodity flow from a source to a destination and choose the least-cost route which meets various capacity restrictions. For this purpose special algorithms have been developed to treat flows in networks. Ford and Fulkerson and Hadley lay out the basic analysis.[19] W. Jewell has extended this model to the case in which the flow is augmented or partly absorbed en route from the source to the destination, an extension which may improve markedly the prospects for handling important classes of marketing problems.[20]

Sales Solicitation; Pricing Rules. The problems of market coverage and adequate warehouse servicing have some analytic similarity to the problems of sales-force deployment, although different cost elements arise in the latter case. Artle and Berglund employ elaborate marginalist reasoning to determine whether a manufacturer would profit by using his

---

[15] J. Andresen and R. Lutz, unpublished manuscript.

[16] W. H. Meserole, "Warehouses and Computers," in Wroe Alderson and Stanley J. Shapiro (eds.), *Marketing and the Computer* (Englewood Cliffs, N.J.: Prentice-Hall, Inc., 1963), p. 54.

[17] John F. Magee, "The Computer and the Physical Distribution Network," in Alderson and Shapiro (eds.), *op. cit.*, pp. 70–76.

[18] G. Hadley and T. M. Whitin, *Analysis of Inventory Systems* (Englewood Cliffs, N.J.: Prentice-Hall, Inc., 1963).

[19] L. R. Ford, Jr., and D. R. Fulkerson, *Flows in Networks* (Princeton, N.J.: Princeton University Press, 1962); and G. Hadley, *Linear Programming* (Reading, Mass.: Addison-Wesley Publishing Co., 1962), chap. x.

[20] W. S. Jewell, "Optimal Flow through Networks with Gains," *Operations Research*, Vol. 10 (July–August, 1962).

own direct sales force or a series of wholesalers to secure sales coverage.[21] Andresen and Lutz also consider this question, in conjunction with the determination of an appropriate physical distribution scheme.[22]

Pricing policies are another important aspect of marketing channel relationships. Here, we refer only briefly to two issues. One, the question of the vertically integrated wholesaler's pricing in sales to "outside" customers versus the shadow prices it may charge to its own establishments at the same marketing level as the outside customers is considered by Hirschleifer.[23]

A quite different problem is faced by the firm which can set not only its own selling price but also the resale price of its customers. Curiously enough, the elaborate discussions of "fair trade" or "resale price maintenance" as an important issue of public regulatory policy do not seem to include much discussion of the manner in which the firm might choose an optimal fair-trade price, given the legality of such a policy and the availability of an enforcement procedure.

This question is a member of a class of pricing problems which arise in the firm's approach to its marketing channels, and a solution to a simplified case will be given. Suppose, first, that there is a maximum population of N^* "dealers" who may stock the manufacturer's product if the margin $M per unit is sufficiently attractive. (We presume that the manufacturer has first set a price to the dealer, P_n, that transport costs are zero, and that there are no quantity discounts.) There is a relation $N = f(M)$ of which the maximum value is N^*, the entire population of dealers. Figure 1 illustrates this function.

Consumers, however, react to the situation in two ways. First, they are negatively affected if P_c, the price they must pay, is high. Second, they are positively affected by the ease of availability of the product. The solid lines of Figure 2 show these two effects, in that for every number of dealers, quantity demanded falls as P_c increases, but, for each given level of P_c, the quantity demanded is greater, the greater the number of dealers.

Now we combine the margin relation and the consumer response relation in the dotted line of Figure 2, which shows the quantity sold at each price P_c, in view of the fact from Figure 1 that only a certain number of dealers will materialize at each level of margin.

Now, if the manufacturer's marginal costs are constant over the entire relevant range, the profit-maximizing objective in the context of this fairtrade situation is that of choosing M so as to maximize sales quantity

[21] R. Artle and S. Berglund, "A Note on Manufacturers' Choice of Distribution Channels," *Management Science*, Vol. 5 (July, 1959), pp. 460–71.

[22] Andresen and Lutz, *op. cit.*

[23] J. Hirschleifer, "Decentralized Decisions and Internal Pricing," in Graduate School of Business Administration, Stanford University, Seminar on Basic Research in Management Controls, *Proceedings*, forthcoming.

(P_M being fixed, by assumption). In Figure 2, the optimum fair-trade price is shown as P_c^*, at which price Q_{max} will be sold.

There are, to be sure, much more complicated pricing aspects of the firm's channel policy than the two considered in this section, but perhaps these examples illustrate the problem area.

Large-Scale Models. Some company research staffs have worked out extremely large-scale models of their production-distribution systems. Hadley refers to a sales district analysis involving four company plants and 2,500 jobbers, the solution of which required approximately two

FIGURE 1

DEALER RESPONSE TO DIFFERENT DEALER MAR-
GINS OFFERED BY THE MANUFACTURER

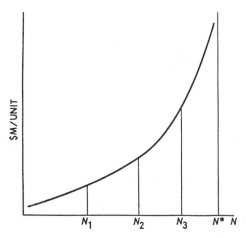

FIGURE 2

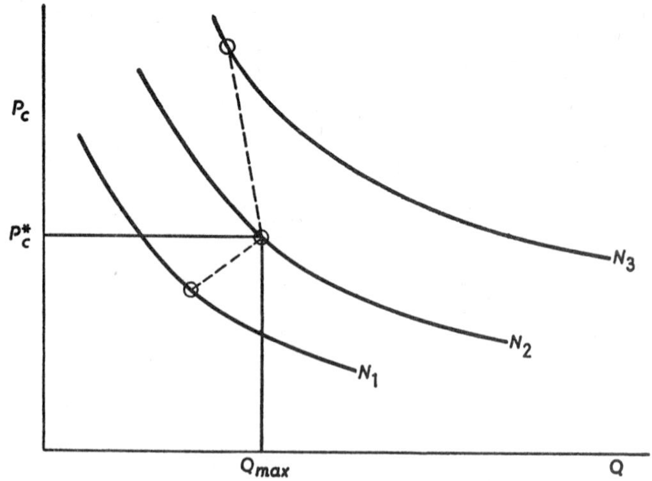

hours of IBM 704 time.[24] The present author has been told of at least one massive production-distribution model of the linear programming type which incorporated more than 30,000 variables. Both of these models were optimizing (presumably, cost-minimizing) models.

Where analysis fails, there is always the comfort (slow, painful and expensive, to be sure) of computer simulation. The present author was a co-worker in one such study.[25] This model was developed in order to test hypotheses concerning the effect of information cost and market loyalty on the structure and performance of a market. It has since been adapted to the testing of alternative pricing rules and to an exploratory test of the desirability of replacing the set of wholesale intermediaries with a central clearing mechanism. The results are not yet fully analyzed.

The preceding review is not an exhaustive catalog of the work being done on various of the partial relationships entering into the firm's channel design problem, but it illustrates what kinds of relationships are available as inputs to new models for analyzing alternative marketing channel policies.

It is the author's view that much more work on channel design is both needed and feasible. This topic is central to our theories of the behavior of marketing systems, and in the context of the individual firm, it is of pressing practical importance.

---

[24] Hadley, *op. cit.*, pp. 433–37.

[25] F. E. Balderston and Austin C. Hoggatt, *Simulation of Market Processes* (Berkeley, Calif.: Institute of Business and Economic Research, Special Publications No. 1, 1962).

13. TOWARDS A THEORY OF RETAIL COMPETITION

*Wroe Alderson and Stanley J. Shapiro**

IN AN ATTEMPT to contribute to the development of retailing theory, a Wharton School research team has been studying competitive interdependence among food chains active in the Philadelphia area. This three-year undertaking was financed by one of many grants made by Sperry & Hutchinson to further basic research in retailing. The changes that occurred over time in scope and research design as well as the studies conducted to determine the validity of various assumptions and hypotheses are outlined in the following paragraphs. No effort is made to conceal from the reader the frustrations encountered during the three stages of the project or the avenues of false promise that eventually lead to intellectual impasses. The present status of the undertaking and the need for additional investigations of certain subject areas are discussed in a brief concluding section. This report is presented in the hope that researchers concerned with similar problems and equally interested in developing a theory of retail competition may find the information of some value and guidance.

STAGE I—NEGATIVE FINDINGS AND POSITIVE INSIGHTS

Pricing, advertising lineage, new-store openings, and innovations in marketing methods were originally to be examined in an effort to discover the patterns of competitive behavior characterizing Philadelphia department stores and grocery chains. A variety of factors combined to restrict

* The authors wish to express their appreciation and acknowledge a debt of gratitude to Professor Reavis Cox of the University of Pennsylvania and Professors William Baumol and Richard Quandt of Princeton University for their meaningful contributions to the first stage of the project, to Dr. Eugene Beem of Sperry & Hutchinson for his patience and encouragement as well as the financial support provided by his employer, to Dr. George Fisk for his efforts from the beginning of the study to the present time, and to the many graduate students who on one occasion or another performed necessary and sometimes intellectually challenging tasks.

190

the scope of this first study to competitive interaction among food chains. The focus of empirical testing became the relevance of the Cournot oligopoly model to pricing behavior as revealed by a study of advertised prices. Considerable effort was also devoted to developing a model for predicting the size of the physical plant of each chain in the various sections of metropolitan Philadelphia. The examination of advertising lineage conducted at this time was quite limited in scope. Nevertheless, its preliminary results influenced the research team's subsequent studies of advertising. The type of data that would make possible meaningful analysis of competitive interaction in the area of marketing innovation proved to be unavailable.

The scope of the first stage of the study, the methodology employed, and the results obtained are set forth in an unpublished report.[1] Aspects of that study most directly relevant to a summary of the entire project are discussed below. Researchers desiring more detailed information on specific topics or on the design and scope of this first study are advised to write for the source document.[2]

The Pattern of Advertised Prices— Relevance of the Cournot Solution

The problem of interest to Cournot was the price decisions to be anticipated when only a few large competitors were active in the market. Cournot's solution is discussed in most of the standard texts on price theory and need not be reviewed at this time.[3] Of more immediate relevance are the results obtained from testing the hypothesis that the competitive moves and countermoves of A & P, Acme, Food Fair, and Penn Fruit—the four chains active in Philadelphia—would demonstrate the existence of Cournot reaction curves.

Prices of thirty-five items frequently advertised during 1958 and 1959 in the *Philadelphia Bulletin* were examined. The items chosen were drawn from four product classes—packaged detergents, meats, produce, and canned and frozen foods. A massive correlation study comparing the price behavior of the four chains with respect to these items was then carried out. Behavior characteristic of a Cournot-type solution was observed in some cases. Also, the pattern of relationships revealed by the correlation analysis was verified by other available data on how the various chains interact. Nevertheless, the empirical findings were inconclusive despite a possible methodological bias conducive to results consistent with a Cournot solution. The occurrence of a fairly low overall percentage of

---

[1] Wroe Alderson, *The Structure of Retail Competition in the Philadelphia Market* (Philadelphia: Wharton School, 1961), mimeographed. The ensuing discussion of research team activity during the first stage of the project is drawn from that report.

[2] For copies of the report, write the author c/o Marketing Department, University of Pennsylvania, Philadelphia 4, Pa.

[3] See, for example, Sidney Weintraub, *Intermediate Price Theory* (Philadelphia: Chilton Company, 1964), pp. 199–206.

price reactions, the feasibility of alternate explanations for those reactions that did exist, and other considerations yet to be discussed convinced the principal investigator that the prevailing market structure could not be characterized as oligopolistic.

The Store Location Study—The Model and Its Limitations

In view of the obvious importance of locational decisions in a study of retail interdependence, this phase of the study was the source of some frustration. Obtaining relevant information even with respect to such basic facts as the dates of store openings and closings turned out to be an unexpectedly complex problem. The analytical model was carefully and thoughtfully constructed, but the interactions which doubtless exist among the locational decisions of the four firms largely fell through the crevices and were lost. The major conclusion reached—that supermarkets follow purchasing power—while valid statistically, was trivial in the sense it had been fully demonstrated years ago by simpler methods.

An elaborate geographical model was developed in an attempt to explain the number of stores and the square footage of store space owned by the various chains in particular areas. The critical independent variables included certain demographic and socioeconomic characteristics and the degree of competition in that area from other stores. Although the formulas that were developed by the use of multiple-regression procedures demonstrated admirable predictive power, they left something to be desired as a reflection of competitive strategies.

Obtaining the necessary data for a locational model was thus an arduous task, and the model itself merely confirmed what was already known. Nevertheless, this study of the geographic aspects of competition was of some value. Hypotheses concerning locational strategy formulated at this time were investigated during subsequent stages of the project.

The Paradigm of Retail Competition

The negative tone of the preceding discussion should not be misinterpreted. Valuable insights into the pattern of competitive interaction were obtained at this time, and the areas requiring further investigation pinpointed. The formulation of the paradigm of retail competition outlined below was one noteworthy contribution.

The first step in structuring retail competition is to recognize two semi-independent domains for decision making. These may be called the product domain and the establishment domain. Each domain comprises several areas or aspects of competition. The linkage among decisions is believed to be closer within a domain than from one domain to another. Indeed that is the primary basis for defining a domain. The product domain is concerned with questions of sales and profits from current operations. If competitive interaction is to be observed within the product domain, a countermove should follow the initial move within a relatively short time interval. The establishment domain, in contrast, covers a class of decisions which relate to retailing facilities rather than current sales. Many of these actions require considerable time for deliberation and implementation. An action may be intended as a countermove even when there is a lapse of several months or a year following the initial move.

The product domain comprises three primary areas of competition—price, assortment, and the size and character of advertising expenditure. These are the areas in which the store competes for sales and profits on a day-to-day basis. The costs of maintaining these operating flows include giving up potential margin to make prices attractive, giving up display space to relatively slow-moving items in order to make the assortment as a whole attractive, and plowing potential earnings back into advertising in the attempt to maximize.

Another dimension of the structure of retail competition is the distinction that can be drawn between levels of competition as compared to the areas embraced by the domain. In the product domain there is first of all the face-to-face relationship of the retailer to the customer in the store. Here behavior is influenced by a variety of sales pressures including a consciousness of alternatives offered by competitors. This might be called the primary or transactional level of competition.

On a secondary or opportunity level of competition an effort is made to draw people into the store, either for the particular sales event or as continuing patrons. Firms are engaged in a kind of meta-competition. They are competing for the opportunity to compete at this opportunity level. Competitors stress featured prices rather than the prices of the entire product line.

The distinctions in levels also applies to advertising expenditures. At the primary level, advertising represents competition to sell goods or to develop patronage for the store as a reliable source of goods. At the secondary level, advertising itself is competing for attention, readership, and acceptance. What has been said about the structure of the product domain is summarized in Figure 1.

The domain of establishment can be segmented into a somewhat simi-

FIGURE 1

THE PRODUCT DOMAIN IN RETAIL COMPETITION

Levels of Competition	Areas of Competition		
	Pricing	Assortment	Advertising Expenditure
Primary	Shelf prices	Items stocked	Product sales
Secondary	Advertised prices	Advertised items	Competing for attention

lar structure again with three areas and two levels of competition. This domain embraces the retailer's decisions concerning his facilities and the constraints under which these facilities are employed in competition. The three areas are store location, store size and layout, and store services and features. The primary level in the establishment domain is the utilization of facilities in the continuing competitive engagement—each store in its own location with a character appealing to its specialized market. The secondary level consists of additions and improvements to facilities.

Changes in facilities are likely to receive most of the promotional attention just as changes in prices or assortments are most likely to be featured in advertising. In both cases the specific items being promoted are often intended to symbolize the overall adequacy or distinctiveness of facilities or the overall attractiveness of assortments and prices. The structure of the establishment domain is summarized in Figure 2.

FIGURE 2

STRUCTURE OF THE ESTABLISHMENT DOMAIN IN
RETAIL COMPETITION

	Areas of Competition		
Levels	Store Location	Store Size and Layout	Store Services and Features
Primary	Existing network	Present selling space	Established pattern
Secondary	Network expansion	Store improvements	Innovations

Strategic Dimensions of Advertising Policy

The study of advertised prices required for testing the Cournot hypothesis led to a reassessment of what retailers were trying to accomplish through advertising. Statistical confirmation was provided for the frequently observed phenomenon that only a relatively few of the 5,000 or more items stocked by a supermarket are advertised. A marked difference in the number of items mentioned by each of the chains in their advertisements was also revealed. Frequency of mention tended to run about twice as high for A & P and Acme as for Penn Fruit and Food Fair. These observations and the results of the empirical testing for Cournot reaction curves led to the following formulation of advertising strategies being set forth as worthy of more detailed examination:

Advertising is not employed primarily to sell the particular items mentioned but rather to promote the success of one weekly sales event after another. The fundamental strategy pursued by each chain in promoting this objective is to differentiate its offerings from the offerings of competitors. The underlying assumption in this approach is that advertising dollars are more effective when used to offer something that other advertisers cannot match immediately rather than to announce that the advertiser is prepared to meet competition.

A secondary advertising strategy is to include a reminder list in addition to the genuine specials. These reminder items are selected because of seasonal interest, their complementary relationship to the featured specials, or as cues to remind the consumer of subclasses of goods within the store's broad assortment.

Finally there is some part of retail advertising that may be devoted to neutralizing the advantage gained by competitors through products mentioned or prices quoted in recent advertising. It is this practice of neutralization which is reflected in the existence of reaction curves.

Neutralization is a relatively minor advertising strategy as compared to differentiated offerings and reminder listings. The major objective of this week's advertising is to push this week's sales. Such a result depends mostly on creating positive impressions currently with only supplementary concern for negative impressions left over from last week. Limitations of the consumer's knowledge of prices and recollection of advertising lend powerful support to this strategic judgment.

The Tentative Model of Consumer Buying Behavior

The first stage of the project also indicated that observation of each firm's behavior might not be sufficient for a study of competitive interaction. Interviews with both chain-store executives and consumers appeared essential for a valid interpretation of what goes on in retail competition. Consequently, the first report contained a model to guide further research on the consumer's expected values in shopping for food. This tentative formulation as outlined below allows for the concept of retail strategies by recognizing the price and assortment aspects of the image the retailer is trying to project. The model also assumes that the advertiser is attempting to maximize the impact of his chain's advertising on the expectations of the consumer.

$$I_E = F(P_1 D_B, P_2 D_A, P_3 C_S)$$

For any given amount of money to be spent on advertising, the impact on expectations, I_E, would be maximized through the most favorable allocation of expenditures against the terms in the right-hand side of the expression. The symbol D_B refers to differential advantage in market-basket cost on a particular visit to a store; the symbol D_A refers to differential advantage in greater product satisfaction derived from the quality and breadth of assortment of the goods displayed. The elements P_1, P_2, P_3, represent subjective probability estimates made by the consumer. It is these probability estimates that the advertiser is attempting to influence through advertising. C_S is the cost of visiting additional stores, if any.

The initial state of mind of the consumer is one in which she hopes to visit a single store and obtain everything she wants at a favorable price. She knows that she will encounter a selection problem and that the conditions under which she makes her choice may differ from those she assumed when she came. Despite the bargain prices in the advertised specials, the consumer may discover that the market-basket cost is not favorable after regular prices are paid for all other items. She may also fail to find some of the things she wanted, such as a preferred brand of coffee, despite the wide variety of items offered. Her expectations concerning the probable outcome doubtless differ from store to store. Once she is in the store, pressure of time may cause her to buy what she wants even though prices are higher than expected. Also the consumer may accept substitutes for preferred items or go without temporarily if no substitute is acceptable.

In the extreme case, she will buy only part of her requirements or nothing at all in the first store and go to a competitive store. Her anticipation of this possibility doubtless has an influence on her initial choice which is not measured directly by market-basket cost or full satisfaction from the products selected. It would reflect some measure of the economic or psychic cost to her in having to spend time shopping in a second store. This part of the consumer's expectation is related in part to the convenience aspect of the store, including its location and the way it is laid out and operated. Convenience is also related to competitive locations. Thus, a consumer might take a chance on responding to the advertising of an unfamiliar chain if the store to be visited was located next door to the consumer's regular store.

Strategy in the Establishment Domain

The inability of the locational model developed during this stage of the project to shed much light on the strategies of individual competitors was previously discussed. More fruitful investigation required a conceptual framework emphasizing the alternatives open to management in making a locational decision and in assessing the moves and countermoves of competitors. The following analytical framework was advanced as an approach of sufficient generality to apply to the actions of department stores and grocery chains:

A chain which was open to consideration of a new site must weigh two objectives: optimal site selection and optimal network expansion. The two objectives would not always lead to the same decision. From one viewpoint the site would be evaluated as an independent opportunity in which the sole criteria were objective measures of the potential business for a supermarket at that spot. From the other viewpoint, the chain is attempting to complete the network of stores with which it covers the market as a whole. Optimal expansion of this network would favor the more effective use of such city-wide merchandising facilities as newspaper advertising. Ideally, all prospective customers exposed to such advertising should find a unit of the chain within an acceptable shopping range.

Suppose that all of the possible supermarket locations as yet unoccupied were set up in an ordered sequence, graded on some objective measure of market potential. Suppose further that this list was available to each chain as a point of reference each time it was ready to invest money at a new location. There are a number of cases in which management would not choose the site at the top of the list since this choice would not be consistent with optimal network expansion. It might appear that too much of the prospective volume would be taken away from other units of the same chain. A competitive chain might enjoy a stronger following in the particular neighborhood. The chain considering the location might have to depart substantially from its standard assortment and operating plan to exploit the opportunity fully. Competing chains might place different values on available parking space, visibility from the stream of traffic, and demographic changes occurring in the neighborhood. Also, one or more chains may be in the position of regarding their existing network as adequate for the market. This would tend to divert their investment funds to other areas or other activities.

These considerations might appear to lead to the conclusion that the decision problem could be reduced to a single objective, with each chain thinking solely of the optimization of its own network. The difficulty here is that this would be equivalent to ignoring the location decisions of other chains. Assume that a management hesitated to acquire a site, fearing that a store at that point would draw from the chain's other stores, might not that firm's executives be even more fearful of the impact of a competitive store located there? Obviously no one chain could afford to buy up all the available sites to keep them out of the hands of competitors. On the other hand, preclusive purchases doubtless do occur.

The Agenda for Basic Research in Retailing

The report on the first stage of the research project contained a discussion of future studies that should be carried out. The basic research program proposed at that time is set forth in detail so that the reader can trace its subsequent impact on the project.

1. A study to determine the adequacy of monopolistic competition as an explanation of the structure of competition among Philadelphia food chains was advocated. (As was indicated earlier, the findings of the first stage had resulted in oligopoly being discarded as an adequate explanatory model.)

2. The paradigm of retail competition was tentatively advanced as an analytical formulation of some merit deserving of further refinement.

3. The following types of empirical studies of advertised prices were proposed:

   a) A comparison of advertised and store prices to determine the extent to which the various chains adjust store prices to meet the advertised prices of competitors.

b) An analysis of chain-store advertising on a given date to determine the frequency with which items are mentioned by more than one competitor.

c) Interviews with consumers to measure advertising impact and with chain executives to determine what advertising strategies were being followed.

d) An identification and listing of the various ways in which a price quotation is presented in an effort to make price interesting to the consumer.

4. A historical study to determine whether each chain had attempted to establish an optimal locational network design as it added to existing facilities in Philadelphia was advocated.

5. The circumstances surrounding the introduction of special features, new services, and merchandising innovations—especially the extent to which fact-finding and experimentation had been used in making decisions in these areas—was judged especially deserving of study.

STAGE II—ADMINISTERED PRICING, ENTERPRISE DIFFERENTIATON, AND THE POLICY STANCE MATRIX

The proposed agenda for basic research in retailing guided the team's efforts during the second stage of the project. Attention was focused on discovering how adequately the received model of monopolistic competition described the market behavior of Philadelphia food chains. Advertisements were analyzed to determine whether the four chains attempted to differentiate their offerings by deliberately not mentioning the same items as their competitors. Food-chain executives were then interviewed to obtain necessary supplementary information on advertising and other policies. To the extent that space and a promise of confidentiality to those interviewed allows, the results of these two related studies are summarized below. Also, a new conceptual tool is introduced and certain conclusions reached by the chief investigator are discussed.

Item Overlap in Newspaper Advertising

Examining the degree of item overlap in food-chain advertisements appearing on the same day had previously been recommended. Such a study was conducted, and the results obtained are summarized in Table 1.[4]

---

[4] This discussion and the following sections on predicting the items and prices to be advertised and auditing the availability of advertised items at advertised prices is drawn from Colin B. Church, "How Is Newspaper Advertising Used as a Competitive Tool by the Chain Grocers in the Philadelphia Area?" (Unpublished Master's Thesis, Wharton School, University of Pennsylvania, 1962).

One finds, for example, that of all the items advertised by Acme during the four-week period, 91% of them were advertised exclusively by Acme while 4% were also advertised by A & P. Food Fair and Penn Fruit each advertised 3% of the items mentioned in the Acme advertisements. Since branding is a deliberate attempt at differentiation, the advertising by two chains of comparable quality private-label merchandising was not considered an example of item overlap.

TABLE 1

PERCENTAGE OF ITEM DUPLICATION IN NEWSPAPER ADVERTISING DURING THE
FOUR-WEEK PERIOD 5/17/61–6/7/61 BY GROCERY CHAIN
Weeks No. 1–4 Average

Chain Grocer	Acme	A & P	Food Fair	Penn Fruit
Acme	91	4	4	4
A & P	4	91	4	6
Food Fair	3	3	90	3
Penn Fruit	3	3	2	87
Total *	100	100	100	100

All figures in the charts indicated conditions of item overlap between two chains. Item overlap between three or four chains occurred 16 times over a four-week period in which there were approximately two thousand items mentioned.
   * Rounding error adjusted in totals.
SOURCE: *Evening and Sunday Bulletin* (Philadelphia).

Upon completion of this study, an unexpected problem of determining its significance arose. Ninety percent of the items advertised by each chain are not simultaneously promoted by its competitors. Does this "prove" that a policy of conscious differentiation was being followed? Probability theory threw little light on this problem. Every item in a supermarket does not have an equal opportunity or even a known probability of being advertised. No conclusion could thus be drawn as to whether the observed amount of item overlap demonstrated conscious differentiation, selection with no regard to competitors' actions, or some other policy.

A new approach was employed to circumvent the statistical impasse described above. A very low percentage of item overlap between a chain and its competitors would indicate conscious differentiation *if both the items and the prices to be advertised by rivals were known in advance.* Was such information on the future advertising of competitors available? To answer this question, a member of the research team attempted to predict the items and the prices of products to be advertised by A & P in a specified week. If a novice could be reasonably successful, it was believed, then the chains themselves could—and probably did—make such predictions with much greater accuracy.

Predicting the Items to Be Advertised

Limitations of space and relevancy preclude a detailed discussion of the techniques used by the novice investigator. Primary emphasis was placed on an examination of A & P advertising for the corresponding week of the previous year and for the four weeks preceding the advertisements to be predicted. Available published information on the supply of meat and produce was also reviewed. Given the assumptions that (1) the A & P newspaper advertising examined was and would continue to be representative of all A & P advertising and (2) that the items to be advertised by other chains can be predicted with more or less equal accuracy, the following conclusions were reached:

1. A novice can predict between 25% and 68% of the items that will appear in the forthcoming ad. The accuracy of the estimate of the number of items to appear and the absolute number of items mentioned in the forthcoming ad will be the factors determining where within this range the percentage of items predicted will fall.
2. There are a small group of items (approximately 33) which are very likely to appear in the forthcoming ad. These items have appeared quite frequently in the recent past, and 68% of them will appear in the ad which is to be predicted. The more frequently any item has been advertised in the recent past, the more likely it will appear in the forthcoming ad.
3. The ability of a novice to predict total advertising space is even greater than his ability to predict the items to be advertised. It is easier to predict a feature item which occupies a large space than it is to predict the average item which occupies a small space.
4. A considerable amount of advertising space will be devoted to a meat or poultry item. In addition, there is a fairly consistent relative percentage of total items which are devoted to any one food class, e.g., meat items will account for 7–17% of the total number of items advertised while cereals and soups will account for less than 1%.

Price Prediction

When informed of the research team's success at predicting the items to be advertised, some food-chain executives claimed predicting the prices to be charged for such items was the real problem. The fear of mentioning comparable items at a higher price was reported to be a factor underlying the high degree of differentiation that existed in advertised offerings. Members of the research team, however, believed the supposed difficulties of predicting the price competitors would advertise were being exaggerated. Earlier tests for the existence of Cournot reaction curves revealed, in the short run at least, little change over time in the price of advertised products. To resolve the issue, a more detailed study of the nature, frequency, and pattern of change in the price of advertised items was conducted.

Chain-store advertisements appearing in the Wednesday *Bulletin* during a four-week period in May and June of 1961 were analyzed. The prices of all items advertised more than once by each chain during that period were recorded, and the extent of any price change determined. Some attention was also given to price variability over a longer period of time. If the sample chosen was a representative one—and there is no reason to believe it is not—overwhelming empirical support was provided for the position that little change occurs in the price of advertised items.

1. In the short run (one month), the prices on over four fifths (81%) of the items advertised do not change at all. Variations in the prices of the few items that do change will fall within the range 1–10 cents; the average price change being 4.6 cents, and the median price change being 2.5 cents.
2. In the short run, almost four fifths of the few items subject to price changes will be meats, fish, dairy products, fresh fruits and vegetables, and soaps. Other types of goods, e.g., canned fruits and vegetables, cereals, and beverages have almost no incidence of advertised price change.
3. In the long run (eight months), prices fluctuate more. However, this fluctuation is only significant in the case of those few foods which account for most of the short-run changes in price. On over half of the items, price did not change more than 1.6 cents over the eight-month period.
4. On the basis of previously advertised prices, over 80% of the prices of items to appear in forthcoming advertising can be predicted to remain constant. Knowing that changes occur among certain foods, such as meats, fish, soaps, etc., and with knowledge of wholesale price trends, it seems reasonable that over 90% of the prices of items to appear in forthcoming advertising can be predicted within ± 1 cent.

Availability of Items at the Advertised Price

The desirability of measuring any discrepancy that might exist between actual and advertised prices also became evident at this time. To obtain information on that point and on the availability of advertised items, a store audit was conducted. The thirty-two stores audited were chosen on the basis of simple random sampling without replacement. Each chain was represented by eight store checks. The study was conducted over the four-week period of January 18, 1962, to February 9, 1962. One store within Philadelphia and one suburban store of each chain was inspected. The four "city" stores were audited concurrently as were the four suburban stores. The weather was such that trucks with supplies could reach the stores, and no other unusual conditions were apparent.

Audits were also made during the summer and fall of 1962. Although the later audits were designed with a somewhat different problem in mind—the cost and complexity of changing prices as a promotional device—information on the availability of advertised items at advertised prices was collected. Consequently, the results of all three examinations are presented in Tables 2 and 3.

The results in Tables 2 and 3 reveal that administering price changes to further promotional objectives is a difficult task. For a variety of rea-

TABLE 2

PERCENT OF ADVERTISED ITEMS NOT ON THE SHELF

Chain Store	Audit I June–Feb., 1962	Audit II July, 1962	Audit III September, 1962
Acme	13.3	6.2	8.6
A & P	10.8	6.0	13.5
Food Fair	7.0	4.2	3.5
Penn Fruit	5.1	4.1	5.4

TABLE 3

PERCENT OF ADVERTISED ITEMS AVAILABLE AT OTHER THAN ADVERTISED PRICE

Chain Store	Audit I June–Feb., 1962	Audit II July, 1962	Audit III September, 1962
Acme	4.4	7.5	9.9
A & P	3.8	2.7	5.5
Food Fair	5.6	12.5	16.3
Penn Fruit	4.0	5.5	15.5

sons, the audits did not reliably measure the relative likelihood of advertised items being correctly priced in the four chains. The following were among the most noteworthy findings of the initial audit and the partial replications:

1. Stores located in Philadelphia were less likely to have advertised items in stock than suburban supermarkets. This fact was attributed to the smaller size and the more limited shelf space of city stores. The exception in this case appeared to prove the rule. Penn Fruit is a relatively new major factor in the market with a majority of large, recently constructed city and suburban stores, equally likely to carry an advertised item.

2. Penn Fruit and Food Fair often do *not* change prices on containers when "6 for" or "4 for" quantity discount specials are offered. Instead, they may indicate the offer on cardboard posters or on the shelf itself. Also, or alternately, those working at check-out counters receive written indication of sale prices. A small number of purchases were made to determine the amount consumers would be charged when advertised and container price differed. In a small, and perhaps unrepresentative, sample, exactly one half of the items were charged at the price marked on the container.

3. The prices advertised will be what the consumer actually pays for merchandise at least 90% of the time. When advertised items are available at other than advertised prices, most of the difference will be at the expense of the consumer. The reasons why this is so were not discovered. Soaps accounted for a large percentage of the items with shelf prices

higher than advertised prices. The frequency of advertised price reductions for this commodity probably explains the large number of discrepancies. Soaps, meats, and frozen foods were the advertised items most often missing from the shelves. These three classes of foods accounted for over one half of the total number of unavailable advertised items.

The Executive Interview Program

Efforts at statistical analysis were supplemented by twenty interviews intended to reveal the policies that underlie competitive behavior. Three of the four chains active in Philadelphia allowed their executives to be queried. Also interviewed were past employees of the fourth chain, representatives of the two major newspapers, and officials of the largest voluntary chain—Thriftway—and the most important retailer owned co-operative—Frankford Stores. Those questioned were assured that their comments on internal operations and competitive behavior would be treated as confidential. The following summary of relevant information obtained from the interviews has been prepared with this pledge in mind:

1. Respondents differed greatly in their professed ability to predict the items to be advertised and the prices to be charged by competitors. As was mentioned earlier, some executives maintained that while the items to be advertised could be predicted, the prices could not. Diverse answers were obtained when respondents were asked how advance information on the prices and items to be advertised by competitors would affect firm policy. The most frequent response was that the majority of items would be disregarded but a special attempt made to embarrass rivals by underpricing them on advertised specials. It was believed, however, that cutting price to match or undersell competitors when one's own supply of merchandise was inadequate would alienate many customers.

2. When pressed, most executives admitted that their chains pursued a policy of deliberately differentiating advertised offerings. The reason most frequently advanced for such a policy was the previously mentioned problem of price prediction and the difficulty of obtaining adequate supplies of items featured by competitors. One high-ranking chain-store official maintained that he was too busy running his own operation to worry about the advertised offerings of his rivals. Executives employed by those rivals, however, insisted with equal vehemence that the chain in question consistently followed a policy of conscious differentiation in the selection of advertised items.

3. Some respondents reported that they could predict how the sale of featured items would be affected by price cuts of differing magnitude. By doing so, they were, in effect, maintaining that they knew the shape of the demand curve for such items over the range of prices most likely to be charged. Occasionally, it was claimed that the "cost" of a particular advertisement could be determined since both the gross margin per unit

that would be sacrificed and the increase in sales of advertised items that would result were known.

4. A & P was viewed by the trade as the unchallenged price leader in Philadelphia even though Acme's share of market was somewhat larger. The interviews provided additional support for the conclusions reached in another study of chain-store pricing.

> A & P is generally regarded as the price leader—constantly exacting a downward pressure on the structure of retail prices in those areas where it operates. The company does not, however, assume the usual responsibilities of a price leader in initiating short-term upward or downward revisions in specific product areas.[5]

5. Those interviewed disagreed as to the intensity of competition that existed among food chains active in the area. Some respondents argued that a condition of overstoring and the fact that three of the four chains were headquartered in the city made the area especially competitive. Others maintained that while Philadelphia was a low-priced market, it was not terribly competitive when compared to such areas as northern New Jersey where A & P's position as price leader was being challenged.

6. Interviewers were frequently cautioned that external considerations cannot be ignored in studying the Philadelphia market. A & P's nationwide strength was repeatedly cited as a factor explaining its ability to serve as price leader. Also, the intensity of competition in the area was allegedly affected by the rate at which the Philadelphia district of A & P was achieving budgeted profit goals and by A & P's fear of being prosecuted for violating antitrust legislation. Changes over time in the profitability of other divisions of chains active in Philadelphia were also reported as having affected the character of competition. One high-level executive emphasized the importance of environmental considerations. Were he and his counterparts to change places, he maintained, the new institutional setting would probably cause the men concerned to follow policies far different from those they are now pursuing.

7. The major advertising medium for food chains in Philadelphia is the Wednesday *Bulletin*. This newspaper will not allow advertised prices to be changed in subsequent editions when the first edition reveals that a firm is being underpriced by rivals. There is time, however, for adjustments to be made in advertisements scheduled to appear in the Thursday *Inquirer*. Often, executives employed by the same chain gave contradictory answers when asked whether *Inquirer* advertising would be altered when the company was underpriced in the Wednesday *Bulletin*. These contradictory replies led to an empirical investigation of the point in a subsequent stage of the project.

8. Marked differences of opinion were expressed as to the effective-

---

[5] A. D. H. Kaplan, Joel B. Dirlam, and Robert P. Lanzillotti, *Pricing in Big Business* (Washington, D.C.: Brookings Institution, 1958), p. 183.

ness of a mock advertisement prepared by the research team. Also revealed was the fact that while the chains advertise each week, the effort devoted to making advertisements "strong"—i.e., especially appealing—differed greatly. For example, cutting price sharply to made advertisements appearing during the summer months particularly attractive was not economically justified. Regular customers not on vacation would come to the store in any case. The purchase of other items by the reduced number of "floaters" still in the city would not compensate for the loss in gross margin of advertised specials. A tendency to make advertisements timed to appear during bimonthly pay periods especially "strong" was also noted.

9. Investigation of site location policies revealed only one clear-cut illustration of preclusive action. To prevent a rival from obtaining a choice location, one chain built supermarkets at opposite ends of the same shopping center. Each chain, however, will purchase and hold sites in areas where a rapid growth in population is expected but a store could not yet be profitably operated. (Although the interviews did not reveal that Penn Fruit was engaging in the preclusive purchasing of sites, financial difficulties recently encountered by this chain have been attributed, in part at least, to such a policy.)

10. Promotional allowances offered by manufacturers were revealed to have considerable influence on advertising policies and net profits. Items on which such allowances were offered were more likely to be advertised in the *Inquirer* than in the *Bulletin*. Only the name and price of most of the products concerned are mentioned. Such listings are buried in what was appropriately called the "obituary" section of the advertisement. The availability of promotional allowances and the special efforts made by manufacturers to have the chains "tie in" with national magazine advertising were often cited as the factors underlying the limited degree of item overlap revealed by empirical studies.

The Policy Stance Matrix

Analysis of the executive interviews revealed the desirability of developing a policy stance matrix.[6] Decisions as to the prices a firm will charge, the merchandise it will stock, the manner in which it will advertise, the size and location of the stores it will build, and, finally, the financial objectives it will pursue are not made in a vacuum. Examination of the competitive tactics employed by the various chains indicated that meaningful differences existed in advertising, pricing, merchandising, locational, and financial policies. Little information was available, however, on either the strategic policies governing the actions of the respective chains in each of these areas or on the specific policies being pursued.

---

[6] The concept of the policy stance matrix was a contribution to the study of Dr. George Fisk, a Wharton School Marketing Department faculty member.

The matrix presented in Figure 3 was designed as a representation of the task yet to be performed. Because the matrix was an "after-the-fact" refinement, the executive interviews and previously conducted empirical studies were of only limited value in providing the desired information. In the third stage of the project, however, a major effort would be made to "fill in" the empty cells of this matrix.

FIGURE 3

The Policy Stance Matrix

Company	*Price*	*Assortment*	*Advertising and Image*	*Location and Capacity*	*Financing*
A & P					
Acme					
Food Fair					
Penn Fruit......					
Thriftway					

Competitive Dimension

The Summary Statement of Findings [7]

In a published discussion of the research team's conclusions at this point in the study, the following propositions were set forth:

1. Competition among supermarket chains in a metropolitan area does not conform very closely to any of the standard models for competition among the few such as oligopoly or monopolistic competition. There is some evidence of oligopolistic interaction but only on a fraction of one per cent of the thousands of items carried. Monopolistic competition, to the extent that it appears to be present, is reflected in ways that are peculiar to retailing rather than by product differentiation, as in competition among manufacturers.

2. Both oligopoly and monopolistic competition fail as general models for the interpretation of competition among large grocery retailers. The system of grocery retailing could not support the administrative costs and uncertainties of competitive behavior which conformed fully to either model. Among the thousands of items sold, an individual item will seldom justify the unrestrained warfare of oligopolistic interaction or the effort required to capitalize on the limited opportunities for product differentation.

3. The tentative conclusion is that chain executives could predict the content of competitive advertising with considerable reliability but are probably not making any systematic efforts to do so. Prediction is not worth the trouble unless there is some systematic pattern of response to be guided by these predictions. The apparent failure to make use of

---

[7] This entire section is drawn from Wroe Alderson, "Administered Prices and Retail Grocery Advertising," *Journal of Advertising Research*, Vol. 3, (March, 1963), pp. 1–5.

readily available methods of prediction is one of several indications that there is no deep sense of urgency to meet the price offers of a competitor or to make unique offers of one's own.

4. With respect to advertised prices, the advertiser does not appear to concern himself directly with supply and demand. Instead he is weighing the relative advantage and cost of various techniques for creating a reputation for satisfactory prices. If it could be assumed that he has a specified goal as to acceptance of prices by consumers, then he may be said to be attempting to minimize the cost of appearing competitive.

5. The conviction still stands that the search for differential advantage is central to the competition of large retailers or any other large organization. Further development of the concept of administered prices seems to offer the best hope of interpreting some of the peculiar variations in the competitive behavior of these chains: . . . the concept . . . will lead to more fruitful questions about promotional pricing in retailing than the theories of oligopoly or monopolistic competition. . . . Promotional pricing does not comprise the whole range of price policy problems but it should be possible to deal with all aspects of price policy within the framework of administered prices.

The term "promotional pricing" was introduced to describe the various methods employed by supermarkets in using price as a promotional tool. These methods include advertising a product at its regular price, cutting prices sharply on featured items or moderately "across the board," cornering supply and offering a desired item at a price competitors cannot match without running out of merchandise, and, finally, offering a special coupon or trading stamp. An attempt was then made to explain the promotional pricing strategy of the competing chains in light of the administrative costs of the promotional devices they had employed. Finally, a study of the relative cost and effectiveness of the various types of promotional effort was advocated.

STAGE III—PROMOTIONAL PRICING AS THE FOCUS OF ATTENTION

Although earlier efforts pointed up many areas deserving of further examination, promotional pricing was the topic most intensively investigated in the project's as yet uncompleted third stage. Additional financial support for the desired study of the relative effectiveness of the various types of promotional effort was sought and obtained. The scope of this new research project is outlined below in some detail. First, however, attempts to provide the information necessary to complete the policy stance matrix are discussed. Even these efforts, however, focused on promotional pricing in that the areas most intensively explored were advertising and pricing.

Empirical Studies of Promotional Pricing Patterns [8]

The investigations carried on at this time to determine competitive strategies in the areas of pricing and advertising have been discussed elsewhere at considerable length.[9] In summary, five aspects of promotional pricing were studied: (1) the extent to which the various types of promotional pricing are used by Philadelphia food chains; (2) the frequency with which prices differ for items advertised by two or more rivals and featured by at least one of them in the Wednesday *Bulletin;* (3) the degree of competitive reaction occurring when such differences in price exist; (4) the ability of a novice to predict the feature items to be advertised by rival chains; and (5) the prices charged by the four chains in the store for national brand and "similar" items advertised by at least one of them. The most significant findings of these five studies can be summarized as follows:

1. As far as promotional pricing patterns are concerned, A & P relied heavily on bold print straight price offers of feature items and long reminder lists of items priced at normal shelf prices. Acme also listed a large number of shelf-priced items, but combined coupon offers, tie-in, and particularly Green Stamp promotion with its feature offers. Food Fair and Penn Fruit offered considerably fewer items per page of advertising and ran much larger percentages of their offer as special weekly sales events and quantity or price discount promotions.

2. Nearly 60% of the items advertised by two chains and featured by at least one of them were priced the same or were not comparable because of some differentiation in units of issue or in packaging. A & P prices differed from those of competitors on 46 of the 110 times it advertised the same item. On 35 of these 46 occasions, the rival chain offered the merchandise at the lower advertised price. Table 7 summarizes in greater detail the results of the study of the relative prices of feature items advertised in common.

3. When competitive reaction to being underpriced on items advertised by more than one firm was examined, A & P showed the greatest concern. On 19 occasions, the underbid item was dropped from A & P's Thursday *Inquirer* advertisement and its price left unchanged in the store. On seven occasions, A & P met the rival's lower *Bulletin* offering in the *Inquirer* the following day. A & P thus reacted 26 of the 35 times it was underpriced. In contrast, Acme was relatively incognizant of or unconcerned with being underbid. This firm dropped only one item from the following day's *Inquirer* and made no adjustment on the advertised price of eight other items. Food Fair and Penn Fruit each reacted on eight of the 15 and 12 occasions, respectively, they were underbid. Four of these eight times, each chain met the lower price in the Thursday *Inquirer;*

---

[8] This section is based upon research findings reported in Lawrence F. Nein, "How Do Chain Grocers Promotional Pricing Patterns in Advertising Relate to Their Competitive Postures in the Philadelphia Market?" (Unpublished Master's Thesis, Wharton School, University of Pennsylvania, 1963).

[9] George Fisk, Lawrence F. Nein, and Stanley J. Shapiro, "Promotional Price Rivalry among Philadelphia Area Food Chains," *Journal of Advertising Research* (forthcoming).

on the other four occasions, they dropped the underpriced item from their *Inquirer* advertisement.

4. When attempts were made to predict the feature items that would be advertised in a given week, primary reliance was placed on an examination of features appearing the corresponding week of the prior year. This method allowed the researcher to predict over a 12-week period, 9 out of 24, or 37.5%, of the leader features that would be advertised by A & P. For Acme, the corresponding figures were 11 out of 39 features, or 28%; for Food Fair, 9 out of 32 items, or 28%; and for Penn Fruit, 4 out of 38 items, or only 10%. These results cast some doubt on an assumption made in an earlier stage of the project—that A & P advertising was no easier or harder to predict than that of other chains.

5. When store prices of items advertised by at least one chain were audited, each competitor was revealed as charging the same price as its rivals between 60% and 65% of the time. A & P was the only chain that underpriced rivals more frequently than it was underpriced by them. When total differences in cost of items priced either higher or lower than competitors are considered, only for Acme and A & P do the savings on items priced lower than competitors exceed the premium paid on comparable items priced higher. An analysis by each of 12 subclasses of food items revealed results generally consistent with the summary figures. The most noticeable exception was Food Fair's apparent determination not to be underpriced on meats. More detailed information on aggregate price differences is presented in Table 5.

TABLE 4

RESULTS OF STUDY OF RELATIVE PRICES OF FEATURE ITEMS ADVERTISED IN COMMON
An Aggregate Comparison of Prices of All Feature Items Advertised in Common between Each Chain Grocer and *All* Other Chain Grocers in the Same *Bulletin* Issue, Accumulated from Chain Advertisements Placed in Twelve Wednesday *Bulletin* Issues over the Period September 3 through November 26, 1962

	Total Advertised Features Common with Three Other Chains *	Total Other Chains' Advertised Features Common	Price Comparison Others' Advertised Features Common		
			S	L	H
A & P	90	110	64	11	35
Acme	62	83	52	22	9
Food Fair	62	81	41	25	15
Penn Fruit	62	80	51	17	12

* "Total Advertised Features Common with Three Other Chains" column total is necessarily less than "Total Other Chains' Advertised Features Common" column total, due to the occurrence of items common to more than two chains' advertisements.

Nonprice Competition and the Policy Stance Matrix [10]

The manner in which Philadelphia's four major food chains competed on a nonprice basis was also examined. This undertaking focused on com-

[10] The source document for this section is Richard P. Ossen, "Merchandise Differentiation and Service Rivalry among Major Philadelphia Food Chains" (Unpublished Master's Thesis, Wharton School, University of Pennsylvania, 1963).

TABLE 5

DETAILED INFORMATION ON AGGREGATE PRICE DIFFERENCES
Comparison of Shelf Prices of Chain Grocers' National Brand and Similar Items,
Aggregate of Twelve Selected Food Categories, Ten Weekly Store Audits, September
17 through November 19, 1962

Chain	Prices Compared to All Other Chains No. of Items			Total Price Difference		Average Price Difference per Item	
	Same	Higher	Lower	Higher	Lower	Higher	Lower
A & P	915	179	326	$7.22	$11.02	$.0403	$.0335
Acme	901	246	243	8.16	8.66	.0331	.0356
Food Fair	818	286	252	11.47	9.63	.0401	.0382
Penn Fruit ...	898	283	173	8.53	6.13	.0301	.0354

petitive interaction with regard to enterprise and merchandise differentiation and service rivalry. The results of the investigation were somewhat
disappointing in that very little of the information needed to complete the
policy stance matrix was obtained. A judgment sample provided data on
the type of services being offered by the various chains. Also, information
was gathered on new product selection procedures, the methods used to
determine the stock a given supermarket would carry, and, finally, the
autonomy and attitudes of store managers. Especially noteworthy was
the frequency with which the views and presumably the actions of managers differed markedly from company attitudes and policies as expressed
by home office representatives. Nonetheless, the attempt to discover governing policies in the areas of enterprise, merchandise, and service differentiation was not successful. Sharp differences in practice were known to
exist in areas where executive interviews revealed an alleged similarity in
the policies being pursued and the goals being sought.

The failure to obtain reliable information may have been due to shortcomings of the interviewer or of the questionnaire he employed. Alternately, the inability or the unwillingness of those interviewed to convey
accurate information may have been at fault. Finally, development of a
policy stance matrix assumes the existence of clearly formulated strategies.
It may well be that such an assumption is unfounded. Whatever the reason, the only difference in policy revealed by this study concerned the
impact on prices and profits when services were added. Representatives
of two chains doubted that new services made a significant contribution
to volume. Consequently, the cost of such services was reportedly covered
either by higher prices or reduced profit margins. In sharp contrast,
executives of the two remaining chains stated that services which are not
expected to contribute to profits will not be added by their firms. Also,
new services that neither increase volume nor cover their cost are, they
maintained, discontinued.

Towards an Optimal Promotional Mix for Food Chains

The desirability of examining the benefits and costs associated with the various forms of promotional pricing has previously been discussed. Such a study is soon to be undertaken in the hope that a meaningful contribution can be made to increasing the effectiveness and reducing the cost of promotion. Emphasis will first be placed on measuring the relative impact on the consumer of alternate forms of promotion employed under a variety of circumstances. The conversion of such measures into data to guide business policy by gathering information on the costs associated with each promotional device is considered a subsequent objective, albeit one to be kept in mind in designing the initial effort. Although the behavior of consumers in only a limited number of market areas will be investigated, the ultimate objective is a methodology of broad applicability.

The study will examine two related but nevertheless distinct aspects of consumer response to promotional stimuli:

1. *The housewife's perception of the various promotional activities of her usual food chain as well as of competitive firms.* In this respect, such factors as halo effects, images, and perceptual thresholds will be considered.

2. *The relative effectiveness of the various types of promotional activity, once they are perceived.* Effectiveness would be determined by measuring the extent to which departures from normal behavior can be induced by systematic variation of the different types of possible promotion.

Three basic research tools will be used to obtain information from consumers:

1. Shopping games designed to reveal the effect on hypothetical behavior of various promotional inducements.
2. Interviews to determine stated consumer preferences between promotional alternatives, and
3. Observations of actual shopping behavior and of how such behavior was affected by a variety of deals and special offers.

The consumer is thus the focus of attention, and the research tools to be employed can be described easily enough. The success of the entire project, however, will depend on the ability to design an experimental program providing quantifiable measures of relative efficiency. For this reason, the research project will be somewhat atypical. A larger percentage than usual of available funds will be expended on the design of experiments and in the analysis of the strengths and weaknesses of the experimental program.

Looking Backward—and Forward

The findings and the frustrations of three years of research have been outlined at length. Consequently, a detailed summary of past successes and failures does not appear in order. The authors hope, rather, to benefit from an independent appraisal made by students of retailing interested in similar problems. Needless to say, development of the desired theory of retail competition has proven to be an even more difficult task than was originally expected. Nevertheless, refinement of the concept of "promotional pricing"—itself a modification of the more familiar notion of administered pricing—seems to hold great promise. The feasibility of measuring the relative effectiveness of the various forms of promotional pricing remains to be determined.

In one respect, at least, this research project has demonstrated its kinship to the vast majority of similar efforts. It raises as many questions as it answers and points up a variety of topics deserving of additional study. An agenda for basic research in retailing was formulated at the end of the first stage of the project. Many of the recommended studies were subsequently conducted, however, and more recent experience has indicated other areas deserving of investigation. A revised program for basic research in retailing might well include the following:

1. A social and managerial appraisal of the locational aspects of food-chain competition.
2. A study of the authority and autonomy, in theory and in fact, of branch-store managers and regional executives.
3. The design of a retailing information system which would provide real time (current) rather than historical data on changing market conditions and the actions of competitors.
4. The development of measures which would indicate the relative competitiveness of market areas and the effect on competition of proposed mergers.
5. An examination of the influence of consumer store images, government policies, and supplier practices on the efforts of food chains to establish a measure of differential advantage.

The fact that an interest in retailing theory has pointed up the need for more information on the operating problems of business executives should not be surprising. Any aspect of marketing theory must serve two masters. It should simplify the task of those concerned primarily with obtaining some understanding of the myriad of events occurring in the marketplace. It must also, however, provide a broader framework within which marketing practitioners can deal with problems they encounter in their day-to-day operations.

14. MARKET STRUCTURES AND FUNCTIONS IN AGRICULTURAL CONTROL PROGRAMS

Henry B. Arthur

THEORY in economics has always given a very eminent place to the phenomenon of the market. In contrast, the concept of *marketing* has been developed to describe a highly sophisticated art or activity that has not become more than an incidental element in economic theory, never fully treated, sometimes almost unrecognized.

Somehow the theorists have bypassed marketing as a dynamic, generative force in economics. They have not ignored the existence of marketing as a business practice or as a fact of life. However, it is usually treated by the economic theorist as a "special case," an incidental in the general theory of imperfect competition.

In order to delineate between the two concepts, markets and marketing —one a noun, the other a verb—one must comment on several terms in a way that may risk doing some violence to conventional definitions. It is not intended to depart from or reject existing definitions, although several points need to be emphasized in a way that is scarcely mentioned in most definitions I have seen. In marketing literature there is a heavy burden of multiple meanings for "markets," "market functions," "market structure," "market behavior," "market performance," and, of course, the activity called "marketing." Sometimes they are ambiguous; sometimes contradictory. The meanings we will use have been selected as appropriate for our particular purpose.

1. Markets

Markets can be defined broadly enough to embrace all of those relationships between firms or individuals whereby necessary inputs of goods and services are brought together to make their contributions toward the emergence and sale of a final end product.[1] In other words, markets provide linkages, and in each case they perform a function relevant to the end purpose at hand—a finished product delivered to an ultimate customer. Such relationships or linkages are primarily "vertical." They bring the goods and services one step nearer to the consumer.

Markets permit the production process to be accomplished in separate and independent stages. At each stage services are performed and value is added. The succession of market transactions that occur as goods move from basic resources toward the consumer theoretically presents us with a succession of appraisals of values added as the stream of goods progresses from stage to stage. These cumulative appraisals give us a constant linkage between the uses to which we put our resources and the ultimate values which the market system expects the final consumer transaction to validate.

In contrast, government-controlled markets (or "State Marketing" as in the Communist countries) often omit this vital check on "discounted" or expected consumer evaluation, and rely most heavily upon cumulative costs or arbitrary allocations. Having said this, we should recognize that almost everywhere, and at practically all stages, the government is a part of the market structure of today's world of commerce, and often a major factor in its transactions.

Markets as they operate, embrace relationships that are *interpersonal* or *interfirm*.[2] These interfirm relationships have, as we all know, a great many dimensions. The one that is likely to come first to mind is the bargaining relationship between a buyer and a seller. Of course, this was the classic concept of marketing in the early days—the bringing together of a buyer and a seller and the "bargaining out" of the terms of a transaction. Henry H. Bakken in his paper before the Futures Trading Seminar in 1959[3] cited, in a most interesting way, the historical development of various marketing arrangements and the historical evolution of the systems and rules which made it possible for markets to evolve from crude gift-giving and barter to extremely refined contract markets and futures trading. The old principles of *caveat emptor* were modified. Orderly procedures and rules were developed to make it possible to introduce specifications in place of spot inspection and delivery.

Bargaining, while perhaps still among the most important relationships that characterize a market, has been vastly modified, sometimes beyond

---

[1] There is a meaning for the word "market" which is unduly restrictive for our purpose—that which is equivalent to a description of the final buyers and their buying habits, as in the case of "the market for television sets" or for cosmetics. We are likely to be using the word in this sense when we speak of being "market-oriented." Traditionally, and in the true economic sense, markets embrace both buyers and sellers and the factors which both take into account.

[2] The conduct of relationships *within* a firm may have analogies to markets and marketing but they are not regarded as a part of our field.

[3] Futures Trading Seminar (Madison, Wis.: Mimir Publishers, Inc., 1960), Vol. I.

recognition. Products have been developed and differentiated to a point where they bewilder consumers (and indeed even the professional industrial buyer). In the case of many staple agricultural products and basic raw materials, the process of classification and grading has minutely divided the total supply on the basis of use categories and by variations in quality, service, and terms of sale. As a result of these and other changes, a consumer today seldom finds himself haggling over a trade. He is confronted with numerous alternatives of brand names, qualities, sizes—and of course competing stores—where he normally makes his selections without personal negotiation to resolve the differences between himself and the seller. At the point of purchase the choice is likely to be unilateral, not a matter of give and take between two parties.

We have mentioned two kinds of market relationships—bargaining and the exercise of choice. There are many others [4] which are interrelated with these two. However, we can regard the other arrangements as being subordinate to the essential features of bargaining and the making of choices. In fact, when we begin to look at market structures we find that most of the arrangements we encounter are devices that have been developed in our more or less civilized world for the purpose of making it more convenient for the bargainer or chooser himself to be more intelligent or better informed.

The bargaining, the making of choices, and the transaction, are at the focus of the market. The broader market area, or the scope *of the market, is the entire area where practical alternatives exist and are given consideration in the process of arriving at a final choice.*

A market has a "focus" and a "scope" for you or me as an individual in the purchase of a new car or a can of tomatoes. But "focus" and "scope" have a more conventional meaning when we think of markets with broader participation of both buyers and sellers. Hence we can use as our definition that *a market (micro) is the relevant environment of a particular transaction; a market (macro) is a conglomerate environment embracing many somewhat similar transactions.* Transactions are the definitive things in either case; the environments can be almost as varied as life itself.

2. Market Functions

Whether it is accomplished through bargaining or unilateral choice, a transaction normally provides for the performance of economic services or the transfer of title to goods. The transaction, and what it provides for, is of course the prime function of a market. It facilitates exchange. However, the functions of a market go far beyond the transaction. Since the terms of a transaction almost always include a price, the market functions include the transmitting of incentives and rewards—the signals that guide our economic production and resource allocation. The market provides

---

[4] For example, long-term contracts, auctions, communications through missionary salesmen or advertising.

access to goods and services on terms that make each buyer equivalent to the "most favored buyer" and each seller to the "most favored seller," assuming competitive conditions exist.

These are the bare fundamentals of market functions.

I like to think of the word "function" as meaning the "job to be done." The job existed before the market performed its function. If a market fails to accomplish one or more of its necessary or traditional functions, then some other arrangement has to be found to fill the gap.

Markets have purposes to accomplish. They also have consequences, some of which may be unrelated to traditional purposes, while others may serve one purpose and thwart another, or introduce new complications in its accomplishment. This is particularly true in instances where innovations such as government-control programs are introduced.

3. Market Structures

Market functions are performed in a particular way largely because of the market structure which exists. We have defined market structures as those parts of the market environment that comprise the *preexisting "institutions" and arrangements* for implementing market relationships.[5] Institutions include entities such as marketplaces, but they also include a great deal more. Market news services can be regarded as institutional parts of a market structure. The same is true of price catalogs, rate books, and the like. All kinds of legal rules defining eligibility or restraints on trading would be a part of the institutional structure. Market structures also include the people who do the trading, but not their actual trading activities.

Thus, market structures embrace the rules, the information systems, indeed all the arrangements for integrating the needed resource inputs in a vertical commodity or industrial complex. They include arrangements to accommodate the peculiarities of the commodity itself—its degree of standardization, its perishability, or its assorted sources and uses. But, they exclude the actual negotiations and the decisions reached.

Within the terms as we are defining them, we could think of a "micro" market structure for a single transaction, even an isolated one. Competition enters into this "single transaction" kind of market structure whenever a buyer or a seller has the opportunity to choose another bargaining partner or another product or service. When we look backward from a consummated transaction, we find that competition represents the series of opportunities, whether accepted or rejected, which were open to the buyer or to the seller. The actual buyer and seller were the successful competitors.

Most authorities would say that a market does not exist unless there is a large mass of transactions and unless considerable numbers of buyers

---

[5] For example, market structures preexist in the sense of preceding, in time and n acceptance by the bargaining parties, the specific transaction.

and sellers assemble to negotiate their trades. In contrast, I am suggesting that such markets represent conglomerations of individual transactions each one of which may be unique in terms of the set of market considerations that surrounded that particular transaction. When we consider many transactions, we tend to obscure widely diverse sets of considerations that are taken into account by individual buyers and sellers. The mass phenomenon of the market creates an often false impression of uniformity and continuity; it is like an average, which obscures the diversity of the items entering it. For some individual transactions the considerations taken into account by a single buyer or seller may be few and simple; for others they may reach far afield. Nevertheless, these considerations, varying from one individual transaction to another, are all relevant to the composite environment that makes up the broader market structure.

In this sense, the conventional market, or marketplace, is very seldom a completely closed system. There are almost always opportunities to take advantage of a wider area or of different offers outside the market system being considered. In fact, some of the participants are constantly exploring or moving to other sources or other outlets.

In other words, markets are useful devices for the very reason that they are loosely defined arrangements. This is one of the basic dilemmas that is faced by anyone who tries to regulate markets. There is a tendency to assume that a market structure is a closed system within which all kinds of manipulation or exploitation can occur without any outside recourse for those who are in the market. The fact of the matter is that both buyers and sellers usually have a great many additional choices by turning beyond the restricted limits of the market being considered, and therefore the degree of flexibility in our market system greatly exceeds that which is assumed by most regulators.

4. Market Behavior and Market Performance [6]

The terms "market behavior" and "market performance" are sometimes thought of as interchangeable terms. However, a distinction may be made between a factual report of what happens or has happened—market behavior—and an analytical statement of the degree to which a market accomplishes its functions—market performance.

5. Marketing

The purpose of the present discussion is not to define the term "marketing"; instead, it will suffice to point out that the term as used in the title of this book refers to a field of human or business activity usually looked upon from the viewpoint of a seller and his efforts to generate or

---

[6] The term "market conduct" is sometimes used interchangeably with one or the other of these terms.

improve sales.[7] However, marketing has a great deal to do with markets, even though the orientation is very different. The environment of the marketing executive can in large part be described in terms of a market structure; his activities involve participation in most of the elementary functions of markets, as well as the specialized considerations of product development, advertising, managing a sales force, etc. One of the distinctions between the two terms may be illustrated if we characterize marketing as the generating of new forces and new market structures, whereas the market resolves forces already in operation in a preexisting structure.

GOVERNMENTAL ACTIVITIES AND "FREE MARKETS"

What has been said is enough to illustrate the breadth of market structures and to establish the terms on which government control activities become a part of these structures. Mr. William McChesney Martin, chairman of the Federal Reserve Board, said in his commencement address at Harvard in June, 1962: "The Government is deeply involved in the conduct of our economy and it could not extricate itself altogether even if it were minded to do so."

The distinctions which have been made between markets and market structures give us at least a small handhold for grappling with the question of the impact of government control programs. The acceptance of government authority in prescribing and defining *parts* of the market structure is long standing and noncontroversial. One of the easiest ways of illustrating this acceptance is to consider the number of inspectors, of market reporters, of court actions to enforce contracts, of registrations, licenses, and the like which we encounter every day.

All of us understand that the term "free markets" does not mean freedom from all restrictions. Most markets, even without government intervention of any formal sort, would be subject to innumerable rules and customs. The two elements of freedom that seem to be most significantly present in "free markets" are *freedom of pricing* and *freedom of access*.

The institutions and arrangements that make up a market structure are sometimes restrictive, sometimes facilitative. It is not always easy to distinguish between the two.

Rules and customs that would generally be acknowledged as facilitating trade include those relating to such things as:

Honesty in dealing (including the law of property and contract)
Physical facilities and conveniences
Definitions of terms to facilitate mutual understanding
Information services
Trading rules

---

[7] When the author mentioned this meaning of marketing to a homemaker and a department-store executive, they both insisted that, to them, marketing meant "going shopping" or seeking out new merchandise to buy.

Grading (voluntary)
Credit information and facilities
Weights and measures

Some restrictive arrangements are:

Licenses
Entrance fees and qualifications
Tariffs
Quotas
Compulsory or arbitrary classification of sellers and customers
Compulsory arbitration
Preponderance of market power
Patents and other exclusive privileges
Copyrights, brands, etc.

Many trading arrangements are initially entered into on a free basis, but because they involve contracts or commitments covering a substantial period of time they may have a variety of restrictive consequences. Included in this category would be—

Franchises
Dealerships
Options
Restrictive covenants
Requirements contracts
Etc.

It seems fairly safe to affirm that *most* of the activities of government which relate to market structures have over the years had a strong influence toward facilitating trade. Some of the highlights of such influences are seen in the all-important market intelligence provided through government channels. This is not just marketing reporting on things like supply and price. It is market intelligence in very considerable depth. More information is available about our heterogeneous agricultural and agribusiness industries—and it is rendered in a more usable form—than is available for nearly any other comparable sector of the economy.[8] Without government information services, the census, market news service, innumerable special studies, and information from regulatory agencies, agriculture and many other industries as well would be floundering in virtual ignorance.

Market structures include not only information, but access to markets by both buyers and sellers. Here again, government activities in the field of highways, mail services, and various market facilities have opened the channels of trade to much broader participation.

In many other ways the role of government facilitates the functioning of free markets. The existence of orderly procedures relating to general

---

[8] This statement might be challenged by people in other fields, such as money and credit, securities, transportation, or labor, where extensive information is available. However, the information in these fields, while extensive, seldom provides the "depth," the facts and factors underlying supply and demand, that are available for agricultural industries.

honesty, as well as the establishment of generally accepted grades, labeling procedures, and terms of trade, greatly increases the efficiency with which transactions can be accomplished.

None of the last-named procedures is considered restrictive if it leaves room for the voluntary meeting of minds as respects final transactions. In other words, grades need not be mandatory; acceptance of customary terms may be optional. When we move to the next step and shift the role of government to that of regulator issuing orders of "thou shalt" or "thou shalt not," we enter the restrictive area.

In appointing Lester P. Condon as Inspector General in charge of a newly established Office of Internal Audit and Inspection in the United States Department of Agriculture, on June 19, 1962, Secretary of Agriculture Freeman said that "the growing complexities and increasing responsibilities assigned to this Department require that we must continually appraise the effectiveness with which we discharge these responsibilities. The highest possible standards of performance must be maintained at all times. Our internal audit and investigation activities are essential to the accomplishment of these objectives.

"As Inspector General, Mr. Condon will report directly to the Secretary. His duties will include review, appraisal and policy direction of independent internal audit operations in 10 major agencies now carried out by some 700 people."

The reason for Mr. Condon's army of auditors, however, is not chiefly the enforcement functions of the USDA in policing markets. It is safe to say that the major reason for the auditors is the fact that Uncle Sam has moved from the role of referee to that of player in the marketplace. The Commodity Credit Corporation, with its seven to eight billion dollars of assets, is one of the world's largest corporations engaged in commerce. Back of this huge corporate operation are the vast number of agency arrangements, guarantees, contracts, and other types of commitment which involve Mr. Freeman's department in direct business arrangements with at least several million farmers.[9] Thus the government has had a direct impact upon market structures, not only because it has developed and policed rules of conduct but also because it has become by far the largest participant in several of our most important markets.

The argricultural control programs of the federal government, of course, have many kinds of impacts upon markets. The activities that take the form of referee or facilitator of orderly marketing and the like have been mentioned. We tend to accept most of them as being part of a free-market system. The same is true of other government activities such as antitrust laws. These are intended to prevent participants from disrupt-

---

[9] Allotments in 1960–61 have been listed as numbering roughly 100,000 for peanuts, 500,000 for tobacco, over 900,000 for cotton, and between 1,500,000 and 2,000,000 each for corn and wheat.

ing orderly market structures, but they do not engage the government as a trader or participant in the transactions of the market.

AGRICULTURAL CONTROL PROGRAMS

The agricultural control programs of the past thirty-five years have helped to make government a major participant, a trader, an active influencer of price levels. Without going into detail, the principal control programs can be classified into five categories:

1. Production controls, acreage quotas, land retirement, and the like are programs designed to direct resource inputs or to limit the supply coming to market, and thus to create scarcity. These controls don't involve the government in actual trading, but they seek to employ the most basic monopolistic device in the book—such control of supply sufficient as to enable prices to be fixed. This of course is done on behalf of the farmers, not to provide any benefit to the government itself.

2. Measures to stimulate or subsidize demand are the corresponding devices on the demand side to be compared with output controls on the supply side. Here the buyer is given the means or inducement to procure more in the regular market channels. Within this category fall stamp plans, advertising and publicity campaigns, and the like. It also includes research programs aimed toward developing new uses for agricultural products (assuming they are successful).

3. Price support purchases and loan programs. These programs make the government a direct trader or the equivalent of one. Generally the primary purpose of government trading is to influence and dominate the price. This is seldom the prime purpose of private traders; if it is, they are likely to be accused of price rigging.

4. As a counterpart of point 3, the government, not being itself a consumer, must dispose of that which it acquires. It must choose between selling, giving away, destroying, or letting its supplies hang over the market. In private trade, many of the practices followed in disposal activities are given names like "dumping," "salvage," or "waste." One disposal channel —resale in the commercial market—is largely foreclosed to the government unless production controls, crop failures, war, or some other catastrophe replaces surplus with shortage, or unless price objectives are modified.

5. Activities affecting access to the market, or permitting and fostering government supervised monopolistic practices.[10] These include nearly all market orders.

What have the several government programs referred to above done to markets and market structure? Can we expect markets to behave in

---

[10] The terms employed in the numbered points are not intended to be prejudicial in any sense; the use of the words "monopolistic," etc., is simply to enable us to compare impacts of these programs with the free-market model.

new and different ways because of them? Will market performance be as effective in accomplishing the functions we normally expect of markets?

1. Production and Acreage Controls

Government control of production and acreage has a more limited impact upon market structures than do most other programs. The control device in this case does not necessarily require the government to enter the commodity market at all. (Usually, of course, production controls have been linked with price supports, but for our purpose they can be treated separately.) Production control is achieved through a contract between the producer and the government, and it is designed to affect the supply coming to market. The market structure for the commodity (excluding the contract by producers to cooperate, which is a new market structure in itself), experiences little change.

The use of the market to give signals that guide production plans is of course sharply modified by the imposition of the quota scheme.

2. Stimulated or Subsidized Demand

At the opposite end of the market stream from the government programs that restrict supplies are those direct measures for building up demand by distributions of purchasing power, stamp plans, advertising programs, and the like. This sort of program does not involve the government as trader, and it may leave market structures almost untouched. Even the present "experimental" food stamp program has not gone beyond the consumer and retailer in the handling of stamps.[11] The degree of interference in the functioning of markets is less than in most other schemes, because the control is introduced at the extreme consumer end of the marketing chain. Dollars quickly replace stamps in the money flow; demand is largely undifferentiated [12] from normal food buying; and the scheme seems to be largely an income bonus to the eligible consumers. Consumers like it (who wouldn't?); dealers can handle it; and demand for food is enhanced to the extent that tax money (a part of which the tax*payer* would have spent for food anyway) is collected by the government and turned over to poor people who may use somewhat more of the money for food. (The percentage of total consumer expendable incomes going for food will no doubt be increased a little under the food stamp plan. There is a question whether, after paying the costs of tax collection, stamp distribution, and administration, we are directing many more dollars into the market for food.) Analyses aimed toward appraising the potential of such programs for enhancing farm income, while inconclu-

---

[11] In contrast, wartime food rationing, a similar device, carried the ration coupons back to *processors* in many cases, and sometimes to producers.

[12] This is an important consideration. The more specifically the food stamp money is restricted or channeled to particular items, the more drastic the impact upon market structures and functions.

sive, suggest that they are a very expensive instrument if this is the sole purpose.

3. Price Support Purchases or Loans

In this category of control measures the government becomes a trader or participant in the market, taking its place along with other traders. The structure is of course affected by the entry of a single preemptive buyer, just as it would be by the entry of a large preemptive private buyer. To the extent that the government can stay on the buying side and not have to resell its supplies, it can affect price.

Private traders tend to deal with this kind of government activity very much as they would with the entry of any other large trader. They can continue to perform most of their individual functions even though a major new price factor is present. They learn to operate in the shadow of the "big guy." They have found ways to deal profitably and to serve their customers even with the government present. They can trade with the government as with anyone else. The functions of the total market are distorted, however, so far as price signals are concerned. With price supports, cotton competes less advantageously with other fibers. Meanwhile, high prices stimulate increased production which is not a reflection of the true demand, and direct output restrictions are usually required.

4. Disposal, Diversion, and Subsidy Programs

Disposal programs are a necessary consequence of prior acquisitions. Their impact upon market structures arises largely from the fact that the government is under great pressure not to have supplies produce their usual impact upon the market. This restriction necessitates special arrangements. In the extreme, the market can be completely circumvented by the destruction of the surplus. Since this is seldom feasible, the supplies usually hang over the market and have to be disposed of in a way that affects commercial channels.

Short of destruction, one of the most frequent procedures is to find diversionary channels where the supplies will not have their usual effect upon the market. Subsidized industrial use of food products is one device. Gifts to those who would not normally be able to purchase is another. Export subsidies have been introduced in many forms, in order to attract trade which would not otherwise be generated. The range of export transactions covers the entire scale from outright gifts to price remissions, from acceptance of inconvertible currency to arbitrary long-term credits.

The impact of the disposal programs upon market structures can vary widely. There have been government statements affirming the intent to use normal commercial channels. Although this has been attained in considerable measure, there is something of an anomaly in the use of normal commercial channels in order to move goods into abnormal outlets. This suggests that market structures are in effect modified substantially. Anyone dealing actively in commodities which come under the Public Law 480 program can testify to the degree of impact. When sales are not based on the high bid, the market structure is surely modified, and sometimes severely warped. The degree of severity depends upon how well the disposal channels are insulated from normal channels of trade.

A government threat to use dumped grain surpluses as a club to induce compliance (called cooperation) with acreage restrictions is an interesting new example of the interplay of controls with market functions. This device could, it appears, force all compliance grain into government hands, leaving noncompliance supplies and government sales to move at prices substantially lower than "support" levels.

5. Market Orders

Market orders usually impose a substantially new set of market structure conditions. Frequently they go beyond what I have defined as market structure and deal directly with *access* and *price*. They may prescribe *who* may trade, *what grades or qualities* may be traded, *what price* may be charged or paid, who shall receive *subsidies* and on what terms. In effect they preempt the most vital of market functions, and may go so far as to fashion their own market structures to accomplish their purposes. A private monopolist employs many of these devices, but we undertake to protect ourselves by our elaborate system for enforcing competition. In market orders this is not our defense; instead, we deliberately create market power and then rely upon a market authority or watchdog to see that market power is not abused.

Market orders may depart from the free or competitive market norm in another way. They may so freeze the price as to make it a part of the market structure—a fixed factor. This inevitably changes the guidelines and signals which lead producers and consumers to adjust output and consumption to keep these two considerations somewhere near in balance. We have thrown away or at least pegged the automatic regulator, and must of necessity replace it with another. Usually this turns out to be an arbitrary authority. Thus we have not only affected the free choices of buyers and sellers in the market. We have also taken on the task of replacing the vast underlying network of self-serving decisions with arbitrary restraints and regulations. This is a big order. The problem is not just a matter of deciding what are the right answers; it also involves getting them carried out. The machinery for doing this is inevitably complex, and we need look no farther than a typical milk market order to learn that resourceful people find loopholes, that conditions constantly change, and that this type of regulation invariably breeds more regulation.

This is not to say that market orders can't be made to work. Some can and some can't. Almost always the complexity of the machinery imposes major supervisory responsibilities. The regulations are usually cumbersome and often lead to inefficiency. Sometimes they place great temptations before the enforcement authorities, either to exploit the regulations for their own profit or to favor their friends. Seven hundred auditors in the USDA may well be an insufficient number.

In summary, we can say that market orders are a device for revamping the market structure. Where they have any substantial effect, they greatly alter the performance of market functions and the role of those in the market.

This brief review of the impact of control programs has distinguished the effect upon market structures according to types of programs which introduce (1) artificial scarcity measures through control of output or resource use, (2) demand stimulating activities, (3) government trading as a preemptive buyer, (4) diversionary disposal of government acquired supplies, and (5) market orders which have the most severe impact on market structures—those intricate fabrics of conditions within which we trade. The government as trader (items 3 and 4) may employ the normal market structure, but the very weight of government trading cannot avoid disturbing the structure as well as pricing and other functions of the market. This is especially true when the government's purpose is so often to preempt or dominate the market. Market structure is least affected when the government itself stays out of markets and applies direct controls to production (item 1) or to the demand and purchasing power of others (item 2).

A CASE OF MUTUAL ADJUSTMENT

Not all market structures are identical, or even similar. They represent the adaptations developed over long periods of time to the peculiar requirements for trading in a particular commodity. The selection of specific devices for accomplishing price or income-raising objectives is very largely governed by the same kinds of factors that brought about the market structure which had historically evolved for the commodity. Therefore, it might have been more appropriate to inquire about "the impact of market structures upon agricultural control programs" than to start, as we did, in reverse. Certainly, agricultural programs have taken their present form in part because of the dictates of the preexisting market structure.

To give an example or two, it is perfectly clear that the possibility of segregating fluid milk from manufacturing milk was a prime consideration in developing use classification, support prices for different classes, and even the practice of pricing by statistical formulas in milk markets.[13]

Or, if this country was not a substantial net importer of sugar, we can

---

[13] See USDA, "Government's Role in Pricing Fluid Milk in the United States," ERS-63.

be sure that a very different kind of sugar program [14] would have developed.

Again, where controls involve the accumulation of surpluses as a part of administering price supports, the product must either be storable or it must somehow be convertible into nonperishable form. Where neither of these possibilities seem practical, ingenuity has been used to find ways of implementing support through indirect means. Perhaps the prime example has been the use of feed grain programs as the primary instrument of avoiding direct controls in the livestock field. If feeds are made scarce, or high in price, the inducements to increase likestock feeding are retarded. In this indirect way livestock markets have managed to escape most of the direct administrative involvement in government farm programs.

The ingenuity with which market structures have been employed in agricultural programs calls for considerable admiration. Many traders have a feeling that the government acts like a bull in a china shop when its programs affect their particular market. Nevertheless, the truth of the matter is that these programs have employed the existing market structures and market arrangements about as fully as they can. Markets *can't be expected* to escape some effect if we realize that the programs themselves exist for the very reason that markets were considered not able to do the desired job (i.e., provide fair prices or adequate incomes).

SOME COMMENTS ON FUTURES MARKETS

Another example of the adjustment of existing market structures in the face of government programs is seen in the interaction of futures markets with the commercial operations of the government. Many of the price support guarantees are in fact future commitments. Repeatedly they have set a practical limit on the range within which futures prices are likely to fluctuate. However, there have been practically no cases wherein futures trading has been outlawed. In fact, futures trading has been vigorous in the recent past, in spite of the fact that the opportunities and the need for futures operations have shifted drastically from one commodity to another.

An organized futures market is unquestionably a part of the market structure for the commodities traded there. Its most important service is to provide an effective time dimension for the market.

The time element is no doubt important in nearly all transactions. Even spot transactions are seldom free of time considerations. The terms of the transaction, including delivery and payment, call for time specification, as do many other trading terms. Past and future trade relations, the

---

[14] See USDA, "Special Study on Sugar," February 14, 1961.

value of reputation or goodwill, are meaningful largely in a time context. When ordinary orders are placed or sales contracts are signed, the importance of the time element becomes even more explicit.

When the span of time is somewhat more extended, however, the futures market can provide very special services. It enables traders to split their commodity transaction into two distinct parts. The futures contract contains a carefully defined set of specifications and terms for a typical or standard transaction, and thus permits the sale (or purchase) of this carefully defined commitment in which the change of price over time is in effect the only variable. The standard futures contract becomes the vehicle for transferring the risks of price change over time. Anyone dealing in actual grain or other products can then negotiate all the other parts of a particular transaction—those relating to such things as location of supplies, quality considerations, blends, packages, shipping routes and arrangements—without reference to a specific dollars and cents price. Rather, the entire transaction is stated in terms of the number of cents over or under the nearby contract price which is used as the "basis contract" for such negotiations.

To the dealer in actual products who normally has a hedged position, a specific commodity sale is expressed in terms of a differential realization, to be compared with the corresponding differential commitment he entered at the time he acquired the product. (The dealer may have bought his grain on a basis of 2 cents per bushel under the futures quotation and later taken a profit by selling on a basis price described as 2 cents over the same futures contract.) He need not concern himself with what has happened to price levels, since someone else (who bought the futures contract the dealer sold) has been carrying the price risk.

The virtual isolation of the time-price factors makes it possible to regard the futures market as a device for opening up an otherwise difficult and restrictive market dimension. The futures market is not just a separate market with its own structure and its own functions; it is a part of the broader market structure which embraces the entire trading in a commodity. The futures market not only broadens the market by providing another trading place, but it makes it possible for market participants— dealers and processors, for instance—to transfer to others the time-price risks. The participants can then concentrate on other factors, such as geography, quality, transportation, customer service, and the like, with comparative freedom from time pressures and risks. In short, the futures market is a market-extender.

These comments on futures are relevant to the main argument of this discussion in view of the similarities between (1) futures trading on organized exchanges, (2) government production control and price support programs, and (3) contract farming or other forms of integration in agricultural industries. All three phenomena—

1. Entail future commitments.
2. Undertake to transfer certain risks from one party to another.
3. Employ the legal device of contractual arrangements.
4. Divide and reassign functions in the vertical production and marketing chain.

It would sound shocking to some politicians to hear that the government is a prime factor in agricultural integration. But consider how many farmers sign contracts which control their planting, grow crops only because of the guaranteed price, secure government guaranteed credit, and store and deliver on government instructions—all this with virtually no recourse to individual bargaining.

As an illustration of integration through risk transfer, the government supports a number of items by giving farmers an open-end offer to take their products at support price levels. There are time limits, delivery conditions, and the like, but the main difference—one which futures markets can't match—is the "heads-you-win, tails-I-lose" feature whereby the seller has a minimum guarantee but can accept a better offer if the price goes up. Many contract farming arrangements fall somewhere between the firm contract of the futures markets and the open option of the support price. They often have floor prices, with a sharing of profits or losses if prices change substantially.

Mr. W. B. Murphy, president of Campbell Soup Company—a strong supporter of contract farming and of what it has done for the producers of many crops—says: "With a sound contract, the grower has a guaranteed price, a guaranteed market, a great incentive to do a good job and the help of an alert research team and up-to-date crop service." [15] The first two or three of these advantages also apply in futures markets and in government-support programs. The reader will find it both interesting and informative to ponder two questions in this connection. First, why has the government steered as clear as it has from the commodity futures markets in its efforts to influence price? Second, is there any basic difference between the effects of agricultural integration through such devices as private contract farming on the one hand and the influence of government decision making implemented by quotas, support prices, nonrecourse loans, and the like on the other? [16]

---

[15] Talk given before the Faculty and Graduate Students, Texas A & M, College Station, Texas, January 18, 1962.

[16] A very interesting discussion of vertical integration appears in USDA Agricultural Economic Report No. 19, issued in February, 1963, titled *Vertical Coordination in Agriculture* by Roland L. Mighell and Lawrence A. Jones. The report contains a very comprehensive discussion of the various arrangements which provide the decision points and linkages in our agribusiness complexes; but, strangely enough, no mention is made of the government as integrator or decision maker.

SUMMARY

It is argued in this essay that government control programs do alter market structure and behavior in ways and degrees that vary over a wide range. The Kennedy Administration's "supply management" proposals of 1962 asked authority to employ practically all the devices discussed above with respect to almost any commodity. The Congress was apparently unwilling to grant such a *carte blanche*. Nevertheless, it is not difficult to find numerous examples of each of the following market impacts of government agricultural control programs:

1. Government control programs often make prices so fixed that they become a built-in part of the *market structure* rather than a balancing force to enable the market to match demand and supply factors.
2. They impose other criteria than consumer free choice as a primary control of resource allocation.
3. They alter cost structures by imposing mandatory new factors—both involuntary costs and "unearned" rewards. (If the purpose of controls is to provide "adequate" or "fair" incomes to farmers regardless of whether or not the goods or services are needed, then at least one function of markets is drastically changed.)
4. Frequently government control programs make the government an active trader, buyer or seller, in the market. (Usually the government, because it is an authoritarian body, undertakes to dominate the market, not just to stabilize it.)
5. The government, since it is not itself a consumer, must assume the role of seller as well as buyer if it enters the market. It can of course destroy (a form of consumption) or give away the products it acquires, but its acquisitions usually overhang the market.
6. Many control activities in which the government does not itself become a buyer or seller (such as acreage quotas or stamp plans) impose rules and restrictions that change the market structure. These changes require substantial adjustments in other elements of the structure or functions of the market.
7. When control programs require the market to be segmented (as in milk orders) or supplies to be diverted (as in other market orders), there is a loss of free access and also a loss of economic efficiency as the term is generally understood.

Whether the purpose in every case justifies the means, and whether the means in fact accomplish the purpose, it is for each of us to try to decide. Even though this essay has made no attempt to appraise the merits or effectiveness of government agricultural control programs in the light of their basic purposes, we cannot ignore the impacts upon market structures and functions. Many industrial sectors of the economy have developed the science or art of "marketing" as a primary device for attaining adequate incomes and growth. The development of authoritarian market controls in agricultural products seems to point out a different course of action about which the "theory of marketing" should also be concerned.

III. Consumer Behavior

15. THE MERCHANDISING FUNCTION

Edmund D. McGarry

THERE is no concept in marketing more controversial than "merchandising." Some would have the term include practically the entire work of marketing; others would restrict it to stock-control activities of wholesalers and retailers. Some would confine its use to the modification of products already in production, while others would also include in it the original design of new products. This confusion notwithstanding, no other word approaches "merchandising" in its aptness to express the process of fitting merchandise to potential consumers' desires. Therefore, the writer proposes to redefine the term and to fit it into a general concept of marketing as an adjustment process.

Marketing is conceived of as that phase of the economy through which man in the modern world adjusts to his environment in terms of physical goods and psychic desires. In this adjustment, marketing is the great intermediary force. Its agencies maintain the contact between producers and consumers. Through their constant search for and selection of products which can be offered to consumers, these agencies modify the products which are to be made. Through their efforts to persuade consumers to take the products which are produced, they condition people's likes and dislikes. Through their pricing methods, they adjust the costs of making and distributing products to what consumers can afford to spend. Through their storing and transporting of products, they adjust the time when products are made and the place where they are made to the time and place where they will be consumed. These fundamental activities are the functions of marketing.

The present statement is confined to an examination of a merchandising function which comprises the various activities undertaken to adapt the product to the users' ideas of what is wanted. It embraces all the adjustments made in the goods and in their presentation to meet the needs of potential customers. Merchandising includes quality determination as well as measurement, packaging, branding, and display at strategic points to stimulate consumer interest. It involves the selecting of the product to be produced or stocked and the deciding of such details as size, appearance, form, dressing of the product, quantities to be bought or made, time of purchase or production, and lines to be carried.[1] In short, the merchandising function adjusts what is practical to produce to what consumers want.

The essential element in this definition concerns the orientation or adaptation of either an individual product or a group of products to conform to consumers' needs and desires. It is the fact that the product or its method of presentation is being changed which makes the definition exclusive. Although the immediate decision as to what is to be offered on the market is made by producers and marketing agencies, the ultimate determination of products and their characteristics is in the hands of consumers, who decide what merchandise will be purchased. Whether considered from an individual or a social point of view, it follows that the empirical test of how well the merchandising function has been performed is the extent to which the goods move off the market and gain consumer acceptance.

Development of Merchandising

From the early days of the Industrial Revolution until the turn of the twentieth century, manufacturers placed very little emphasis on merchandising. It is commonly said that throughout most of this period goods were sold in a sellers' market. Stress was placed on production, for practically all kinds of goods were in such demand that the seller had merely to keep his price in line and customers would be forthcoming. Theoretically, it was assumed that the retailer would analyze and interpret consumer demand and pass his suggestions to a wholesaler who would in turn relay them to the manufacturer. In this way, product improvement would come about automatically. It is doubtful, however, if this system ever worked very effectively. The range of choice facing the consumer with limited income was still rather narrow. The margins of profit per unit were so wide that retailers and wholesalers gave little attention to merchandise turnover and seldom attempted to convey the reactions of customers upstream to the manufacturer.

Merchandising became a separate, distinct, and specialized activity when growing competition among numerous products designed for the same use convinced producers they should try to find what consumers wanted before goods were placed on the market. The foundation of merchandising lay in the recognition that literate consumers with adequate means of expressing their desires and incomes which could provide more than the bare necessities of life were tending to become ever more discriminating

---

[1] This definition approximates that used by Copeland and Learned, except that it does not include pricing, which is here considered a separate function. It also approximates what Professor Chamberlin calls "product differentiation." Cf. M. T. Copeland and E. P. Learned, *Merchandising of Cotton Textiles* (Cambridge, Mass.: Harvard Bureau of Business Research, 1933); and Edward Chamberlin, *The Theory of Monopolistic Competition* (Cambridge, Mass.: Harvard University Press, 1933).

in their tastes and preferences. It became evident that a great deal of time, effort, and money could be saved and consumer goodwill attained with less expenditure on promotion, if preferences could be determined before the goods were offered for sale. At the same time, as a by-product of the merchandising process, ideas for profitable new products were often developed.

As the concept of merchandising took root and the techniques of researching consumer preferences were refined, businessmen came to realize the enormous profit possibilities inherent in knowledge of what consumers wanted. As a result, merchandising or product planning became the central feature of the entire production and marketing program. Not only the design of the product but also the design and location of facilities for marketing the product were based on studies of market potential.

Perhaps no better illustration of the significance of merchandising can be found than the transformation of marketing in the cotton textile industry. The change that has occurred in the attitude toward merchandising has been a leading cause of an almost revolutionary integration of the industry. For generations before the great depression, cotton textile manufacturers produced grey goods which were sold by sales agents to converters and cutters. The stress was almost completely on production and price differentials, with the result that many of the manufacturers were kept on the verge of bankruptcy. In order to meet price competition, finishers skimped on materials and workmanship, and consumers were misled into the purchase of cotton goods of poorer quality than they desired.[2]

Within recent years, emphasis in this industry has been placed on the consideration of merchandising factors. Mills have integrated with finishers to keep in close touch with consumer preferences, and have differentiated and specialized their products. As a result, manufacturers have avoided destructive price competition and gone much further in giving consumers a wider range of choice. Merchandising has become even more influential in the competing man-made fabric field. Consumers' desires serve as the basis not only of the fabrics woven but also of the specifications of the fibers from which fabrics are developed. In order to meet the practical needs of consumers, new characteristics, such as drapability, resistance to grease and chemicals, and ability to hold crease, have been built into these fibers.

The merchandising function is performed at all levels of marketing, but it takes a somewhat different form at each level. At the producing level, it consists chiefly of the discovery and development of new products, new qualities in old products, new combinations of products, and new uses for existing goods. At the wholesale level, merchandising takes the form primarily of finding and securing a proper assortment of goods to offer to

---

[2] See Copeland and Learned, *op. cit.*

retailers. At the retail level, it includes the selecting of appropriate assortments of goods for the retailer's particular clientele as well as the location and presentation of these goods in a manner convenient to customers.

Segmentation of the Market

Economists and marketing writers, accustomed to thinking in broad generalities, tend to consider markets as consisting of all the people in a given geographical area. This is a perfectly satisfactory concept of the market for some broad category of goods, such as clothing. In this context, the market consists of everybody in the area, and it may be considered as homogeneous. However, the individual marketer of a specialized item (and most products today are specialized) is concerned not with goods in general or even with a major category of products, but rather with a single item or brand. Consequently, the market must be defined much more narrowly. A market segment consists of that group of people who have a preference for a certain item or brand or for certain characteristics in a product that is different from the preferences of others. Thought of in this way, the people in a given geographical area comprise not a single market but hundreds or even thousands of segmented markets, one for each of the differentiated products.

Each of these segmented markets consists of few or many people. For a yacht priced at $100,000, the market is very thin and the potential customers may be counted on one's fingers. On the other hand, the market for "Mars" candy bars could run into the millions. But it should be noted that in neither case is the market universal. It is segmented by institutionalized patterns of behavior. The basis of market segmentation lies in the nature of man. Although plants or animals of a given species or subspecies may superficially appear alike, comparative studies of characteristics reveal them to be of infinite variety. Applied to man, were this not obviously true in a physical sense, we would not be able to distinguish one person from another. More important from the marketing standpoint, it is just as true of man's habits of thought, his mental attitudes, and his reactions to given stimuli. These factors are spoken of by psychologists as individual differences. And it is to these individual differences that the product must be adjusted, if it is to be successfully marketed.

The process of matching goods to individual differences in human wants is made possible by the fact that the wants of many different individuals fall into patterns. Although no two people are wholly alike, many often have the same pattern of desires. People may be grouped by age, race, religion, incomes, education, etc., and their choices of goods may fall into patterns based on these groupings. Consequently, such groupings are often used as criteria for segmentation into markets for differentiated products.

In an economy of affluence, with its better communication and higher standards of living, producers find a competitive advantage in discovering new segments of the market that need a product somewhat different from the general run. Often, new characteristics of the population must be determined in order to identify and define the segment which can be appealed to by a product. Thus social habits, such as types of automobiles owned, professional as against amateur status in sports, and many other criteria are used as bases of segmentation. In this way, the market is segmented and resegmented to discover new niches of demand, and products are proliferated to meet them. A considerable part of market research is devoted to the discovery and definition of the exact segment that will need the characteristics of specific products.

The attainable degree of segmentation, however, is limited by the fact that modern production facilities are geared to mass production of standardized products. If the market segment contains an inadequate number of potential customers, the inefficient scale of production which results will cause costs to be prohibitive, i.e., too great to be adjusted to the consumer's pocketbook. Thus, it would be impractical to make products to each individual's specifications. In brief, the purpose of merchandising is to seek a market segment of sufficient size to warrant the commitment of production facilities to a particular item.

Although it is impractical in a mass-production economy to make products that meet each individual need or preference, an approximation to these individual needs can often be achieved by the standardization of parts and the assembly of these parts in different combinations. Such action provides a wide variety of attributes from which the consumer may choose. It is said that the Chevrolet car offers over a million variations, including perhaps a hundred color combinations, different types of tires, etc.[3]

If the role of modern merchandising in marketing and in the culture generally is to be understood, the nature of human wants and of the products that are designed to satisfy them must be clearly delineated and the patterns which people develop for choosing from among the great diversity of products offered for sale must be explained.

The Nature of Human Wants

According to Alfred Marshall, "Human wants and desires are countless in number and very various in kind: but they are generally limited and capable of being satisfied. The uncivilized man indeed has not many more than the brute animal; but every step in his progress upward increases the variety of his needs together with the variety in his methods of satisfying them. He desires not merely larger quantities of things he has been accustomed to consume but better qualities of those things; he desires a greater choice of things, and things that will satisfy new wants growing up in

---

[3] "Carl Helm of Wayne University's mathematical computation laboratory has figured that the 1955 Chevrolet car offers 1,152,000 possible combinations, not including standard accessories" (*Detroit Free Press*, December 28, 1954, p. 16).

him." [4] It will be noted that Marshall uses the terms "wants," "needs," and "desires" interchangeably and synonymously.

In terms of marketing, a "want" is a desire or need of a particular person for a specific item; and the preference for one item over another is a purely personal matter. In other words, a person's want or need is whatever he thinks it is. It is something that fills a lack, and it is assumed that if a person puts forth an effort to get something or pays something of value for it, then in his mind he has a need for the product. Thus, there is no such thing as buying something one does not need. Wants are subjective, exist only in the mind, and the only way we can actually know what others want is to observe what they choose to buy. A want is universally and almost exclusively expressed in the terms of the good that satisfies it.

An individual's wants are influenced by the interaction of his physical or mental state, his background of conditioning, the immediate situation which confronts him, and, most importantly, the goods he knows about either directly through their use or vicariously through communication with others. People do not usually think of their needs until they learn about something which will satisfy them. This is the reason why the inhabitants of the so-called backward countries appear to be perfectly satisfied until civilized peoples bring them new goods to make them unhappy. Balzac said, "Herein lies the whole story, races who have no wants are always poor." [5]

In the modern world most people satisfy their material wants as well as many of their intangible wants by purchasing goods in the marketplace. They select from the assortment of goods offered those they prefer. It is in this way that they express their individual personalities. In making such choices not only is each individual's attitude toward a given item inherently different from others, but the difference is fostered and accentuated by the individual himself in his attempt to build a personality which is unique and distinct from all others. At the same time, the individual is conscious of belonging to a certain group and desires to preserve his association by conforming to group mores. Thus, the individual is constantly faced with the dilemma of how far he should conform as against how far he should express his individual personality. He wants to be different but not so different as to be considered conspicuously odd. He seeks his identity with the group by circumscribing his wants within the group's boundaries. The desire to be different and at the same time to conform to the group is perhaps one of the reasons that consumers pay so much attention to small differences in products.

Wants are of different values. For any individual they differ in in-

---

[4] Alfred Marshall, *Principles of Economics* (London: Macmillan & Co., Ltd., 1947), p. 86.
   [5] Honore de Balzac, *Le Medecin de Campagne*, quoted in Paul Cherington, *Peoples Wants and How to Satisfy Them* (New York: Harper and Brothers, 1935), p. 31.

tensity, in urgency, and in importance. A college education is a most important want for many people, but it is usually not very urgent, nor very intense; the want for a stick of chewing gum may be intense, but neither very urgent nor important; the want for a "Band-Aid" may be urgent, but not especially important or intense. In making a decision concerning the thing he needs, the buyer must consider all relevant values in terms of his purchasing power and the effort required to obtain the item. The values which people assign to their different wants are based on their internal drives, their previous conditioning, and their careful weighing of the relevant facts. Any one of these elements cannot be considered independently of the others. Needless to say, the more important the want, the greater the amount of thought that will be given to satisfying it.

Fortunately, the problem of deciding what one wants is made somewhat easier by the fact that most wants are of a recurrent nature and the means of satisfying them has become patterned and more or less habitual. Admittedly, specific choices may appear stereotyped and irrational when purchases are repeated without any consideration of existing alternatives. In such cases, however, much thought may have been devoted to the initial selection of an appropriate item and the later purchases reflect this earlier decision. Even when the pattern of recurrent purchases changes, the image of what by experience was found to be satisfactory becomes the yardstick by which to measure the value of the new product for the same use.

Although there is often a degree of fixity in the choice of recurrent purchases, changes do occur from time to time. Environmental shifts bring new needs into the picture and make old ones obsolete. Increased maturity and the aging process tend to outmode products formerly used, and changing status brings additional requirements into play. New products in themselves have an attraction simply because they are new. Men's minds are flexible, and their attitudes are changed by innumerable factors.

The desire for a particular item is influenced by the relationship of its accessibility, defined to include price, the funds available and the trouble and effort required to secure it. As one's disposable funds increase or as the goods become more accessible, the limitations on his desires are lifted and he is able to broaden the horizon of his choices. With the increasing availability and accessibility of goods to the individual, he pays less attention to the intrinsic characteristics of the product, which are now taken for granted, and more attention to how well the product fits his incidental and often intangible objectives.

In considering how one makes a choice from the vast inventory of products presented to fit his needs, it is well to recognize that there is usually a certain tolerance in human wants. Within this tolerance, individuals are willing to accept near substitutes. Just as in the case of mechanics, there is no such thing as a perfect fit, so in the case of goods sold to consumers there is probably never a perfect satisfaction of a need.

In other words, the consumer makes part of his adjustment to the goods he wants by compromising his ideals. As consumption reaches higher levels and larger numbers of products compete to satisfy specific needs, the allowable tolerances become narrower and choices are made among products that objectively appear to be similar or identical.

The Nature of Products

Because of the nature of human wants, an object offered for sale is likely to be seen in a different perspective by the buyer or potential buyer than by the seller or casual observer. It may be the same physical product with the same objective features capable of being seen and felt and sometimes heard. Nevertheless, the buyer must fit the item into a personal frame of reference which is likely to be different from that of the seller. The fact that the product does what it is supposed to do is not enough. It must, in addition, be consistent with the buyer's social position, lend prestige and meaning to the individual and his family, and fit the mode of life to which the buyer is accustomed or to which he aspires. Thus, the acceptable product is imbued with a halo of subtle and invisible qualities beyond its mere physical attributes.

Nor is it correct to assume that buyers generally are all looking for the same characteristics in a product. In fact, the most acceptable characteristics for one person or segment of the market may be entirely unacceptable to another. The frame of reference for each individual is somewhat unique because of variations in background, experience, and previous conditioning and differences in the situation in which the product is to be used. The purchaser of a garbage can, for example, if he has to handle the can himself, probably wants one that is light and easy to handle. If he hires someone else to handle it, he is likely to be more concerned with its durability under heavy use. The fact that durability means an increase in weight is now unimportant.

The frame of reference within which consumers evaluate the products they buy will change as a result of changes in more basic social and economic patterns of behavior. An example of this is the change in attitude of consumers toward the most desirable features in a pair of shoes. When people did a great deal of walking, they demanded shoes which were comfortable and durable. They wanted shoes that were waterproof and would stand up under hard usage. The automobile, paved sidewalks, and rubber overshoes, however, have caused the old idea of comfort and durability to be replaced by certain aesthetic features as the leading criteria of value. The customer now asks how well do the shoes look, how long will they keep their shape, and whether or not they are compatible with his or her ensemble.

Any given product has innumerable dimensions, features, and attributes—many products would require a book to describe the product accurately and fully. Obviously consumers do not have the time nor will they make the effort to analyze all the features of the item or to compare it carefully with other products. Instead, they tend to generalize and simplify the situation into loose terms of little real meaning. They see the product as either black or white, good or bad, high quality or low quality. Such terms are simply value judgments of the person using them. To assume that such judgments have some universal validity is neither logical nor realistic. One man's meat may be another man's poison.

The determination of whether a product is acceptable to any segment of the market depends on the value judgments of the many consumers who constitute the specific segment as to how well the product suits their individual purposes. Marketing men know all too well that products, which from some objective point of view are of high quality, may not sell simply because potential customers are not looking for this particular type of quality. On the other hand, the manufacturers and vendors of a product may be unaware of "qualities" in the item with a special appeal to consumers.

Buying Behavior

Although it is impossible to describe the wide variety of motives that lead people to buy what they do, one can point out and classify some of the major patterns of their behavior. In view of the nature of their wants and the nature of the goods, these broad patterns of behavior appear to be both rational and consistent. People go to the market primarily to seek out certain products for which they feel a need or to discover new needs by exploring what is offered. These trips are either planned or unplanned, and the needs may be either well defined in their minds or vague and inexplicit. In some cases, the shopper feels the lack of something which is within his means. At other times, he has the means to expand his wants and is searching for the direction which his expenditures should take.

In considering the behavior of purchasers, it is well to make a distinction on the basis of who is to use the product. On this basis, goods fall into three categories: (1) goods bought for the use of the household as a unit, (2) goods bought by individuals for their own use, and (3) goods bought by individuals for the use of other individuals. These three types of purchasing, although often combined in a single shopping trip, represent three distinct approaches to the buying situation and should be considered separately. For brevity, these three types of buying may be termed "household purchasing," "personal purchasing," and "fiduciary purchasing," respectively.

Household Purchasing. Household buying, the largest proportion of consumer buying, is done principally by the housewife who acts as purchasing agent for the household unit. In such purchasing, as Wroe Alderson has pointed out, she acts very much like the purchasing agent of a business firm.[6] Starting with a given inventory of goods on her shelves and in her cupboards, she attempts to maintain this inventory by replacing items that have been consumed. From time to time she may replace items with substitutes, drop some of those she has previously used, or add some that are entirely new to her inventory.

Most of the items purchased by the housewife are well known to her as she has used them before. Consequently, her buying is in the nature of routine behavior established by habit and requiring but little effort. She may carry a shopping list, but this is merely a reminder of what she lacks. This list is likely to be in generic terms rather than in terms of specific items or brands, thus enabling her to substitute freely as she desires. She fulfills generic needs by walking down the aisles of the supermarket or department store, surveying the goods on display, and making up her mind as to the specific item she wants.

In the case of substitution, the housewife must make somewhat more effort. She considers how well the item previously used has satisfied her needs, the cost of the substitute, and the possible risk of getting something she does not like. She frequently reads the label on the new item and considers its economy in use.

When the housewife attempts to add to her inventory, she takes even more care in selection. She thinks in terms of the increased variety and flexibility of her inventory and of the alternatives offered by other goods that might be obtained. Price is usually a major factor simply because an extension of her inventory means total expenditures will exceed their customary level.

Personal Purchasing. In buying for her personal needs, the consumer, whether a housewife or some other member of the family, may be buying for replacement or buying something the like of which she has not previously selected. In the case of the replacement purchase, the consumer considers how well the item presently in use has satisfied her. If it has been fully satisfactory, she is likely to seek out the same product or brand. Even if improvements have been made in the product, she will probably want the older variety. If she cannot get the identical item, she will want the same brand.

In buying a product that has not been used before, the consumer will give much more weight to her own personality. She will try to determine how well the product fits her image of what she aspires to be or to do. She will think of the product in the use-situation with herself as the user. Finally, she will consider the satisfactions which she assumes the product will give in relation to other products that she might buy for the same outlay of money.

Fiduciary Purchasing. In fiduciary purchasing, the buyer is buying for someone else, and, in consequence, must place himself in "the other

---

[6] See Wroe Alderson, *Marketing Behavior and Executive Action* (Homewood, Ill.: Richard D. Irwin, Inc., 1957), p. 165.

person's shoes" so to speak. Except in cases where the purchaser is simply acting as an errand boy, this is obviously the most difficult type of buying. It requires that the purchaser imagine what is in another's mind, and fit the product to the user's situation. Also to be considered is the personal reaction of the potential user toward the individual who selected this item. Within the family, purchasing the right item is often not difficult. In other cases, where knowledge of the recipient's likes and dislikes is incomplete, the risk of buying the wrong item is great. The large number of neckties received as gifts and never worn testifies to this fact. In such cases, the items selected are those which would have been chosen if the purchaser were buying the goods for her own use.

Characteristic of all three types of purchasing is the selection of a considerable number of items which the customer did not have in mind when she started. This can be termed serendipity purchasing—the discovery of items the customer was not seeking and the decision, on the spur of the moment, that these items would fit previously unrecognized needs. In other words, the sight of the goods themselves created the need for them.

In many cases, purchases are made simply to gratify the buyer's curiosity. If the shopper is feeling affluent and the price of the goods is small relative to her purchasing power, she may be willing to try a new product simply to see if its use is satisfying. If the product does not satisfy a desire, she knows what to avoid the next time and will not replace the item. This type of purchasing is greatly stimulated by advertising, bargain offers, and the packaging and display of goods on the shelves.[7]

Conditioning Influences

People differ widely in their purchasing behavior and in their attitudes toward spending money, with some of the determining factors being economic circumstances, age, and status in society. Some individuals are spendthrifts who must use their income as fast as it comes in; others are savers with a strong liquidity preference and a desire to have their money rather than use it. These attitudes are major factors in determining shopping behavior. Older people are accustomed to their mode of life and, consequently, they find adjustment of new goods to their needs more difficult than do younger people. Some individuals are more status conscious than others, and the strength of social influences tends to vary from group to group.

There are also changes in moods from day to day and even from hour to hour. If people cannot find what they want, they tend to be frustrated and are inhibited from buying anything. If they are upset by personal problems, in poor health, or not feeling up to par, they are likely to be

---

[7] "An aspect of product presentation which gives expression to some hidden desire of the consumer can be effective in getting buyers to try it." Alderson, *op. cit.*, p. 182.

in a poor buying mood. Many people are highly sensitive to things which are not objectively apparent.

The selecting of products by the consumer to fill his needs is not an easy one. It requires effort and thought to make satisfactory decisions. Most products are purchased for use in the future, so the buyer must consider whether he should buy now or wait for some future opportunity. He must decide whether this particular product is the best available to fill his particular need or whether he should search further; whether this outlet is the best place to buy the product or whether he should go elsewhere. In making these decisions, the consumer is trying to adjust the product offered to his value judgment of his needs.

In spite of the effort required to get what he wants, there are balancing compensations. For many consumers, shopping is what Wroe Alderson calls "congenial behavior." There is an exhilarating effect in seeing new items and learning of new possibilities for using them. Moreover, many consumers appear to enjoy being in the marketplace where one can watch what other consumers are doing, see what they are wearing, eavesdrop on their conversation, and reflect on their tastes.

Dynamics of Merchandising

Probably the most difficult problem in modern merchandising is to determine just what the consumer wants, or, to be more specific, what he will want by the time the goods reach him. Actually, the producer must always build his product for a forward demand. As Father McInnis has so cogently pointed out, this rapport with consumers' desires becomes progressively more difficult as the gap between consumers and producers is extended by the complex division of labor and the increase of differentiated consumer wants in the modern world.[8]

When one considers the large number of new products reaching the market each year, he is likely to assume that the analysis and interpretation of the market is of little consequence. That such is not the case, however, is clearly evident if one reflects on the enormous number of new products which never gain market acceptance. It is estimated that only one out of five of the new products put on the market ever proves profitable. When it is further considered that only about 1.5 per cent of patented items are ever worth their patent fee, the statistical probability of successfully marketing a patented product becomes less than one in three hundred.[9] Obviously, much of the time, effort, and money that must have gone into the making of these unmarketable new items could have

---

[8] From an unpublished abstract of "General Theory of Marketing" by Rèv. William McInnes, S. J., 1954.

[9] "At an outside estimate 1½ per cent of them (patents) are worth the filing fee" ("After Hours," *Harper's Magazine*, August, 1950). "Peter Hilton, President of Hilton and Riggio, which specializes in promoting new products, estimates that four out of five fail to meet consumers' acceptance" (*New York Times*, February 6, 1955, Sec. 3, F7).

been saved if a careful analysis of market desires had been made in advance.

The merchandising function, however, is dynamic not only in the sense that new products are introduced to meet the rapidly changing culture, but also in the sense that the new products themselves create a type of chain reaction. One need only point to the development of the automobile and its effect on road building, plaza developments, and social habits generally to demonstrate the far-reaching effects of a single major innovation. Less obvious, but equally significant from the theoretical point of view, are the effects of minor changes which follow the improvement of a product. Thus, the improvement of antifreeze has not only made possible the year-round use of cars, it has also eliminated the need for garages and added to the problems of snow removal from streets.

Initiative in Merchandising

Although in the last analysis consumers as a group determine the characteristics of merchandise, they usually play a passive role in the initiation of changes. Consumers with interests dispersed over a vast number of items in their inventory of wants are not likely to do anything about a single item. Other things being equal, they will accept what they are accustomed to have rather than attempt to think of something new. With the increasing complexity of products, they prefer to leave the initiation to others. Moreover, they usually have the easy alternatives of either buying something else for the same use or of not buying anything.

If consumer inertia is to be overcome, someone else must take the responsibility for change and spend the time and effort required to see that the change is accepted. In our economy, businessmen operating at some point in the channel of distribution take on this responsibility. The hope and expectation of profits serves as their incentive. If the innovation is in the item itself, the profit-making possibilities are greatest for the producer, with interests concentrated in a relatively few products; if it is in a group of items and in terms, say, of display at the retail level, the initiative is most likely to be taken by the retailer. But the conditions described do not universally hold true. Often the manufacturer reaches down through the channel to see that his goods are properly displayed and presented at the point of sale. On the other hand, the retailer not uncommonly sets up specifications for a product which he asks some manufacturer to make for him.

To be more specific, it may be said that the initiative is taken by that agency in the channel which has identified itself with the goods—in other words, the owner of the brand. If it is a national brand, the manufacturer determines what characteristics should be incorporated into the products which he offers the public. Then, working back through the channels which provide his supplies, he selects the raw materials which will meet his specifications and, to the extent necessary, controls their quality. At the same time, he works forward and attempts to control the handling, display, and presentation of the product through the various agencies to the public. With the brand owner as the leader, the entire channel is organized as a team, expected to cooperate in distributing the product to the consumer in the manner in which the brand owner has decided to market it.

The problem of coordinating the process of merchandising throughout a channel of distribution composed of many independent agencies is a difficult one. Each agency has different interests and different ideas of how to attain its objectives.[10] Clashes of interest have led to many innovations in the marketing structure. The use of exclusive agencies, tie-in contracts, consignment selling, and even the integration of the entire process has often been motivated by the desire to secure a consistent and articulated merchandising policy. When the process is integrated, it is possible for the initiator of the program to exercise complete control over merchandising decisions.

Conclusion

An effort has been made to present a theory of merchandising. The conceptual scheme attempts to tie together innumerable strands of information in a manner which enables one to see the complicated relationships that connect them. If the assumptions used are real and the logics applied are sound, the results should give some real insight into a process which is too often taken for granted. As in the case of most theories, the analysis raises more questions than it answers. Left unresolved are such issues as who shall decide what items are to be produced, to what extent should experts be employed in this choice process, and what should be the role of government in aiding or compelling individuals to make the "right" choice. The whole age-old question of socialized versus individualized action is bound up in this theory.

Then, too, there are the practical aspects of the problem. How can the merchandiser engaged in presenting his product to the public avoid the enormous wastes of trial and error—wastes which run into billions of dollars annually? How can he determine or rather predetermine what the consumer will want, when often the consumer himself does not know? How can consumers themselves determine what is best for them? And when they know what is best, how can they communicate their ideas to the marketer? These are some of the problems to which more attention must be given.

---

[10] For an elaboration of this process see the author's "The Contactual Function in Marketing," *The Journal of Business of the University of Chicago*, Vol. 24, No. 2 (April, 1951).

16. CONSUMER ACCEPTANCE THEORY

Leo V. Aspinwall

THE CONSUMER acceptance theory is being rewritten at this time in the interest of a better orgnization of the material. It was originally written in 1954 and mimeographed for students attending a graduate seminar in marketing theory. Prior to that time, it was used, beginning about 1934, in the classroom to explain certain marketing relationships involving producers, middlemen, and consumers. The changes which have taken place over the years have made this reorganization necessary. Certain arguments contained in the earlier version of the theory are now well accepted, and a substantial amount of that material need not be restated.[1] The main tenets of the theory have not changed—they are as important today as they were when first formulated—nor has any change occurred in the reason why I write theories.

My attempt at theory construction is aimed at bringing together related material, from diverse and scattered sources, so as to afford a concise statement of relationships helpful in obtaining a better understanding of marketing.

Thesis

The thesis of the consumer acceptance theory can be stated as follows: *"The obligation of consumer acceptance generation is that of the manufacturer or the owner of the brand."*
The theory recognizes that there are three levels of intensity which the consumer achieves in his relationship with a product. These are: acceptance, preference, and insistence. These three levels are important in the execution of a promotional plan used in marketing a product or a family of products. Marketing men recognize that promotional funds are often dissipated and that such losses have serious economic effects on our society. The consumer acceptance theory is formulated with the view of

---

[1] Leo V. Aspinwall, "Consumer Acceptance Theory" (Boulder. Colo.; School of Business, University of Colorado, 1954), mimeographed.

decreasing marketing costs and affording a better understanding of relationships in the marketing process.

Consumer Acceptance Defined

The terms "acceptance," "preference," and "insistence" are used with their generally accepted dictionary meaning, and special definitions will not be necessary. Consumer acceptance means, in the marketing sense, that the consumer has had some contact with the product or with the promotional effort offering the product. This contact has caused a decision to be made by the consumer as to the acceptability of the product in his normal demand schedule. This is the normal mental process of sorting stimuli with respect to the needs and goals of the subject.

The human mind operates constantly in its attempt to identify whatever comes to it from our environment. This sorting process relates stimuli to some experience of memory that we have had and rates them as either a positive or a negative value in terms of our current goal. Whatever thinking or sorting process the mind accomplishes, as regards these stimuli, terminates in a resolution which is nothing more or less than a summation. This resolution is stored in the mind along with earlier experiences or memories. The total of these resolutions is the knowledge we have gained and serves as the universe which is scanned whenever a stimulus presents itself in the sorting process.

Resolutions have magnitude based upon the number of experiences or minor resolutions that are related together in a sort of connected chain, all the parts of which may come up for review whenever the sorting process operates to add a new resolution. If a limited experience is stored in the reservoir of the mind, then a minor resolution is the result, and, conversely, if a vast experience has been had, a major resolution is laid down.

This whole area of major and minor resolutions cannot be considered without some mention of the cross relationships that exist between chains of resolutions. These cross relationships may be an index to the mental capacity of an individual. The greater the storage capacity, the greater the mental potential of the individual. Yet, without a large amount of organization by the individual, utter mental chaos exists. We commonly speak of the well-organized mind and, similarly, recognize the disorderly, unorganized mind. We conclude that the mind of great capacity is that mind that has a large reservoir of classified knowledge.

Consumer Preference Defined

The second stage of intensity in the relationship of the consumer to a product or family of products is called the preference stage. The term "preference" indicates that the product will be favored, when available, over other competing products. This fact demonstrates a satisfactory reaction based upon a firm mental resolution that resulted from a less satisfactory experience in the use of a competing product. If, however, the preferred product is not immediately available, some other competing product will be chosen, provided the alternate choice does not involve a large economic outlay. To reduce this situation to concise terms, the second stage preference position of the consumer is that substitution will be tolerated.

Consumer Insistence Defined

The final stage of intensity in the consumer product relationship is called consumer insistence. A full knowledge of the product based upon substantial experience in use has produced a firm resolution in favor of this product over all other competing products. The full consumer satisfaction which the product affords might be called a consumer's surplus. Although a difference in price might tempt the consumer to purchase a lower-priced brand or even a substitute product, behavior is governed by the firm resolution mentioned above, indicating that despite greater initial cost, the product which has achieved consumer insistence offers the greatest utility and satisfaction. Reducing this situation to concise terms, we can say that consumers in the insistence stage brook no substitution and will endure some measure of hardship in order to purchase the exact product.

Stages of the Advertising Spiral

The advertising spiral, as recognized by Otto Kleppner, provides a means of undertaking a program that will produce the desired results.[2] Embodied in this concept is a systematized approach, closely keyed to the consumer's mental processes, which aids in eliminating uneconomic efforts in the promotional program.

The advertising spiral has three distinct stages, each aimed at producing a special end result—first, creating consumer acceptance; second, creating consumer preference; and, lastly, creating consumer insistence. The cumulative effect increases the intensity of consumer loyalty and establishes the basis for the continuation of a promotional program. The time element of any program is unpredictable, since constant changes in technology, together with changes in consumer tastes, require much research and development to maintain a share of the consumer market. It is often said that the value of a brand is the sum of the promotional effort invested in it. This is not as simple as it appears to be, since promotional effort may be good or bad. The value of bad promotional effort and, hence, even the value of the brand may be negative. The true value of the brand is the net profit realized over a reasonable period of time, and a direct correlation exists between sound promotional effort and brand value.

---

[2] Otto Kleppner, *Advertising Procedure* (New York: Prentice-Hall, Inc., 1964), pp. 9–35.

Pioneering Promotion. The three stages of promotional effort—pioneering, competitive, and retentive—are the sequential steps in a campaign designed to achieve maximum sales for a product, brand, or family of products. Each step in the promotional campaign is keyed to the normal mental processes of the consumer, so as to build a fund of information that will lead to a firm resolution. The first stage, pioneering, aims at providing new and unique facts, which show that the product will meet a need in a more satisfactory manner. The advertisement or sales message aimed at providing the consumer with clear-cut, new information is definitely of a pioneering nature. In this stage of the campaign, all possible means are used to gain the attention of the consumer. Color, soundly constructed display advertising, and sampling are all employed to gain attention and afford the consumer the opportunity to rationalize, since without rationalization, there will be no resolution. In short, the aim and objective of the pioneering effort is first to gain attention and then to provide the new unique facts about the product.

It is clear that without a resolution base against which to compare the offerings of competitive or retentive motives, nothing will take place in the mind of the consumer. The stimuli will be subject to the normal process of consumer mental sorting and either passed by as being unrelated to any past experience that could possibly benefit the consumer in achieving his personal goal or that of his family or friends, or, alternately, seized upon as being important and useful. Keep in mind that mental sorting of stimuli is a constant activity of a human mind, which seeks out and evaluates everything reaching it and stores the value of such stimuli as resolutions in its reservoirs. Even a weak, almost fragmentary, resolution is stored in the mind and operates as a signal that latches on to anything that comes as a stimuli related to it. The sorting process might reinforce or weaken the original resolution with the effect depending on whether subsequent signals prove beneficial or otherwise.

This is the true area of theory and, to my mind, demonstrates the important role of the theorist, that of bringing together sometimes fragmentary bits of information or, at other times, massive amounts of information and relating it all to a simple thesis. The capacity of the mind is expanded by having ready for immediate use the total experience relating to a central thesis. A wide range of central theses affords a greater sorting capacity. Individuals equipped in this way are able to receive more out of their everyday experiences. Almost everything has some significance. Thus, the role of the theorist is that of the teacher who enables students to build mental models upon which related facts and experiences can be fitted to provide speedy recall.

This mental sorting process begins at an early age in normal human beings and continues throughout life. Early resolutions of childhood are often canceled out by subsequent information, but even canceled-out resolutions remain and may be reinforced and revived, dependent upon such stimuli as may be found useful from later experience. Cases have been reported which support the idea that such canceled-out resolutions can be revived long after they have been forgotten by the subject. Electrical stimuli, transmitted by means of a needle probe used in brain surgery, have caused patients to recall, in minute detail, long forgotten past experiences, the occurrence of which was later verified by the patient's close relatives. Surgeons, in their attempt to control areas of the brain from which tumors were being removed, have reported these recall experiences. In other cases involving mental patients undergoing brain surgery, similar experiences have been cited.

This system of forming resolutions is an area in which considerable research has been done and much more is required. For example, although there is conclusive evidence that forgotten experiences exist in a dormant state in the human mind, further clinical testing is needed before positive acceptance of the idea can be relied upon in the design of promotional campaigns. Marketing, in order to perform its greatest service, must first know the consumer's mind and how it works. As a strictly lay psychologist, this writer thinks of resolutions in terms of a common "T" account. Debit and credit entries are made into the account. Then, these are summed up to show which side holds the greatest value. When that has been determined, a resolution has been formed. The mind then microfilms the whole account and stores the negative in an appropriate area. Whenever any entry of the account is activated by a stimuli, the resolution and the whole account come up for review. The resolution then becomes an entry on a new account, which, in turn, leads to a new resolution. The process is repeated, and a new microfilm is sent to the proper storage area. How much time does all this take? Just about as much time as a computer takes; that is, if the subject's mind is well organized by having large masses of experience and factual information well integrated into theories and models. Scattered, unrelated bits of experience and information tend to get lost in the mental storage areas just as a fine coat would, if stored in a vast stock of nuts and bolts. The time aspect of these mental operations is not known, but some of the research indicates that it may well be less than one second.

Another element of this operation—attention—is closely related to both time and intensity of resolution making. The writer has found it helpful to think of attention in terms of a bull's-eye diagram. The very center of the target diagram is black and occupies only a very small space—theoretically only a dot of infinitesimal small size. Outward from this minute, blackest of black dot, the color passes through various shades of gray, becoming white at infinity in the outward direction. The degree of attention intensity is measured by the degree of blackness, with the center as 100% black. Thus, moving through the gray areas, we have lesser and lesser degrees of intensity, until at infinity, there is zero degree of intensity or no attention.

The time element at 100% attention intensity is near zero, probably approximating the speed of light or electricity, but in that instant of time, a resolution is laid down. Keeping in mind the flash at the center, it must be understood that the pattern of attention originates usually in the gray area where greater amounts of time are required, and as more information pours into the mind, the attention pattern shifts towards the center. It may stop some place in the gray area, and a weak, indecisive resolution is formulated to await additional evidence which may be gleaned in some later scanning operations. The very center of the bull's-eye pattern of attention is called perfect rapt attention, where the mind's scanning and sorting operation is concentrated wholly upon the specific area, to the exclusion of all other stimuli that may be available. This exclusive concentration is operative only over the period of the flash; then, scanning takes over, and attention intensity will vary over the longer periods of time. Thus, if we ran a movie of the happenings on the bull's-eye, we would have a few flashes of almost complete darkness, followed by longer periods of degrees of grayness. When the mind blanks out and ceases to operate, our screen would be completely white—absolutely a blank. All this is intended to indicate that the time element of mental operations consists of flashes. No one has determined exactly the duration of these flashes, but it is safe to say that they are extremely short.

Marketers are aware of the difficulty in achieving rapt attention; yet, without such attention, nothing happens. The scanning activity of the consumer's mind brushes aside, as unimportant and unrelated, stimuli that do not afford the advancement of the goal objectives. Promotional effort in the pioneering stage must gain attention and then offer new ideas. The communication must be filled with unique, different, and better ways of achieving greater human satisfaction. Such stimuli offer the consumer a chance to operate a "T" account and draw down a resolution.

Competitive and Retentive Promotion. The second stage in the promotional program is tied to the gaining of consumer preference. The intensity of this level of consumer-product relationship determines whether repeated purchases occur of products which require replacements and whether a sustained loyalty is maintained for products purchased less frequently.

The mode of communication is intended to show that the product is better than other competing products. This is the competitive stage of promotion and it is aimed at reinforcing the earlier resolution gained in achieving acceptance. The "T" account receives more entries, and greater areas of receptivity are developed. The duration of this stage of promotion is governed by the competitive situation. Everything is done to head off possible ventures on the part of the consumer to try competing products. It is recognized that such experimentation is a real possibility, but if such a trial should eventuate, then the number of advantages offered should clearly demonstrate that the prime product is best. In uncontrolled situations, such as when the prime product is unavailable, substitution will occur. This is the real difference between the competitive stage and the insistence stage, wherein the consumer's loyalty is such that he will allow no substitution.

The third stage in the promotional program has for its aim the firming up of the resolution to the point of intensity that maintains complete loyalty. The means employed to achieve this end is a condensation of the full import of all the campaign into a slogan—some short phrase which will recall for review the whole "T" account, so that the consumer will continue to purchase the product. Each recall of the earlier resolutions has the effect of reviewing earlier decisions to determine the consumer's best interest. Should the sales results indicate that a competing product has gained some acceptance, then the promotional program must be shifted into the pioneering mode. This means, the product must be improved in a major way so that it can qualify as a real innovation. Once a promotional program is carried through three stages, there is no place to go except to pioneering which starts the whole process anew, but upon a much expanded scale. This gives the model the character of a spiral.

Programs vary with types of goods. It would be unfair to leave this important area of marketing without calling attention to the fact that differences in promotional programs vary with the types of goods. The three [3] main types this writer is identified with—red, orange, and yellow goods—serve very well as a framework for campaign differences. The aim is, as in all marketing activities, to make the best disposition of resources, and this aim is accomplished through the adjustment of program to type of goods.

---

[3] Leo V. Aspinwall, "Four Marketing Theories" (Boulder, Colo.: Bureau of Business Research, University of Colorado, 1961). Originally published in *Cost and Profit Outlook* (Philadelphia: Alderson & Sessions, 1956).

17. UTILITY, UNCERTAINTY, AND THE CONSUMER-BUYER

William S. Peters

INTRODUCTION

ANY ACCOUNT of current developments of importance to marketing theory must surely give attention to the trends of thought that are converging upon the problem of decision making under risk and uncertainty. Economists concerned with utility, psychologists concerned with learning theory, subjective probability, and probability preference, and statisticians and logicians concerned with decision theory have for a number of years been making significant theoretical and experimental contributions to the same central problem. In this essay the author traces in nontechnical terms what from the viewpoint of marketing theory are the central strands of these converging threads.[1] Applications to the study of consumer buying are suggested. Finally, the survey of major contributions and the marketing applications suggested by them is drawn upon to indicate some of the possibly critical variables in a comprehensive program of research in consumer decision making under uncertainty.

A VIEW OF RATIONAL DECISION MAKING

The classic distinction of decision situations is made by Frank Knight, who differentiates among the kinds of knowledge available to the decision maker regarding the consequences of alternative courses of action.[2] When these alternate consequences are known, there is of course complete certainty; when they are known only in the sense of expectancies based on repeated trials (as in life and casualty insurance), the term "risk" is applied. When it is impossible to apply a relative frequency

---

[1] The author wishes to express his indebtedness to the Western Management Science Institute of the University of California at Los Angeles for a grant in support of work leading to the essay presented here.

[2] Frank H. Knight, *Risk, Uncertainty, and Profit* (New York: Houghton Mifflin Co., 1921).

probability notion to a decision problem, one uses "uncertainty." "Uncertainty" in this sense connotes noninsurable risks.

Knight enumerates several causes of error in decision making under uncertainty as distinct from certainty and risk. These center about sources of imperfection in knowledge that are not present under certainty and risk. He states that decision errors arise because of (1) faulty perception of the present, (2) faulty inferences about the future, (3) lack of knowledge as to consequences of our own actions, and (4) faulty execution of our own intended actions.

Wroe Alderson discusses the motivation of consumer buying in terms quite compatible with Knight's enumeration of sources of decision error.[3] For Alderson, consumer buying problems arise from uncertainty as to the best course of action to pursue in a purchasing situation. Solution of a buying problem is "to reduce uncertainty to the point where a course of action can be adopted with some confidence."[4] In this process, "the problem solver is trying to see the *essential structure* of a complicated situation and trying to make the best gamble in being prepared for future requirements which are subject to chance variations."[5]

Alderson views the consumer-purchaser as buying agent whose problem is to adjust the flow of goods and services to present and prospective needs of the family unit. Habitual buying patterns are viewed as "deliberately chosen routines designed to save time and energy for rational consideration of more important matters."[6]

Alderson further contends that the consumer-buyer is conscious of the notion of *performance* in regard to his role as purchasing agent. He claims "the desire and ability to improve are clearly in evidence."[7] Not only does the consumer-buyer attack existing problems rationally, but "rationality is exhibited in ability to learn from experience and adopt new methods."[8]

Both Knight and Alderson take the viewpoint that consumer buying decisions are the consequence of rational considerations in the fitting of alternative goods and services to consumption goals. Incomplete information as to ends and means injects many uncertainties into the process, and the decision maker may have to make do with the grossest of approximations. Nevertheless, rational, purposive action prevails, though clouded by uncertainty.

If this viewpoint is valid, then an understanding of how the consumer-buyer deals with uncertainty constitutes a keystone to understanding consumer buying behavior. The whole area of human behavior under

---

[3] Wroe Alderson, *Marketing Behavior and Executive Action* (Homewood, Ill.: Richard D. Irwin, Inc., 1957), p. 167.
[4] *Ibid.*
[5] *Ibid.*
[6] *Ibid.*, p. 166.
[7] *Ibid.*, p. 167.
[8] *Ibid.*, p. 166.

probabilistic and uncertain conditions becomes a fertile field for generating testable hypotheses relating to consumer behavior in the marketplace. This essay reviews some major contributions to this field and draws upon this work to suggest applications to the problem of the consumer-buyer.

ELEMENTS OF THE UNCERTAINTY PROBLEM

The Expected Value Approach

A traditional criterion for selection among alternative risky propositions is the expected value criterion. Familiar to gamblers and forming the basis of statistical methodology, it asserts that maximizing probability-times-payoff is the proper basis for choice among alternative risky propositions.

Doubt was cast early on the universality of the expected value criterion by the famous St. Petersburg paradox of Daniel Bernouli, a problem involving the fair value of a certain gambling proposition.[9] Bernouli devised an ingenious but simple gamble with an expected value that was infinite. The gamble involved an infinite series of smaller and smaller expectancies of proportionately larger and larger gains. However, most persons will pay only a finite sum and a modest one at that, for the privilege of playing the game. Although Bernouli "resolved" the problem by arbitrarily positing a constantly diminishing marginal utility of incremental money gain, the St. Petersburg paradox sounds a warning against zealous application of normative rules of behavior in the absence of evidence that individuals behave in the prescribed fashion. How persons react to risky and uncertain propositions is equally as important as how they ought to act according to accepted probability calculations. By rational behavior, one can only mean some kind of consistent behavior that can be predicted within tolerable limits by factors with a relevance to the acts involved that is at least plausible.

The Marginal Utility of Money Gain

Strict adherence of choice behavior to the traditional expected value criterion presupposes a constant marginal utility of money gain to the decision maker. Since utility is assumed to be strictly proportional to money gain, expected money gain can be used in place of expected utility as a norm of behavior. Friedman and Savage deduce from the behavior of individuals in purchasing insurance and lottery tickets that the "utility of money" curve might typically have a generalized reverse "S" shape.[10] If individuals will pay more than the fair value for a sweepstakes ticket, the marginal utility of large money gains must be high. Similarly, if per-

---

[9] Duncan R. Luce and Howard Raiffa, *Games and Decisions* (New York: John Wiley & Sons, Inc., 1957), p. 20.

[10] Milton Friedman and L. J. Savage, "The Utility Analysis of Choices Involving Risk," *Journal of Political Economy*, Vol. 56 (1948), pp. 279–304.

sons pay more than the actuarial value for the protection from large money losses afforded by insurance, the marginal disutility of large losses might be high. This means that the marginal utility of a large gain must exceed the marginal disutility of the cost to the individual of the chance at the gain. Also, the marginal disutility of the large loss must exceed the marginal utility of the cost of the insurance. This accords with common sense in that it pictures the individual as less concerned with relatively small changes in money position than the possibility of large changes that would completely alter his level of living.

Von Neuman and Morgenstern introduced an operational method of measuring the degree of preference (or utility) of alternative payoffs.[11] Given payoffs A, B, and C, where A certain is preferred to B certain which is preferred to C certain, they say that the utility of B to a subject is numerically equal to a probability $(\bar{p})$ such that the choice between the expected gain $\bar{p}(A) + (1 - \bar{p})C$ and the certain payoff of B is a matter of indifference to him. Given this statement of the "standard gamble," and an arbitrary designation of the utilities of A and C, it is possible to impute the utility of B from observed choice behavior. Mosteller and Nogee determined in a related manner the utility attached to different money prizes by players in an experimental situation.[12] They found some subjects whose marginal utility decreased for increasing prizes, and others whose marginal utility increased.

Note that although the St. Petersburg paradox led to a suggestion that individual marginal utility of money curves might be constantly diminishing, Friedman and Savage offered support for high marginal utility of large gains and large loss avoidance and low marginal utility of small changes. The "standard gamble" proposition offers a basis for utility measurement, but experiments employing it with small money sums have not yet revealed any fixed form of the utility curve.

Probability Preferences

Implicit in the utility approach introduced above is the notion that choices are a function of expected utility, or, more precisely, that choices reflect expected utility which, in turn, is a function of money value. Probabilities serve only to discount utilities of uncertain prizes so that expected utility may be compared with the cost of the prize. Preference for an uncertain over certain gain reflects a personal valuation of the prize, not a preference for the uncertain over the certain. Probability serves as a mechanism for equating alternatives with varying risk, but that is all. Individuals are not assumed to have a different attitude toward varying probabilities.

---

11 R. Duncan Luce and Howard Raiffa, *Games and Decisions* (New York: John Wiley & Sons, Inc., 1957), pp. 20–22.

12 Frederik Mosteller and Phillip Nogee, "An Experimental Measurement of Utility," *Journal of Political Economy*, Vol. 59 (October, 1951), pp. 371–404.

A classical experiment on probability preferences was conducted by Preston and Barratra.[13] In their experiment, two or four contestants bid for the opportunity of participating in 42 gambles representing exhaustive combinations of six prizes offered at seven different odds. The prizes ranged from 5 to 1,000 points, and the probabilities from .01 to .99. The highest bidder won the opportunity to participate in the gamble, with the amount bid being provided from an original "endowment."

Preston and Barratra found consistent overevaluation of long odds and underevaluation of short odds. That is, the winning bids on probabilities under .25 tended to exceed expected value, and winning bids on probabilities over .25 failed to equal the expected values on balance.

Francis W. Irwin offers an explanation of the behavior pattern observed by Preston and Barratra. Favorable events are assigned a higher subjective probability than unfavorable ones.[14] The individual really believes the likelihood of a large gain at long odds is greater for him than objective probability or relative frequency indicates. Subjective probability theory suggest that gambles involving long objective odds would be overvalued even if the individual's marginal utility for money were strictly proportional to money value.

Evidence also exists that individuals faced with experience data tend to overestimate the relative frequency of occurrence of rare events and underestimate the relative frequency of common events. Griffith provides an interesting example in horse-race betting behavior. He studied the percentage of winners among horses placed by betting in various odds groups in American horse races.[15] The odds groups represent aggregate psychological probabilities, while the associated winning experience represents objective probability. He found a systematic underevaluation of the chances of short-odded horses and an overevaluation of the chances of horses at long odds. The breaking point occurs at odds of 6 to 1 or 5 to 1 which, Griffith points out, are approximately the same as the indifference points found in the Preston and Barratra experiments.

Excepting the historical viewpoint of constantly diminishing marginal utility of money, the descriptions of choice behavior under differential risks discussed thus far find general agreement in observed preference for low probability of large gain. However, three alternate explanations of this behavior have appeared: (1) increasing marginal utility of larger money gains, (2) persistent overestimates of the frequency of winning at long odds, and (3) psychological overestimation of personal chances of winning.

13 M. G. Preston and P. Barratra, "An Experimental Study of the Auction-Value of an Uncertain Outcome," *American Journal of Psychology*, Vol. 61 (1948), pp. 183–93.

14 Francis W. Irwin, "Relation between Value and Expectation as Mediated by Belief in Ability to Control Uncertain Events," paper read before the Annual Meeting of the American Psychological Association, Chicago, 1960.

15 R. M. Griffith, "Odds Adjustments by American Horse-Race Betters," *American Journal of Psychology*, Vol. 62 (1949), pp. 290–94.

Repetitive Behavior and Learning

Much of the previous discussion has centered about choices in which the probabilities of the outcomes or payoffs were known. Lack of knowledge of objective probabilities has been introduced as a factor qualifying behavior, but we have not considered available evidence on learning in a probabilistic environment.

A classic experiment in this field is the binary choice experiment under conditions of probabilistic reward or reinforcement. In these experiments a subject upon a given cue makes one of two choices, *a* or *b*. Choice *a* is rewarded with probability p_1 and choice *b* with probability p_2. Sometimes *b* is simply "not *a*," and $p_2 = 1 - p_1$, as when light *A* goes on (cue), the subject predicts that light *B* will then go on (*a*) or that it will not (*b*). Light *B* then goes on with relative frequency p_1 in an appropriately selected random sequence. Reinforcement may simply be the satisfaction of having guessed correctly, may involve a punishment of incorrect responses, or may involve a monetary incentive. A common pattern of response, termed asymptotic matching behavior, has been observed in the binary choice learning experiment. After a period of learning, the subjects tend to choose alternative *a* with relative frequency p_1 and alternative *b* with relative frequency p_2. Where this happens, it appears we must conclude that the subjects estimate objective probabilities correctly but do not maximize expected value. One could maximize the likelihood of a correct prediction by simply ascertaining the more frequently reinforced alternative and always selecting it.

Event matching behavior seems to be another example of failure of individuals to maximize expected gain in the classical sense. Estes notes that a strategy of always choosing the more frequently rewarded response would not permit discovery and adaptation should the reinforcement probabilities be subject to change.[16] Failure of reinforcement of alternative *a* does not mean that alternative *b* would have proven "correct," since the reinforcement series are independent of one another. He has also observed that existence of differential monetary incentives (rewards) and risks in the binary choice situation leads to relative frequencies of choice that overshoot the matching values. The extent of departure from matching behavior is apparently greater as differentials in risks or payoffs increase.[17] Edwards suggests that if the rewards are trivial, the subject will not really care if he is right, and the choice probabilities will

---

[16] W. K. Estes, "Individual Behavior in Uncertain Situations: An Interpretation in Terms of Statistical Association Theory," R. M. Thrall, C. H. Coombs, and R. L. Davis (eds.), *Decision Processes*, (New York: John Wiley & Sons, Inc., 1954), pp. 127–37.

[17] W. K. Estes, "A Descriptive Approach to the Dynamics of Choice Behavior," *Behavioral Science*, Vol. 6, No. 3 (July, 1961), pp. 177–84.

tend toward the reinforcement probabilities.[18] The subject sees the trials as a game, and tries to outguess the experimenter on each choice. As the reward or desire for reward increases, choice behavior deviates from event-matching toward consistently choosing the favored alternative. However, this tendency stops short of always choosing that alternative. Precisely because desire or motivation is present, the subject becomes distressed over the inevitable occasions when his favored choice is unrewarded, and directs some proportion of his choices to the unfavored alternative. He might also do this to determine if the reinforcement level has changed.

APPLICATIONS TO CONSUMER BUYING DECISIONS

Advertising and Probability Preferences

The adoption of new products and new brands by consumers appears to be an area where attitudes toward differential risk propositions may prove to have considerable relevance. The consumer-buyer is familiar with certain products or brands either through personal experience or through reactions of those for whom she acts as purchasing agent. The net advantages of these products are well assessed, and the consumer-buyer intuitively attaches a high probability that future purchases will bring similar psychic gain. However, the merits of untried products and brands are surely known with less certainty, and in all likelihood the claimed advantages are believed with less assurance. It is a commonplace that merchandisers must present strong reasons why consumers should buy a new product or switch to their brand. But it is not clear how credible these reasons need be. A claim of extravagant advantages that a buyer feels has only a small probability of coming to pass may have a greater subjective expected value to the consumer than more modest, highly credible claims. The marginal utility of the remote payoff may be higher than more certain gain, and the consumer may, for some psychological reason, overestimate the objective magnitude of the lower probability. Both of these possibilities predispose the buyer to prefer the small chance of large gain. Such a probability preference offers an explanation for the persistent tendency toward unbelievable exaggeration in the advertising of highly competitive branded products. There may really be some probability, however low, that use of Brand X face cream will bring Prince Charming to a proposal, and who can deny that the value of this outcome may be high indeed.

A related application is suggested by the higher subjective probabilities attached to favorable as compared with unfavorable outcomes of equal

---

18 Ward Edwards, "Reward Probability, Amount, and Information as Determiners of Sequential Two-Alternative Decisions," *Journal of Experimental Psychology*, Vol. 52, No. 3 (September, 1956), pp. 177–87.

objective probability.[19] This raises the question of the relative merits of positive and negative advertising appeals. If we are more predisposed to believe that favorable events will come our way than that unfavorable outcomes will befall us, we will attach greater value to the chance of enjoying possible gain than we will to the opportunity to insure against possible comparable loss. It may follow that negative appeals, to be effective, must have great and general credibility. They must be addressed to universal and omnipresent conditions that we are desirous of avoiding and offer convincing evidence of the effectiveness of the product as a remedy.

Cumulative Performance

The context in which decision behavior has thus far been discussed is that of a series of similar decisions. The personal and environmental determinants of decision behavior have been regarded as homogeneous from occasion to occasion. Hermann and Stewart, from experiments involving gambling preferences of the kind already discussed, observe that individuals are more willing to take speculative long odds when losing than when winning a game.[20] Simon considers what happens when an individual's performance fails to measure up to his own expectation or aspiration level.[21] Search for new alternatives for action (perhaps new rules for decision) ensues, and at the same time there is a tendency for adjusting the level of aspiration downward in accordance with more readily attainable goals. Where performance and aspiration are not sufficiently adjusted, irrational rather than rational adaptive behavior may well ensue. It is quite possible that the taking of increasingly long chances when losing a game represents just such a shift in behavior. If, as Alderson says, the consumer is quite conscious of her level of performance as a buyer, behavior under performance-aspiration discrepancy may be a fruitful area to study experimentally.

Attitudes toward Success and Failure

Littig introduces into differential risk calculations the decision maker's motivation for success and his anxiety over failure.[22] He suggests that where outcomes depend on the skill of the decision maker, these motivational elements operate as coefficients that modify the subjective proba-

---

19 Ward Edwards, "Interactions between Utility and Subjective Probability and the Variance Preference Problem," paper presented to the American Psychological Association meetings, Chicago, September 1, 1960, by the Engineering Psychology Group, University of Michigan.

20 Cyril Hermann and John B. Stewart, "The Experimental Game" *Journal of Marketing*, Vol. 22, No. 1 (July, 1957), pp. 12–20.

21 Herbert A. Simon, "Theories of Decision Making in Economics and Behavioral Science," *American Economic Review*, Vol. 49, No. 3 (June, 1959), pp. 253–84.

22 L. W. Littig, "Motivation, Probability Preferences, and Subjective Probability." Paper read before the Annual Meeting of The American Psychological Association, Chicago, 1960.

bility-times-payoff criterion discussed previously. The result is that an individual with a high motivation for success and a low anxiety over failure will prefer alternatives involving intermediate probabilities of success. On the other hand, high failure anxiety combined with low motivation for success will produce more extreme behavior. The individual will prefer either relatively sure modest gains or low chances of great gain. Either of these will present the decision maker with a low chance of ego damage through failure. In the first instance, assurance of success is high, and in the second failure can be easily explained away by reference to the long odds involved. The extent and character of the consumer-buyer's experimentation with alternative products and brands may be closely related to perception of performance and attitudes toward achievement of success and avoidance of failure.

Quality of Information

Daniel Ellsberg finds some interesting behavior in the following situation.[23] Urn I contains red and black balls in unknown proportion while Urn II contains 50% red and 50% black balls. He offers the following sets of alternative bets regarding single draws from the urns, with the subject to indicate his preference or indifference in each case.

1. Bet on red (Urn I) or black (Urn I).
2. Bet on red (Urn II) or black (Urn II).
3. Bet on red (Urn I) or red (Urn II).
4. Bet on black (Urn I) or black (Urn II).

According to axiomatic utility theory as developed by Savage, one should be indifferent in all four choices given. Yet Ellsberg finds many who would rather bet on the draws from Urn II in alternatives 3 and 4, and a smaller number who prefer to draw from Urn I on these alternatives. The critical difference is in the quality of information provided. In Urn II one knows what the chances are, while in Urn I, though some would act as if the chances are 50–50 on red and black, there is no real knowledge present. Thus the amount of confidence, or standard error of a probability estimate, appears as a relevant decision criterion. This is clearly related to quantity and adequacy of information in a shopping decision. It also relates to credibility, which we have already discussed, albeit in suggesting that high credibility may not be required in connection with high utility payoffs. One can visualize, in fact, that individuals may be willing to give up certain amounts of payoff in return for increased credibility or confidence as well as for increased probability, and that trades are possible between probability and confidence given a stated payoff. Either of these may be a means of assessing the value of information to a decision maker.

---

[23] Daniel Ellsberg, "Risk, Ambiguity, and the Savage Axioms," *Quarterly Journal of Economics*, Vol. 75, No. 4 (November, 1961), pp. 643–69.

Ellsberg touches on this same point in suggesting that status quo or present behavior strategies are often pursued in the face of alternatives with greater expected value because of a differential in the quality of available information. Businessmen stick to strategies with outcomes that are well known to them, and consumers continue to purchase products and brands with familiar performance characteristics. It is in ambiguity and inadequacy of information that real uncertainty in the Knightian sense lies. Ellsberg's example spotlights the difference, and points to a potentially valuable avenue of consumer research in the interaction of pure risk and uncertainty. It should be possible to devise gambling choice and simulated shopping experiments in which costs are subject to some indeterminateness, either random or purposive. How much variation in cost (which need not change expected value) will be tolerated without some change in decision behavior? When variation is recognized and acted upon, what changes in choice behavior occur? In purchase experiments involving coincident information seeking, realism would dictate that information or shopping costs be subject to some random variation. Indeed, one might find some buying situations in which product price or information costs were subject to more uncertainty than payoff. How the consumer-buyer behaves in the face of various sources of uncertainty could prove to be a fruitful avenue of investigation.

Learning and Brand Preference

The parallelism between learning experiments and brand preference, purchase frequencies, and search behavior is inviting. Changes in the environmental conditions of learning-choice experiments with probabilistic reward can be introduced that simulate the conditions of brand choice behavior. One could introduce sudden changes in probability of reward that correspond to product innovation and gradual changes that resemble steady comparative quality improvement. The effect of information of varying reliability could also be studied in this context. Information could be made available, prior to each decision, about the occurrence of reinforcement. If this information were reliable, and this was perceived by the "shopper" through experimentation, then presumably it would be used, even at some cost. But if the information is not perfectly reliable, would it be used? What degree of inaccuracy will be tolerated, and how much value is put upon increments of accuracy? The possibilities for experimentation in many facets of communications related to buying decisions are considerable.

Finally, the probability choice experiment suggests a measure of brand preference as an alternative to studying the effects of price variation. The framework would be a brand preference experiment offering alternative brands as prizes with varying probabilities. The brand chosen with lowest probability is the preferred brand, and the strength of preference can be measured by the extent of further reduction in probability of payoff that will be endured by the choice maker without shifting his choice.

Interrupted Tasks

In interrupted task situations, investigators have looked for factors associated with subsequent recall of completed and uncompleted tasks. Alper finds that a preponderance of uncompleted tasks are recalled when the task situation is informal while recall of completed tasks predominates in formal settings.[24] Motivation is more positive in the informal setting. In general, Atkinson feels that the greater the motivation to achieve, the greater will be the tendency to recall uncompleted rather than completed tasks.[25] Again the connection with Alderson's performance-conscious consumer-buyer is evident. Many shopping tasks are interrupted. Time runs out without enough opportunity to view alternative choices, or a few out of a set of related items may have been purchased, leaving until later the purchases required to round out the assortment. Both of these phenomena appear to be susceptible to incorporation in shopping games in which the shopper is faced with a sequence of decisions about acquisition of "products" to fill a set of programmed needs.

Closure and the Costs of Indecision

The "closure" principle seems to bear some kinship to the incompleted task phenomenon. It is based on the notion that people perceive things in familiar completed patterns. Presentation of incomplete patterns, as in unfinished advertising slogans, stimulates recall.[26] This happens because the very incompleteness of the slogan motivates the observer to complete it, and apparently this involvement contributes to greater recall. The drive to finish what is perceived as incomplete appears to set up a sort of tension that is resolved only by the individual's providing the missing element. May one say that any decision involving the fitting of alternative means to preconceived ends presents itself as an unfinished pattern, and that the closure principle operates as a spur to resolve the problem through a decision? Because continued tension is undesirable, there is value attached to decision per se. Further, could not this value be assigned to whatever alternative is selected? If this interpretation is meaningful, then any analysis of preferences based on choices will contain this imputed utility of a decision. If these costs are high, apparently inconsistent choices may occur over a considerable range of alternatives. Conceivably, for some individuals great differences in probabilities or prizes in gambling-type situations

---

[24] T. G. Alper, "The Interrupted Task Method in Studies of Selective Recall; a Re-evaluation of Some Recent Experiments," *Psychological Review*, Vol. 59 (1952), pp. 71–88.

[25] J. W. Atkinson, "The Achievement Motive and Recall of Interrupted and Completed Tasks," *Journal of Experimental Psychology*, Vol. 46 (1953), pp. 381–90.

[26] Norman Heller, "An Application of Psychological Learning Theory to Advertising," *Journal of Marketing*, Vol. 20, No. 3 (January, 1956), pp. 248–54.

induce such tension. For others, similarity of probability-prize combinations create greater tension. It may be possible to apply considerations of this kind to the problem of imitative versus differentiating product strategy in brand competition.

GROUP INFLUENCES ON ATTITUDES TOWARD RISK

Reference Groups

Many writers place great stress on the role that reference groups play in determining consumption patterns and brand preferences of individuals. Choices will tend to conform with the norms set by groups with which the individual identifies himself or to which he aspires. In a real sense, the group norm as perceived by the individual is part of the information he brings to a decision-making situation. Unfortunately, as with prior experience, this is an internalized information source, and it is difficult to know when it is being used. Bourne feels that reference group norms are particularly potent when other information is absent.[27] When the individual has little direct knowledge of product attributes, reference group influence is thought to be at a maximum. Although group norms may thus at times be a substitute for other kinds of information, in some instances these norms may compete or conflict with other information. Bourne states that reference group studies tend to show that persons enjoying the greatest prestige and status within a group, while generally conforming to the group norm, will feel freest to deviate from it when other criteria conflict with the established norm. Those less secure within the group will feel more constrained to conform regardless of special circumstances, even though they may harbor resentment when the group norm overrides other considerations.

The introduction of group influences suggests another direction for decision experiments. This is the influence that group decision making may have on probability choice behavior. It might be expected that group participation would lead to more conservative behavior in probability choice experiments. What effect would the group have, for example, on individual disposition to overvalue long odds, or on the tendency to extreme behavior motivated by individual success or failure attitudes (Littig) or by position in a game (Hermann and Stewart)? With proper design, much might be learned by comparing shopping game decisions as made by husbands and wives separately with decisions made jointly. Other "teams" appropriate to differing situations could be formed by various members of a family.

---

[27] Francis S. Bourne, "Group Influences in Marketing and Public Relations," Rensis Likert and Samuel P. Hayes, Jr. (eds.), *Some Applications of Behavioral Research* (Paris: UNESCO, 1957).

Age and Sex

Wallach and Kogan concern themselves with the effects of age and sex on probability estimates placed on events.[28] The characteristics of estimates of interest to them are extremity, or the deviation from a 50–50 estimate of the chances of an event, and the confidence expressed by the subject in his probability judgment. They find a greater tendency among the young to venture extreme judgments with high confidence. Women appear to make more extreme judgments with high confidence than men, but among the young, men have more confidence than women over all judgments combined.

Wallach and Kogan also devised an index of disutility of failure based on twelve situations in which the respondent indicated the lowest probability that he felt justified undertaking the riskier of two alternative propositions. A high critical probability level here represents high disutility of failure. Generally speaking, disutility of failure was found to increase with age. If the more elderly are less inclined to extreme probability judgments, less confident in their judgments, and more concerned with consequences of failure than the young, then their patterns of response to purchase decisions carrying disparate risks could be quite different from the young.

Occupation

Vidich and Bensman, in a socioeconomic study of a small town, find that small businessmen, traditional farmers, and old aristocrats are hoarders in contrast to professional and skilled workers and "shack people," who are consumption minded.[29] Interestingly, this different attitude toward accumulation and spending might well be found to be associated with attitudes toward risks involved in alternative consumption choices. An orientation toward accumulation corresponds to a conservative attitude toward risk bearing, for the savings involved form an insurance reserve against future contingencies of all kinds. These contingencies may be either of a consumption or an investment nature. Some who practice this accumulation may do so out of a discipline growing from a tradition of investment and capital creation. Of the groups studied by Vidich and Bensman, only the prosperous farmers had this ideological tradition.

Klein finds that a variety of consumer expenditure studies show entrepreneurs have both a higher average and a higher marginal propensity to

---

28 Michael A. Wallach and Nathaniel Kogan, "Aspects of Judgment and Decision Making: Interrelationships and Changes with Age," *Behavioral Science,* Vol. 6, No. 1 (January, 1961), pp. 23–36.

29 Arthur Vidich and Joseph Bensman, "Social and Economic Dimensions of Class in Springdale," *American Journal of Economics and Sociology,* Vol. 17, No. 3 (April, 1958), pp. 261–77.

save than do other segments of the population.[30] Some economists have suggested that this arises from a desire to save as a hedge against fortuitous changes in income level. We wonder if the consciousness about risk represents an attitude that would make for different behavior of this group within the area of risky consumption choices.

Although these are only isolated examples, the effects of occupational backgrounds on attitudes toward risk deserve the attention of the serious student of consumer buying behavior.

Social Class

The association of social class position and saving-spending propensities forms the basis of a set of socioeconomic determinants of consumption behavior developed by Pierre Martineau.[31] He views individuals as located somewhere on a continuum from accumulators of money (savers) to accumulators of goods (spenders). Martineau describes the behavior of mobile and stable groups within social classes formed by W. Lloyd Warner's criteria of occupation, source of income, and kind of housing. Mobile groups are characterized by spending for symbols of upward movement while stable groups put more emphasis on saving and security. The form that savings take, however, differs among classes. Within the middle class, investment savings, particularly intangible investments, are preferred and take on some of the aspects of status symbols. Among lower social classes the saving that occurs tends to be of a noninvestment, low-risk, readily convertible kind. When investments are made, lower status persons tend to prefer real estate, business property, and other visible and tangible forms.

Martineau draws psychological portraits of middle and lower status groups that have implications for decision making involving risk and uncertainty. He finds middle-class persons future-oriented, possessed of a sense of rationality and awareness of purposive choice making, willing to tolerate risk, and capable of abstract thinking. In contrast, lower-status individuals are more concerned with the past and present, have a more limited sense of rational choice making, are concerned more with security, and are inclined to think concretely and perceptively rather than abstractly. The relevance of these factors to choice behavior indicates the importance of using social class as a control variable in any experimental program in consumer decision making.

---

[30] Lawrence R. Klein, "Entrepreneurial Saving," in Irwin Friend and Robert Jones (eds.), *Study of Consumer Expenditures, Incomes, and Savings,* Vol. II (Philadelphia: University of Pennsylvania, 1960), pp. 297–335.

[31] Pierre Martineau, "Social Classes and Spending Behavior," *Journal of Marketing,* Vol. 23, No. 2 (October, 1958), pp. 121–29.

TOWARD A THEORY OF THE CONSUMER BUYER

This review of contributions to the explanation of consumer decision making under uncertainty has developed the thesis that existing concepts in the field of decision making can form the basis for an operational theory of consumer buying behavior. In discussing these concepts, some of the directions that applications in consumer decision making might take have been suggested. What remains to be developed is a comprehensive and logically exhaustive framework for an entire program as it moves from analysis of elemental relationships to interactions among a diversity of factors. To attempt this would be clearly premature, but some value might accrue from an indication of the possible dimensions that might be incorporated into such a guiding framework.

Having adopted an instrumental framework of rational decision making, one should expect to recognize distinctions between means, ends, selection criteria, and the actions or events produced by the decision process. Further, it must be recognized that individual behavior with respect to means, ends, and selection criteria is conditioned by the social and personal values, attitudes, and beliefs held by any individual or class of decision maker. Personal and social values may, for example, either rule out explicitly or prevent the recognition of some among the available means to given ends as well as some among all possible ends. The study of permissible ranges of action may thus be a necessary prerequisite to studies designed to find what selection criteria are being employed within the range that is free from such restraints.

Other dimensions need to be carefully outlined for inclusion as factors that distinguish one decision-making context from another. Various writers have called attention to some of the psychological, social, and economic characteristics of decision makers that might have an important bearing on decision behavior. Some of these may be viewed as determinants of personal and social values and some might form independent dimensions. Such concepts as aspiration level, performance orientation, ambiguity tolerance, resolution drive, discrimination, the psychology of spenders versus accumulators, and environmental factors affecting risk tolerance must be more closely examined. A search must also be made for those personality traits that correlate highly with attitudes and preferences regarding differential risks and uncertainties.

Useful distinctions between kinds of decision situations need to be found. This review has suggested what some of these might be. The amount and reliability of relevant information, skill versus chance-dominated settings, competitive versus individually established bases of performance evaluation, single versus sequential decision environments, number and variety of alternatives presented, single versus multiple search objectives, constant versus changing underlying reinforcement parameters, and group versus individually established decisions are among these differentiating factors.

Finally, different aspects of decision behavior may be at one or another time the focus of experimental effort. Estimation of probabilities, probability preferences, payoff preferences or utility, consistency of choice, the handling of price, payoff, and informational uncertainties, and trade-offs between uncertainties arising from different sources are among the pertinent factors.

It would appear, then, that no satisfactory operational theory of consumer choice is available at the present time. If this is so, no promising avenue should be left unexplored. The author has tried to show on an intuitive level that research centering on how the consumer deals with uncertainty is indeed such an avenue. Statistical decision theory and learning theory provide a guiding frame of reference. The determinants of subjective probability and probability preference bring to this abstract framework the varied forms of human behavior as conditioned by psychological, social, and economic forces. Marketing students and practitioners should bring their insights to bear in suggesting new forms and extensions of experimental work in decision making. In turn, they would be well advised to bring to their market survey work an increasing use of a probabilistic background for the interpretation of consumer decision making.

18. INTERACTING ROLES OF THE HOUSEHOLD PURCHASING AGENT

Henry O. Whiteside

WOMEN have been the objects of observation from time immemorial. Aside from poets and philosophers, however, there is some doubt as to how systematic the observers have been. The normal girl watcher is, for example, not usually concerned with deriving marketing principles or constructing marketing strategies as these terms are normally used.

No one would question the fact that the systematic observation of women is an important marketing function. There are significant limits on the use in marketing of the experimental method. Consequently, the preponderance of existing knowledge in this field is obtained from observation. As observations become more acute and reporting more vigorous, our understanding of woman as a shopper slowly increases.

One of the factors pointed up by careful observation is the ever increasing duties of the wife who serves as household purchasing agent. As an urban industrial society has developed, the economic role of the husband has become more precisely and narrowly defined. At the same time, the role of the wife as the steward of family funds has been more openly recognized. A decline in the number of homes that are largely self-sustaining units has been matched by an increase in the amount of income available to purchase the family's expanding requirements from outside sources.

As the role of the family purchasing agent became more specialized, the economic strength of that role was enhanced. We are concerned here with an examination of how this role is prepared for and how it is expressed under a variety of conditions that, for all their uniqueness in a given household, are the shared experiences of the great majority of American families. An understanding of these conditions and a realization that the concerns of this buyer change markedly with time and situation should serve to sharpen the insights of all those who market goods or services destined for home consumption.

The Influence of External Factors

Much, if not most, of the housewife's training and education for her role as family purchasing agent is received informally. No school is yet presumptuous enough to offer to teach her all she needs to know in so many areas. Our jokes and cartoons about women and bank accounts offer an ongoing commentary on the limits of one aspect of this training.

Her first real training comes from the informal and inquiring observation of a mother whom she follows around the house or accompanies to the store, observing and asking, time without end, "What?" and "Why?". As the child moves out into the larger world of school, church, and playground, she compares her own clothes and other property with that of her peers. She exchanges information, plays games that mimic adult family life, constructs and operates stores, and begins to simulate the roles that she will play as an adult under different roles and for higher stakes.

The cultural environment of her childhood will strongly shape her conceptions of the wife/mother role and her behavior as she lives this role. Religious precepts influence the beliefs of some as to desirable family size. Others, as a result of ethnic patterns still holding on from different cultures, note varying degrees of passivity/dominance in the women's role. The values of the social class in which the child is raised contribute to her personality and affect the perspectives that she will bring to her adult role. The character of these and related influences have been extensively recorded. They are mentioned here in the briefest way, since they form the matrix out of which the housewife develops her values and her means of expressing these values in her purchasing behavior. (One other environmental condition must be noted here, though it is still too early to assess its potency. Television, bringing as it does, day after day, intense and concentrated interpretations of worlds quite different from that observable to the child in her own house, may be holding up values in conflict with and possibly more attractive than those visible in her home. The maturation of the first full generation to grow up in a TV environment may well see marked value reorientations, particularly in the lower and lower-middle class.)

Once, values were derived largely from the immediate and extended family operating in a reasonably stable environment. Increased mobility of families, longer school experience, and exposures through the mass media to a heterogeneous assortment of ideas and concepts have brought about a weakening of the family example. Advice columns in newspapers and magazines increasingly assume the responsibility of interpreting roles to the young woman.

Opportunities in the labor force, ranging from baby sitting to retail-store checking, lessen dependence on the parental allowance. Where once the earnings of all family members were contributed to a common budget, this concept has been weakened to the point of vanishing from the average family. In its stead, the concept "my money from my effort" opens the way to more independent behavior as a consumer. With such spending comes the dawning of understanding of "value." Her first extended purchases probably will focus on very personal items—cosmetics, clothes, baubles, bangles, beads. An apparently strong belief in magic will empty the teen-ager's purse while filling her bathroom shelves with "beauty aids." This experience may well be the beginning of her education in the discounting of advertising claims!

During high school days she is exposed to a certain amount of formal training having as its intention her preparation for an adult role as housewife. The relative remoteness of this role appears to minimize the amount and value of such learning. The young girl anticipates further years in college or X years in full-time employment before assuming the housewife role. Either or both of these post–high school experiences further her sense of economic independence and help to prepare her for her future role.

Purchasing Behavior at Different Stages of the Life Cycle.   The life cycle stages through which the female moves are only roughly chronological. Rather, they relate to major changes in her personal environment. Such changes may occur at any time over a very long span of years. Our concern here is with the fact that her entry onto each succeeding stage has its repercussions in her economic behavior. Her role is affected markedly by each change, and her behavior as purchasing agent expresses these changes in subtle as well as obvious ways.

Prologue to family or household behavior is the period as young, single, adult female. Frequently independent economically, she may or may not be sharing the parental home. With at least a high school education, she has been exposed to many different influences that have shaped her values and goals. Whatever additional goals may seem attractive, the central goal usually is marriage, home, family. Her focus of concern is primarily self —the satisfaction of uniquely personal wants. Her purchasing behavior naturally reflects this self-centeredness. She does not have to be too concerned with others since our society demands that the expenses of courtship be borne exclusively or primarily by the male.

With marriage comes a major change in her status in society and in her economic role. Whether her marriage comes at 18 or 28, she moves into a different world, and her interest shifts from pleasing self to pleasing husband. More and more frequently she continues to work after marriage, but the goal of such labor becomes the speedier acquisition of shared goods—goods desirable for a newly established home. Personal consumption items occupy a lesser share of attention, and it seems natural to set about acquiring furniture and the thousand-and-one items needed to furnish a home or apartment. Food is selected, purchased, and prepared, not with her own figure but rather the happiness of her man uppermost in mind. How will her cooking fare in comparison with what he remembers of his mother's table? How far can risks be taken with canned and already prepared foods before she demonstrates her competence in "making it from scratch?" In terms of the budget and high-ticket items, how much can be paid for prepared foods? For clothes of quite limited utility? For purely personal indulgences?

This first stage in the housewife's life has frequently been characterized as "nest building." From an economic point of view this is an apt term. In this period, the basic appurtenances of a home are being acquired. The housewife is developing familiarity with the problems of caring for another's wants. She experiments rather freely in many directions and is fairly open about her ignorance and errors. Just as she is developing dependable and orderly patterns (*sometimes before*), along comes the first child, and the housewife enters a new stage in her life cycle.

Concern must now be expressed for husband *and* child. (With the first child there comes a whole new pattern of economic relationships that will grow and develop until the children in their turn have grown and left home.) Both must be cared for, but, as the infant is more obviously helpless, husband gets less attention. And so it will be with each succeeding child. As the family grows, father and concern for his welfare is allotted less and less attention.

Out of the family income, there now must come funds to satisfy needs not felt by an adult family, and the responsibility for this legerdemain rests on the housewife. Consideration of her own needs commonly is placed last. Family needs, as expressed in requirements of child/husband, become controlling considerations.

First, there are the physicians and other professional specialists who must be retained for an unbelievable array of aches and pains. Medicines, special clothing, furniture, foods, and other new items find their way into the family budget. In most cases, the housewife no longer works outside the home, so there is frequently enlarged demand on restricted income. On top of everything else, there comes the heightened interest in and concern for the future. With the arrival of a child, something of a rudimentary long-range planning process begins. Today's expenditures are made with an eye to a distant tomorrow.

Enlargement of the family with additional children is no more than an extension of the second stage. More and more time and energy is spent on the wants of children, and rare is the family income that expands precisely on the same scale as family needs. Against a limited budget new needs must be satisfied. Children grow, and clothes are outgrown before they are worn out. Durability, cleanability, and other such value considerations increase in importance, and the housewife spends 80% to 90% of the family income with growing sophistication.

A time comes when the children have grown up and left home. The family shrinks back to its original twosome and concern for the husband and self again dominate purchasing behavior. Fears of not pleasing the husband, however, seem to be materially lessened, and the housewife can more overtly engage in self-gratification. By this time, however, the manner in which needs are satisfied is so patterned that much purchasing appears to indicate reflex behavior. The days of experimentation are past, the days of routine established.

Finally, the housewife may reach a stage increasingly common to the American woman, her last years being spent alone with her concern again focused solely on herself or, in a happier version, on her grandchildren if they are not too far away.

Whether we classify in this detail or in the somewhat simpler one sometimes used—*the child-bearing, child-rearing, and deserted years*—it is apparent that the housewife's position at any one time in this life-span has a marked effect on her role as family purchasing agent. Her values undergo profound changes, and these changes are expressed in her purchasing and consumption behavior. The marketer should assess his wares in terms of the life cycle stage in which the housewife will find his goods most or least meaningful. He is increasingly compelled to choose one stage in the cycle, appeal to it in its own language and in a manner which does not challenge existing values, and abandon the old dream of a single, universal appeal to all ages at once.

Stratification of the market by age poses a real dilemma to the marketer who, over the years, has established a strong brand image for his product. That very reputation which gives him such strength with the older population may be interpreted in another way by the young. Reputation for quality may be high but the product may appear old-fashioned and dated to a generation captured by the magic of change. The marketer must reinterpret his brand in a contemporary language, even while he holds on to the loyal consumers of yesteryear. It is a difficult assignment at which many fail, not because of product deterioration but because of failure to reinterpret old values in new terms. An understanding of these several stages in the life of the household purchasing agent can increase efficiency in product and service design, in sales and advertising media selection, and in the interpretation of product utility.

The Areas in Which Important Decisions Are Made

Up to this point, emphasis has been placed on a rather broad but pervasive set of influences that operate on the household purchasing agent. So many and so varied are the purchase decisions of an adult lifetime that a broad background is necessary for a general understanding of the purchasing role. To this discussion, we can now add another dimension—the type of purchase and the area of family need it satisfies.

Food and nutrition consumes the largest share of budget and energy and produces the greatest amount of psychological involvement. Over a period that may last 50 years, the housewife can expect to prepare two, sometimes three, meals every day for one or more persons in addition to herself. At a minimum, this will figure out to over 36,000 meals, or 72,000 servings. A beverage and two or more food items will appear at each meal. It is no exaggeration to say that the number of choices open to her under such conditions is astronomical. Only the low level of expectation on the part of the husband simplifies the selection problem.

What are the considerations that influence food purchases? First, funds are limited, although the housewife may spend 25 cents out of every family dollar on food. Since Americans tend to assess meals in terms of the meat course, she must acquire skills in manipulating this part of the food budget. There is a predictable relationship between the splurge on steak and the meat sauce–spaghetti frequency. There seems to be no limit to the ways ground meat can be stretched to feed the family and keep the meat budget under control. Over and above the choice of any one single item, though, is the basic concern for family nutrition. Is the family fed in such a way as to keep it healthy? Is it well fed?

At a more readily observable level is the housewife's concern for the enjoyment of food. Although eating is a pleasant experience, reluctance to eat is an unpleasant experience for the cook as well as for the balky noneater. The pattern of grocery purchases must reflect a balance between foods that are "good for you" and foods that are "good" in the sense of "enjoyed by the family." The product possessing both attributes is especially well received by the housewife.

In the course of her food purchases, the family purchasing agent accumulates an enormous store of information on prices, qualities, and quantities. Without apparent planning, she feeds a family on a food budget that varies only slightly from month to month, except when it is adjusted upward as new faces appear in the household. She unsentimentally gives up old items if the new perform equally well (margarine over butter) or even enhance her prowess in an area where she was weak (cake mixes). She adopts a new food that promises health and is palatable (orange juice) and steps up her purchases when the food is made more convenient (frozen concentrate). She uses food to reward and punish and, except for the minor indulgences of father in the supermarket or the children selecting ready-to-eat cereals, is the sole arbiter of how the food budget is spent. Her own tastes get the least consideration in the process.

The next most important item after food is clothing, where a different pattern is visible. The housewife purchases all of her own clothes, all of the children's clothes until they are well in their teens, and frequently votes on the clothing purchases by the husband (suits and ties) where appearance counts. The husband, while buying his shoes and hats, may delegate to his wife the purchase of those articles of clothing that are standardized as to size and that must be replaced at regular intervals—

socks, underclothes, shirts. Children are given no choice in the selection of their clothes until they are well along in school. Mother selects or dictates the selection of every item of apparel from the skin out. She distinguishes between "everyday" and "dress-up" clothes, economizing on the former for occasional splurges or frivolous indulgences on the latter. Her own wardrobe is an attempt at combining the durable with the fashionable. Her indulgences in shoes or hats may not appear rational to her husband whose own world makes low demands on him to keep in style. They are, however, her relatively inexpensive modifiers of a more expensive wardrobe.

The outer clothing that she purchases for herself and her family provide a visible statement of her interpretation of the family's position in the society. Clothing has a way of being relatively durable, and the economic task is to extract the maximum benefit from it without appearing to the surrounding society as either poor or out of style. The housewife never has enough money to buy all the clothes she desires. The decision for the little extra expenditure commonly goes to the clothing of the children, since they have such a long time ahead of them, and, in her judgment, are entitled to the best start possible.

In a third major area, the purchase of shelter and its furnishings, she deals alternately with the problem of too much and too little space. At the beginning of married life, there is much to acquire in furnishing even minimum living quarters and little with which to acquire it. Many purchases involve large sums and, if she makes a mistake, she must be prepared to live with it for a long time. Not uncommon is the discovery that few furniture designers have small children in mind. The husband participates in these major purchase decisions. At least, he is invited to say what he likes, to go through the motions of examining furniture, testing mattresses, box springs, etc. Chances are that at least one chair will be chosen because he likes to sit in it. That item will be known henceforth as "his" chair. Aside from this single selection, however, and a participation in the agreement as to the maximum monthly payments to be made, the husband's role is likely to be minor. More often than not, he hides his confusion and ignorance behind such statements as "whatever you like, since you will have to live with it."

At a later stage, when children have grown past the hard-wear stage, the housewife will buy with a considerable body of experience to guide her whenever furniture is replaced. Her tastes will be more firmly fixed, her disposition to buy "sets" and complete furnishing schemes less likely.

Expenditures for health will be governed partly by necessity, partly by choice—an aching tooth must be treated, a crooked tooth may or may not be straightened. Health expenditures for the adult members of the family will probably be slighted except for inescapable and incapacitating illness. Children, on the other hand, especially the first child, command professional medical attention without too much of a struggle. Except for hospital insurance, however, most expenditures in this area are for illth rather than for health. Selection of the professionals to serve the family needs is usually the responsibility of the wife, the husband professing immunity from illness and indifference to medication and practitioners.

Expenditures for education will largely be left at that portion of earning claimed by the government for school taxes. Beyond this, however, there is, particularly in the middle majority, a lively concern that the children be given educational advantages. Sets of books designed to enrich their educational experience appear to be desirable investments, and budgets are rearranged to admit such items. In this case, the husband is given an influencing role, and the purchase decision is made to appear as a joint one. The more ambitious may plan ahead for a private college experience, and those of a particular religious persuasion may send their children to private schools, even at the primary and secondary levels. Expenditures on education may be accepted as a joint responsibility, but their extraction from a limited budget is frequently effected by the housewife, who must trim, eliminate, or delay purchases in other areas of the family life. It is clearly a part of the American middle-class value system that the children receive a better education than the parents. Furthermore, the parents expect to forego personal satisfaction in order to bring this about. Even when students are earning considerable sums, this income is frequently viewed as "over and above" the basic parental obligation.

A major reversal of role is apparent when we come to family expenditures for recreation. Shared recreation of husband and wife is usually quite limited. The husband is expected to satisfy his recreational needs in any of a number of independent ways. Expenditures for his bowling, fishing, hunting, tavern visiting, or what-have-you, will come from that share of the income known as "his" and not be accountable beyond that point. The wife's attention is for so long committed to her children that it hardly ever occurs to her to spend for personal recreational needs. The husband will make most of the decisions which affect her leisure time. So far as the recreational expenditures for the children are concerned, the housewife usually limits her concern to the size of the allowance. How the allowance is spent is left up to the child. Occasional large or unusual demands are dealt with as they arise. Depending upon many factors, her decision may alter radically from occasion to occasion.

With the spread of paid vacations and longer vacation periods, more and more families find themselves considering each year a major expenditure in the recreational area. The housewife plays a critical role in such decisions, frequently being the voice of conservatism against the combined arguments of husband and children. Against the expenditure for transitory and uncertain fun of limited duration, she may press for the resolution of other needs not otherwise to be squeezed from the budget. House repairs, major equipment, a needed but put-off operation for some member of the family, a savings account either for a specific purpose or that proverbial "rainy day" may weigh heavily with her as she considers the vacation expenditure. Whatever the decision, it will not be her own pleasure, her own need for recreation that determines her vote. Her concern will be expressed in terms of relative value to her family.

There are two major areas of family expenditure where her influence and involvement is minimal—the purchase of transportation and of future economic security. Even though the housewife will have to adjust many other purchases to make certain that the monthly payments are met and that there is always gas in the tank, it is the husband who decides which car shall be purchased and when maintenance expenditures are in order. No guarantee exists that the husband is necessarily better informed and will purchase more shrewdly. In this one area, however, his status as husband and head of family is involved. He will be the principal user of the auto and, presumably, he can bargain more effectively with the salesman. Also, he is expected to know what is needed for its upkeep and be better able to diagnose the car's ills. The housewife appears to have no interesting in mastering this mechanical complex, and she is at a loss to provide an alternate solution for the husband's problem of traveling to and from work daily. Usually she keeps her participation in the purchase to the peripheral issues of color and upholstery. Sometimes, she delays the decision until she can figure out a way to juggle an already tight budget.

In the area of insurance, the housewife plays a negative role. She accepts the O.A.S.I. and possibly company group insurance as necessary and, in any event, decided upon before the paycheck gets home. Life insurance, for all the euphemisms employed in its promotion, still calls her attention to a future certainty that she would rather not face. She will rarely consider it for herself or the children. Fire and casualty insurance is accepted as an inevitable companion to the mortgage rather than as an item which may or may not be purchased. In this area, as in that of transportation, the husband plays the active, decision-making role. The housewife finds herself anticipating the periodic premium notices and again searching the budget for places where purchases may be reduced or delayed without serious threat to the family. Generally, her concerns are with the many, immediate demands that must be dealt with rather than any distant future event. It appears likely that in many households the outlay for security of the type represented by insurance is a compromise reflecting conflicting value judgments between husband and wife.

It is not practical in a brief essay to deal in greater detail with all classes of purchases made by the average family. The broad categories sketched above serve to highlight the major shifts of emphasis in the purchasing consideration. An additional value scale previously hinted at, however, calls for specific mention. With many purchases, the degree of privacy of the purchase enters into the buying decision. If the purchase is for purely private consumption, one in which neither she nor some member of the family will be judged, the housewife will express her choice more freely on economic and other dimensions. If, on the other hand, there will be public exposure and, in consequence, social evaluation of the purchased item, the problem becomes more complicated. A mattress for a child's bed, notwithstanding its implications for health, will be purchased with far more assurance than a lamp to put in front of the picture window. Intermediate on this scale, which might be described as one of possible social tension, is the purchase for family consumption. Criticism at the family level, while undesired, can be dealt with on rational or even irrational grounds that will not suffice when dealing with the world of neighbors and friends.

It should be pointed out that this social dimension cannot be tied to the simple axis of economy-affluence. In some areas, it is highly appropriate to indicate shrewdness by making an economical purchase. In others, a wedding, for example, money must appear to be no object. An interesting cross between these two extremes is frequently seen in entertainment of the occasional guest. Here the artistry of the housewife in purchasing, preparing, and serving may be given free play as she takes ground meat, that for the family would have been hamburger, and turns it into Salisbury steak for the guest.

The Magnitude of the Task Performed

Throughout this essay, the housewife has been identified as the purchasing agent. The accuracy of this assumption is generally accepted. Numerous studies have described the extent of her involvement in some areas. In others, it has been assumed from overwhelming evidence of observation, e.g., grocery purchases. Aside from her own purchasing activities, however, the housewife plays a role in influencing the purchases of her husband and children. Her restraining power must be exerted on all family members if the family is to remain sufficiently solvent and always act in a manner that will avoid censure by society.

In the early years of marriage, the housewife often must attempt to deflate her husband's romanticism. She may well blunt his urge to buy a fur for her by suggesting that the money is needed for some more utilitarian purchase. As was mentioned earlier, her influence on recreational and entertainment expenses may, likewise, be to restrain and reduce. (The impulsiveness and suggestability of the male in the supermarket is even better understood by his wife than by the grocer.) With children, her first major task is to deny permission to spend on unacceptable objects. Later, her role becomes one of influencing choice, directing her daughter to buy this dress rather than that. In such ways, she instructs the next generation in a value system that they will carry into their own homes and families.

The more one studies the economic behavior of this household purchasing agent, the more impressive appears her performance. She must satisfy family, societal, and personal needs with monetary resources that are, for a large part of her married life, limited to what her husband earns. Should he have a productive life of 45 years and average $8,000 per year in that time, she will be responsible for spending well over $300,000 on a variety of goods and services of far greater range than those confronting the industrial purchasing agent. All during this period, the promotional pressures of an unbelievable number of marketers of goods and services will be focused upon her. Many will try to reach her through her husband and children. Others will approach through friends and neighbors, some through the social institutions that are meaningful to her.

There is no likelihood that family wants and family resources will ever be brought into balance. The former are sure to stay well ahead of the latter. And yet, against impossible odds, the housewife performs her task day after day, year after year. To a remarkable degree, she achieves her goals of providing for the more important physical and psychic needs of her loved ones and of achieving fulfillment as wife and mother of a happy family.

19. SYMPTOMATIC FACTORS IN CONSUMER BEHAVIOR

Otto Pollak

IN THE FIRST edition of *Theory in Marketing*, it was pointed out that "rationality in action, as defined by the usual assumptions of economic motivation, is notoriously honored in the breach." [1] The discussion of economic irrationality at that time was restricted to a consideration of entrepreneurial behavior which was not dominated by the profit motive. In this essay, a generally neglected type of irrationality in consumer decision making is explored. Involved is the use of merchandise not primarily or at least not solely for the purpose it is intended to serve or for the status needs it satisfies. From the utilitarian point of view, a vehicle meets the need for transportation, food the need for nutrition, housing the need for shelter, and so on. Also, the higher priced the product, the more likely it is to satisfy the need for the display of status symbols. [2] A high price is also interpreted as an indication of quality in an era of specialization in which very few customers have the ability to evaluate the product with the knowledge of an expert.

Although the need for nutrition, shelter, and transportation is not questioned in our society, the service of products as status symbols sometimes is. Value systems which extol austerity conflict with the value system of an open-class society. Also, our relative abundance does not allow us to distinguish classes by their ability to meet basic needs. For this reason, the use of price as an indication of quality is sometimes the only criterion which can be used to to identify social class. For example, it is often said that the vast majority of American women are well dressed and that differences in their class membership do not express themselves so much in the appearance of their clothing as in its price. (Women assert that this

---

[1] Wroe Alderson and Reavis Cox (eds.), *Theory in Marketing* (Homewood, Ill.: Richard D. Irwin, Inc., 1950), p. 90.

[2] Thorsten Veblen, *The Theory of the Leisure Class* (New York: Modern Library, 1934), pp. 68–101; and Vance Packard, *The Status Seekers* (New York: David McKay Co., Inc., 1959), pp. 128–38.

is not so, but to the male observer the proposition seems to have considerable merit.)

The purchase of status or the use of price to establish class membership cannot be considered irrational because such action meets a need which is related to the structure of our society. Undoubtedly, it produces gratification in many customers. There is, however, another area of consumer behavior that is not related to life maintenance, status seeking, aesthetic enjoyment, or any other commonly recognized value system. It is the central proposition of this essay that many purchasing decisions are made not in order to acquire but in order to destroy, in order to gratify hostility rather than to attain comfort or enjoyment. These purchasing decisions can be judged to be symptomatic because they do not facilitate living but make it more burdensome for the purchaser and his associates.

Given the framework of our Judeo-Christian tradition, it is difficult to gain acceptance for an argument which claims equal power for hate as well as for love; for destructiveness as well as for acquisitiveness; for damage as well as for maintenance; for deterioration as well as for growth. Consequently, the reader must follow the illustrations presented below with a readiness to venture forth into the shadows of his own psychic structure. He must be willing to cope with the resulting anxiety in terms of attack rather than in terms of flight. Anxiety can be a stimulus to coping as well as to repression or denial. In the present case, a spirit of coping rather than one of repression or denial is clearly in order. The ethical implications of the material to be discussed as well as the cognitive problems presented provide ample cause for alarm. A recognition of the destructive purposes of purchasing decisions will produce mental anguish and disapproval within the framework of our culture. It will disturb our self-image and the image which we have of our associates in family and business life. It also suggests a source of customer motivation of considerable effectiveness, the exploitation of which, however, would be incompatible with the traditional value system of our culture.

A Theoretical Frame of Reference

The concepts with which the central proposition will be elaborated are partly taken from modern behavior theory as developed by Clark Hull and his associates at Yale and partly from Freudian psychoanalysis. The human act—under which purchasing can be subsumed—is seen as circumscribed by two boundaries: (1) an activated need, and (2) a drive reduction due to the satisfaction of that need. Since human beings are "open systems," activated needs usually are followed by the appearance of thought images about possible need satisfiers. These thought images are based on past experience and can be viewed as "goals." The goal of the hungry person may be a steak, soup, ice cream, or cheese. It can be any of the processed and cooked forms of nutritional substance which the organism, in the process of its socialization, has experienced as matter which reduces the sensation of hunger.

When a deficit in body intake produces a need for food, hunger satisfiers consumed in the past will come to mind along with some awareness of the location where such items can be obtained. Behavior will result when the human organism utilizes his capacities in order to establish closeness between himself and an opportunity, the reality behind a goal which occurred to him when his need was activated. When behavior has produced contact with the opportunity for the satisfaction of a need, the organism still has to exercise the capacity for consumption. Difficulty along this line is experienced by anyone who tries to chew solid food without teeth, grasp something when he has Parkinson's disease, or swallow when he suffers from inability to take food.[3] At any rate, when an individual has the capacity to bring about proximity between himself and an opportunity and the ability to avail himself of this opportunity by consuming the item, tension reduction will occur, human behavior will be rewarded, and the human act will come to an end.

In order to develop the original proposition—that many purchases are made to gratify hostility—in logical fashion, one must recognize that the human organism is equipped not only with maintenance and growth creative urges but also with urges of destructiveness and hatred.[4] Anybody who has seen a child destroy a structure of toys, a sand castle, or any object accessible to him will gain the impression that destruction is a primary need, a form of self-expression of the growing organism, rather than a reactive form of behavior.

Every phase of psychosexual and social development requires, at least in part, a destruction of earlier tendencies toward gratification. In that sense, the primary need to destroy has to be seen as self-directed or actually as "self-past directed." Anality has, in a sense, to destroy orality and genitality to destroy anality.[5] Over and beyond primary destructiveness there is also reactive destructiveness as elaborated in the theoretical nexus of frustration and aggression.[6] The human organism is set up, potentially at least, as a fighting machine. When this organism encounters obstacles in the process of establishing contact with a gratifier of its needs, activation of the adrenal glands will change the blood chemistry in a manner that

---

[3] Neal E. Miller and John Dollard, *Social Learning and Imitation* (New Haven: Institute of Human Relations, Yale University Press, 1941), p. 26; Otto Pollak, *Social Adjustment in Old Age* (New York: Social Science Research Council, 1948), pp. 32–34; and Ernest Jones, *Life and Work of Sigmund Freud* (New York: Basic Books Publishing Co., 1953), Vol. I, p. 223.

[4] Edward Bibring (1936), "The Development and Problems of the Theory of Instincts," *International Journal of Psychoanalysis*, Vol. 22 (1941), pp. 116–17.

[5] Karl Abraham, *Selected Papers*, edited by E. Jones (1927) (London: Hogarth Press, 1952), pp. 370–93; and Robert Waelder, *Basic Theory of Psychoanalysis* (New York: International Universities Press, 1960), pp. 109 ff.

[6] John Dollard, Neal Miller, *et al.*, *Frustration and Aggression* (New Haven: Institute of Human Relations, Yale University Press, 1939), pp. 1–54.

facilitates efforts to destroy the obstacle. The possibility of masochism in the making of purchasing decisions must also be considered. Tension reduction experienced by persons suffering from guilt-based anxiety when they are punished for violating social norms may lead to self-defeating purchases.[7]

Up to this point, emphasis has been placed on the process of need satisfaction in general and the importance of destructive needs. Before emphasis can be placed specifically on consumer behavior, consideration must be given to the "principle of multiple function" which suggests that as a rule psychic phenomena have many determinants.[8] On the conscious level eating provides nutrition. On the unconscious level, one may eat to seek gratification for disappointment encountered in one's family life or professional career. The determinants do not have to belong to different realms of the psychic structure; they can both operate on the conscious level. Nevertheless, where a human act has both a culturally acceptable and a culturally unacceptable goal, the culturally unacceptable goal is likely to be hidden from the actor by the forces of repression or denial.[9] Finally, a human act can essentially serve a single function, which, however, due to its cultural and personal unacceptability, must be "rationalized" by the actor.[10]

In analyzing purchasing decisions, we have, therefore, to consider the different possibilities as covering a spectrum. One end of the possible range of variation is represented by rationality of a one-functional nature; the other end by irrationality of a one-functional nature. The middle-range positions will be occupied by multifunctional acts which may combine two rational purposes, a rational and symptomatic purpose, or two symptomatic purposes. This model even provides a position for "immobilization," i.e., lack of decision making because of an internal "double-bind" situation.[11] In such cases, the unconscious symptomatic goal is incompatible with the rational goal. This condition produces either self-defeating behavior or no behavior at all. From a topographical point of view, the double-bind situation would probably have to be located in the middle of the spectrum. Most important for present purposes, however, is the fact that rational excuses can be used to obscure symptomatic (aggressively motived) purchasing behavior.

---

[7] Gardner Murphy, *Personality* (New York: Harper & Bros., 1947), p. 557.

[8] Robert Waelder, "The Principle of Multiple Function," *Psychoanalytic Quarterly*, Vol. 5 (1936), p. 49.

[9] Anna Freud, *The Ego and the Mechanisms of Defense* (New York: International Universities Press, 1948), pp. 52 ff., pp. 89–99.

[10] Robert Waelder (ed.), *The Living Thoughts of Freud* (New York: Longmans, Green & Co., 1941), pp. 3–4.

[11] For a definition of the concept of "double bind" in communication, see Gregory Bateson, "Formal Research in Family Structure," in Nathan W. Ackerman, Francis L. Beatman, and Sanford N. Sherman (eds.), *Exploring the Base for Family Therapy* (New York: Family Service Association of America, 1961), pp. 137–39.

Categories of Symptomatic Motivation
in Purchasing Decisions

In American society, the possession of tangible property is largely confined to the family home and its furnishings.[12] In consequence, many purchasing decisions for the home result in purchases which express the nature of family relationships. It has been observed with great psychological shrewdness that "relationships in which social distance is reduced have far greater potentialities for the development of intense hatred" [13] than do relationships in which closeness is not very pronounced. If that is true, purchases decided upon by the wife may express hostility and destructiveness toward the husband, and possibly even the children, more frequently than is generally assumed. The housewife can use her social role of the shopper for the expression of hostility in what may appear, not only to others but even to herself, as acceptable forms. Where the husband is the provider and the wife the shopper, the purchase of consumer goods can be turned into a method of destroying the fruits of the husband's earning power. The pattern of purchases can be used to make his income seem inadequate and, thus, produce damage to the self-image of the husband as a provider. These purchasing decisions of the wife may also be used to express hostilities toward product preferences which the husband formed as a child. They, thus, may express an attack against mothers-in-law which is waged on the battlefield of the husband's canalizations.[14]

The concept of canalization refers to the acquiring of taste preferences as a result of the experience of gratification which follows contact with and consumption of specific need satisfiers. All individuals start with a background of general nonspecific hunger cravings. The encounter at an early age with specific types of food produces personal preferences that have a tendency to persist and to be elaborated on in later life. A child may become a meat-eating, corn-eating, or rice-eating child. When he later marries a person whose canalization system has developed along different lines, nutrition may become a field of potential conflict in the household. One person is likely to become frustrated, angry, and hostile. Such secondary hostilities may also lead to conflict over purchasing decisions in other areas, to refusal to agree with the purchasing wishes of the partner, or to purchases which will bring into the home things known to be disagreeable to the spouse or incompatible with his ideal of expense management.

Irrationality can influence not only the relationship that exists between the members of a family making the purchasing decision but also the

---

[12] Otto Pollak, "A Family Diagnosis Model," *The Social Service Review*, Vol. 34, No. 1 (March, 1960), p. 24.

[13] Henry V. Dicks, "Clinical Studies in Marriage and the Family," *British Journal of Medical Psychology*, Vol. 26 (1953), pp. 181–96.

[14] Murphy, *op. cit.*, pp. 161 ff.

relationship established between the buyer and the salesman. The phenomena of "displacement" [15] may operate in that relationship. A woman who cannot afford to express antagonism toward her husband or her children may find the salesman a convenient target. In a buyer's market, the salesman is notoriously vulnerable, and vulnerability always attracts the displacement of aggression. Market researchers concerned with the product preferences of consumers have to disregard this phenomenon by the very nature of their design. The sales manager of a firm does so at his peril.

Apart from hostility and aggression directed at specific persons, purchasing decisions may also reflect a feeling of generalized hopelessness and defeatism. A group of tenants who were chronically tardy in paying their rent to the New York Housing Authority expressed their defeatism by such statements as: "Live today because tomorrow you may die," "We are trapped," "We're in a blind alley." In the group discussions of these people, all expressed their resentment at the hopelessness which characterized their lives and viewed their unrealistic buying as an expression of anger against their situation. [16] A special light was thrown on the compensatory fantasies of attaining control and power through instalment buying. The low-income person apparently considers instalment buying an attempt to attain an experience of acquisitive power, an attempt which is not justified by financial conditions and which actually leads to victimization and further experience of defeat.

A final expression of irrationality in human behavior is expressed in the attempt to chase gratifications which have not been sufficiently provided in the past. People with deprived childhoods long for gratifications which they should have enjoyed earlier. These gratifications are pursued at a later stage when subsequent developments have made them inappropriate. The aging woman who buys a youthful hat, the retired executive who buys a bright and shiny sports car, the person who with high blood pressure indulges in a high cholesterol diet are likely to be pursuing, inappropriately and belatedly, goals which they did not attain sufficiently at earlier phases of development. One could consider purchasing decisions made on such a psychological basis as reflecting "arrest buying" with the term signifying that growth in making purchasing decisions has been arrested at a certain level of development. Previous patterns prevail in later stages of development without adjustment to age changes, need changes, and condition changes.

A somewhat related irrationality refers to the purchase of securities on the basis of the past record of a company. Certain investment decisions are frequently made on the assumption that the trend of business performance which characterized the past will continue in the future. The assump-

---

15 Dollard, Miller, *et al., op. cit.,* pp. 41–44.

16 Mrs. Muriel Nelson Rogers, "A Group Education Program for Marginally Adjusted Families," *Social Casework,* Vol. 43, No. 4 (April, 1962), pp. 178–84.

tion at work seems to be related to the "law of good continuation" in Gestalt psychology. When we perceive segments of a line which follow a definitive direction without break, we are likely to disregard other lines which connect with the perceived line but break its clarity of direction. It should be obvious to the rational investor that he is to share in the future rather than the past of the company. To project future earning strength on an assumption of the law of good continuation is to disregard such factors as social change, changes in competition, and mortality in management.

From an overall point of view, it might be suggested that in our culture the rise in impulse buying and in buying determined or codetermined by hostility and destructiveness is due to an increase in the number of persons afflicted with "character disorders." In the practice of psychiatry, social work, and education, it has been observed that more and more people are suffering not from a neurosis reflecting something of which they disapprove in themselves but rather from nonsatisfaction of their demands by their associates.

When people blame others instead of themselves for their discomforts, they are unlikely to work to improve their condition. They deny the necessity of "input" in their personal life, demand "output" from others without reciprocity. Such people are bound to fail in problems of interpersonal competence and will be unable to maintain the equanimity required to make rational decisions. Since they deny that the relationship between themselves and others is one of give-and-take, they are also likely to deny the relationship between their present and their future. In consequence, they will be impulse buyers and they will frequently be instalment buyers without considering whether or not they can meet the schedule of debt repayment.

Implications for the Ethics of Selling

It is characteristic of our culture that many areas of business life are showing an increasing trend toward professionalization. This has been demonstrated in the fields of accountancy, insurance, and management, and is also becoming more pronounced in marketing. All professionalization, however, is characterized by more than the possession of specialized information and the ability to use specialized techniques. There is also an affirmation of ethical concerns. In the last analysis, ethical action involves self-limitation, a renunciation of pursuit of self-interest in the interest of others.

If professionalization is to take place in marketing, the personnel engaged in this activity will have to become aware of the types of irrational consumer motivation discussed in this article. Furthermore, they will have to refuse to sell to individuals so motivated. Such a decision may seem very difficult, if not absurd, given the frame of reference of the "economic man." In fact, however, the profit motive as an overriding basis for "selling decisions" is already exposed to considerable limitations. Government regulations and self-regulation by management work in the same direction. The "well-tempered corporation" has to meet more interests than those of the owners.[17] Admittedly, it is easy for government employees working in regulatory agencies and for management personnel in a business corporation to modify or dissociate themselves from the profit motive. By and large, the income of neither group is immediately affected by a decline or arrest of profit development in private corporations. For the salesman working on a commission or the owner of a firm, a refusal to sell under certain conditions or in certain situations has more immediate consequences. A conflict of interest situation which makes ethical considerations harder to follow may arise. In the last analysis, however, it might be proposed that a customer who damages himself or members of his family by a purchase with destructive consequences will not remain a customer over any extended period of time. Consequently, the development of marketing ethics along the lines herein defined may demand a smaller renunciation of profit than the proposal seems to imply.

In conclusion, can a salesman be expected to recognize irrational motivation of the type discussed in this essay? In mail-order selling or selling based on ephemeral contact with strangers in a department store, such a recognition of motivation is unlikely to occur, even though careful study of charge accounts would produce amazingly telling clues. In house-to-house selling or selling to a customer who is personally known to a salesman, some recognition of motivation can be expected. Ours is a psychological age in which people become increasingly perceptive of the negative aspects of human behavior, of the self-damaging character of decisions, and of destructive tendencies in others. Since our culture is allowing for the expression of an ever increasing amount of hostility, customers will be freer in the future to reveal their motivations than they may have been in earlier stages of our business civilization. Consequently, sales personnel who recognize that purchasing decisions can be motivated by the factors discussed in this essay will be alert to and should be able to identify many illustrations of this type of consumer behavior. The extent of professionalization eventually reached in marketing will depend in large part on the action taken on the basis of this awareness.

---

[17] Richard Eels, *The Meaning of Modern Business: An Introduction to the Philosophy of Large Corporate Enterprises* (New York: Columbia University Press, 1960), pp. 307–38.

20. A MARKETING ANALYSIS OF SUBURBAN AND URBAN EXPENDITURE PATTERNS

Donald F. Blankertz

EARLY in 1951, the Bureau of Labor Statistics made a field survey to provide the information needed for revising the expenditure weights in the Consumer Price Index. Data on expenditures in 1950 for some 15,000 budget items were collected from 12,500 families in 91 representative areas. These data were tabulated later by the Bureau of Labor Statistics for the Wharton School of Finance and Commerce and published in 1956 in 18 volumes.[1] The wealth of information on expenditures and related factors, particularly for suburban areas, is almost unrivaled. Even today, these data remain fully useful for some forms of basic marketing investigation.

The findings and proposals given here are drawn from an earlier and far more exhaustive study. Regional and small-city-size data have been eliminated. Demographic analyses and details of expenditure patterns, such as are useful for individual marketing applications, have been minimized. The data presented are taken from urban and suburban areas of the North to represent the most typical relationships. Emphasis is placed on uniformities and similarities rather than on differences. Marketing opportunities also are stressed, and special attention is given to the potentials of demand analysis based on necessity and luxury patterns of expenditure.

Some Urban and Suburban Differences and Similarities

The assortments of types of families domiciled in large cities and suburbs differ in many respects. Suburban living has little appeal for some

---

[1] *Study of Consumer Expenditures, Incomes and Savings,* tabulated by the Bureau of Labor Statistics, U.S. Department of Labor, for the Wharton School of Finance and Commerce, University of Pennsylvania, Philadelphia, Pa., 1956.

types of "families," and prejudice is a factor tending to reduce the number of representatives of other types. The net effect is what might be termed selective migration to the suburbs. In the suburbs of the North, there are fewer single-person families (7.2% of total suburban families versus 13.9% in the large cities), fewer Negro families (2.8% versus 12.3%), and fewer unskilled workers who are heads of families (9.3% versus 15.4%). These groups are, of course, characteristically low-income families. For example, the majority of single persons (58% in suburbs and 55% in large cities) had income of less than $2,000 after taxes in 1950.

For many marketing purposes, therefore, *the most significant difference between cities and suburbs is in income distribution or the mix of income classes.* This difference is shown in Table 1.

TABLE 1

DISTRIBUTION OF FAMILIES BY INCOME CLASS, 1950 *
(Percent of Families)

Income Class	Large Cities	Suburbs
0–$999	5.3	4.0
$1,000–$1,999	11.5	6.8
$2,000–$2,999	19.4	14.0
$3,000–$3,999	24.5	24.6
$4,000–$4,999	17.8	19.4
$5,000–$5,999	9.7	11.6
$6,000–$7,499	6.2	9.4
$7,500–$9,999	3.3	6.0
$10,000 or more	2.3	4.2
	100.0	100.0

* Data is for the North; income is after taxes.

This is not to claim that demographic factors are unimportant. Those already noted undoubtedly influence store patronage and the demand for individual commodities and services. So, too, does higher home ownership in the suburbs (62.6% versus 39.1%), higher educational levels, and the presence of more families with young children. The following are among the notable differences in expenditures which may be influenced by differences in the urban and suburban social settings: considerably higher suburban expenditures in all income classes for fuel, light, and refrigeration; lower suburban expenditures in the bottom half of the income scale and higher suburban expenditures in the top half of the income scale for housing; lower suburban expenditures in most income classes for food eaten away from home; higher suburban expenditures in most income groups for automobile purchase and operation but somewhat lower expenditures for other transportation and travel; and somewhat larger suburban expenditures for men's and boys' clothing.

Marketers are and need to be cognizant of the differences previously mentioned. These differences, however, should not obscure the very great similarities which exist among families of the same type regardless of location. In general, as the data in later tables indicate, locational difference (residence in large cities or their suburbs) makes little difference in the expenditures of families of like type, size, and composition. Differences in income distribution explain why identical behavior can cause wide variations in per capita expenditures. Even if every family of like type in both cities and suburbs made absolutely identical expenditures, their aggregate expenditures for goods and services would differ sharply as between city and suburban markets. Intriguing and useful as is the analysis of differential behavior, the emphasis here is placed on underlying uniformities. Using overall averages and playing fast and loose with cause-and-effect relationships can be dangerous. The fact that suburbs have proportionately far more children in the total population than do large cities is well known. Some people deduce from this fact that something about the suburbs is conducive to child bearing or promotes philoprogenitiveness. The true situation seems to be that a higher percentage of the suburban population consists of husband-and-wife families (76.4% versus 67.6% in the North). Even though both areas have about the same proportion of husband-and-wife families without children (23.3% to 22.9%) and those families with children are the same average size (3.80% to 3.79%), the higher perecntage that husband-and-wife families with children constitute of the suburban population (53.1% to 44.7%) kites the average. In sum, child-bearing families prefer the suburbs to the large cities, but nubile females are not more fecund in one place than another.

Market Power

For many, perhaps most, marketing purposes, the expenditures made rather than savings or income, either before or after taxes, is the truly important phenomenon. Income can be completely misleading as a measure of market potential because of the effects of progressive taxation and of dissaving (spending more than they make) by lower-income families. The expenditures actually made by consumers sometimes are compared to votes, or dollar ballots, cast in the marketplace to determine what goods and services, and in what quantities, will be offered. This concept of dollar voting can be a useful analytical tool, even though data do not permit identification by expenditure as against income classes.

The share of total expenditures made by any given class can be called its *market power*. Table 2 shows the market power held in 1950 by the different income classes in the large cities and suburbs of the North. These data make clear how market power is concentrated in the middle-income classes of both the cities and the suburbs. The great difference between city and suburban markets, however, lies in the shift to the right on the income spectrum. In the large cities of the North, the $2,000–$2,999 income class has the third highest market power (13.8%); in the suburbs it is but seventh in power (with 8.8%). Families with incomes below

TABLE 2

MARKET POWER: SHARES OF TOTAL EXPENDITURES FOR
CURRENT CONSUMPTION, 1950, BY INCOME CLASS
(Percentages)

Income Class		Large Cities		Suburbs	
		%	Rank	%	Rank
0–999	....	1.9	9	1.1	9
$1,000–$1,999	....	5.4	8	2.7	8
$2,000–$2,999	....	13.8	3	8.8	7
$3,000–$3,999	....	22.4	1	19.9	1
$4,000–$4,999	....	20.9	2	19.1	2
$5,000–$5,999	....	13.4	4	13.6	3
$6,000–$7,499	....	9.5	5	13.1	4
$7,000–$9,999	....	6.2	7	9.7	6
$10,000 or more	....	6.5	6	12.0	5

$3,000 account for 21.1% of total expenditures by city families but for only 12.6% among suburban families. Conversely, families with $6,000 or more income have a 34.8% share of suburban totals but only 22.2% of city totals.

As later analysis of expenditure elasticities for individual service and commodity classifications will make clearer, it is necessary to remember these variations in the distribution of market power when examining demographic factors. Otherwise, what is due primarily to different assortments of family types, particularly income classes, will be ascribed to differences in living and buying habits.

Aspects of Uniformity

Budget Allocations. Table 3 reveals that families in the various regions and in cities of all sizes allocate their budgets or distribute their expenditures in very similar ways. This fact suggests that some strong forces for uniformity are at work in American society. In 1950, as everywhere in all times, food ranks first in American family budgets. More remarkably, expenditures for travel and transportation are always second or tied for second; expenditures for education are always last (fifteenth); expenditures for newspapers, magazines, and books always fourteenth; expenditures for house furnishings and equipment are always in fifth place; and expenditures for personal care are always tenth. Because percentage allocations for some categories are very similar, some minor shiftings in rank exist. Thus, housing and clothing expenditures play roles of twin stars varying from third to fourth rank among city size by regions. Expenditures for medical care, household operation, and recreation rank sixth, seventh, or eighth in family expenditures.

Another notable similarity is that after purchasing food, transportation, housing, clothing, and house furnishings and equipment, families in the

TABLE 3

AVERAGE FAMILY EXPENDITURES AND RANK OF EXPENDITURES
(Percentages)

Major Categories of Goods and Services	Large Cities		North Suburbs		Small Cities		Large Cities		South Suburbs		Small Cities		Large Cities		West Suburbs		Small Cities	
	%	Rank	%	Rank	%	Rank	%	Rank	%	Rank	%	Rank	%	Rank	%	Rank	%	Rank
Food	30.1	1	28.9	1	30.1	1	29.6	1	28.8	1	30.6	1	28.1	1	27.9	1	29.1	1
Transportation	12.0	2	13.1	2	12.7	2	12.9	2	14.8	2	12.9	2	14.9	2	18.1	2	15.7	2
Housing	12.0	3	11.3	4	11.3	3	11.6	4	10.9	3	9.7	4	12.0	3	10.4	3	10.6	4
Clothing	11.5	4	11.8	3	11.0	4	12.0	3	10.9	4	12.2	3	11.1	4	10.2	4	10.8	3
House furnishings and equipment	6.2	5	7.0	5	7.3	5	6.8	5	7.2	5	7.3	5	7.4	5	7.2	5	7.6	5
Medical care	5.1	6	5.0	7	4.9	7	4.8	7	5.0	6	5.4	6	5.5	6	5.5	6	5.4	6
Household operation	4.6	7	5.1	6	4.4	8	5.2	6	5.0	7	5.0	8	4.6	7	4.6	8	4.2	7
Recreation	4.6	8	4.6	8	4.2	9	4.2	8	4.6	8	3.1	9	4.5	8	4.8	7	4.1	8
Fuel, light, refrigeration	3.9	9	4.6	9	6.0	6	3.8	9	4.0	9	5.3	7	3.3	9	3.2	9	4.1	9
Personal care	2.0	10	2.1	10	2.1	10	2.4	10	2.2	10	2.4	10	2.2	10	2.1	10	2.2	10
Tobacco	1.9	12	1.6	12	1.8	11	2.0	11	1.8	11	2.0	11	1.6	12	1.5	12	1.7	11
Alcoholic beverages	2.0	11	1.8	11	1.3	12	1.6	12	1.5	13	1.0	13	1.8	11	1.5	13	1.4	13
Miscellaneous	1.3	13	1.5	13	1.3	13	1.5	13	1.7	12	1.6	12	1.5	13	1.7	11	1.6	12
Newspapers, books, magazines	.9	14	.9	14	1.0	14	.9	14	.9	14	1.0	14	.9	14	.8	14	.9	14
Education	.6	15	.7	15	.4	15	.7	15	.6	15	.6	15	.7	15	.4	15	.5	15

North have made between 71.8% and 72.3% of their total expenditures; families in the South 72.6% to 72.9%; and families in the West 73.5% to 73.8%.

Distribution of Families, Persons, and Children by Family Income; and Per Capita Expenditures. Traditionally, the most basic economic unit is taken to be the family unit or household. But single persons living alone, young married couples without children, and larger family units have differing needs and differing life styles; and income is distributed differently among them. For some marketing analyses, it is better to consider the individual as the important unit or to consider the presence (or absence) and number of children of differing ages—or even to consider children alone. Table 4 shows the rather amazing, and gratifying, differences in the distribution of wealth and poverty in America (1950) when family income is assigned to family units, to persons, and to children.

TABLE 4

PERCENTAGE DISTRIBUTION OF FAMILIES, PERSONS, AND CHILDREN BY FAMILY INCOME
CLASS FOR LARGE CITIES AND SUBURBS OF THE NORTH

Income Class	Large Cities			Suburbs		
	Families	Persons	Children	Families	Persons	Children
0–$999	5.3	2.6	.7	4.0	1.9	.4
$1,000–$1,999	11.5	7.1	3.9	6.8	4.2	2.1
$2,000–$2,999	19.4	16.8	14.3	14.0	12.3	12.4
$3,000–$3,999	24.5	25.8	28.4	24.6	24.3	26.4
$4,000–$4,999	17.8	20.9	23.9	19.4	20.3	20.2
$5,000–$5,999	9.7	11.6	11.8	11.6	12.8	11.2
$6,000–$7,499	6.2	7.6	8.3	9.4	11.5	12.6
$7,500–$9,999	3.3	4.6	5.0	6.0	7.7	9.0
$10,000 or more ..	2.3	3.0	3.7	4.2	5.1	5.7

Obviously, we depress ourselves overly much—whether members of the dismal sicence or not—by concentrating on income distribution by families. People are better off than households; and children select with fine discrimination parents able to support them in the fashion to which so many modern children are accustomed. In the large cities of the North, 5.3% of all families had less than $1,000 in income after taxes, but only 2.6% of all persons were part of such families, and only .7% of children were so located. In the suburbs, conditions were better all along the line.

Even more clearly indicative of the real ability to buy and therefore to enjoy a satisfactory standard of living are per capita *expenditures.* Far less variance exists in fact in per capita expenditures in America than is usually assumed. As shown in Table 5, per capita expenditures made by those in the lowest income class (0 to $999 annual income) are not doubled until one reaches the $7,500-to-$9,999 income class. For the middle two thirds of all people, per capita expenditures vary by less than 50%. Certainly this relative uniformity in effective purchasing power exerts a very strong force toward market uniformities. Reducing the differences are the increases in family size associated with additional income, progressive taxation and higher rates of saving as income increases, and the ability of the poor to borrow.

A Law of Uniformity?   Beyond these statistics, there are reasons for proposing a law of uniformity. Simon Nelson Patten [2] stressed the importance of modes of consumption as opposed to income. Among the insights provided in *Middletown*, the following is of particular interest: "In 1890, Middletown appears to have lived on a series of plateaus as regards standards of living. . . . Today the edges of the plateaus have been shaved off, and every one lives on a slope from any point of which desirable things belonging to people all the way to the top are in view." [3]

Even more explicit is the following: "For today, it is our belief, a general lowering of barriers is going on: between the age grades, between the sexes, between regions of the country, and between social classes, with the prospect in view of a fairly uniform middle-majority life style becoming a major American theme with variations." [4]

From such roots, a more formal hypothesis or law of uniform consumption in an economy of relative abundance may be worded: *All families, except those at the extremes of the income range, are seeking to obtain the same categories of goods and services in the same relative proportions; and they fail entirely to accomplish this common goal only because of the expenditures they "must" make for "necessities."*

The Role of Scarcity and the 100% Fallacy.   The stated hypothesis need not carry all the sociological freight found in the cited article by Riesman and Roseborough. The chief qualification relates to the continuing role of scarcity, or need. For social acceptance, if not for outright survival, those with low incomes must use a large share of total expenditures for food. A more compelling reason for the qualification, however, involves what might be called the 100% fallacy. The relevant problem may be clarified most easily, perhaps, by an example. If a clothier is particularly successful in selling men's suits, his sales of men's suits as a percentage of total sales will be far above average. Perforce, however, sales in some other line or lines—shirts, pajamas, or shoes—will have to be shown as less than average. This is true even though by other measures, such as sales per square foot of selling space, sales of these items also are above the average for all stores. In reasoning as to share of total sales, success in some category will force other categories to show up poorly.

---

[2] Simon Nelson Patten, *Essays in Economic Theory* (New York: Alfred A. Knopf, Inc., 1924).

[3] R. S. and H. M. Lynd, *Middletown: A Study in American Culture* (New York: Harcourt, Brace & Co., 1929), pp. 82–83.

[4] David Riesman and Howard Roseborough, "Careers and Consumer Behavior," in Lincoln H. Clark (ed.), *Consumer Behavior: The Life Cycle and Consumer Behavior* (New York: New York University Press, 1955), Vol. II, pp. 1–2.

TABLE 5

PER CAPITA EXPENDITURES BY INCOME CLASSES
(In Dollars)

Income Class Income	No.	Large Cities	Suburbs
0–$999	1	963	855
$1,000–$1,999	2	988	899
$2,000–$2,999	3	1,078	1,010
$3,000–$3,999	4	1,129	1,160
$4,000–$4,999	5	1,301	1,331
$5,000–$5,999	6	1,506	1,505
$6,000–$7,499	7	1,633	1,620
$7,500–$9,999	8	1,782	1,780
$10,000 or more	9	2,781	3,353
Average		1,313	1,415

For expenditure data the relevant problem is that some categories, especially food, take a large percentage of total expenditures for the poorest families. These categories decrease steadily in importance as a percentage of total expenditures as income rises. This fact can be viewed either as evidence of what families "must" do when poor or as the remnant role of scarcity in our society.

A fairer test of the law of consumption uniformity, therefore, may be had by subtracting the actual dollar expenditures made for food prepared at home; for housing; and for fuel, light, and refrigeration before percentaging. As is seen in Table 6, such action does not "force" a conclusion, since the differences in dollar expenditures are increased not decreased by this substraction. What remains may be called "discretionary" expenditures. Results indicate a very large measure of uniformity for the great middle majority of 80% to 90% of all families. From a family income level of about $2,000 to that of $10,000 or more, there appears to be a definite life style, an American theme—but not without variations.

Expenditure Elasticities

In this age of relative abundance, very few categories of goods or services are the exclusive province of either the rich or the poor. *Each succeeding increase in income among groups of families is accompanied by increases in dollar expenditures for each major category of goods and services.* (Also, because of larger average family size and higher family income, the dollar expenditures of suburban families for all categories of goods and services will tend to be higher than the expenditures of families in large cities.)

But this does *not* mean that dollar expenditures increase at the same rate for every type of purchase. For some goods, such as food prepared at home, the dollar increases in expenditures that accompany increases in income are relatively small; and for some, such as clothing, they are relatively great. These different expenditure patterns and the previously discussed differences in income distribution among families are strongly determinant factors in shaping suburban and urban markets. Compared to these two factors, such demographic differences as occupation, age, and nationality are in general but modifying forces.

Necessities and Luxuries. Expenditures have traditionally been classified as to whether they were made for the purchase of a necessity or a luxury. In an economy of scarcity (or, in marketing terms, of mass markets and class markets), the distinction is painfully easy. Neither producers nor marketing agencies have difficulty in sorting out differential opportunities between rich (class) and poor (mass) customers. With the rise in average purchasing power and the increasing dominance of the middle class, the concepts of necessity and luxury goods blur.

Families of Belgian workingmen in 1853 (see Table 7) allocated from 85.4% to 91.3% of their budgets for the old trilogy of need: food, clothing, and shelter. In America in 1950 (see Table 3), such expenditures, even after taxes, took little more than half of family budgets. This is an entirely different world of consumption from that investigated by Engel.

Neither the importance to survival nor the size of budgetary share adequately characterizes necessities. Moreover, in almost every category there is an increased mixture of necessity and luxury components. Oranges are no longer a luxury food, but the common purchase of them as concentrated, frozen juice is partly a purchase of "built-in maid service" or "time in a package."

Marketing Definitions of Necessity and Luxury. The concepts of necessity and luxury need not be abandoned. For marketing analyses the following definitions would seem to be useful:

A necessity is any good or service, or combination of both, for which, as income increases, a decreasing percentage of total expenditures is made. Its hallmark is a regressive pattern.

A luxury is any good or service, or combination of both, for which, as income increases, an increasing percentage of total expenditures is made. Its hallmark is a progressive pattern.

Actually, the patterns are not linear, and the 1950 sample data at the extremes of the income classes are limited. A simple ratio of expenditures by lower- and upper-income groups, however, will give a fair indication. Table 8 shows ratios for the income group of $1,000 to $3,999 versus the $5,000 to $9,999 group. In general, the upper group spends about $2.00 per family to every $1.00 spent by the lower-income group average family; but whatever actual ratio existed has been taken as 1.00, or unity.

As of 1950, the important necessities were food, housing, and fuel, light, and refrigeration. Tobacco is the only other clear necessity, although expenditures for personal care, for medical care, and for newspapers, magazines, and books show a primarily necessitous pattern.

TABLE 6

DISCRETIONARY EXPENDITURES FOR MAJOR CATEGORIES OF EXPENDITURES

Income Classes

Large Cities in the North

Expenditure Categories	0–$999	$1,000–$1,999	$2,000–$2,999	$3,000–$3,999	$4,000–$4,999	$5,000–$5,999	$6,000–$7,499	$7,500–$9,999	$10,000–Plus	All
Total expenditures	1,405	1,807	2,742	3,533	4,534	5,375	5,940	7,334	10,974	3,871
Less: Food at home	389	502	765	982	1,144	1,241	1,264	1,520	1,741	960
Housing	277	334	381	423	507	544	615	707	1,281	465
Fuel, light, etc.	99	100	125	147	173	189	191	239	271	152
Discretionary expenditures } $	640	871	1,471	1,981	2,710	3,401	3,870	4,868	7,681	2,294
%	100	100	100	100	100	100	100	100	100	100
1. Trans. and trav.	18.3	14.5	16.9	20.3	22.1	22.6	21.8	22.3	17.4	20.4
2. Clothing	14.4	18.1	19.3	19.3	19.5	20.6	20.9	20.1	21.1	19.9
3. House fur. & equip.	7.5	8.3	10.3	10.8	11.8	11.1	10.2	9.6	7.9	10.5
4. Food—away	12.3	15.8	12.1	8.4	8.5	9.0	10.4	11.0	11.4	10.0
5. Medical care	14.8	10.6	9.3	9.7	8.4	7.5	7.9	9.0	5.5	8.6
6. Recreation	4.7	4.9	6.8	8.2	8.7	7.8	8.3	7.2	8.1	7.8
7. Household op.	9.7	10.0	8.0	7.1	6.5	6.9	6.7	8.2	13.0	7.7
8. Personal care	4.1	4.9	4.6	4.2	3.8	3.5	3.4	3.1	2.8	3.8
9. Alcoholic bev.	2.2	3.6	3.8	3.4	3.4	3.4	3.4	3.4	3.2	3.5
10. Tobacco	2.2	3.9	4.4	3.6	3.3	2.9	2.7	2.2	1.5	3.2
11. Miscellaneous	6.6	3.0	2.1	2.0	1.6	2.2	2.1	1.7	4.4	2.2
12. News., bks., etc.	2.5	2.1	2.0	2.2	1.5	1.4	1.4	1.1	1.0	1.5
13. Education	.9	.4	.8	.8	1.0	1.0	.9	1.1	2.9	1.1

Suburbs in the North

Total expenditures	1,302	1,799	2,841	3,661	4,458	5,299	6,296	7,213	12,965	4,522
Less: Food at home	364	542	822	1,012	1,150	1,214	1,373	1,478	1,758	1,071
Housing	242	261	338	416	473	588	689	790	1,432	510
Fuel, light, etc.	103	156	180	183	214	225	252	245	391	207
Discretionary } $ expenditures } %	593	840	1,501	2,050	2,621	3,272	3,982	4,700	9,384	2,734
	100	100	100	100	100	100	100	100	100	100
1. Trans. and trav.	19.9	17.1	21.2	22.8	25.1	22.3	23.2	21.4	15.2	21.7
2. Clothing	11.5	17.5	17.5	19.3	19.4	19.2	20.4	21.8	19.4	19.5
3. House fur. & equip.	7.5	9.4	12.3	11.5	12.5	12.3	11.3	9.1	12.3	11.6
4. Food—away	15.7	9.5	8.0	6.8	7.0	8.5	9.0	11.7	11.0	8.7
5. Medical care	15.6	11.1	11.2	9.7	8.2	8.9	7.4	6.7	5.8	8.3
6. Recreation	2.2	6.1	6.5	7.9	8.1	7.2	8.6	8.0	6.9	7.6
7. Household op.	9.7	10.8	7.5	6.9	6.5	6.7	7.3	7.9	16.6	8.5
8. Personal care	3.5	4.4	4.1	4.2	3.7	3.5	3.3	3.2	2.3	3.5
9. Alcoholic bev.	.8	3.9	2.0	3.3	2.8	3.2	2.4	3.0	3.0	2.9
10. Tobacco	2.5	4.3	3.5	3.6	2.9	2.7	2.5	2.0	1.5	2.7
11. Miscellaneous	8.5	3.0	3.5	1.6	1.9	2.9	1.7	2.0	3.7	2.4
12. News., bks., etc.	2.7	2.5	1.9	1.7	1.5	1.3	1.3	1.3	1.0	1.5
13. Education	-	.5	.9	.8	.6	1.3	1.7	1.8	1.5	1.1

TABLE 7

PERCENTAGE COMPOSITION OF BELGIAN WORKMEN'S
FAMILY BUDGETS, 1853 *

Category of Expenditure	On Relief	Poor but Independent	Comfortable
Food	70.9	67.4	62.4
Clothing (including cleaning)	11.7	13.2	14.0
Housing	8.7	8.3	9.0
Heat and light	5.6	5.5	5.4
Tools and work supplies	.6	1.2	2.3
Education, religion, etc.	.4	1.1	1.2
Taxes	.2	.5	.9
Health, recreation, insurance, etc.	1.7	2.8	4.3
Personal services	.2	.2	.4
Total	100.0	100.0	100.0

* Borrowed from Benjamin S. Loeb, "The Use of Engel's Laws as a Basis for Predicting Consumer Expenditures," *The Journal of Marketing*, Vol. XX, No. 1 (July, 1955), p. 21.

The most important luxuries in family budgets are clothing, auto purchases, auto operation, recreation, and household operation.

Care must be exercised in assuming that the pattern for a commodity group will hold for all subgroups. Expenditures for women's and girls' hosiery, for example, follow a strong necessity pattern, but expenditures for outerwear (both men's and boys' as well as women's and girls') are strongly progressive.

Among the many interesting features of such analysis, as well as the important social, economic, and marketing implications, only two will be highlighted. For present purposes the most significant aspects concern (1) the effect which the divergent patterns of necessity and luxury expenditures have on suburban and urban markets and, therefore, on our ability to understand, measure, and predict market opportunities; and (2) the strong influence which supply factors (other than quantity) seem to have on demand in shaping market size and structure.

Expenditure Patterns, Market Power, and Market Size. A typical suburban market is characterized by a considerably higher average family income than that of a typical urban market. This makes for a general tendency toward higher dollar expenditures per market unit in the suburbs. If the pattern of expenditure is that of a necessity good or service, however, then the difference will be greatly dampened down or even obliterated. But if the pattern of expenditure is that of a luxury good or service, a multiplier, accelerator, escalator, or staircase effect results. Charts 1, 2, and 3 demonstrate for a representative necessity expenditure (food prepared at home) and luxury expenditure (women's and girls' outerwear) how vastly different is market structure (or the market power by income class) and total market size—and *not*, it should be stressed again,

TABLE 8

Necessities and Luxuries among Major and Minor Categories of Expenditures for Large Cities and Suburbs of the North

| | Large Cities | | | Suburbs | | |
	Ratios		Classification	Ratios		Classification
Fuel, light, refrig.	.75		N	.69		N
Tobacco	.83		N	.78		N
Food—total	.85		N	.87		N
Food at home		.79	N		.77	N
Food away		1.14	L		1.48	L
Housing	.75		N	.86		N
News., bks., mags.	.85		N	.83		N
Education	1.67		L	2.36		L
Trans. and travel—total	1.44		L	1.19		L
Auto. purchase		1.71	L		1.28	L
Auto. operation		1.39	L		1.12	L
Other trans. and travel		1.02	S		1.08	S
Recreation—total	1.27		L	1.25		L
Purch. of rad., etc.		1.07	S		1.15	L
Admissions		1.18	L		1.15	L
Other recreation		1.48	L		1.46	L
Clothing—total	1.27		L	1.26		L
W & G clothing—subtotal ..		(1.26)	(L)		(1.28)	(L)
W & G outerwear		1.31	L		1.35	L
W & G underwear, etc.		1.24	L		1.19	L
W & G Hosiery		.98	S		1.03	S
W & G footwear		1.10	L		1.16	L
W & G hats, etc.		1.58	L		1.76	L
M & B clothing—subtotal ..		(1.33)	(L)		(1.24)	(L)
M & B outerwear		1.36	L		1.30	L
M & B underwear, etc.		1.18	L		1.11	L
M & B footwear		1.06	S		.94	S
M & B hats, etc.		1.73	L		1.51	L
Clothing materials		1.12	L		.92	S
Cothing services		1.19	L		1.28	L
Clothing—child under two ..		.67	N		.75	N
Household operation	1.09		L	1.13		L
Alcoholic beverages	1.13		L	1.11		L
Personal care—total	.92		S	.94		S
Personal services		.98	S		.96	S
Toilet articles		.85	N		.90	N
Medical care—total	.98		S	.96		S
Group plans		.93	S		.94	S
Dir. pay, medical care		1.00	S		.88	N
House furnishings and equip. ..	1.25		L	1.11		L
Household tex.		1.16	L		1.31	L
Floor covering		1.67	L		1.41	L
Furniture		1.53	L		1.40	L
Equipment		.97	S		.76	N
Other housewares		1.10	L		.76	N
Miscellaneous	1.14		L	1.19		L

because of differences in basic buying behavior by families of the same type and size in cities and suburbs.

In the case of food prepared at home in 1950, the dampening down effect of a necessity pattern can be seen visually by comparing Chart 2 with Chart 1, the latter being for total expenditures by each income class. Market size per family is 11.6% higher in the suburbs because per capita expenditures for food happen to run higher ($33.47 to $32.04), family income is greater, and families are larger. The difference is not due to an increase in the proportion of income spent for food, since this is lower (22.9% to 24.3%) in the suburbs.

CHART 1

MARKET POWER OR PERCENT OF TOTAL EXPENDITURES BY
EACH INCOME CLASS

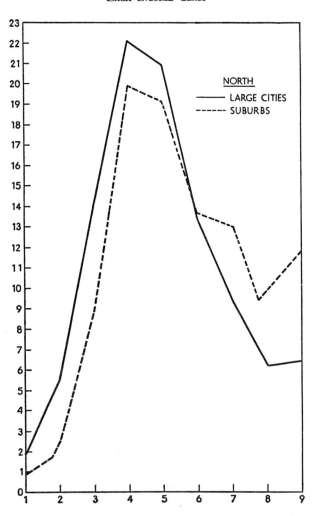

In sharp contrast are expenditures for women's and girls' outerwear. Comparison of Chart 3 with Chart 1 shows the very great shift in market power to the upper-income classes, which in turn makes the suburban market per family 29.1% higher than the city market for the same class of expenditure.

Obviously, market estimates made on a population or an income basis have to consider carefully both the differences in family composition by income groups and family size and the great changes in the market power of each income class as between cities and suburbs.

The Interaction of Supply Characteristics on Demand. For a more detailed analysis of necessity and luxury expenditure patterns, it seemed desirable to distinguish subcategories.

Continuous necessities are those goods and services for which percentage expenditures decline throughout all increasing income classes. Most necessities follow this pattern, as in 1950 did food (both in total and food prepared at home); fuel, light, and refrigeration; tobacco; and newspapers, magazines, and books. *Discontinuous necessities* are those goods and services for which early declines in percentage expenditures come to a halt or even are reversed slightly among higher-income classes. Expenditures for housing decline steeply until about the $5,000 level of income, after which percentage expenditures decline no further.

Continuous luxuries are those goods and services for which percentage expenditures rise throughout all income classes. As of 1950, these included women's and girls' outerwear; women's and girls' clothing as a total; all clothing as a total; food eaten away from home; all recreation as a total; and other recreation (toys, hobbies, etc.) as well as education.

Discontinuous luxuries are those goods and services for which the rise in percentage expenditures slows to a halt or declines slightly among higher-income classes. As a group they suggest that satiety in purchasing and consumption is a definite force in our economy. Goods and services included, in 1950, were alcoholic beverages; men's and boys' underwear, nightwear, and socks; women's and girls' underwear and nightwear; clothing services; automobile operation; automobile purchase; men's and boys' footwear; and transportation and travel as a total.

Some patterns of expenditures of rather bizarre types seem to result from the grouping of goods and services within a single category. Expenditures for household operation and medical care form *dish curves*, percentage expenditures declining at first and then rising. Perhaps this is due only to the inclusion of such disparate expenditures as those for mops and for maid services. A number of patterns are the reverse order, called *humpback curves*, starting as luxuries and then continuing as necessities. These include expenditures for household equipment, furniture, floor coverings, and home furnishings and equipment as a total.

CHART 2

Food Prepared at Home

Dollar Expenditures by Income Class in Large
Cities and Suburbs in the North
(per 1,000 Families)

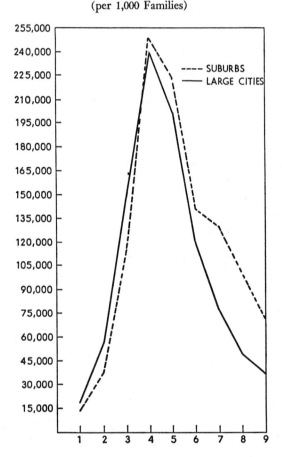

Some Inferences

Such expenditure patterns do not reveal given demand or immutable
forces. If we were knowledgeable enough, we might read in each of them
particular telltale symptoms of desire and need, of ability to buy, of social
pressure, technological change, promotional influence, and all else that
pertains. A marketing analyst can hardly escape the conclusion that in
these patterns are portrayed various interactions of supply and demand
factors in plastic markets fully susceptible to technological innovations,
style changes, market segmentation through broad price ranges, and marginal differentiations. Pattern analysis may provide clues to opportunities
and to danger of saturation; and if pursued over time, it should reveal how
product, market, and demand mixes shape and change individual markets.

DATA FOR CHART 2

Income Class	Large Cities	Suburbs
1 = under $1,000	$ 30,600	$ 14,700
2 = $1,000–$1,999	57,800	36,700
3 = $2,000–$2,999	148,500	115,200
4 = $3,000–$3,999	240,300	248,500
5 = $4,000–$4,999	204,700	224,000
6 = $5,000–$5,999	120,100	140,800
7 = $4,000–$7,499	78,400	129,300
8 = $7,500–$9,999	50,100	89,300
9 = $10,000 and over	40,200	73,600
	$960,700	$1,072,100

	Large Cities	Suburbs
Market size (per 1,000 families)	$960,700	$1,072,100
Per capita expenditure	$32.04	$33.47
Percent of total income expended	24.3%	22.9%
Percent of total market held by—		
0–$2,999 income class	23.6	15.6
$5,000 + income class	30.1	40.4

One of the few laws of marketing pertains to the fact first discovered by Engel that as income rises, the percentage of income spent for food declines. Every static analysis has supported this law. When used for prediction, however, as shown by B. S. Loeb in the article quoted earlier, the law seems fallible indeed. Why has this long-standing truth been turned into an apparent running falsehood? Two factors seem important with the first being changes in income distribution.

A rise in total national income always will reduce the percentage of that income spent for food so long as the income rise is spread among families in the same proportions as present national income or is so distributed as to benefit the higher-income groups. This is a truism as long as food expenditures are regressive, and no one has disputed this regressiveness. The historical trend in all nations, at least until recently, has been for such a percentage reduction in food expenditures to occur.

If through progressive taxation and social legislation a given amount of national income were to be redistributed in favor of the lower-income classes, the percentage expended for food would rise. This again is a function of the regressive expenditure pattern. The same principles would apply to increases in total national income distributed in favor of lower-income groups. The period of the test made by Loeb was one of peaceful economic revolution. Under these conditions of rapid changes in income distribution, Engel's Law cannot be applied indiscriminately. Nevertheless, it would seem inappropriate to discard this analytical and predictive tool too quickly. Allowing for changes in income distribution as well as for changes in total income might do much to aid forecasting.

The other important factor implicit in Engel's Law is that food itself

CHART 3

WOMEN'S AND GIRLS' OUTERWEAR

Dollar Expenditures by Income Class in Large
Cities and Suburbs in the North
(per 1,000 Families)

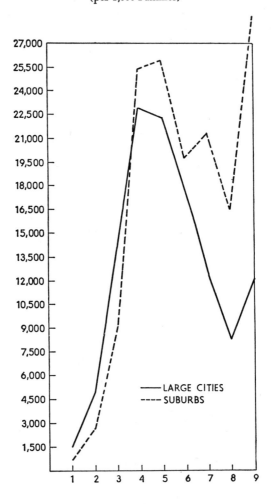

does not change fundamentally in character. We have long been under
the sway of Marshall in considering products and industries as essentially
homogeneous when in fact they are not. It is convenient to talk of a steel
industry and a price for steel. In reality, there is no one identifiable product such as steel but rather hundreds of types of steel and alloys in a wide
variety of shapes and sizes sold in widely differing manners with a host
of services. And in food, we have an example of a "product" changing in
character. With the advent of frozen foods, prepared mixes, and special
packaging, consumers are able to buy food with a wide variation in built-in

DATA FOR CHART 3

Income Class	Large Cities	Suburbs
1 = Under $1,000	$ 1,500	$ 600
2 = $1,000–$1,999	5,100	2,500
3 = $2,000–$2,999	14,200	9,100
4 = $3,000–$3,999	23,000	25,500
5 = $4,000–$4,999	22,400	26,000
6 = $5,000–$5,999	17,900	19,800
7 = $6,000–$7,499	12,500	21,700
8 = $7,500–$9,999	8,300	16,700
9 = $10,000 and over	12,200	28,600
	$117,100	$150,000

	Large Cities	Suburbs
Market size (per 1,000 families)	$117,100	$150,500
Per capita expenditures	$3.90	$4.72
Percent of total income expended	2.96%	3.22%
Percent of total market held by—		
0–$2,999 income class	17.8	8.1
$5,000 + income class	43.6	57.4

maid service or other conveniences. TV dinners and raw meats and vegetables are quite separate things. Yet, statistical measures of food will tend to incorporate these changing quantities of food processing and allied food services. Such action puts a considerable strain on Engel's Law. The solution again would seem to involve not the discarding of this analytical tool but instead an attempt to sharpen it.

Adequate reason exists for striving to refine this aid to analysis. Engel's Law is presently concerned with the changes in markets associated with changes in national income. Attention should also be paid to two closely related changes in markets: changes in the distribution of income and changes in the percent allocated over time by each income group for the purchase of given categories of goods and services. Ability to isolate out the effects of changes in income distribution, for example, would provide clues to those changes due to food processing and other technological improvements and to differential use, if any, of such new food products among income classes. That the analysis is far more difficult than it was in Engel's day should not forestall the attempt.

Expenditure patterns reflect basic modes of behavior; and it would be amazing if they did not change at all, for they are not givens. Being relatively stable, expenditure patterns provide a basis for estimating and forecasting. Since they are subject to change, a study of the extent and nature of differences over time could provide an understanding of how and why changes occur and point up future trends.

Of greatest potential use to marketing, perhaps, is an understanding of how technology and marketing together change and shape expenditure patterns. This is not merely a problem of product differentiation or the shifting of demand curves á la Robinson, Chamberlin, and monopolistic competition theory generally. The interaction of technology and marketing can change the consumption function, accelerate the rise and fall of products and industries, and rival, perhaps, monetary controls in the determination of economic change.

If a product, cigarettes for example, has a relatively low unit price and is in widespread use, then the pattern of expenditures probably will be regressive. But much can be done to change this pattern. The production and popularization of widely varying qualities at widely varying prices could transform the market into one with a highly luxurious pattern. On the other hand, products which have been considered luxurious for the relatively few, such as silk hosiery, cars, classical music, or good books, can expand by transforming the market (usually accompanying technological innovation with lower prices) into a broader one.

The extreme of mutability probably exists in those products of widely varying but relatively high price which depend heavily on style and planned obsolescence. Much has been said of the stabilizing factors in today's economy as contrasted, say, to that of the 1920's. The general stability effected by social legislation, however, is not the whole story. Important instabilities also have been added. The rise in the amount and dispersion of discretionary income has created a potential volatility which did not previously exist. The economy is now much more at the mercy of the decisions of consumers to spend, to buy now or to postpone the purchase, and to shift purchasing power rapidly among classes of goods and services. The durable-goods sector seems particularly vulnerable and has been driven to dependence on frequently and radically changed styles. This increased uncertainty and reliance on the choices of consumers has projected marketing more and more into the management and organizational limelight. Factories rarely shut down for lack of materials, machines, money, or manpower, but poor market forecasting and defective marketing efforts can close them.

Marketing has found it somewhat difficult to prove or to dramatize its dynamic powers and its ability to create demand. It still lies under the old cloud of suspicious economic doctrine which says that demand is given and that an advertisement or salesman can do no more than divert the purchase from one seller to another. The ups and downs of the automobile market may reveal marketing's weaknesses; but these swings clearly indicate also the function and the power of marketing. The adaptation of products to the true needs and desires of consumers and the successful cultivation of potential markets is a strong creative force.

Consumption being so largely time-dependent is in the end a scarce resource. Although one might buy every conceivable type of sports equipment, he could make little use of each item; and if he were an ardent sportsman, other leisure pursuits would be reduced. Time sets a barrier to many forms of consumption and, therefore, creates a deterrent to purchasing. Even laborsaving devices for the busy housewife demand care, storage, and ability to locate them when needed. Limits thus tend to exist on what can be expected from technological change. Although wants may be infinite, the desire for many specific things may at any given time be dormant, postponable, or otherwise inoperative—and not for lack of ability to buy or fear of insecurity. The data show a very common tendency among luxury goods and services for the increase in percentage expenditures not to continue indefinitely. At moderately high income ranges, the percentage expenditures either stabilize or fall off suggesting the existence of generalized satiation. While we have considered that savings accumulate as the result of conscious decisions, they may be a mere residual after desired expenditures are made. Necessity may be the mother of much consumption, and desire a stimulant to more. As the philosophers have urged, however, satisfaction in what we possess may be the key to happiness. Even in a materialistic economy, an end to, or a palling of, acquisition could occur. Marketing cannot afford to neglect these implications of expenditure patterns.

IV. Marketing Theory and Marketing Management

21. MARKETING THEORY AS MARKETING MANAGEMENT

C. West Churchman

OF ALL the ideas that man's genius has created, perhaps none have been so frustratingly elusive as "theory" and "fact." The frustration comes about because we seem so sure at times what these ideas must mean, only to have them shattered by the next breakthrough in man's history.

As Professor Martin's essay assumes, there is a perfectly reasonable sense, historically justifiable, in which "theoretical" is a property of the language man uses to describe and predict the world about him. But there is also a reasonable sense, also historically justifiable, in which "theoretical" is a property of the way in which man makes decisions in his world. It is this second sense that will concern us here. We wish to explore the concept of theoretical behavior.

The historical justification of the concept of theoretical behavior goes back many centuries, to the early Greeks. In more modern times, it arises in the fascinating notion that knowledge is a way of doing, or, as we shall prefer to say it, a certain kind of management of affairs. The underlying philosophy is pragmatism, itself an elusive but highly profitable idea occurring in man's intellectual development.

To say that knowledge is a type of management is to imply that the validity of our ideas can only be tested in the context of decision making. If the decision making is uniformly good, then the principles that led to the decisions are valid, i.e., known.

Now "theory" and "fact" are aspects of knowledge; they represent some of the things that are known well or badly. If we regard knowing to be a type of management, then we will feel impelled to regard "theory" itself as a certain kind of management activity.

In other words, to discuss a "theory of marketing" is to discuss a mode of managing marketing functions. Thus, our aim is to distinguish between "theoretical" and "nontheoretical" marketing management, and to judge to what extent the distinction makes a difference in the practical management of marketing in firms.

In order to find some guidelines, we should traverse briefly the old pathways of man's pursuit of the elusive concept of theory. Perhaps the best beginning is Democritus of the fifth century B.C. Here was an attempt to describe the behavior of all Nature in terms of a very few properties; the size, shape, and velocity of particles. Few would deny that Democritus sought a "theory" of Nature. What makes his work seem theoretical is (1) the parsimony of properties (Nature is "basically" made up of very few properties) and (2) the utter rationality of the laws (events must happen in one way only).

Both points are important in the subsequent history of ideas. When Plato describes the universe in his *Timaeus* and Euclid writes his *Elements*, both writers try to reconstruct the whole or a part of Nature by means of the fewest basic properties, and both writers assume that Nature is inherently rational in its structure.

If we were to characterize Euclid as a manager, we would say that he operated his enterprise with a strong policy theme based on an assumption that the underlying structure of the world could be recognized, and, once recognized, that his policy would operate successfully thereafter.

This conviction that Nature is inherently rational characterized the early theorists of the Greek period. The irrational for them is inherent in men and their attitudes towards Nature; the goodness of man consists in man's learning the true rationality of his environment and adapting the right attitude towards it.

The same spirit pervades in the renaissance of science and philosophy in the seventeenth century. Leibniz tells us that there are various ways in which decision makers manage their affairs, but the most perfect manager is God. God requires no information from outside and perceives all things analytically, i.e., deduces all events precisely and perfectly. He is an ideal, self-contained inquiring system; for example, the time required to compute any finding, no matter how complicated, is exactly zero. The less ideal minds of Leibniz' world perceive less clearly, compute more slowly, make more errors, and have to use information as a crutch to compensate for their inadequacies. Reality is supremely rational: minds of finite intelligence introduce noise, uncertainty, obscurity, irrationality.

It was the empiricists of the seventeenth and eighteenth centuries who argued so strongly against this type of theoretical manager. For John Locke, the mind starts with very little, and only after a long struggle does it come to learn about the rationality of the world. It starts by being meagerly theoretical. Nevertheless, Locke did maintain the other facet of Platonic theory: there are only a few basic qualities with which the mind begins. Everything is constructed from these few types of inputs for the system.

The most significant thing that Locke did was to place the rationality of the world in the inquirer himself. Or, rather, to be historically accurate, it was Hume and especially Kant who showed that a mind that learns only from raw inputs must construct its own connections between these inputs. In Kant's philosophy, the inputs are so raw that the inquiring system cannot tell them apart unless it imposes a rationality upon them. "Telling apart" requires a concept of space and time, and the laws of space and time are the contribution of the inquirer.

In management terms, Kant's thesis is that information is as much a matter of managing as are the other practical decisions the manager makes. The most important managerial decision to be made about information is interpretation. The interpretation of information is a matter of inferring what the information means. If the manager is willing to assume a great deal about reality, he will interpret information in very rich terms, whereas if he is skeptical about how reality is going to behave, he will interpret information in very sparse terms. For example, a sales manager may assume that his markets are all stable; he interprets last year's data to imply an accurate picture of this year's demand. Another manager may not want to assume anything at all about the stability of demand; he interprets last year's sales to be last year's sales and nothing else. It is to be emphasized that these two managers could not resolve their conflict by hiring an expert statistician according to today's concept of statistics. The statistician himself adopts either strong assumptions about reality or very weak assumptions; what makes him an expert is not contained in his willingness to assume or not to assume.

Now, both these managers understand their problem to be one of using information that is in some sense "given." The question is: "given" by what? By a rational outside world? If all we have is what is given, then this "outside" world is unknown, unconscious, unreflective, and (as Berkeley put it) unnecessary.

David Hume tried to show that the so-called regularity of these inputs and the conviction that they will reoccur in the same patterns as they had in the past is a matter of habit for the mind. The manager simply becomes used to regularity.

The tactical problem of these managers is, therefore, one of deciding how much order to impose on what is given. Immanuel Kant tried to provide one guide for the manager in this connection. His thesis is that the manager must impose a minimal rationality, because otherwise he won't be able to recognize any information at all. Specifically, he must assume that he can divide the world into the past and the future and that objects can be structured in space. In order to do this, the information system requires a clock and geometrical measuring rods. The clocks and the rods presuppose a modicum of logic, arithmetic, geometry, kinematics, and mechanics. In other words, numbers, points, lines, planes, spaces, times, and masses exist because the information system operates that way, and we know of no other way for it to operate.

Although Kant showed to his own satisfaction that there must be a future if there is a past, he provided no help in showing what this future must be. It must be a future with a clock, a ruler, and a compass. But this is small consolation to a skittish manager who believes that Nature—including his competitors—may trick him, unless one could show (which Kant could not) that a world with a clock must be highly predictable.

Thus, there are two types of information managers: the bold and the cautious. Since neither manager is "theoretical," in the sense of Democritus, Plato, and Leibniz, let us call the bold one the generalizer, and the cautious one the particularizer.

The particularizer says that one cannot forecast. He likes to show how past attempts to forecast prices have been no better than random predictions, and then—very inconsistently to be sure—he asserts that therefore no one can forecast: *he* forecasts an infinity of failures to beat chance. The generalizer believes that the task is to interpret the data, and that interpretation includes the art of making a priori assumptions. So he tries—over and over—to predict what will happen, and he acts on his assumptions. Both particularizer and generalizer are fundamentally skeptical about the basic rationality of Nature: the flow of inputs may be—or may not be—a pattern. The flow itself is essentially nonrational, that is, does not originate from known rational causes.

Thus, the bit of the history of thought we have just reviewed reveals three types of management:

1. Theorizer—A management based on the assumption that reality is rational (predictable), and hence the task of the manager is to remove the randomness and obscurity of his own thinking in order to become as much like reality as possible.
2. Generalizer—A management based on the assumption that reality is nonrational, but that the task of the manager is to construct a strong structure within which the raw inputs from reality may be given the fullest possible weight.
3. Particularizer—A management based on the assumption that reality is irrelevant, and that the task of the manager is to permit maximum flexibility of decision making so as to meet the requirements imposed by the data.

In language more familiar to the student of management, the particularizer is an opportunist; the generalizer, a planner; the theoretician, an idealist.

As is true of all lessons learned from history, it is necessary to go beyond what our forebearers said and try to capture their intent in our own language. The three descriptions given above are vague and somewhat useless, until we couch them in a language more familiar to current analysis.

The life of any decision maker may be considered as a string of decisions made at specific points of time. At these points of time, the decision maker has choices. Therefore, throughout his history he is creating his life by choosing one decision rather than another. At the beginning, he confronts a fantastic array of alternatives lives; as he nears the end, he finally decides just one life, which is his biography.

Attached to any life-in-prospect for the decision maker is a value or perhaps a set of values, depending upon the viewpoint of the observer. For purposes of discussion, assume that this value, or these values, can be fully described by a number on a scale, or a vector of numbers. Thus, each life L_1, L_2, L_3, etc., is a member of a set L. Associated with each L_i is a value V_i. Each L_i is a string of decisions D_{jk}. The subscript j refers to the point in time, the subscript k to the particular, physical decision that might occur at such a point. Thus j ranges over the decision-making episodes of the life, while k ranges over the alternative decisions that can be made at any episode. The total set of D_{jk} is designated by D.

We shall want to assume some things about decision-making lives. Indeed, we have already assumed that their values can be represented along appropriate scales. Furthermore, we shall want to say that an act is a decision only if its adoption changes the value of the life to which it belongs. Suppose L_i is a life with a string of decisions D_{jk}. The notation "$L_i - D_{jk}$" designates a class of lives in which, at time t_j, the decision D_{jk} does not occur, though every other decision in L_i remains. In other words, at time t_j, $L_i - D_{jk}$ contains a decision other than D_{jk}. We note that the operator "$-$" is intended to be closed with respect to L; that is, given any L_i with D_{jk} at time t_k, there exists at least one L_m belonging to L which is like L_i in all respects except that it contains no D_{jk} at t_k. The assumption we have made about decisions is that the value of L_i differs from the value of any member of $L_i - D_{jk}$. In effect, this assumption simply groups together into one decision all physically distinct acts that have the same effect on the value of a life. We assume that the points of time are so chosen that every life contains a decision at every point of time.

Next, we introduce the concept of a policy. A policy is a life with an underlying theme. That is, an observer of the life can depict the pattern of the life by some rule. He sees, for example, that the life was trying to accomplish a goal or avoid a certain kind of act. Apparently, we are struggling to define something here that is quite obscure. To avoid the obscurity, without really solving the problem, we introduce a set of rules R. A rule is a device that, at any time t_k, selects a proper nonempty subset of the alternative decisions. If it selects one and only one decision at each t, it is a rigid rule; if it selects more than one (but not all), it is a constraining rule. Thus, each rule selects a proper subclass of L. We say that a life is governed by a policy if it belongs to the subclass selected by some member of R.

This way of defining policies does not really solve the basic problem, because one can always define a rigid rule for any given life by simply having the rule select the decisions that actually were made. The intent, of course, is that R contains only rules that the decision maker himself generated at the outset of a series of decisions.

In order to make this stipulation more precise, we introduce the concept of a "preparatory" decision. One decision prepares the way for another decision if it makes the latter possible. This notion is not too difficult to capture within the symbolism already adopted. Imagine a life with decision D_{11} at time t_1 and D_{22} at time t_2. Suppose D_{11} is removed; i.e., we consider the class of all lives $L - D_{11}$. If none of these contain D_{22}, we say that D_{11} prepared for D_{22}. A more general and more useful way to define preparation is to say that D_{11} prepares for D_{22}, if all lives containing both have higher value than the corresponding lives containing D_{22} but not D_{11}.

I have chosen this fairly elaborate way to define preparatory decisions in order to be able to describe any kind of decision maker and his life, whether living or machine, individual or social. In lives with a heavy emphasis on preparatory decisions, the decision maker is a planner. He devotes a great deal of his potential resources to setting up for later decisions. Indeed, if we think of preparatory decisions in the same way in which we think of setup procedures in production, then we can say that the setup cost is a decision itself, and that the planner tends to decide to make this cost high. Continuing the analogy with production, this means that he tends to make strong commitments, just as a high setup in inventory theory implies large inventories.

In order to make the concept of a commitment clearer, we can return to the formalism introduced above. The lives of decision makers are pathways of decisions. Sometimes the pathways break into many choices at each episode, while at other times, there are very few choices. In some cases, the decision maker will start to follow one path, i.e., to adopt one theme, but may find that this theme is unsatisfactory. If he has left himself flexible, he can change his theme without drastically changing the overall value of his life; if he has committed himself, he cannot feasibly reverse his theme. Thus, a life is reversible if, once a decision has been made, it is possible later on to adopt other decisions that nullify the cost of the first decision.

To make this concept of reversibility clearer, suppose a decision maker has adopted decision D_{11} at time t_1. He now pursues his life until time t_j, when he comes to regret his earlier choice. At this point, there may be a decision D_{jk} available to him that nullifies the effect of D_{11}. In other words, at t_j he can choose a life containing D_{jk} with a value equal to a life not containing D_{11}. He can pursue his life "as though" D_{11} had never occurred. Thus, a decision D_{11} is reversible at time t_j if there exists in L two lives with the following properties: (*a*) one contains D_{11} and the other does not; (*b*) both contain the same decisions between t_1 and t_j; (*c*) the one containing D_{11} does not contain D_{jk} at time t_j, while the other does; (*d*) the lives are the same after t_j; and (*e*) the value of the two lives is the same.

A decision is irreversible if no decision can reverse it at a later period of time during the life of the decision maker. Evidently, reversibility could become a matter of degree, depending on how much a later decision can erase the value introduced by an earlier one. I assume that the more a life tends towards preparatory decisions, the greater the irreversibility of its decisions. In other words, one who plans thoroughly commits himself to the decisions his plan dictates.

The planner, then, is one who adopts policies (lives with a theme) with preparatory and consequently irreversible decisions. The opportunist prepares minimally and commits himself least; the theme of his life is much more difficult to discern, except in vague terms like happiness or profit maximization. The opportunist, therefore, lets the day-to-day data tell him how to respond. He is the operationally oriented manager in the sense that he tries to overcome the difficulties as they occur. One could find a theme for his life only if one could forecast the difficulties; but forecasting is a preparatory decision he tends to shun.

Nothing in the above discussion indicates which manager is "best," and man has always recognized the problem of prejudging by posing contradictory maxims: "Rome (O Great Irreversible Decision!) was not built in a day," and "He who hesitates (plans?) is lost."

The planning manager leads a life very much like the cognitive life of a so-called theoretical scientist. The opportunistic scientist plans minimally for the next experiment and lets the results of the experiment tell him what to do next. Nowadays, he finds contentment in the application of experimental designs and the analysis of variance and covariance. He thinks of himself as exploring a vast area and being able to travel from one site to another with no loss of energy. Since he has no real a priori conviction about the outcome of an experiment, he is rarely disappointed intellectually. The generalizer, on the other hand, works for months building up an elaborate conceptual structure; only then does he permit himself to test his concepts. He can be terribly disappointed or marvelously overjoyed. But in either event, the next choice becomes an outcome of his preparatory structure building. Like it or not, his intellectual decisions tend to become less and less reversible the older he gets. A single datum, on the other hand, tends to become more and more important.

As for the generalizing manager, he believes in long-range planning, operations research, systems design, and all the other tools of management that emphasize the larger point of view. The opportunist believes in cases, daily or weekly accounts, and other factual reports. He believes in seeing his subordinates on the scene. He believes that on-the-spot tactics are more important than vague and general strategies.

If one were to try to characterize the shift in management that has occurred in the last two decades in America, it would be safe to say that it has become less opportunist and more planning. In recent years, the shift has become most apparent in marketing management.

What of marketing theory, then? At the beginning of the essay, it was argued that there is a distinction between the true theorizer and the generalizer. In ordinary academic discussions, the distinction is rarely made. This is because the American scientific community has practically forgotten the rationalist philosophy that initiated its modern history. The theorizer believes that reality is rational, and that irrationality, randomness, and the like are the making of the inquiring mind. The generalizer, on the other hand, believes in order, too, but he believes that order is what he imposes on chaos.

To the mind of Leibniz's God, there is no "given." "Data," for Leibniz, are the devices that poorer minds use to cope with reality; data are contingent, uncertain, obscure. Yet, a modern scientist would argue that objectivity, the cornerstone of science, is to be found in data—what is given. The planning manager tries his best to prepare for what will come, but he ultimately believes that what will come will be given to him, as an "input." "Information" is the input he cannot plan. Or can he?

Suppose he asks himself this question: after all, since my plans do change the world and hence also the information I eventually receive, what is it that my plans cannot change? What is really, fundamentally, irretrievably given? If he does ask himself this question, he is on the way to becoming a theorizer as well as a generalizer.

One response he may make is this: the past is irretrievably given. It is *given* that last year we sold 1,000 items of so-and-so. But is it? In the life of the manager, it is not what was sold that matters but why it was sold. Can he create an answer to the "why"?

Suppose we are observing a man looking at a white swan. One question the man could pose to himself is: *given* this white swan, are all swans white? Another and more interesting question is this: to what degree is this a white swan? A manager may ask: *given* these sales last year, what will the sales be next year? Another and far more interesting question is: to what degree is this a sale? As soon as we begin to regard nature in depth rather than extension, we ask why rather than what. To learn that a swan has degrees of whiteness is to learn why the swan appears white to our eyes. To learn that a customer is sold in degrees of conviction is to learn why he appears to be someone we sold to last year. In both cases, the "given" becomes the start of a problem, not the answer. To ask why a swan appears white is the start of an inquiry in which the so-called induction to "all swans are white" is irrelevant. It is to understand that recording a swan as white is a delicate decision. To ask why a customer appears to be sold is also the start of an inquiry in which forecasts of next year's sales based on this year's sales are irrelevant. It is to understand that recording a sale is a delicate decision. To record some transaction as a sale when the customer is truly dissatisfied, or truly erratic, or truly dead, is to make a foolish decision.

The theorizer is therefore the supreme questioner. He questions in depth as well as extension. One of the greatest insights of modern philosophy is E. A. Singer's dictum that to ask a question is to assume an answer. The question-asker assumes that answers "exist." He also assumes that any reply he may give to a question is no more than one response among many. *The* answer is an ideal, and yet, it must exist. Reality is the ideal end of all question asking.

When a decision maker lives his life, he asks a question. The empiricist believes that when the life is over, then finally the answer to the question will be given. At this point, at life's end, the question asker is, for the planner and opportunist, completely passive. To the theorizer, a life is also a question, but at its end, there is only a response, one part of the whole that makes up the final answer. He believes that all these responses, in some rational but obscure way, go to make up the meaning of a life. The way is obscure, because we cannot accept the simple rationality of our philosophical predecessors, who defined the rational in terms of the logically consistent. Whatever modern rationality is, it must be far richer in meaning than the logically consistent: it must include contradiction, opposition, conflict, evil, as well as consistency, sameness, cooperation, and good.

Marketing theory is at least a proposal for a generalizing rather than a particularizing marketing management—for planning rather than for opportunity. It may sometime become a proposal for a theorizing marketing management as well—for a management that knows how to ask questions.

22. COMPANY GOALS, GROWTH, AND THE MULTIPRODUCT FIRM

William J. Baumol

It is all too tempting and easy to impugn the utility and realism of the generally accepted models of the theory of the firm. Students of marketing have found that these constructs describe only the bare bones of a real business firm and tend to focus attention on aspects of the company's operation which are not of primary interest to marketing analysts. Yet, despite these reservations, even the textbook model of the firm can be, and indeed has been, of immeasurable help to investigators attempting a rigorous analysis of any actual business operation. Moreover, a number of recent developments in the theory have sought to enrich it and to add to its applicability. This essay undertakes to describe one such development.

The discussion of limitations of the standard theory when contrasted with the proposed model should not be misinterpreted. If it is true that the construction described in this essay can serve purposes beyond the capabilities of the more standard analysis, it is only because the author had this analysis available to him to build upon. Moreover, the more standard static model still offers invaluable assistance and insight both into the analysis of the workings of the economy and to the applied work of operations research. In sum, the two models are designed for different purposes and are certainly not intended to be competitors.

1. The Textbook Model of the Firm

The textbook version of any body of theory is bound to be a vast oversimplification which avoids most of the subtleties and complications of the analysis upon which it is based. Nevertheless, a textbook description is often indicative of the salient features of such an analysis. It sets forth the material which remains in the minds of those who are not specialists in the area.

With these preliminary remarks out of the way, we can describe the bare outlines of the static analysis of the theory of the firm in a rather excessively simple manner. Management is taken to pursue a single objective using a single instrument for the purpose. Its sole goal is the maximization of profits, and other aims are either treated as subsidiary or more often ignored altogether. This abstract firm is usually designed to have a single decision variable—either output or price, where one may interchangeably be substituted for the other. Thus, management is taken to consider the alternative levels of output which it can produce and to calculate for each such level what costs will be incurred, what market price can be obtained, and what level of profits will therefore result. Once the optimal or profit maximizing output level has been determined, the firm will continue to produce this quantity in perpetuity. The level of output will not change until some fortuitous circumstance causes a shift in consumer attitudes or in technology which modifies the cost or demand structure and makes some alternative production level more profitable. Thus, once the equilibrium level of output is found, the operation of the firm can be considered a routine exercise. There is no really essential decision-making role to be performed by management so long as market conditions and technology remain the same.

Moreover, in this analysis, the firm is typically taken to produce a single commodity. There are, indeed, models of the multiproduct firm, but one can hardly avoid the impression that the managerial choice between one and many products is largely accidental or capricious in the static model. There is nothing inherent in the workings of the model which would lead the firm to go into the production of a substantial number of different commodities.

All of this is illustrated in Figure 1, which shows how total costs and total revenue might be taken to vary with the magnitude of output. For example, point C shows that to produce 2,000 units of output (say per week), it would cost the firm $40,000, and point D shows that this level of production could be sold for a total return of something slightly less than $60,000. CD, the difference between these two, of course, represents total profit, in this case approximately $20,000. We observe that the profit level at a 1,000 unit output, AB, is smaller than the 2,000 output profit, and that, similarily, profits at a 3,000 level of output, EF, is also smaller than CD. In fact, the graph indicates that CD is the largest total profit that the firm can obtain and that it will achieve this level by producing 2,000 units of its product per week. This then is the equilibrium profit maximizing level of output.

2. Modification of the Textbook Model

Several features of this standard model may well be questioned by those with marketing experience. For one thing, the objectives of management are not likely to be as well defined or as monistic as the model presupposes. A variety of alternative goals are apt to influence the operations of any company in a manner which is not precisely specified nor clearly determined. Second, the company has before it much wider

FIGURE 1

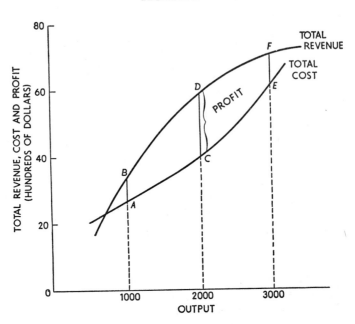

varieties of decisions than just the determination of production level, even if we ignore complex problems involved in choice of technology. Advertising, sales force, product mix, packaging, and many other variables play a most important part in company planning. Indeed, there is much evidence that in the thinking of management, price determination is frequently assigned a far less significant place than that accorded to decisions on these other matters. Third, it may be objected that the history of few firms is as static as the textbook model would appear to suggest. Expansion is highly characteristic of a large variety of business enterprises, and this growth does not seem to take place only sporadically and by happenstance when there occurs an autonomous change in consumer desires or in technology. Finally, the extreme rarity of the single-product firm suggests that there is something inherent in the structure of business operation which makes for a multiplicity of products and that this should be explainable in terms of our basic model.

Let us examine some of these items in greater detail. The idea that companies may have objectives other than simple profit maximization, and that it is possible to incorporate these alternative objectives in a formal analysis, has been discussed adequately elsewhere. I must only remark that it is rather difficult to document such a view, particularly when the defenders of the standard model argue that the pursuit of alternative objectives such as sales and market share is only a manifestation of the desire to maximize profits over the *long run*. That is, the firm may seek to expand its sales today primarily because it considers this to be a good means to earn money tomorrow. But one may well suspect that the very meaning of such a long-run objective is questionable in a large firm in which there are many centers of power of varying potency and where goals have never explicitly been discussed and formulated (except for purposes of public relations releases in which the promotion of virtue itself is in effect described as the ultimate aim of the corporation). Moreover, observed corporate behavior seems, typically, to be equally consistent with the view that the firm is seeking to maximize long-run profits and the allegation that it wishes to maximize long-run sales. Thus, the observed facts seem not to lend unambiguous support either to the one hypothesis or the other. Therefore, if we are to avoid claiming insight into a corporate unconscious which has adopted goals without their being revealed to management, must we not simply give up the search for long-run objectives and file it under the heading "not relevant" or at least "not settled"?

Looking at the matter from a more short-run point of view, it would appear that expansion itself is frequently an important objective of management. One has seen the pride with which executives regard the growth they have been able to achieve for their company. Certainly the growth of the firm is given adequate publicity and attention in the financial journals and in releases to stockholders. There is every reason to believe that rate of growth is closely correlated with prestige and morale within the firm and with the way it is regarded by outsiders. If this is so, it would seem appropriate to devise models in which the rate of growth of the company is its prime objective and in which profit becomes an instrument variable. In such a case, profit becomes a means out of which the corporation can retain earnings to finance its further expansion and with the aid of which it can induce the money market to make more funds available to it for the same purpose. Thus, profits, like price and advertising, become a means rather than an end, and it is not difficult to construct a mathematical model in which profit determination is described accordingly.

But even if this view is taken to be rather extreme, if profit is considered to be a very important objective of the company in and of itself, it is possible to question the adequacy of the static textbook model for many purposes. For it is by no means obvious that in practice there will be any single output level which will maximize profits for the indefinite future, even in the absence of exogenous change.

Figure 2 is very similar to the preceding diagram except that the revenue and cost curves are of somewhat different shape. The total revenue curve is a straight line, indicating that the market for the commodity is still far from saturated. It suggests that the company can increase the money it obtains from selling a commodity roughly in proportion with the amount of the item which it produces. The total cost curve is shown to curl downwards, that is, it ascends less steeply as we move over to the

FIGURE 2

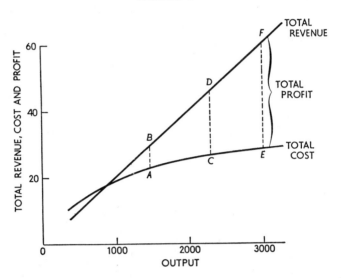

right. This means essentially that the productive process is characterized by economies of large-scale operations. Costs do increase as the company adds to its output, but less than in proportion. It costs more to produce three thousand units of output than to produce one thousand units, but it does not cost three times as much.

In these circumstances, it will be noted that as we move along the diagram toward the right, profits continue to increase. *CD* is larger than *AB* and *EF* is larger than *CD*. That being the case, the larger the production level of the firm, the more profits it will earn. If this is so, it would appear to be in the firm's interest to expand indefinitely and without limit. Certainly, in these circumstances, no stationary solution seems to be possible and growth apparently becomes an integral requirement of profit maximization.

More will be said about this construction in the next section, and the reasons why a multiplicity of products is offered by the typical company will be considered after the growth model of the firm has been outlined briefly.

3. An Equilibrium Growth Model

Figure 2 seems to have forced us to the ridiculous view that the sky is the limit for the company whose circumstances are depicted in that diagram. It would appear to suggest something at least as unrealistic as the static model—that the management of that company can, and undoubtedly should, decide to expand many fold *and to do so precipitously*. There are several fairly obvious reasons why things do not work out this way in practice.

First of all, sheer construction costs involved in providing physical facilities increase disproportionately as expansion is accelerated. If it normally takes two years to complete the erection of a certain type of factory, a crash program to get it finished in one year is likely to be far more expensive, and any attempt to build many factories of the same sort at once is verly likely to strain the capacity of those who construct them and is also apt to add substantially to costs.

A second reason for increasing costs of expansion is financial. The capital market which faces any one company is usually far from perfect. As its demand for funds increases, it is likely to find that the cost it must pay for them goes up. The amount of expansion which can be financed out of retained earnings is limited. Too large an issue of new stocks or bonds will drive down their price, and financial institutions may place absolute limits on the amounts they are willing to lend or will increase their lending only if they are offered extremely attractive terms.

Third, and perhaps most important, are the internal limitations to expansion, the fact that administrative and organizational costs are almost certain to rise disproportionately with the rate of expansion of the firm. As the growth of the company increases, managerial capacity must also expand. Members must be added to the executive group, and there must be time for their training and opportunities for them to acquire experience. All of this means that costs are virtually certain to be a function, and a sharply rising function, of the firm's rate of growth. This is illustrated in Figure 3 where the total cost curve rises more and more rapidly as we move from left to right. That is, as the firm considers a rate of growth of 5% or 10% or 15%, management is confronted with the fact that its total costs at a 15% rate of growth will be far higher than those which would apply if a 10% rate of growth were decided upon.

FIGURE 3

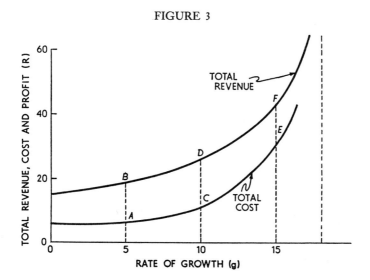

Total revenue, which may be defined as the discounted present value of the future stream of returns, is also a rising function of rate of growth. That is, a company which selects a more rapid rate of growth over its lifetime may expect higher receipts than one which chooses to expand more slowly.[1]

Now it will be observed in Figure 3 that as was the case in Figure 1, total profits first increase and then decrease as we move toward the right. That is, *CD* is larger than *AB* but *EF* is smaller than *CD*. This means that there will be an optimal rate of growth in the model shown in this diagram. It will be the *rate of expansion* of the firm's output rather than the *level* of its production which is to be determined by an equilibrium analysis. Each company will find it unprofitable to expand either too slowly or too quickly, and there will be a rate of expansion (in the case of the diagram, 10%) which makes a maximum contribution to the company's long-run profits.

Thus in the model which is described in this diagram, firms grow not *despite* the effect of expansion on the profit return but *because* such growth makes the firm more profitable. Growth occurs and continues out of the very logic of the analysis and not as a result of some *post hoc* observations which are subsequently imposed upon the model.

4. Increasing Marketing Costs and the Multiplicity of Products

Let us return now to the observed prevalence of the multiproduct firm —the fact that the single commodity company of the textbook model is so rarely, if ever, observed in practice. Up to this point, our growth model has not cast any light on this matter.

I shall argue that this is one of those subjects where our first intuitive guess turns out to have been entirely correct. One would naturally feel that a firm which is dedicated to continual expansion, as is the company

---

1 In simplified circumstances, this revenue function may be described more explicitly with the aid of a little algebra. Let R represent the initial net revenue of our company, g be the percentage rate of growth whose magnitude is to be determined, and, finally, let i be the rate of interest relevant in discounting future revenues. Then at rate of growth, g, per period, we may expect that t periods from now, the firm's net revenue will be increased to $R(1+g)^t$ and the discounted present value of that net revenue will be $R(1+g)^t/(1+i)^t$. The present value of the expected stream of revenues will be, therefore, the sum of these terms for all values of t from the initial zero period up to the firm's horizon. This is the function which describes the total revenue curve in Figure 3. It can be shown that this function crawls upward as we move to the right and that it increases without limit as g approaches the value of i. This last observation has led some writers to the conclusion that there is something paradoxical in this construct, for it would appear to say that if the firm's rate of growth approaches the relevant rate of discount, its expected future yield will be infinite if the firm does not have a limited horizon. Of course, this is not a serious problem in practice because firms' horizons are indeed limited, that is, the revenue function is not an infinite series. Moreover, if the expected earnings of any firm did shoot up without limit, this could cause a major increase in the demand for funds which would automatically raise interest rates sufficiently to make i greater than g.

depicted in Figure 3, must ultimately run into difficulties in marketing its single product. At this point it is faced with two alternatives: either it must retrench substantially on its expansion plans or it must turn to the production of other items. In other words, the multiplicity of products which is typical of today's company can be explained as a combination of two facts: its dedication to a program of long-run expansion, and the increasing difficulties and costs which are involved in marketing ever larger quantities of any given product or fixed set of products.

In practice, even if there are economies of large-scale production, the costs associated with any particular output are virtually certain to expand with its scale of production. Ultimately, a doubling of output will more than double costs because the markets for the company's products will become increasingly saturated as production expands. It will require disproportionate increases in sales force, advertising outlays, promotions, and other marketing expenditures to find customers for these expanded supply flows. As more and more of these commodities find their way to market, their prices will have to be reduced. Consequently, increased quantities of these products will not even bring in proportionate gross revenue increases.

Our intuitive judgment that the increasing costs of marketing a fixed product line lead the firm to introduce new products can be substantiated by more formal analysis. In technical terms, what we have been asserting is that the larger number of products is accounted for by the absence of constant returns to scale. Let us first look more closely at what would happen in the constant returns case.

Figure 4 depicts a production function characterized by constant returns to scale. The heavy curve labeled PP' is called the company's *Production Possibility curve*. It represents the maximal combinations of two commodities, x and y, which the company can produce with its initial level of resource utilization. That is, with its current capacities, it has just enough resources to produce any combination of outputs such as that represented by the point B which lies on curve PP'. There are more than enough resources for a combination like A, which lies below PP', while point C, which is above the production possibility curve is beyond the company's productive capacity.

A program of investment, however, can add to the company's maximal scale of operations, and as a result the production possibility curve shifts upward to RR'. A well-known proposition tells us that with constant returns to scale the production possibility curve shifts outward exactly in the same proportion along any straight line through the origin, for outputs can then increase in exact proportion with the added resources. Thus, as the firm expands, and the production possibility curve moves outward from PP' to RR', it retains the same slope at point R that it had at point P. Its profits are represented by the family of parallel isoprofit lines such as those labeled ii and ii'. Hence, if, as is the case in the diagram, it pays

FIGURE 4   FIGURE 5

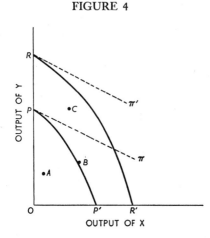

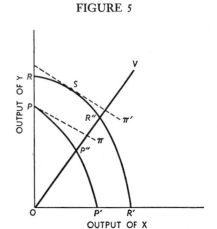

initially to produce commodity y exclusively (point P) because the iso-profit curves have smaller (absolute) slopes than does the production possibility curve, the same thing will be true when the firm expands.[2] Because slopes have been preserved in the expansion process, the new optimal point, R, will again involve a zero output of x.

But suppose, as is the case in Figure 5, that the curvature of the production possibility curve increases as output rises. This means that we can only increase output by a smaller proportionate amount if we concentrate on the expansion of either output x or y alone by moving along one of the axes, rather than on a combination of the two products by moving along a ray such as OV interior to the positive quadrant. That is, we have $P''R''/OP'' > PR/OP$. Then, with diminishing returns of this sort, an increase in the magnitude of operations can easily call for an expansion in the product line, as this second diagram shows. For, while with the initial scale of operations (point P) it pays to produce only y (as was the case in Figure 4), with expanded activity the production of both x and y now becomes profitable (point S).

5. Corporate Financial Practices and the Growth Objective

I have already referred to the fact that the modern firm is not a monolithic entity and that its objectives are necessarily compounded out of the divergent views of a variety of individuals and groups within the firm.

It may be that those of us who are concerned with marketing problems are overimpressed with the extent of the company's dedication to expansion. After all, by its very nature, the objective of marketing is to sell more. Growth is almost the ultimate justification for the existence of the

---

[2] For then any point on PP' other than P will be on a lower isoprofit line than ii.

sales manager. Other groups within the firm may well have more conservative aspirations. If this is so it is important that it be recognized by all concerned, if the danger that company executives will be working at cross purposes is to be minimized. It is also well for us to recognize this possibility as a reminder that our own impression of the goals of a typical firm is likely to be biased by the nature of our frame of reference.

There is, for example, some evidence that financial practices of most, or at least many, of our larger corporations are such as to place very severe limits on their rates of expansion. In recent years established corporations have relied, with a very few exceptions, almost exclusively on internal financing out of retained earnings to obtain the funds necessary for their growth. They have assiduously avoided floating new issues of stocks or bonds for this purpose. Conceivably, some companies will have found the flow of funds out of retained earnings to be more than adequate for the achievement of their optimal rate of expansion. But it is hardly plausible that this will universally have been the case. During recent years there was a period of stock prices so high that the resulting price-earning ratios could be considered truly exceptional. Money could have been obtained to finance new expansion at almost negligible cost by the flotation of new stock issues. However, during this period and despite the general buoyancy of the economy, there was no noticeable increase in stock issues and large firms continued largely to avoid it. It is hard to believe that many of these companies could not have found profitable opportunities for investing their money in expanded facilities which would have produced a yield many times the cost of this additional capital. As the author of one important study in this area comments, ". . . for some mature and generally successful companies the customary debt capacity rules of thumb imply a concern for events of extremely remote probability and an extreme conservatism . . . these same companies appear to be far more aggressive in assuming the risks of new product development, expansion of markets, inventory accumulation—all of which hold potential hazards for cash solvency just as debt does." [3]

There would thus appear to be a split personality within many corporations. Not that financial management is opposed to growth; rather, it is willing to expand but only up to a point where financial risks are kept extremely low. It may well be suspected that sales management is much more aggressive and much more reconciled to the risks which are involved in a program of long-term expansion consistent with maximum profits and even with maximum rate of long-term growth.

It is to be emphasized that the conservatism of financial management which acts as a deterrent to growth is also inconsistent with profit maximization. If a firm refuses to raise funds at a cost lower than the yield which they produce, that firm is sacrificing profits. It may be doing so in

---

[3] Gordon Donaldson, *Corporate Debt Capacity* (Cambridge, Mass.: Harvard University Press, 1961), p. 262.

order to increase safety or for any of a variety of other reasons, but it is certainly not profit maximizing.

It follows from the discussion of this section that the determination of the objectives of a firm are no simple matter. Casual observation and discussion are likely to be extremely misleading. It is not even clear that the divergent aims of the managers of a firm can meaningfully be aggregated into something called the goals of the corporation. It does, however, appear that pure profit maximization is an oversimple characterization of company objectives and that growth plays a significant role in the aspirations of some managerial groups.

6. Conclusion

This essay has described a model of the firm capable of accounting for a variety of observed phenomena which are not explained by the standard static theory of the firm. In particular, it can rationalize the continuing growth pattern which characterizes so many companies in practice and the very large variety of products which are typically carried.

It is possible to formalize the model, translating it into explicit mathematical terms. This has in fact been done in another essay, and the analysis has been used to derive a number of illustrative theorems about the operations of the firm and the effects of different government policies designed to influence its rate of expansion.[4]

It is also not very difficult to expand the model to take into account a number of other marketing decisions, such as the level of advertising expenditure and the magnitude of the sales force. However, such details are not of importance for my present purpose—to demonstrate that our understanding of market phenomena need not be restricted by the limitations of the standard economic models and that extensions of these models in relatively straightforward ways can make them instruments which shed illumination on many marketing practices.

---

[4] W. J. Baumol, "On the Theory of Expansion of the Firm," *American Economic Review*, Vol. 52 (December, 1962).

23. UNCERTAINTY, INFORMATION, AND MARKETING DECISIONS

Paul E. Green

MARKETING's potential as a scientific discipline is the subject of much current debate. Probably less moot, however, is the assertion that the continued development of marketing theory will depend in large part on the adaptation of concepts and techniques drawn from other fields.

The present state of marketing theory already reflects the impact of other disciplines. Portions of microeconomic theory play a large part in contemporary normative marketing. The value of a behavioralistic approach to marketing has been ably demonstrated by Alderson.[1] The efforts of Kuehn and other mathematically oriented researchers have resulted in the use of Markov processes as models for the prediction of brand-share levels over time.[2] The area of physical distribution appears particularly amenable to the construction and testing of mathematical models.

Still another pair of disciplines, decision theory and information theory, show promise for contributing to the growth of marketing theory. The nature of these new developments and their potential applicability to managerial decision making in marketing are discussed in this essay. Considerable emphasis will be placed on the applicability of these techniques to the theory and design of marketing research activity. At times describing, at other times exhorting, the author attempts to show how applied decision theory and information theory can provide a useful prescriptive framework within which the data gathering and cost incurring activity of marketing research can be fruitfully analyzed. The *informational value* of marketing research rather than the mechanics of carrying out such research—given that its anticipated value is worth the cost—is emphasized in this essay.

---

[1] Wroe Alderson, *Marketing Behavior and Executive Action* (Homewood, Ill.: Richard D. Irwin, Inc., 1957).

[2] R. E. Frank, A. A. Kuehn, and W. F. Massy, *Quantitative Techniques in Marketing Analysis* (Homewood, Ill.: Richard D. Irwin, Inc., 1962).

Although these techniques are of rather recent development, the literature on both decision theory and information theory is already extensive. No attempt is made herein to cover even a modest portion of this literature.[3] Rather, emphasis is placed on Bayesian decision theory, a specific segment of the literature in which concepts of both decision and information theory have been combined in an effective and elegant form. The contributions made by Schlaifer and Raiffa to developing the relevance of Bayesian theory to both information theory and decision making under uncertainty are so exhaustive that anyone writing on this subject is obliged to consider his own efforts as largely expository or slightly extensive to their more basic work.[4]

A brief overview of information theory as propounded by Shannon, Weiner, Nyquist, and other noted contributors is provided at the beginning of this essay. Initial efforts focused on the development of concepts to measure the amount of information. Shannon concentrated on those aspects of information dealing with the design of *physical systems* and the relationship of information to the technical problems of encoding, transmitting, and receiving the symbols of communication. In the discussion of Shannon's contributions, some rudimentary concepts of information theory, such as the logarithmic measure of information, the amount of average information, and noisy and lossy information channels, are described in a marketing context. Both in its own right and as an analogue to some of the information concepts of Bayesian decision theory, this earlier work constituted a significant breakthrough.

Attention then shifts to a discussion of the *value* of information in decision making under uncertainty. Concepts of information theory become imbedded in the broader framework of decision theory. Once marketing research is recognized as an important area for the application of these techniques, both decision theory and the modified concepts of information theory can be used in the evaluation of the three main information-gathering functions of marketing research:

1. Information gathered to support the existence of a business problem.
2. Information gathered in the developmental process of structuring a problem, i.e., the activity incurred in searching for alternative courses of action, identification of objectives to be achieved, etc.
3. Information gathered (or capable of being gathered) in the evaluative process of choosing among alternative courses of action.[5]

---

[3] In particular, an apology is offered for our failure (due to space constraints) to include a description of the behavioralistic theory of communication as developed by Ackoff. Readers interested in this specific extension of information theory should see R. L. Ackoff, "Toward a Behavioral Theory of Communication," *Management Science*, Vol. 4, No. 3 (April, 1958).

[4] R. Schlaifer, *Probability and Statistics for Business Decisions* (New York: McGraw-Hill Book Co., Inc., 1959); and H. Raiffa and R. Schlaifer, *Applied Statistical Decision Theory* (Cambridge, Mass.: Harvard Business School Press, 1961).

[5] In effect, all three categories involve choice. Our reason for separately identifying these activities is that the *character* of choice is quite different among classifications. These distinctions will be brought out in a later section of the chapter.

Such decision theory concepts as the expected value of perfect information, the expected value of sample information, the cost of obtaining information, and the employment of preposterior analyses in determining how much (if any) marketing research should be undertaken are illustrated by simple numerical examples.

In the final section, the author comments in a more philosophical and speculative manner on the potential contribution of decision and information theory to the advancement of both descriptive and normative marketing theory.

INFORMATION THEORY FROM THE SYSTEMS' VIEWPOINT

Probably most of us have some intuitive idea as to what is meant by possessing "a lot" versus "a little" information. We might expect that a primary objective of information is *to reduce our uncertainty* as to the occurrence of several possible events. For example, if we were driving along some relatively unknown route and came to a fork in the road, the statement of a seemingly reliable gasoline station attendant as to which road we should take in order to proceed to our destination would be informative. If the attendant not only assisted us in making this choice but, in the spirit of true service, proceeded to tell us the name of the best restaurant in the town which was our destination, we would consider this combined message as constituting even greater information (assuming our notions about the best eating place in town were also subject to uncertainty).

This illustration suggests that the *amount* of information is related to our degree of uncertainty. That is, the greater our uncertainty as to which possible event will occur, the greater is the amount of information conveyed by the occurrence of the event. Being told the correct route out of five equally likely routes should be more "informative" than being told the correct route out of two equally likely possibilities. And, if we already know which fork to take in order to reach our destination, being told that this route is "correct" provides *no* information.

In the special case where all contingencies are considered equally likely, it would seem reasonable to assume that the amount of information contained in a particular message could be measured as some function of the *number* of possibilities which we envision *before* that particular message is conveyed. However, we might also desire that our measure of the amount of information be additive. That is, whether the message conveyed to us consisted of two simple parts, route number and best restaurant in town or the compound expression of these two events, we should like to end up with the same total amount of information. Fortunately, the logarithmic function provides this desirable property of additivity when we deal with the joint occurrence of independent events.

Information theory, as developed by Shannon, is concerned with the *amount* of information measured by the extent of the change in event probability produced by the message, whether or not the message is perfect.[6] In words, the measure for this general case is

$$I(X) = \log_2 \left[\frac{\text{Probability of event after message is received}}{\text{Probability of event before message is received}} \right]$$

In the *special* case of a perfect message (or the actual occurrence of the event), the above expression reduces to

$$I(X) = \log_2 1 - \log_2 p(X) = 0 - \log_2 p(X) = -\log_2 p(X)$$

where $I(X)$ equals the informational content of the event X, and $p(X)$ equals the probability assigned to its occurrence prior to the receipt of the perfect message.

As a marketing setting for our discussion, consider the case of a marketing manager concerned with forecasting unit sales volume for the coming month. Suppose that the manager is certain that forecasted sales will be within ± 10,000 units of actual sales, but as he considers more narrow ranges of error, his forecasting ability diminishes, as shown in the first portion of Table 1. Columns (1), (2), and (3) refer to the forecasting

TABLE 1

CALCULATION OF INFORMATIONAL CONTENT—
SALES FORECASTING ILLUSTRATION

(1) Event X_i	(2) Description of Event	(3) Probabilities $p(X_i)$	(4) Units of Information $I(X_i)$
X_1	± 10,000 units	1.00	.00
X_2	± 5,000 units	.75	.42
X_3	± 2,000 units	.50	1.00
X_4	± 1,000 units	.25	2.00
X_5	± 500 units	.05	4.32

accuracy of our hypothetical marketing manager. In past endeavors, he has always managed to be within ± 10,000 units of actual sales, i.e., $p(X_1)$ equals unity. The probability of his forecast being within ± 5,000 units drops to .75, however, while the probability that his forecast is within ± 500 units of actual sales is only .05.

Suppose the manager were to receive a "message" that his forecast will really be within ±500 units of actual sales. Intuitively, we would suspect that more information is contained in this message than in a message indicating that his forecast is within ±10,000 units. As noted earlier, information theory, as developed by Shannon, formalizes this notion of the

---

[6] C. E. Shannon and W. Weaver, *The Mathematical Theory of Communication* (Urbana, Ill.: University of Illinois Press, 1949). Also, see S. Goldman, *Information Theory* (New York: Prentice-Hall, Inc., 1953).

amount of information contained in a "perfect" message and expresses it
as a number defined as:

$$I(X) = -\log_2 p(X)$$

To illustrate, the informational content of $-\log_2 1$ is zero, while $-\log_2 .05$
is 4.32 units or, more typically, 4.32 bits (an abbreviation for binits, since
logarithms to the base 2 are used). If the message is perfect, the number
representing $I(X)$ specifies the informational content of this special case
or, equivalently, the information after the event X has occurred. As intuition would suggest, if one were certain that an event was going to
occur, being told that the event has occurred provides no information. It
does not alter the probability attached to the occurrence of the event
before the message was received. On the other hand, if the chances attached to the occurrence of an event were very low, a communication
that the event has occurred (or is certain to occur) carries a large amount
of information.

The Shannon measure can be easily extended to deal with both (1) imperfect messages, and (2) the receipt of more than one message. To illustrate
the first case, suppose that before final sales results are tallied, a *preliminary*
report is received by the marketing manager which indicates that his
forecast will be within $\pm 1,000$ units. Based upon past experience with
preliminary figures, the probability that sales will really be within $\pm 1,000$
units, given the results of the preliminary report, is .75. The informational
content of this message can be defined as either the difference between
the perfect information potential before the message and after the message
or the logarithm of the ratio of the after-message probability to the before-
message probability. That is, if $p_1(X)$ equals the prior probability (.25
from Table 1) that the manager's forecast will be within $\pm 1,000$ units of
actual sales, and if $p_2(X)$ equals the probability, after the message, that
the manager's forecast will be within $\pm 1,000$ units of actual, then

$$I(M) = \{-\log_2 p_1(X)\} - \{-\log_2 p_2(X)\}$$

$$= \log_2 \frac{p_2(X)}{p_1(X)} = \log_2 \frac{.75}{.25} = \log_2 3$$

$$= 1.58 \text{ bits.}$$

Had the message been perfect, its informational content would have
amounted, of course, to 2 bits $(-\log_2 .25 = 2)$.

The Calculation of Average Information

To extend the Shannon measure to deal with the possible occurrence
of *several* events, a few new concepts are needed. To illustrate this extension, suppose our marketing manager assumes that the sales potential of a
given marketing area will fall within one of the intervals noted in Table 2.

TABLE 2

CALCULATION OF AVERAGE INFORMATION
(Annual Sales Potential)

(1)	(2)	(3)	(4)	(5)
	Description			Weighted
Event	of Event	Probabilities	Information	Information
X_i	(000's of Units)	$p(X_i)$	$I(X_i)$	$p(X_i) \cdot I(X_i)$
X_1	$100 < X \leqslant 120$	.10	3.322	.3322
X_2	$120 < X \leqslant 140$	.40	1.322	.5288
X_3	$140 < X \leqslant 160$	.25	2.000	.5000
X_4	$160 < X \leqslant 180$	.20	2.322	.4644
X_5	$180 < X \leqslant 200$	.05	4.322	.2161
			$H(X)$ =	2.0415 bits

As noted in Table 2, the marketing manager assumes that the events of column (2) are mutually exclusive and collectively exhaustive, i.e., they form a partition over the set of all possible events. Column (3) represents the probabilities assigned to the occurrence of each event, while column (4) represents the informational content of a perfect message regarding the occurrence of each possible event, respectively.

Although the manager can receive messages regarding the occurrence of *any* of the events, he might well be more interested in the amount of information received *on the average*. For example, a message could be received indicating the occurrence of X_5 (resulting in a large amount of information). Before the fact, however, it is more likely that a message indicating, say, X_2 (resulting in a smaller amount of information) would be received. The *average* information, called $H(X)$, is defined in the general case as

$$H(X) = - \sum_{i=1}^{n} p(X_i) \log_2 p(X_i)$$

or, since $I(X) = -\log_2 p(X)$, the average information is, equivalently,

$$H(X) = \sum_{i=1}^{n} p(X_i) \cdot I(X_i)$$

The average information for the hypothetical data of Table 2 is obtained as the sum of column (5), a figure which was derived by multiplying each perfect message entry of column (4) by its respective probability of occurring.

Lossy and Noisy Channels

Information theory can also be easily extended to deal with the situations of channel loss and/or channel noise. These concepts can be explained in terms of the following illustration. Assume that customer attitudes toward a specific firm can be expressed as either "good" or "poor." Assume further that the firm's salesmen purportedly convey these attitudes (e.g., by means of call reports) to the marketing manager. In terms of this simple illustration, the information "transmitted" in the channel can be viewed as the attitude toward the firm which the consumer really expresses to the salesman. The call report which the marketing manager gets from the salesman can be considered as the information "received" in the channel. From the marketing manager's point of view, the interesting feature is the extent to which the salesman serves as a lossy and/or noisy channel in communicating—via the call report—the attitude actually expressed by the customer.

To be more specific, let us first assume that the probability that a customer's attitude toward the firm falls in the "good" state is .50 and, similarly, the probability that his attitude toward the firm is "poor" is .50. We shall also suppose that the salesman serves as a perfect channel, i.e., a channel which contains neither loss of information nor noise. These assumptions are noted in Table 3.

TABLE 3

Loss-free and Noise-free Channel—Joint Probabilities

Customer Attitude—X_i	Salesman's Report—Y_j		
	Good	Poor	Marginal Probabilities
Good	.50	0	.50
Poor	0	.50	.50
Marginal probabilities	.50	.50	1.00

The entries of Table 3 are joint probabilities, i.e., $p(X_i$ and $Y_j)$. In the loss-free and noise-free case, the salesman is assumed to convey the "true" attitude of the customer without error. In terms of conditional probabilities, $p(Y_1 \mid X_1) = p(Y_2 \mid X_2) = 1.0$; and $p(Y_1 \mid X_2) = p(Y_2 \mid X_1) = 0$. Hence, the joint probability of, say, Y_1 and X_1 occurring is $p(Y_1 \mid X_1) \cdot p(X_1)$, or $1.0 \times .50 = .50$, as noted in the first cell of Table 3.

We can next examine the question regarding how much information is generated, on the average, by X_i and/or Y_j. To do this, we shall have to introduce four new measures: $H(X,Y)$, $T(X,Y)$, $H(X|Y)$, and $H(Y|X)$. The first measure, $H(X,Y)$, is the information contained in the *joint* occurrence of the stimulus (attitude actually expressed by a customer) and the response (customer's attitude as reported by the salesman). The measure $T(X,Y)$ stands for the amount of information *shared* by X and Y. The measure $H(X|Y)$ is that portion of the stimulus which is lost in the salesman's report, the average uncertainty still attached to the stimulus when the response is known, and is typically called the *equivocation* of the channel or channel loss.[7] Finally, $H(Y|X)$ measures the average uncertainty of the response, given the stimulus. This measure is usually referred to as ambiguity or channel *noise*.

The calculation of these measures first proceeds by specific application of the more general formula for determining the amount of average information:

$$H(X) = - \sum_i p(X_i) \log_2 p(X_i)$$

$$H(Y) = - \sum_j p(Y_j) \log_2 p(Y_j)$$

$$H(X,Y) = - \sum_{i,j} p(X_i \text{ and } Y_j) \log_2 p(X_i \text{ and } Y_j)$$

When the appropriate entries of Table 3 are substituted in the three preceding formulas, we arrive at $H(X) = 1$ bit; $H(Y) = 1$ bit; and $H(X,Y) = 1$ bit.

The measures $T(X,Y)$, $H(X|Y)$, and $H(Y|X)$ are derived from the preceding measures as follows:

$$T(X,Y) = H(X) + H(Y) - H(X,Y) = 1 + 1 - 1 = 1$$
$$H(X|Y) = H(X,Y) - H(Y) = H(X) - T(X,Y) = 1 - 1 = 0$$
$$H(Y|X) = H(X,Y) - H(X) = H(Y) - T(X,Y) = 1 - 1 = 0$$

The data in Table 3 illustrate the case of perfect transmission and, hence, a loss-free and noise-free channel. In this case, $H(X) = H(Y) = H(X,Y) = T(X,Y) = 1$, while both $H(X|Y)$ and $H(Y|X)$ are zero. This should agree with what we would intuitively expect. If the sales manager knows *either* the stimulus or the response, he, in effect, knows both inasmuch as the call report perfectly "calls" the customer's attitude. (Incidentally, if the salesman consistently transposed results by calling *all* "good" attitudes, "poor," and vice versa, no change in the measures would result. This reflects the fact that the manager has merely to reverse the labels in order to have a perfect predictor of stimulus, given response.)

In the case of this specific loss-free and noise-free channel, both $H(X)$ and $H(Y)$ contribute 1 bit each. However, their *joint* information, $H(X,Y)$, is less than the sum of $H(X)$ and $H(Y)$ indicating that X_i and Y_j share information; that is, $T(X,Y)$ is greater than zero. In fact, in this case, $T(X,Y) = 1$. We can now consider the other three logical possibilities which remain: lossy and noisy; lossy and noise-free; and loss-free and noisy. The appropriate joint probabilities for these variations are shown in Table 4.

---

[7] Expressed somewhat more technically, $H(X|Y)$ is the *prior* expectation of the information potential in the posterior distribution of X; more will be said on this point in the second section of this essay.

TABLE 4

TABLES OF JOINT AND MARGINAL PROBABILITIES

Customer Attitude—X_i	Salesman's Report—Y_j			
	Good	Poor	Marginal Probabilities	Type
Good	.25	.25	.50	Lossy and
Poor	.25	.25	.50	noisy
Marginal probabilities	.50	.50	1.00	
Good	.50	0	.50	Lossy and
Poor	.50	0	.50	noise-free
Marginal probabilities	1.00	0	1.00	
Good	.50	.50	1.00	Loss-free
Poor	0	0	0	and noisy
Marginal probabilities	.50	.50	1.00	

Calculation of appropriate measures for the other three cases proceeds analogously. In the lossy and noisy case, the salesman's response is independent of the attitude expressed by the customer. Hence, $H(X,Y) = H(X) + H(Y) = 2$ bits and *no* information is shared; $T(X,Y) = 0$. Moreover, $H(X|Y)$ and $H(Y|X)$ produce 1 bit each. In this case, knowledge of some response, Y_j, provides no predictive help about stimulus, and vice versa.

In the lossy but noise-free case, the salesman provided just one response, "good," whether the attitude expressed by the customer was good or bad. Although there exists no ambiguity about the response, i.e., $H(Y|X) = 0$, neither is any information provided by the response; $H(Y)$ also equals zero. The stimulus and response share no information and, hence, $T(X,Y) = 0$. The other measures, $H(X)$, $H(X,Y)$, and $H(X|Y)$, equal 1 bit each. The sole source of uncertainty is then provided by the stimulus X_i.

In the loss-free but noisy case, the opposite conditions prevail. In this instance, we assume that the stimulus is always X_1 (the customer's attitude is "good") and, hence, knowledge that X_i equals X_1 provides no information. However, the salesman is assumed to have a .50 probability of responding with "good" and a .50 probability of responding with "poor." The measure $H(Y)$ thus provides 1 bit of information and $H(Y|X)$ and $H(X,Y)$ equal 1 bit each. Analogous to the preceding case, the other measures, $H(X)$, $T(X,Y)$, and $H(X|Y)$, equal zero.

Information measures of the type illustrated in the simple cases above can be extended to deal with more than two variables at some increase in computational labor. Measures analogous to partial correlation coefficients can be calculated without the need to satisfy the latter's assumption of interval scales.[8] This suggests that some of the measurement techniques

---

[8] A discussion of the similarities between information measures and the analysis of variance may be found in W. J. McGill's paper, "Isomorphism in Statistical Anal-

of information theory may be useful in statistical analysis, independent of their potential for dealing with some of the theoretical aspects of information in marketing.

Limitations of Information Theory in Decision Making

Information theory as developed by Shannon goes well beyond the simple, introductory treatment found in the preceding paragraphs. For present purposes, it is sufficient to note that Shannon is primarily concerned with the informational aspects of physical systems—channel capacity, message encoding and decoding, channel noise, channel loss, and the like. Emphasis is placed on the *amount* of information rather than on whatever *value* it may have to the receiver.

To illustrate the difference between these two points of view, suppose that our marketing manager of Table 2 is now concerned with only two possible levels of annual sales potential, viz., $100 < X \leqslant 140$ and $140 < X \leqslant 200$ (in thousands of units). If the former event occurs, the sales manager would not wish to market some new product in the territory; if the latter event were to occur, he would. Suppose further that if the former event (which we shall call X_a) occurs and the producer *does* market the product, he would lose \$10,000, while if the latter event (X_b) occurs and the manager markets the product, he can gain only \$2,000. These highly simplified ground rules are noted in Table 5.

TABLE 5

PAYOFF TABLE—SALES POTENTIAL ILLUSTRATION
(Payoffs Refer to the Act—"Market the Product")

(1) Event: X in 000's of Units	(2) p(X)	(3) V(X)	(4) I(X)
X_a: $100 < X \leqslant 140$	.50	— 10,000	1.0
X_b: $140 < X \leqslant 200$	.50	2,000	1.0

If we were concerned with only the amount of information generated by a perfect message, Table 5 indicates that such a message indicating event X_a would be equivalent in *amount* of information with a perfect message indicating event X_b. From the standpoint of value, however, the manager who received—before he marketed the product—a perfect message (e.g., the result of a "perfectly reliable" market survey) indicating X_a might well consider this a much more valuable message than one indicating X_b. In the former case, he could avoid a loss of \$10,000; in the latter case he could gain only \$2,000. This distinction between the amount of information and the value of information becomes quite important as

---

ysis," in H. Quastler's *Information Theory and Psychology* (Glencoe, Ill.: The Free Press, 1955), pp. 56–62.

we now turn to the use of Bayesian theory and the information concepts which are associated with this normative approach to decision making under uncertainty.

BAYESIAN DECISION THEORY AND THE VALUE
OF INFORMATION

Bayesian decision theory represents one prescriptive procedure for making decisions under uncertainty. Like other theories of rational decision making, certain assumptions underlie application of the theory. Specifically, a decision problem under uncertainty is made up of the following components: (1) a decision maker; (2) a set ($n \geq 2$) of alternative courses of action; (3) a set ($n \geq 2$) of mutually exclusive and collectively exhaustive events which can occur; (4) a payoff function which assigns a value to the occurrence of each event; and (5) an element of doubt regarding which one of the possible events will occur.[9]

Bayesian decision theory assumes that the decision maker can assign numerical weights (which obey the postulates of probability theory) to each of the possible events. These probabilities may be based on either long-run experience with the event in question, or, in the case of unique events, they may reflect the more subjective judgments of the decision maker, or a combination of the two.[10] In either instance, the theory assumes that the decision maker chooses that act which maximizes expected value (or, more generally, expected utility), where expected value is a weighted average over all possible payoffs for a given act. Hence, maximization of expected value is the rationality criterion of Bayesian theory.

A key feature of this theory is the notion that the decision maker may elect to secure more information regarding the probabilities attached to each possible event by conducting "experiments." In the context of marketing, these experiments may consist of market surveys, pretests of new products, trial pricing studies, and so on. Typically, these experiments will cost something to conduct and seldom will they yield perfect information concerning the probabilities attached to alternative events. Bayesian decision theory provides a prescription for determining the size and type of experiment to conduct (if any should be conducted at all) and a means of using the sample findings of the experiment to modify prior probabilities attached to the alternative events.

The application of Bayesian procedures to marketing decisions offers provocative possibilities. Marketing problems are noted for high uncer-

---

[9] In the general case, payoffs are expressed in von Neumann–Morgenstern utilities, a function which measures the decision maker's attitudes toward risky outcomes. In practice, monetary measures (e.g., net profits, discounted cash flow) are usually employed. An introductory discussion of utility theory may be found in Schlaifer, *op. cit.*, p. 24–49.

[10] A discussion of the "subjective" school of probability may be found in L. J. Savage, *The Foundations of Statistics* (New York: John Wiley & Sons, Inc., 1954).

tainty attached to the occurrence of alternative events, paucity of relevant information, and lack of control over the outcomes of decisions. Consequently, the marketing manager must frequently resort to hunch and intuition in choosing among courses of action. The primary function of marketing research is to reduce this uncertainty by providing information relevant to decisions. Bayesian decision theory provides a systematic framework which considers both aspects, viz., the role of judgment *and* "objective" information (actual or potential) in choosing among alternative courses of action.

But marketing research is a more continuous activity than the preceding paragraph would suggest. Marketing research activity may be undertaken for purposes of (1) providing feedback information on currently pursued courses of action; (2) developing new courses of action (and the possible consequences related thereto) when a need to change present policies may exist; and (3) providing information on the likelihood of possible events, given the choice of each alternative course of action. It is also apparent, however, that each of these activities involves decisions and, consequently, the possibility of erroneous choice.

To illustrate, suppose the sales volume of a supermarket is declining relative to some goal level. A marketing research report which ascribed the decline in sales to failure of the store's merchandising policy could be in error. Sales could be declining as a consequence of a falloff in total sales for all supermarkets in the trading area. This particular supermarket may even be increasing its share of total sales. Another case in point is the nylon leotard craze in 1960. Producers of textile nylon suddenly faced a marked downward shift in demand from knitting mills, a development which producers initially took to indicate that the fad had run its course. Actually, consumer demand was still holding up well. Inventory imbalances in the long channel from fiber producer to consumer had created the sharp fall in the derived demand for the fiber used in the leotards. Demand at the fiber producer level later increased and then gradually leveled off.

The task of marketing research in correctly interpreting feedback is not easy. Marketing research can be compared to a noisy and lossy channel that produces two types of errors: (1) failure to signal a problem when one really exists; and (2) false signaling of a problem when none really exists.

The marketing research manager is also faced with choices in the search for alternative courses of action when there is a possible need for changing the currently pursued course. Search activity delays decisions and incurs cost.[11] In addition, all problems are subject to incomplete optimiza-

---

[11] The reader interested in the relationship of both information theory and search theory to decision theory should see D. F. Mela, "Information Theory and Search Theory as Special Cases of Decision Theory," *Operations Research*, Vol. 9, No. 6 (1961), pp. 907–9. In addition, a path-breaking paper concerned with the value of

tion. The marketing researcher must somehow try to chart a middle course which balances the cost of too extensive a search with the lost opportunity costs attached to terminating his search too quickly. A pricing problem encountered by a firm introducting a new man-made fiber illustrates this difficulty. In the haste of introducing the new fiber, a price was chosen which turned out to be too low relative to customer demand and the firm's ability to supply. A (purportedly superior) alternative course of action which involved coupling a somewhat higher price with a prestige labeling policy was uncovered *after* the original pricing decision had been implemented.

After courses of action are formulated, marketing research can play an important role in the evaluative process—the estimation of probabilities attached to the consequences of taking alternative courses of action. Most pretests are designed to facilitate this aspect of the problem solving process.[12] Again, the decision maker must weigh the cost of securing additional information against the cost of taking action in the light of his current uncertainties. As an illustration of the Bayesian approach, the remainder of this section is devoted to a discussion of this third or evaluative stage in the problem-solving process. By means of a simple and hypothetical example, we introduce such concepts as: (1) the cost of uncertainty; (2) the expected value of perfect information; (3) the expected value of sample information; (4) sequential decision making; and (5) the use of preposterior analysis in evaluating the effectiveness of alternative strategies.

A Numerical Illustration

Consider the following oversimplified problem. The marketing manager for the Beedle Brothers Brewery is concerned with the sales appeal of the firm's present label for its quart-size bottled beer. Marketing research studies indicate that supermarket consumers find little "eye-appeal" in the drab, somewhat cluttered appearance of the label. The firm has hired a design artist who has produced some prototype labels, all of which have been evaluated by the firm's executives. One label design has consistently won out in all preference tests which have been conducted among Beedle executives. But the marketing manager is still in doubt as to whether the new label would increase sales appreciably. He considers the costs associated with converting his firm's machinery, inventory, point-of-purchase displays, etc., to the new label and notes that an out-of-pocket cost of $500,000 would be involved.

---

information is J. Marshak's "Towards an Economic Theory of Organization and Information" in R. M. Thrall, C. H. Coombs, and R. L. Davis (eds.), *Decision Process* (New York: John Wiley & Sons, Inc., 1954).

12 What is described above as an orderly, sequential process of problem recognition, structuring and evaluation is obviously a gross simplification of the real world. In reality, a problem may undergo almost continuous reformulation. Identification of just when a decision was made is frequently a difficult task, as well.

If the new label were really "superior" to the old, Beedle's marketing manager estimates that the present value of all *net* cash flows related to increased sales generated over the next three years by the more attractive label would exceed by $800,000 the cash flows anticipated under the old label.[13] Based on his prior experience with merchandising changes of this type, he is only willing to assign a 50-50 chance to the event "new label is superior to old." Table 6 summarizes these data.

TABLE 6

Beer Label Problem—Calculation of Expected Monetary Value
(Payoff Entries in $000's)

Acts	$p(S_1)$	S_1—New Label Is "Superior"	$p(S_2)$	S_2—New Label Is Not "Superior"	Expected Monetary Value
A_1—adopt new	.5	800	.5	−500	150
A_2—keep old	.5	0	.5	0	0

As noted in Table 6, calculation of expected monetary value for this simple two-act, two-state case merely involves calculation of a weighted average payoff for each act, i.e., E.M.V. $= \sum_j p_{ij} O(A_i, S_j)$ for the A_ith act, where $O(A_i, S_j)$ represents the payoff associated with the conjunction of the ith act and jth state of nature. In the absence of any further information, the marketing manager who wished to maximize expected monetary value would choose act A_1; he would adopt the new label.

More realistically, the decision maker may elect to delay his terminal decision in order to gather more information regarding the probabilities attached to alternative consequences of each course of action. For purposes of exposition, suppose that the decision maker possessed four data-gathering alternatives prior to making a terminal choice.

1. Experiment e_0—do not experiment; make terminal choice now.
2. Experiment e_1—purchase a "perfect" survey service; cost of this service equals $300,000.
3. Experiment e_2—purchase a survey which is 80% reliable; cost equals $100,000.
4. Experiment e_3—purchase a survey which is only 70% reliable in the first stage, but if a second stage is required, the reliability increases to 80%; cost of first stage equals $50,000 while cost of second stage, if needed, equals $80,000. (Since some setup costs need not be duplicated, the second stage, 80%

---

[13] In practice, of course, incremental cash flow would be a function of how "superior" the new label turned out to be. (Moreover, selection of the appropriate planning horizon over which to discount future revenues would require study.) In the interest of keeping this illustration reasonably tractable, we shall heroically assume a two-event structure and a three-year planning horizon.

reliability survey can be done cheaper if preceded by a first-stage survey than if conducted alone.)

Under these simplified ground rules, we can now proceed to a discussion of some of the measures of information underlying Bayesian decision theory.

Figures 1 and 2 represent tree diagrams which summarize the pertinent payoffs and probabilities associated with each experiment. By following the path, e_0 (the dummy experiment) of Figure 1, we note the same data which were shown in Table 6. It is clear that in the absence of experimentation, the decision maker would select A_1 leading to an expected monetary payoff of $150,000; hence, the path labeled A_2 is blocked off by the double slash.

The path labeled e_1 traces out the strategy associated with the opportunity to conduct a perfectly reliable survey at a cost of $300,000. By "perfect" survey is meant one which would disclose without error which event, S_1 or S_2 is the correct state of nature. If $Z_1(e_1)$ and $Z_2(e_1)$ are the outcomes which indicate S_1 and S_2, respectively, in a perfectly reliable survey, the conditional probabilities $p\ [Z_1(e_1)\ |\ S_1]$ and $p\ [Z_2(e_1)\ |\ S_2]$ equal unity; $p\ [Z_1(e_1)\ |\ S_2]$ and $p\ [Z_2(e_1)\ |\ S_1]$ equal zero. Analogous to the channel loss and channel noise concepts of information theory, a perfectly reliable survey would be both loss-free and noise-free. Given each survey response, the decision maker would take the best act for that response—A_1, if the survey results indicate $Z_1(e_1)$, and A_2, should the survey results indicate $Z_2(e_1)$.

Before the fact, however, the decision maker must still apply the prior probabilities attached to S_1 and S_2, since the survey result can report results related to either state. (The calculation of these marginal probabilities is shown in the first part of Table 7.) When the prior probabilities are applied, the gross expected monetary value of the e_1 strategy is $400,000. But without conducting the perfect survey, the decision maker's expected value associated with taking A_1 is $150,000. The difference of $250,000 represents the *cost of uncertainty* associated with taking A_1 and also the *expected value of perfect information*—the upper limit which a decision maker could afford to spend for a perfectly reliable survey. Inasmuch as the perfect survey costs $300,000, the strategy e_1 is definitely inferior to e_0. The perfect information costs more than it is worth.

The branch labeled e_2 traces the path of the next strategy under consideration. This survey, which, more realistically, carries only an 80% reliability, is assumed to cost $100,000 rather than the $300,000 associated with the attempt to gather "perfect" information. Conditional probabilities, $p[Z_1(e_2)\ |\ S_1]$ and $p[Z_2(e_2)\ |\ S_2]$ equal .8 and $p[Z_1(e_2)\ |\ S_2]$ and $p[Z_2(e_2)\ |\ S_1]$ equal .2. In terms of information theory, we are dealing with both a noisy and lossy channel since the stimuli, S_1 and S_2, can imply either "response," Z_1 or Z_2, and conversely.

TABLE 7
CALCULATION OF RELEVANT PROBABILITIES ASSOCIATED WITH
EXPERIMENTS e_1, e_2, AND e_3

		Joint Probabilities S_1	S_2	*Marginal Probabilities*	*Posterior Probabilities* $P(S_1\|Z_i)$	$P(S_2\|Z_i)$
e_1	Z_1	.5	0	.5	1.0	0
	Z_2	0	.5	.5	0	1.0
		.5	.5	1.0		
e_2	Z_1	.4	.1	.5	.8	.2
	Z_2	.1	.4	.5	.2	.8
		.5	.5	1.0		
e_3 (first stage)	Z_1	.35	.15	.5	.7	.3
	Z_2	.15	.35	.5	.3	.7
		.50	.50	1.0		
		$S_1\|Z_1(e_3)$	$S_2\|Z_1(e_3)$		$P(S_1\|Z_i,Z_j)$	$P(S_2\|Z_i,Z_j)$
	Z_1Z_1	.56	.06	.62	.90	.10
	Z_2Z_1	.14	.24	.38	.37	.63
e_3 (second stage)		.70	.30	1.00		
		$S_1\|Z_2(e_3)$	$S_2\|Z_2(e_3)$			
	Z_1Z_2	.24	.14	.38	.63	.37
	Z_2Z_2	.06	.56	.62	.10	.90
		.30	.70	1.00		

The probabilities attached to the branches emanating from experiment e_2 are derived from Table 7. The entries labeled joint probabilities (e.g., .4, .1, etc.) represent the probability attached to the combination of each survey result, Z_1 or Z_2, with each state of nature, S_1 and S_2. For example, the joint probability, $p[Z_1(e_2)$ and $S_1] = p[Z_1(e_2) \mid S_1] \cdot p(S_1) = .8 \times .5 = .4$. Marginal probabilities are also calculated in a manner analogous to the examples covered under the section on information theory.

The posterior probabilities, however, are found through application of Bayes' theorem.[14] To illustrate, suppose $Z_1(e_2)$ *is* observed. This survey

---

[14] What is shown above descriptively may be computed by application of Bayes' formula:

$$p(S_i|E) = \frac{p(E \mid S_i) \cdot p(S_i)}{\sum_{j=1}^{n} p(E \mid S_j) \cdot p(S_j)}$$

where the S_j form a partition over some set of "states of nature" and E stands for some event where an S_j is a necessary condition for its occurrence.

FIGURE 1

TREE DIAGRAMS -- BREWERY PROBLEM PAYOFFS IN $ 000'S

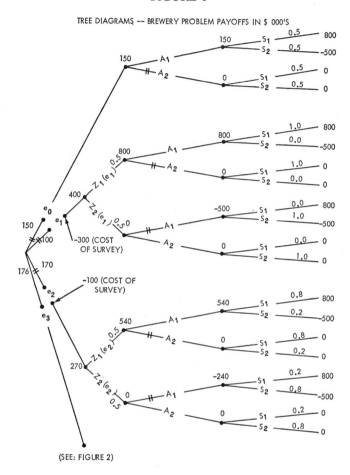

(SEE: FIGURE 2)

result suggests (with less than perfect reliability) that S_1 is the underlying state of nature. Intuitively, we should wish to revise our prior probabilities, .5 and .5 associated with S_1 and S_2, respectively, in the light of this survey result. This can be done by merely dividing the joint probabilities making up the $Z_1(e_2)$ row by the marginal probability, i.e., $p[S_1 \mid Z_1(e_2)]$ = $p[Z_1(e_2)$ and $S_1] / p[Z_1(e_2)]$ = $.4/.5$ = $.8$ and $p[S_2 \mid Z_1(e_2)]$ = $p[Z_1(e_2)$ and $S_2] / p[Z_1(e_2)]$ = $.1/.5$ = $.2$. If $Z_1(e_2)$ is observed, then act A_1 would be selected leading to an expected payoff of $540,000, and if $Z_2(e_2)$ is observed, then act A_2 would be selected leading to a zero payoff. Since before the survey is undertaken each sample result could be observed, the marginal probabilities, $p[Z_i(e_2)]$ are next applied leading to the expected payoff of $270,000. The $100,000 cost of the survey is deducted from this payoff with the result being a net expected monetary payoff of $170,000.

FIGURE 2

TREE DIAGRAMS -- BREWERY PROBLEM PAYOFFS IN $ 000'S

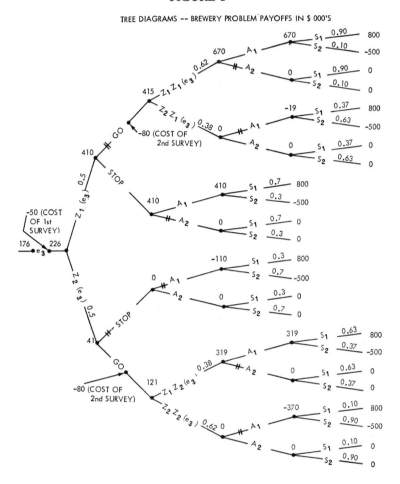

Strategy, e_3, is traced out in Figure 2; associated probability calculations are shown in Table 7. No new principles are involved in this sequential strategy. Notice, however, that the decision maker *again* revises his posterior probability after the first-stage survey *if* he decides to undertake the second stage. If $Z_1(e_3)$, is observed (a survey result favorable to S_1), the decision maker would not undertake a second survey but would proceed with act A_1 and change over to the new design. If $Z_2(e_3)$ is observed (a survey result favorable to S_2), the decision maker should undertake the second survey. When, if another Z_2 is observed, i.e., $Z_2, Z_2(e_3)$, the decision maker should select A_2; while, if $Z_1, Z_2(e_3)$ is observed, he should select act A_1. By starting from the right and working backwards, and always choosing the highest payoff path, the expected value of this whole strategy turns out to be $176,000; hence, all other main paths are blocked off. (In practice, of course, it is not mandatory that the decision maker stop at a two-stage experiment. An evaluation of additional stages would involve calculating the expected payoff of proceeding, i.e., the expected value of additional sample information versus the cost incurred to obtain the additional information.)

In following through the preceding illustration, the reader has probably observed that both probabilities *and* conditional payoffs affect the value of information as formulated under Bayesian theory. Furthermore, this value is an expectation rather than a sum certain.[15] Roughly speaking, the expected value of new information represents the difference between the expected payoff associated with taking the *best* act in the absence of the new information and the expected value of the strategy involving both information collection and best terminal action. The *net gain* from information collection is the expected value of the information less the cost of obtaining it. If the net gain is positive, the decision maker—according to Bayesian theory—should "purchase" the additional information.

Many additional complications could have been included in the illustration. The costs associated with information collection could have been treated as a random variable. Sensitivity analyses could have been run in which probabilities and/or payoffs were changed in order to ascertain the sensitivity of the payoff associated with the best strategy to these changes in assumptions. Hopefully, however, enough has been covered to give the reader at least a basic grasp of the concepts underlying Bayesian theory and the mechanics of applying it.

The Amount versus Value of Information

As has been described, information theory as developed by Shannon is concerned with the *amount* of information. The information measures of Bayesian decision theory are concerned with the *value* of information. Although application of both schemata involves revision of probabilities, Bayesian theory considers payoffs as well as probabilities. In this latter theory, information measures are imbedded in a much broader framework.

Many similarities, however, exist between the two theories. For example, the concepts of a channel loss and channel noise are common to both schemata. Bayes' theorem enters into the calculation of the measure of equivocation, as discussed in the section devoted to Shannon's information theory. Equivocation, $H(X|Y)$, can be defined as the prior expectation of the information potential in the posterior distribution of the stimulus X given Y, the response. On the other hand, the concepts of channel loss and noise can be useful in the interpretation of Bayesian theory. The conditional probabilities associated with the results of a "perfectly reliable" survey are analogous to those related to a channel which is both loss-free and noise-free. In more realistic cases, however, the "channels" in Bayesian decision problems will be both lossy (given a particular survey

---

[15] This distinction is important if the individual's utility were not linear with money.

result, uncertainty may still exist regarding the underlying state of nature) and noisy (given a particular state of nature, uncertainty may still exist regarding the sample outcome).

The purposes for which these two theories have been designed are quite different. Information theory was developed by Shannon to cope with design problems involved in the construction of physical systems and to provide predictive criteria useful in channel transmission and receiving and in message encoding and decoding. Schlaifer used information measures to provide criteria of a prescriptive nature which would enable the decision maker to approach the problem of buying information as part of the overall framework of making rational decisions in the face of uncertainty. Although neither theory has been applied extensively as yet to actual marketing problems, the potential of both appears promising.[16]

Potential Usefulness of Information Measures in Marketing

Information theory has already been employed as a descriptive measure by several experimental psychologists.[17] From the psychologist's viewpoint, information theory has provided measures useful in experimental studies of learning, perception, and stimulus discrimination. As far as marketing is concerned, information theory might be useful in measuring the informational content of advertising messages and in determining the effect of various levels of redundancy on reader interest and recall. For example, how is consumer recall of various advertisements related to their informational content? How is a consumer's loyalty to a given brand related to the level of his information about this brand versus other brands? Do advertising messages containing relatively high information content attract and hold the reader's initial attention and favorably affect his attitudes? Is the informational content of advertising related to the price of an item and/or its length of time on the market?

The use of information theory in the study of marketing organizations and industrial systems would also seem to offer potential as a descriptive measure. For example, the design of such routinized documents as salesmen's call reports, sales forecasts, reports on competitive activity, and various sales statistics might be aided by a conceptual understanding of information theory. It would also appear that some concepts, e.g., the principle of "management by exception" and budget variances (in the accountant's sense of the word), might be studied within the framework of information theory. These areas, of course, are only illustrative of the potential contribution of information theory as an analytical technique in

---

[16] For some early applications of Bayesian decision theory to actual marketing problems, the following articles by the author might be of interest: (1) "Bayesian Decision Theory in Pricing Strategy," *Journal of Marketing*, January, 1963; and (2) "Decision Making in Chemical Marketing," *Industrial and Engineering Chemistry*, September, 1962.

[17] See Quastler, *op. cit.*

the study of business communication. Suffice it to say that an operational definition of information is now available for coping at least partially with the complexities of these problems.

Bayesian theory and its related information concepts might hold even greater potential as a device for dealing with decisions under uncertainty and as an analytical framework in which the data gathering services of marketing research can be evaluated from an economic standpoint.

Although the applicability of traditional statistical techniques is well known to many marketing researchers, it is interesting to note that Bayesian decision theory provides a useful bridge between conventional statistical reasoning and economic reasoning. By explicitly introducing the economic costs of wrong decisions and the decision maker's prior judgments, Bayesian theory offers a direct rationale for choosing among alternative sampling plans and provides insight into the determination of economical sample sizes. In classical statistics, with its emphasis on hypothesis testing and type I and type II errors, losses due to wrong decisions enter the model only externally and incompletely through selection of appropriate alpha and beta risks. (Some levels of significance like .05 and .01 have achieved almost sacred status.) In contrast, Bayesian decision theory enables the researcher to view the costs of wrong decisions that are associated with values of the parameter(s) of interest and, by assigning prior probabilities over the values of these parameters, to choose that act leading to the lowest opportunity loss. Bayesian statistics also provides a natural procedure for statistical estimation which is not restricted to the usual assumption of a quadratic loss function.

Of especial interest to the market researcher, however, is the potential value of preposterior analysis in determining whether any survey is worth the cost and, if so, the type and size of survey in order. Bayesian procedures can be extended in a natural fashion to deal with the important case of making sequential decisions where various information states exist between decision steps.

Although the outlook may appear sanguine for the future application of Bayesian decision theory to real marketing problems, this is not to say that these procedures will be—or should be—speedily adopted without reservation. Bayesian computations are frequently complex and time consuming. In the author's experience, most problems of any size required computer simulation in order to determine the relevant conditional payoff functions. In addition, Bayesian procedures do not yet exist for all traditional statistical procedures with which the analyst works. Nor in many cases can the relevant prior distributions be developed easily. In practice, the analyst will frequently resort to sensitivity analyses of prior distributions and payoff entries in order to show the decision maker how the "best" choice is affected by changes in the variables of interest.

In summary, Bayesian decision theory is entirely consonant with the incorporation of new data provided by activities like marketing research.

Marketing research is thus viewed as a potentially valuable—but cost incurring—source for reducing the costs of uncertainty associated with decisions made in the absence of the research findings. Research can then be channeled into those areas where the potential informational gain is worth the cost of obtaining it. Somewhat ironically, considering the current trend toward greater use of the behavioral sciences in marketing, the venerable marginal analysis of microeconomic theory may find regained stature in the modified garb of statistical decision theory.

24. PRICE WARFARE—A FORM OF BUSINESS RIVALRY

Ralph Cassady, Jr.

I. INTRODUCTION

VERY LITTLE has been written about price warfare, and much of what has been written is superficial. Consequently, this type of competitive behavior has been misunderstood. One factor contributing to this confusion is an imprecise use of the term "price war" by writers and practitioners in the fields of economics and marketing, which has resulted in there often being no way of knowing what phenomenon the expositor is discussing. Another reason for the inadequacies of most discussions of price warfare is the failure of writers to examine actual conditions microscopically in order to find out how price warriors actually behave.

After considerable thought relating to the subject and much field study in various product areas, this writer feels that he is able to generalize about certain aspects of price warfare. As a preliminary step toward a broad understanding of the subject, he has provided a taxonomic basis for a rather precise definition of this type of competitive activity. He has concluded that price warfare (1) can be distinguished from normal competitive behavior and, in fact, (2) must be recognized as a particular species of a genus which includes various types of abnormal competitive patterns.[1] The term should no longer be considered as a catchall for any type of soft-market condition but should be confined, instead, to a specific form of price-competitive activity.

---

[1] Marketing, unlike such disciplines as botany, zoology, and geology, has suffered from an absence of morphological (structural) and taxonomic (classification) studies that precisely analyze and identify different competitive behavior patterns. Although the Definitions Committee of the American Marketing Association, Edward S. Mason, and Joe S. Bain have made some attempts in these directions, relatively little organized research effort has been devoted to studying the precise structure of competition and the actual, as opposed to preconceived, business behavior patterns which develop out of such structures. Consequently, we are unable to distinguish precisely between subtly different forms of competitive effort, and our thinking about such matters is perforce imprecise.

Technically, a price war may be thought of as multilateral pricing behavior involving two or more vendors seeking to achieve opposing goals. Rival vendors, using price as a weapon, make successive moves and countermoves in an attempt to gain an advantage or to resist the attainment of an advantage by others. Such action results in prices spiraling downward to low levels. The essence of price warfare is, therefore, head-on conflict between (or among) vendors who are (temporarily) determined to achieve opposing goals; it is characterized by successive moves and countermoves with resulting downward spiraling of prices. Thus, opposing forces are engaged in a kind of "war."

Although the term is generally descriptive—price warfare is a type of conflict—it is not a precisely apt designation for the type of conflict that is generally given this name.[2] Price wars are not typically long drawn-out conflicts during which particular engagements or battles are fought at various points, as is usually the case in actual warfare. Neither are they like individual engagements or battles, because there is usually no overall campaign that provides a basis for individual engagements, unless one thinks of everyday normal competitive effort as warfare, which is certainly not precisely accurate.[3]

Thus, price wars are like actual wars in certain respects and unlike actual wars in other respects.[4] They are on the one hand conflicts—although usually bloodless—for the attainment of some end.[5] Such conflicts may involve strategic (general plan or purpose) as well as tactical (actual maneuver) considerations.[6] On the other hand, physical annihi-

---

[2] See Ralph Cassady, Jr., "Price Warfare and Armed Conflict: A Comparative Analysis," Michigan Business Review, November, 1956, p. 3.

[3] But see General Carl von Clausewitz (On War, Vol. I, originally published in 1832, new and revised edition published in London by Kegan Paul, Trench, Trubner & Co., Ltd., and in New York by E. P. Dutton & Co., in 1918, p. 121), who argued that all business activity may be likened unto real warfare. "... War ... is a conflict of great interests, which is settled by bloodshed, and only in that is it different from others. It would be better, instead of comparing it with any Art, to liken it to business competition, which is also a conflict of human interests and activities; and it is still more like State policy, which again, on its part, may be looked upon as a kind of business competition on a great scale." For a contrary point of view, see Cassady, op. cit., p. 3.

[4] Cassady, op. cit., pp. 2–5.

[5] Violence and even bloodshed developing out of price conflict is not unheard of in business competition. This seems to have been particularly true in the service trades, e.g.. cleaning and dyeing and barbering. Such conflicts appear to develop out of attempts by organized groups to coerce individual operators into ceasing price-cutting activities. One such case several years ago involved two East Los Angeles barber shops which were attacked with home-made bombs and odorous chemicals for the apparent purpose of forcing the cut raters to raise their prices. See "Chemicals Hurled at Bargain Barbershops," Los Angeles Times, August 24, 1954, Pt. I, p. 2.

[6] Cassady, op. cit., pp. 2–3. See also Ralph Cassady, Jr., "Taxicab Rate War: Counterpart of International Conflict," Journal of Conflict Resolution, December, 1957, pp. 365–66. For a broad historical treatment of competitive business tactics, see Ralph Cassady, Jr., and William F. Brown, "Exclusionary Tactics in American Business Competition: An Historical Analysis," UCLA Law Review, January, 1961, pp. 88–134.

lation is not the end sought in a price war. Also, the weapon used in a price war—price—is in a sense self-destructive and cannot very well be employed without causing damage to the aggressor. That is, the dropping of one's price is likely to have an adverse effect on the "enemy," but it may harm the initiator as well.[7] However, the aggressor may be in a better position than his "enemy" to withstand the loss involved because of the hedge of normal operations in other areas. Moreover, when the "war" is over, he may find himself in a stronger competitive position than he held previously (e.g., price differentials between his offerings and those of competitors may be more favorable).

It should be clear even at this early stage of our study that there are many puzzling aspects of price warfare. The following study is devoted to an analysis of such conflicts in an attempt to throw light on the inner workings of this atypical form of competitive behavior. Having defined the phenomenon and considered other preliminary matters in Section I, we shall attempt to look in abstract terms at various facets of price warfare in Section II (e.g., how price wars start and how deep prices go in price war situations). Section III will be devoted to a case example of a price war from its inception to its termination during which the various aspects of price warfare will be pointed up. Finally, Section IV will attempt to provide the student with some generalizations regarding the impact of price wars on various functionaries and on consumers and society generally. It also will consider the remedial steps, if any, that should be taken to prevent price warfare.

II. ANALYSIS OF PRICE WARFARE

In analyzing price warfare, one might first select segments of the subject that he particularly wishes to study and then place these aspects of the subject under glass, as it were. Such a study of price warfare might include analyses of (a) the competitive structure most conducive to price warfare, (b) the initiation of price warfare, (c) the number of items involved in price warfare, (d) the depth of price reductions in price wars, (e) the spread of price cutting during wars, (f) the duration of price wars, and (g) the termination of price wars.

Competitive Structure Most Conducive to Price Warfare

Price wars have been found by the author to occur in a score or more fields, including alcoholic beverages, books, bread, canned food, cigarettes, drugstore items, fresh milk, gasoline, hamburger, home appliances, meals (in gambling establishments), packaged grocery items, portland cement,

---

[7] Cassady, "Price Warfare and Armed Conflict: . . . ," *op. cit.*, p. 4.

railroad transportation, soft goods, and taxicab service.[8] In some of these fields, price warfare is rare; in others, numerous wars have been fought over the years.

It is perfectly clear that price wars would not develop in pure (or even quasi-pure) competitive situations.[9] Under such conditions, each vendor is able to sell his entire stock at the market price, and hence, no seller needs to undercut another in order to move his merchandise into the market. Similarly, price wars are not apt to develop in pure monopoly situations, since by definition a monopolist has no opponent against whom to wage "war." To be sure, a monopoly might have been *created* by means of such a "war," and monopolists may become involved in a price war in an attempt to repel the invasion of new competitors. However, since monopolies are rare phenomena in a competitive society, it follows that price wars developing out of such conditions, if they exist at all, are uncommon.

Careful examination of the competitive circumstances surrounding the various "wars" reveals that these are all oligopolistic or, in some few instances perhaps, monopolistic-competitive situations.[10] That is, these cases are largely characterized by the existence of few sellers—so few that the competitive activities of any one have a substantial effect on the others.[11] It is conceivable, also, that a price war might develop under oligopsonistic conditions (where *buyers* are few). This might occur, for example, if canners—who post prices at which they will purchase raw products—turned on one another in striving for needed raw materials. It

---

[8] For a study of price warfare in various fields see Ralph Cassady, Jr., *Price Warfare in Business Competition: A Study of Abnormal Competitive Behavior*, (East Lansing: Bureau of Business and Economic Research, Michigan State University, 1963).

[9] In such situations, there are numerous well-known sellers of homogeneous commodity–services. Quasi-pure competition may suggest incomplete information on the part of traders or near-homogeneity rather than perfect homogeneity of product-services.

[10] It might appear that some of the fields mentioned (e.g., gasoline) are monopolistic-competitive in nature rather than oligopolistic, i.e., the competition is characterized by numerous sellers of differentiated products rather than by fewness of sellers. However, the determination of the number of sellers in a market depends on the criterion employed in judging the number. For example, if one considers all of the thousands of service stations in a large metropolitan area as rivals of one another, this may be deemed an example of monopolistic competition. However, if only the stations which are directly competitive with one another are considered, the situation might better be designated as oligopolistic in nature.

[11] For a succinct technical statement of oligopoly theory, see George J. Stigler, *The Theory of Price* (rev. ed.; New York: The Macmillan Co., 1952), particularly pp. 220–40. For an account having a somewhat closer application to actual business competition, see Joel Dean, *Managerial Economics* (New York: Prentice-Hall, Inc., 1951), particularly pp. 68–73, 152–53, and 427–44. It might be mentioned in this connection that competition theory serves as a valuable guide in conducting empirical market studies but, conversely, that the findings of empirical research might serve to sharpen the theoretician's tools of analysis.

is an interesting fact that a price war between oligopsonists (if such occurred) would drive prices up rather than down.

It should not be surprising to discover that price wars are most prevalent in oligopolistic situations. The evidence suggests, however, that price wars occur generally not where nondifferentiated oligopolistic conditions prevail (where there are few sellers of a homogeneous product), but, rather, where differentiated oligopoly conditions obtain (where there are few sellers of a differentiated product or service). Gasoline wars, for example, involve different brands of product as well as different stations, and there may be considerable consumer adherence to particular vendors' offerings.[12]

This finding would seem to be in accord with orthodox competition theory. Under oligopolistic conditions with no product differentiation, buyers would be indifferent as to their source of supply; therefore, a reduction in price by a single seller would attract a substantial amount of trade to price-cutters from competitors. Thus, the degree of cross-elasticity for the product of a single seller would be very high. Under such circumstances, however, the probable reactions of competitors may be easily predicted, and the consequences in terms of effect on profits are apt to be quite apparent.

Because competitors are almost certain to react, an oligopolist selling a homogeneous product usually considers price to be too sharp a weapon for *indiscriminate* use in attracting trade. Consequently, "war" in this kind of situation would not be expected to occur often as a result of open price cutting.[13] This is not to say, however, that such behavior could not occur, or even that it would be irrational under certain circumstances. Nevertheless, the exercise of self-restraint in making open price reductions tends to result in the avoidance of price wars in such an industry.[14]

Conversely, where differentiation prevails either in the product or service, or both, there will be some adherence of buyers to certain sellers. In such instances, the degree of cross-elasticity of demand for the product of any one seller will be sufficiently low so that price reductions may be made without inevitable retaliation by rivals. A seller may then feel that he can use a price cut to expand his trade because he believes that the effect on his competitors will not be so severe as to cause them to resort to countercutting. If his estimate is correct, the entire price level will not

---

[12] There is no question but that the gasoline field is unique as far as prevalence of price warfare is concerned. In no other field is there nearly as much open price conflict. See Section III for an intensive analysis of an actual gasoline price war.

[13] To the extent that a cut can be secretly made, an oligopolist may be able to make gains at the expense of his competitors without pulling the price structure down on his head, but the possibility of exposure may make such practice very hazardous.

[14] This does not mean that price warfare cannot develop in such an industry. See *Price Bases Inquiry* (Washington, D.C.: U.S. Federal Trade Commission, March, 1932), p. 102.

be lowered. If the price cutter errs in his judgment, counterreductions will follow his price cut, either immediately or in due time, and price warfare *might* follow.[15]

An additional point of clarification is required here: Although price warfare is not likely to develop in pure oligopolistic situations, neither is it apt to break out among companies whose brands are so strongly entrenched that they are able to retain clienteles despite substantial reductions in price by rival sellers. This situation may obtain because of the low degree of cross-elasticity among brands (i.e., a price change of one brand has little effect on sales of another) because of brand loyalty as well as an association in the minds of consumers of low quality with low price in "substitute" brands. This does not mean that well-and-favorably-known brands of merchandise are immune from price warfare but only that warfare is not apt to break out among suppliers of such products. Conflict involving such brands may, however, develop at the retail level among institutions competing with one another in the sale of the same well-and-favorably-known brands even though such institutions are themselves to some extent differentiated in the minds of consumers. Indeed, many price wars are precisely of this type.[16]

One final point in this connection: Although price wars appear to develop most often out of differentiated-oligopoly competitive conditions, they are relatively rare even where such conditions prevail. Since the overall competitive structure per se thus has little determinative effect on the prevalence of price wars, it follows that some other, perhaps more subtle, factors are influential as regards the occurrence of price wars. One such factor might be the aggressiveness of certain of the vendors—one of the sellers may be determined to gain a certain market position, using price as a weapon, while another is equally determined to prevent such a move, with the result that conflict becomes inevitable. The point is that the type of competitive structure in its simplest aspects alone does not trigger the price war.

How Price Wars Are Initiated

If one accepts the definition of price wars given in the first section of this chapter, one must agree that such wars are not unilateral in nature. They involve, rather, bilateral or even multilateral competitive relationships. That is, one firm cannot conduct a war against another although one firm may *attack* another; rather, under price war conditions, two or

---

[15] It is an interesting fact that sellers may gain a competitive advantage if their price reduction is *effective but not too effective* in attracting custom and thus inviting retaliation of rivals. If a seller's prices are too attractive, he may find it disadvantageous in longer-run terms because of the reaction of rivals who must at least meet his lower-price offerings.

[16] Ralph Cassady, Jr., "The New York Department Store Price War of 1951: A Microeconomic Analysis," *The Journal of Marketing*, July, 1957, pp. 3–11.

more firms act in opposition to one another. It takes at least two to make a price war.

Although there are various ways in which a price war can be initiated, basically, (1) some sort of market disturbance must occur (e.g., an invasion by a new competitor or market expansion by an established firm), (2) one or more of those vendors who are affected by the move must react to the initial move by the use of the price weapon, and (3) the vendor against whom the countermove is made must react to the first reaction, i.e., *not* capitulate.[17] It is, of course, in the process of cutting and undercutting that price warfare can be distinguished from other types of intensive price behavior patterns. It should be clear from this that (*a*) any type of aggressive move might cause the start of a price war but that (*b*) some such moves might cause retaliation or might not, and that (*c*) even at this point the antagonists might stop short of war. It should be clear also that the chances of retaliatory action might differ according to (*a*) the competitive position of the several sellers, (*b*) the personality patterns of the vendors involved, and (*c*) the market conditions prevailing at the time in that particular trade.

Probably the most common type of precipitating factor leading to price warfare is the invasion of the market by a new seller [18] or the adding of a new line to an existing operation—an action with some of the characteristics of an invasion.[19] More often than not, however, market invasion by the use of penetration pricing techniques occurs without any "bloodshed." This emphasizes the fact that it is the very important but subtle differences among market structures and rival vendors which produce different market results. Unfortunately, we have little precise knowledge about the impact of these variables on the outbreak of price conflict.

One further point in this connection: One might inquire on a basis of the foregoing as to the responsibility for initiating price wars. Is the vendor who makes the first price move responsible in view of the fact that he may simply be trying to gain or regain volume? Should the blame be placed on the shoulders of the vendor whose success in attracting volume from competitors has caused those adversely affected to reduce prices? Indeed, can the price cutters or their competitors be blamed when they are merely trying to successfully compete—should not the competitive system itself be blamed?

The Number of Items Involved in a Price War

It must be kept in mind that antagonists who become engaged in price wars will attempt to prevent one another from achieving the ends sought.

---

[17] Otherwise the countermove would have simply stymied the opposition, and price warfare would have been prevented.

[18] See "Prices Collapse in War between Chains," *Life*, May 16, 1949, p. 47.

[19] See "Fruit and Vegetables Given Away in Price War on Upper Broadway," *The New York Times*, March 11, 1953, Pt. II, p. 31.

The merchandise items used by antagonists will be those expected to attract business from rival concerns. Generally speaking, products that become involved in price warfare are high-demand, frequently purchased, items to whose vendors consumers are attracted when the goods are reduced in price. Sometimes only one item is utilized in a price war; at other times, several, perhaps many, items are employed.

In the service-station field, where price wars are most prevalent, the high-demand product, gasoline, is normally the only item around which wars are fought. In the grocery field, where price warfare occasionally occurs, price conflicts do not usually revolve around one product.[20] They are, however, confined to a relatively few fast-moving items that are commonly used as "leaders" (e.g., shortening, eggs, coffee, and detergents).[21] The Macy-Gimbel price war of 1951 is the only "war" that this author knows about that was fought on the basis of a wide merchandise offering.[22] Even in that war, the price cutting was confined to only a *relatively few* popular items (i.e., hundreds) as compared with the total offerings of the stores involved in the war (i.e., tens of thousands).

One might conclude, therefore, that price wars typically revolve around one or a relatively few items for two reasons: (1) the number of high-demand items stocked by a given type of vendor is limited, and (2) the "warring" vendors will tend to practice restraint in expanding the number of cut-price items because of the increased markdown losses resulting from such a move.[23] In some instances (e.g., the Macy-Gimbel price war), price cutting is confined largely to well-and-favorably-known brands of popular lines.

Depth of Price War Reductions

Price quotations under price war conditions generally spiral downward on a basis of successive reductions and counter reductions. It is not unheard of for prices to go down to zero (i.e., the price-cut item is temporarily given away). Indeed, it is not inconceivable that prices could go to a minus figure (i.e., the patron would not only be given the item free, but a small cash payment might be made which would serve as a promotional stunt).[24]

---

[20] However, a grocery war *may* be fought over only one product such as milk, bread, or cigarettes.

[21] For a full discussion of the use of price leaders in the food field, see Ralph Cassady, Jr., *Competition and Price Making in Food Retailing* (New York: The Ronald Press Co., 1962), particularly pp. 135–38 and 167–77.

[22] See Cassady, "The New York Department Store Price War . . . ," *op. cit.,* pp. 3–11, particularly pp. 5–8.

[23] A combatant may at first worry about whether he can hold out in a long drawn-out action. As times goes on, he is apt to become more concerned with the loss figures with which his accountant confronts him as a result of this price struggle.

[24] A friend, who remembers the Los Angeles milk wars during the depression years, recalls that two stores were competing with daily drops in prices of milk until one vendor's price was down to 1 cent per unit; whereupon his competitor across the

Generally speaking, however, price reduction in price wars do not go below the invoice cost level which acts as a sort of price floor. If such is the case, the merchant does not suffer out-of-pocket losses, even if his prices are drastically cut. Nevertheless, he may be headed for real trouble because of reduced margins out of which he must pay his operating expenses, especially if the sales volume of the price-cut item is substantial in relation to total sales. In some fields (e.g., gasoline), the cost of merchandise is considerably lower for some vendors than for others, in which case some participants may be operating below cost while others are not.

It is interesting to note that in the case of multiple-item "wars," reductions may differ considerably among products involved in price warfare. Some may be reduced only slightly, while others are reduced drastically. When this situation obtains, it would appear, a priori at least, that the deepest reductions would be in the most popular items—those on which vendors could not afford to be undersold. In such a fight, a very popular brand, such as *Bayer* aspirin, might conceivably go to 1 cent or at most a few cents per unit. On the other hand, less-well-known medicaments might be sold at only slightly less than or even at normal levels. Price warfare involving high-demand items such as bread, milk, and cigarettes thus tends to be extremely drastic because a vendor cannot afford to be undersold on such universally demanded items. As a result, vendors of such items will practice restraint in the undercutting of rivals' prices.

Gasoline is a very high-demand item over which price wars are commonly fought. When warfare occurs in this field, prices generally are driven to levels below dealer costs, and normal margins disappear. In fact, unprotected station operators often operate on an out-of-pocket loss basis.[25] Because of the drastic nature of such warfare, suppliers, who require a network of retail distributors to get their goods into the hands of the ultimate consumer, often subsidize their dealers. Even though prices drop to very low levels, the retail outlets are protected, at least in part, from the ravages of war. But subsidization does not protect them fully against margin loss, and operating during such times may be anything but profitable. Also, some dealers who have no regular suppliers but who purchase their requirements wherever they can do so most advantageously, may be unprotected under price war conditions and may even be forced to the wall.[26] The protection provided might well be an important cause of

street advertised free milk. On entering the "free milk" store, the customer found only a sign on the counter with instructions to take a penny from a bowl containing 1-cent pieces, go across the street and buy the 1-cent milk from his competitor.

[25] Some service stations operating on an out-of-pocket loss basis actually close their doors during a price war and by so doing lose less money than they would if they continued to operate.

[26] A Dallas, Texas, informant reported to the author in late December, 1954, that he had been an independent gasoline dealer in his community but had "gone broke" in a recent price war. He had bought his gasoline from a major company on a private-brand basis and, hence, was not protected by a supplier (major-company dealers in his area were guaranteed a 4-cent margin during the "war").

price wars in this field. Retail vendors thus might not practice restraint if they do not have to bear the full burden of involvement in price warfare for which they may be partially or even fully responsible.

The Spread of Price Wars

The geographical extent of price wars appears, in part at least, to depend upon the intensiveness of price cutting and the duration of the conflict. Price wars that involve only modest reductions or that come to an end quickly do not, of course, spread very far. However, unless price wars are not violent or have terminated within a short time, they tend to spread from neighborhood to neighborhood and even in certain circumstances from community to community, unless the "war" is waged in an isolated market area.[27] This is particularly true if the price reductions are severe.[28]

The spread of price wars results from competition among retail institutions and even trade areas for customers as well as the fact that price reductions tend to attract customers from normal-price areas, thus causing reactions on the part of those adversely affected. Theoretically, at least, the critical segment of the market in relation to the spread of price cutting is the overlapping of areas. As a result, customers may be attracted for the purchase of goods and services toward either one of two institutions or market areas. A shift of custom tends to cause a reaction on the part of the outlets affected. The conceptual pattern of overlapping market areas (indicated by the eccentric circles) together with the chain reaction that occurs as a result of a change in price in one of them (indicated by the arrows) is illustrated as follows: [29]

There is no question but that modern transportation and communication methods are factors in the spread of price wars. Because of such facilities, the isolated village or community of yesteryear is now prac-

---

This independent dealer sold gasoline on a basis of a 3-cent margin before the price war and earned $400–$450 net a month. During the price war, he sold the product at a 3-cent negative margin and lasted only for a few weeks of what appears to have been a six-week price war.

This man reported that he and a couple of dozen similarly situated dealers conferred at one time or another during the conflict with district managers of major companies in the hope of bringing the struggle to an end, but these meetings did not result in prompt termination. He said that only two out of twenty-five survived the "war," and that these two were able to hold on because of their greater resources.

[27] The one-day Manhattan war involving the sale of groceries some years ago (footnote 19, p. 361) was confined to two warring stores because it was brought under control within a few hours after its inception. It is an interesting fact in this instance that the "war" was brought to a conclusion by the landlord of one antagonist who forced him to cease selling the line of products that precipitated the conflict, on the ground that the handling of such products violated the terms of the lease.

[28] One reason for this is the fact that such "wars" are widely publicized and, hence, the degree of price elasticity of demand is intensified by such publicity.

[29] An opponent might well drop his prices before his business was actually affected either because he would assume that such an adverse effect would be bound to result and/or because he reacted emotionally to his rival's action.

tically nonexistent (in the United States at least). It follows that whereas at one time price warfare could be confined to an extremely limited market area, any existing intensive price disturbance, unless terminated immediately, is now likely to affect other areas. The effect on other areas, however, may not be severe enough to create open "war" conditions.[30]

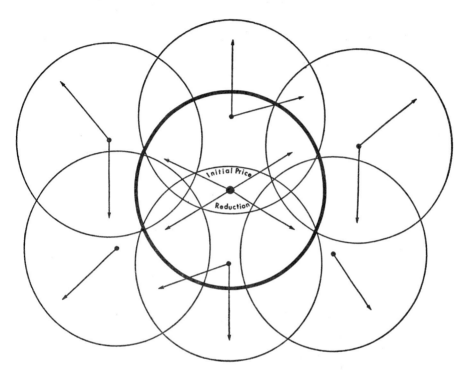

The extent and rapidity of the spread of a price war depends not only on communication and transportation but on the particular type of product involved. A very drastic bread war, which spreads rapidly to various stores in the community, might well be confined to a single locality, since few out-of-town consumer-buyers will be attracted to the scene of the conflict for the purchase of this low-unit-price item. On the other hand, the opportunity of saving money on the purchase of a tankful of gasoline is such that consumers might well be drawn to (or at least induced to purchase in) a community in which a gasoline war rages. As a result,

---

[30] During the Macy-Gimbel price war of 1951, although no open warfare actually prevailed in outlying communities, the war had a considerable effect on the sales of stores in such shopping areas. In the Bronx, for example, one outlying store advertised that it would cut prices to meet or beat prices of Manhattan competitors on such well-known items as *Toastmasters, Mixmasters,* and *Lewyt* vacuum cleaners. Such action indicated a sort of defensive price-cutting activity. In some instances, however, prices in outlying institutions were made on a negotiated basis between buyer and seller, such bargaining having been provoked no doubt by the deep-cut quotations in downtown New York.

price reductions are transmitted from one community to another, and gasoline "wars" tend to spread rapidly and over wide areas.[31]

The Duration of Price Wars

Theoretically, the duration of price wars depends upon the relative determination of contending parties to gain (or prevent the gaining of) the advantage each seeks. It should be obvious that if only one of two belligerents is determined to prevail, the "war" will not last long. It should be equally obvious that if both parties—or in the case of several, all parties —are adamant, the "war" might last indefinitely.

A further influence on the duration of a price war, of course, is its costliness. The vendor who is suffering most is apt to hoist the "white flag" in such an encounter. However, this vendor may be influenced by the longer-run gains to be made if victory is achieved and as in real war decide that he can stand some short-run losses in order to achieve ultimate profits. Such a decision may be especially appealing because he may know that if his profits are adversely affected, those of the opposing forces may be even more seriously impaired.

Unlike real war, in which the cost may be overlooked in an all-out effort to destroy the enemy, vendors involved in price warfare are apt to be sobered by the adverse operating figures that come over their desks as the "war" continues week after week. Although a vendor may think bravely about being able to hold out longer than an opponent in the early stages of the "war," he soon begins to be sensitive to the heavy costs of the "war." At this point, one or more opponents may be amenable to a "cease-fire" agreement even though the basic issues have not been resolved.

Termination of Price Warfare

Just as it takes two or more to start a price war, it takes two or more to bring a price war to an end. There must be, therefore, a move on the part of one opponent and a similar move on the part of another (or others) if a cease-fire is to go into effect. The actual cessation of hostilities might come about in any one of several ways. The simplest situation would be a two-vendor "war" in which one opponent would go across the street and say, "Let's call it quits." The problem of bringing a price war to an end by collusive means becomes more difficult but by no means impossible when there are numerous combatants. Such methods, however, are at the least legally suspect, since price fixing is per se a violation of the antitrust laws.[32]

---

[31] That is, the vendors in the area from which consumers are drawn would be expected to reduce prices in order to retain or regain the patronage of the bargain seekers.

[32] In *United States* v. *Socony Vacuum Oil Co., Inc.,* 310 U.S. 150 (1940), the court said (at 223): "Under the Sherman [Anti-trust] Act, a combination formed for the purpose and with the effect of raising, depressing, fixing, pegging, or stabilizing the price of a commodity in interstate or foreign commerce is illegal *per se.*"

Sometimes, an intermediary may be employed who will discuss the matter with antagonists on an "iffy" basis (i.e., suppose so-and-so were to make such-and-such a move, would you follow?). Termination may even conceivably come about by noncollusive leader-follower procedures.[33] If such a course were applicable, it would possess the advantage of being quite legal. Consequently, those restoring prices to normal levels would not be as apt to become involved in an antitrust action.[34]

Concern about the legality of competitive moves designed to restore prices may not be especially relevant in actual price war conditions for at least two reasons: (1) competitors who are operating on an unprofitable low price basis, and who are thus desperate, are not apt to worry about the niceties of noncollusive behavior; (2) very often—perhaps most often —the competitive activities out of which restoration is to come are intrastate rather than interstate in nature, and hence the seldom-enforced state antitrust laws have little, if any, restrictive effect.[35] It is this author's opinion that while normal price levels could be restored by noncollusive price moves, in actual practice there is usually some sort of communication among combatants before the upward move is made.[36] Whatever collusive activities do obtain, however, they are not necessarily employed at the supplier level (if only because the large companies are "gun-shy" about discussing pricing matters with competitors). They are more apt to be found at the retail level where vendors are less sophisticated about such matters and are less vulnerable to antitrust enforcement because of the intrastate nature of their activities.

III. CASE EXAMPLE OF AN ACTUAL PRICE WAR

Having examined the several facets of price warfare in general terms, let us now turn to a specific example of an actual war. Although it is impossible to select an example that would typify all price wars or even all wars within a particular field, it is possible to provide a microeconomic picture of one "war" that will serve to illustrate some of the generalizations set forth earlier.

The price war we are considering is the California gasoline "war" of early 1961. Price battles in this "war" took place almost simultaneously in (among other communities) San Francisco proper, San Francisco East

---

[33] One firm might first announce its intention of moving upward and thus give the others an opportunity to fall into line.

[34] For an extensive discussion of the legality of leadership pricing, see Ralph Cassady, Jr., *Price Making and Price Behavior in the Petroleum Industry* (New Haven: Yale University Press, 1954), pp. 105–8.

[35] See Note, "The Cartwright Act—California's Sleeping Beauty," *Stanford Law Review*, Vol. 2 (December, 1949), pp. 200–10. But see Will Wilson, "The State Antitrust Laws," *American Bar Association Journal*, Vol. 47 (February, 1961), pp. 160–62.

[36] The author does not believe, however, that collusion is generally employed in normal leader-follower situations.

Bay, and Greater Los Angeles. It is interesting to note that this war was more like international conflict than many other price wars because of the fact that it was fought on several battle grounds rather than just one.

Initiation

For some years in the California market, a 2-cent differential existed between major and minor company gasolines (and even more for certain individual vendors).[37] Single-flag vendors who did not sell to rebranders thought that this differential was too wide and that major and independent company sales imbalances resulted therefrom. This opinion was intensified when two leading independent operations were acquired by eastern major concerns,[38] and certain of the major companies operating in the California market were adversely affected.[39] The single-flag suppliers felt that a 1-cent differential was more in keeping with the new market structure. At least one of these single-flag firms decided to challenge the independents' pricing policies, thus placing itself in a position of becoming engaged in price conflict.[40] The pattern of the resulting "war" is depicted in Figures 1 and 2.

Unlike some other "wars," for which detailed records of price moves are available,[41] the precise initial price-cutting pattern for the early 1961

---

[37] One very important aspect of gasoline price making in the California area that should be mentioned is the existence of several types of supplier-vendors: These include (1) major companies that sell their product under their own brand but also sell gasoline through the "back door" to private branders (e.g., Standard Oil Company of California); (2) major companies that sell their product only under their own brands (e.g., Shell Oil Company, Mobil Oil Company, and Texaco, Inc., which are one-flag sellers, so-called); (3) minor companies that have an affiliation with out-of-state majors (e.g., Wilshire-Gulf, and Douglas-Continental); and (4) unaffiliated vendors that purchase from various suppliers and sell their product under their own, usually little-known, brands.

[38] According to a reliable informant, Gulf acquired Wilshire in July, 1960, and Continental acquired Douglas in January, 1961.

[39] "Shell Oil Co., Mobil Oil Co., and Texaco, Inc., have clung to a major-brand-only policy that has apparently cost them a considerable market share in California. . . ." ("Price Dispute Rages in California," *Petroleum Week*, March 17, 1961, p. 44.) However, according to a confidential report by one reliable informant, prior to the invasion by Gulf and Continental, the battle had been fought in cities outside of the big metropolitan areas of Los Angeles and San Francisco, but it was not until mid-February, 1961, that the issue was joined in the Los Angeles market.

[40] If there is no engagement (i.e., involvement), there, of course, will be no price war. A firm might cut the price and competitors ignore the cuts, or a firm might cut and another make countermoves that discourage the initiator who either moves back up or makes no further move downward. In either of these cases, there will be no price war.

In order that a price war develop, one firm must cut, another must make a countercut, and the first must cut again, etc. That is, the firms must become *engaged* in conflict. Now, the fact is that in some market situations no challenges the price-cutter or the price-cutter is easily scared off by a countermove, while in other situations one vendor who is very hungry for business does challenge the price-cutter who in turn stands by his guns, with a result that a price war is precipitated.

[41] In early 1960, a price war or perhaps better "skirmish" broke out in El Cerrito, California (just north of Berkeley), when a discount house advertised regular-grade

gasoline price war (i.e., who moved how much and when) is somewhat obscure.[42] Certain facts are available, however, regarding the initial price moves: (1) The first gun was fired in the Los Angeles market late in February, 1961.[43] (2) The reductions were made by certain major company outlets, allegedly in an attempt to check shifts in volume to independent outlets (especially to certain "independents"). (3) The individual price reductions making up the downward spiral were very small, consisting of 1-cent or at most 2-cent cuts designed to bring the major-station prices within 1 cent of the independent-station prices. These reductions by the majors resulted in counterreductions. The latter, in turn, caused retaliatory cuts, so that the prices of both independent and major-company stations spiraled downward over a period of several weeks. As might be expected, the price cutting involved more and more stations until the large bulk of retail vendors had become participants by the time price levels reached the bottom.

One particularly interesting aspect of the initiation of the 1961 California gasoline price war should be mentioned at this point. The different types of firms operating in the California market described above [44] do not compete directly with one another. Consequently, a reduction by one may not "draw the fire" of another. For example, dual marketing suppliers in the California market (e.g., southern California) do not normally

---

gasoline at 17.9 cents. While this price was a "gimmick" (because the customer had to have a special ticket issued by another department of the store in order to purchase the product at this price, the price to nonticket holders being 22.9 cents), it had the effect of triggering a price war.

The price war was so vicious that major prices dropped to as low as 19.9 cents (12 cents below normal). At one point in the war, some *majors were underselling independents* by 2 cents a gallon. This "war," which observers considered somewhat of a freak because gasoline stocks were relatively low, lasted for several weeks. See "Discount House Triggers Price War," *National Petroleum News*, April, 1960, pp. 26–27.

[42] Although the author does have available the price data for the period under study (as evidenced by Figures 1 and 2), these data are the result of weekly observations that obscure the daily and even hourly price changes that occur under price war conditions. However, if the researcher had a powerful enough "glass," he would be able to discover more detailed competitive patterns such as (1) the impact of the price change on the volume of direct and indirect competitors, (2) the sequence and timing of the reaction of competitors (e.g., what types of stations reacted first), (3) the precise nature of the reaction (e.g., whether the initiator merely met or undercut the rival's reduction), and (4) the precise sequence of subsequent moves and countermoves by competitors near and far.

[43] The 1961 California gasoline price war appears to have started on February 22, 1961, in the Los Angeles market, when price adjustments were made by a major-company station that were designed to challenge purported gains by certain of the independents. While this move suggests that the major-company station started the price war, one might argue with a certain amount of confidence that this was a normal competitive move in an attempt to correct competitive imbalances by reducing price differentials between independent-company outlets and major-company outlets, including under-the-canopy discounts. In any case, the independent-company stations challenged the major-company outlets, and the war was on. See "Gasoline Price War Develops in Southland," *Los Angeles Times*, February 23, 1961, Pt. I, p. 1.

[44] See footnote 37, p. 368.

FIGURE 1

RETAIL PRICES OF REGULAR-GRADE GASOLINE FOR SAN FRANCISCO EAST BAY AREA
ON A BASIS OF WEEKLY OBSERVATIONS, JANUARY–SEPTEMBER, 1961

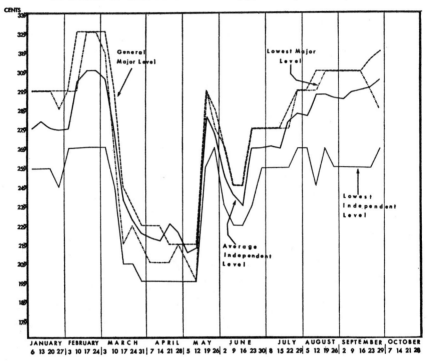

SOURCE: Dan Lundberg, Hollywood, California.

react directly to the price cuts of unaffiliated independents. However, one-flag suppliers (who are more sensitive to price reductions of independents because they are not hedged against the loss of sales to such vendors) [45] may meet price reductions of such firms.[46] Thus, in early 1961, a price reduction by an unaffiliated independent would normally have been met by an affiliated independent, since they were in direct competition with one another. Such reductions might well be met by one

---

[45] One wonders how a company using a single brand would be able to compete with companies operating under a dual-brand policy without competing intensively on a price basis with their major brand.

[46] Actually, *one* of these firms (e.g., Shell) reacts and the others (e.g., Texaco and Mobil Oil) follow. Shell's policy regarding price competition as reported in the *National Petroleum News* ("The West: 'May the Best Plan Win,'" January, 1961, pp. 22–23) is as follows: "'. . . Our policy is simply to be competitive in pricing gasoline sold at our service stations. We recognize as a competitor *any* seller who competes with us in the sale of products of comparable quality.'" The article goes on to say, "Marketers cite Shell's '1¢ plan' as one strategy to improve market share; in this case at the expense of the independents." It appears, however, that inconsequential independents are permitted to price their gasoline at two cents or even more below Shell's level without necessarily causing a reaction from Shell.

FIGURE 2

RETAIL PRICES OF REGULAR-GRADE GASOLINE FOR THE GREATER LOS ANGELES AREA
ON A BASIS OF WEEKLY OBSERVATIONS, JANUARY–SEPTEMBER, 1961

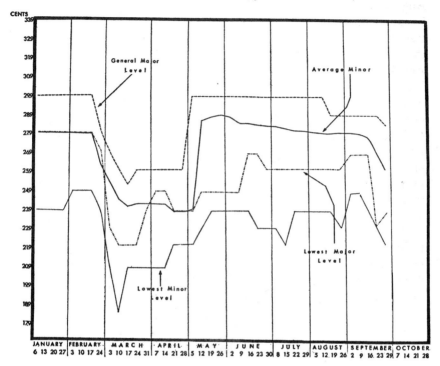

SOURCE: Dan Lundberg, Hollywood, California.

hypersensitive single-flag major supplier. This price reduction in turn
would be met by other single-flag majors as well as by major companies
operating on a dual marketing basis. Thus, direct and indirect competitors ultimately come into conflict with one another.

Depth of Reductions

The problem of measuring the depth of price reductions in the 1961
price war is complicated by the fact that the "war" was waged in numerous market areas. Generally speaking, the total drop in the price level
ranged from about 5 cents to 10 cents a gallon during the 1961 California
gasoline price war, the precise amount depending upon the market area
involved in the conflict. (See Figures 1 and 2, which depict the price
changes for two areas affected.) These reductions were not, of course,
produced by a simultaneous one-step move. They were the result of competitive action and reaction over a period of several days or even weeks.
This pattern of interaction caused reductions to be made in piecemeal
fashion.

As may be seen from the charts in Figures 1 and 2, the depth of the price cutting in the 1961 gasoline price war differed substantially between the San Francisco East Bay region in northern California and the Los Angeles area in southern California. The mean price reduction in the San Francisco East Bay area (Oakland, Berkeley, Richmond, and Hayward) was 10.2 cents (11 cents for the major company outlets and 9.4 cents for the independent company outlets). The average price reduction in Los Angeles was only about 4.8 cents (4.7 cents for the major company outlets and 4.9 cents for the independent company outlets).[47] One must hasten to point out, however, that in the latter situation there was at least one major company outlet (perhaps more) selling at times as much as 6 cents under the average major company level, and for brief periods as much as 3.5 cents under the average independent company level. One can only assume that for some reason or other the price reduction of such isolated vendors could be disregarded by the market at large; otherwise such reductions would have become general and the average major price levels would have been forced to much lower levels.

This difference in the depth of reductions between the two battle fronts is difficult to explain. It is undoubtedly due to subtle differences in the competitive structures of the two market areas. The dealers in the San Francisco Bay region may be more aggressive or the consumer market more price conscious. The difference in competitive structures, though imperfectly understood at this stage of our knowledge of price warfare, may even be the key factor in the triggering of a price war.[48]

Spread of "War"

As we have seen, one important aspect of a price war is the spreading of the "war" from the point of inception outward through the medium of contiguous areas and then from one submarket to another.[49]

------

[47] It may be noted that the typical retail margin of gasoline dealers in this market is about 5.0 cents.

[48] For some years, in the Pacific Northwest gasoline market, reportedly, even though there was considerable price cutting, there were few price wars because no vendors found it necessary to *engage* the price-cutters. Several years ago, however, a major company that had been operating in the mountain states invaded this market. In attempting to establish a beachhead, the firm had to meet the competition of the price-cutters who, in turn, undercut the market again and, thus, precipitated price warfare.

Once there was conflict and the cutting became deeper and more widespread, others were drawn in. But the key factor was the involvement of the firm which was perforce sensitive to price cutting. Without such involvement, there could be no price war. Interestingly enough, the newcomer, after becoming established in the market, may no longer be sensitive to price cutting and, thus, a long period of commercial peace may follow. But by then a new aggressive competitor may have appeared with a result that continued, although very likely intermittent, warfare would be in order.

[49] At any one time a price reporting agency (such as the one that actually exists in the California market) is able to measure the intensity of price cutting not only in terms of the depth of reductions but also in terms of the percentage of participa-

The geographical coverage of the 1961 California gasoline price war was predetermined to some extent by the severity of the price cutting and by the fact that consumers of this product are mobile and could shift patronage among institutions and even among markets with ease.[50] Important, too, was the fact that large "screaming" signs publicized the price reductions and thus intensified the price elasticity of demand for this product.[51] Even more important as a spreading factor, perhaps, were the reductions at widespread geographical points with the result that spreading movements began at multiple locations.[52]

Considering the depth of the cuts and the other intensifying factors mentioned above, it is not surprising that the 1961 California gasoline price war extended beyond the borders of California into Oregon and Washington.[53] This does not mean, however, that the "war" was equally intensive in all areas in terms of the depth of price reductions among the various markets or that all vendors within each market area were equally low. As can be inferred from the charts (pp. 370 and 371), the amounts and timing of reductions differ considerably among vendors within market areas as well as between one market area and another. It appears from

---

tion of competing retailers and the extent of the infected area. However, the price observations that serve as the basis for the charts in Figures 1 and 2 (pp. 370 and 371) were of necessity made not simultaneously but at different times. Hence, some of the price uniformity indicated by the charts may have been more apparent than real. That is, since it takes time to gather price data in a market area, price differences that may have existed at a given moment of time might have been smoothed out by the competitive process by the time the observations were made.

[50] One major-company gasoline executive informed the author that credit-card customers (as much as 80% of the patronage of many stations) are much less responsive to price cuts than cash customers. The reason for this, one would assume, is that credit customers have made a major decision regarding gasoline-station patronage and will not as a result be usually alert to price reductions, especially when no money changes hands. Over a period of time, however, one would expect price awareness to increase. A shift in patronage from high-priced to lower-priced outlets in accordance with the principle of price elasticity as it relates to price elasticity could be expected. See Ralph Cassady, Jr., "The Time Element and Demand Analysis," chap. xii of *Theory in Marketing*, Reavis Cox and Wroe Alderson (eds.) (Homewood, Ill.: Richard D. Irwin, Inc., 1950), particularly pp. 201–3.

[51] There is little question about the effect of publicity on price elasticity. One executive of a major company reported that a 10,000-gallon-per-month station which became involved in an intensive price competitive situation announced the reduced price through the means of large price signs and increased volume to 16,000 gallons per month. It is an interesting fact, however, that when the signs were removed without any upward change in the price, the gallonage went back to 10,000.

[52] For examples of the spreading of price warfare to certain areas, see "Gasoline Price War Extended," *Los Angeles Times*, March 1, 1961, Pt. I, p. 1; and "Gas Price War Spreads to Lompoc," *Los Angeles Times*, March 7, 1961, Pt. I, p. 16.

[53] Usually, when the spreading of price warfare is considered, one thinks of the relatively simple situation of a "war" breaking out in a certain neighborhood of a particular community and quickly spreading to other neighborhoods in that community and to other communities, which, of course, does happen in actual practice. In the 1961 "war," however, the spread of the "war" was accentuated by price moves made by a certain supplier company's service stations in many areas simultaneously. Thus, the 1961 gasoline "war" soon extended from the Canadian to the Mexican border.

confidential information made available to the author that the large bulk
of the gasoline dealers were actively involved in the 1961 price war by the
time the price level had hit bottom.

Duration

In considering the length of the 1961 California gasoline price war, it
is interesting to note that the duration of such a conflict depends on its
impact on belligerents and the determination of the opponents to gain or
to prevent the attainment of some end. As was suggested earlier, some
"wars" break out and are over in a few days or even hours, some last for
two or three weeks, and some extend over many weeks or even months.

The 1961 gasoline "war" broke out in late February (in Los Angeles)
and early March (in the San Francisco Bay region) and lasted until early
May. The upward move in the San Francisco Bay area, however, proved
to be only temporary and the restoration to normal levels did not really
begin until late June. Fighting in some areas, such as the San Joaquin
Valley, may have continued for a considerable time after June, 1961.

There are three phases to a gasoline price war and perhaps to all price
"wars": (1) the period during which prices are declining, (2) the period
during which prices remain stable at the low level, and (3) the period
required for the recovery of prices to the normal level. On the basis of
data derived from the 1961 "war," one may conclude that the first two
stages are of longest duration and the last the shortest by far. A study of
the price-behavior data in Figures 1 and 2 suggests that prices that have
sagged over several weeks might be restored to normal or thereabouts
almost over night,[54] although such a recovery might be anything but
permanent.[55]

Since the gasoline price level sank below dealers' costs during the 1961
gasoline "war," it should be perfectly obvious that this extensive "war"
would have a very heavy impact on competitors and especially on certain
types of vendors.[56] In this instance (as in most gasoline price war situations), much of the burden of the "war" was shifted from those on the
firing line to their suppliers through the medium of dealer assistance or
subsidies. A subsidization system, though justifiable as a channel-protecting

---

[54] Some vendors reportedly dislike the large one-step increases because of (*a*) the
possibility of adverse public reactions created by the large increase from a low price
and (*b*) the chance of speculative gains by owners of large storage facilities who
buy at the low market and sell at the high and, indeed, the fact that a price sag might
have been created by these functionaries in hope of providing for just such an
opportunity.

[55] An examination of the price war chart for the San Francisco East Bay region
(Figure 1, p. 370) indicates that there was a momentary increase in May of 1961 of
one step of 8 cents that almost immediately slipped back with the result that prices
declined a total of 5 cents over a period of two or three weeks before starting to
climb once again.

[56] See "Independents See Ruin in Gasoline War," *Los Angeles Times,* March 8,
1961, Pt. I, p. 1.

device, may actually succeed in extending the duration of price wars because some of the incentive for termination is eliminated by the shifting of the brunt of soft-market conditions from dealers to suppliers.[57]

Termination

A price war is costly to participants; hence, termination becomes more and more desirable as time goes on. Termination of a "war" involves both a decision to end hostilities and the actual implementation of such a decision. If the evidence of the 1961 gasoline price war is to be relied upon, restoration of prices takes place promptly once termination is begun. The upward price change may be the result of a leader-follower move or of some sort of collusive arrangement.[58]

The first move toward termination of the California price war came in early May, 1961.[59] However, in this instance, as in others, the actual task of restoring peaceful conditions was not carried out without a hitch. This attempt to restore price levels was a bit premature and could not be maintained. In the East Bay phase of the 1961 California gasoline price war, for example, an upward move of 8 cents in mid-May was only momentarily successful. Actually, the price slipped back 1 or 2 cents at a time over a period of three weeks by a total amount of 5 cents, before moving up again by 3 cents on the way toward normality.

As to who made the first move upward in the 1961 "war"—it was, as

---

[57] Beginning in late August of 1961, the Los Angeles gasoline market began to deteriorate once again. ("Deteriorating Prices Causing Concern at L.A.," *The Oil Daily*, August 30, 1961, p. 1.) In the early part of October, after the softening had brought the prevailing major brand regular-grade price down to 23.9 cents (from 29.9 cents), one of the single-flag suppliers reportedly decided to take the lead in strengthening the market by reducing the amount of aid given dealers. This move was supported by other suppliers, and regular-grade prices moved up to 28.9 cents for majors and 27.9 cents for independents. But this scheme is not as practicable as it might seem as a device for ending price warfare because of (*a*) the difficulty of withstanding the pressure of the important dealers for assistance and (*b*) the constant worry about competitive capitulation to such demands, which would, of course, cause even the most adamant vendor to give in. But see "Are Gasoline Wars Suffering a Death Blow?", *Los Angeles Times*, September 3, 1962, Pt. III, p. 6.

[58] In a two-vendor "war," (*a*) conceding defeat momentarily, one says to the other "I quit," or (*b*) they agree in so many words (overtly) to raise prices, or (*c*) one raises his price and the other follows. In a multivendor "war," the aggressor having achieved his purpose (i.e., regaining gallonage or chastening a maverick, say) raises his prices with the hope (if there is no understanding) or the knowledge (if there is) that others will follow. According to the *Gasoline Retailer* (May 3, 1961), the "armistice" was preceded by a California Petroleum Marketers Council meeting in which the independents "reluctantly" indicated "they might be willing to live with a 1-cent differential below major brands instead of the 2 cents they have had" because the latter appears to "cause market instability." This, of course, would serve as a signal to the opposing forces that a lead upward but with a narrower differential might well be followed.

[59] According to a confidential report: "The Los Angeles war, which in the meantime had spread northward to San Francisco, came to an end early in May 1961 'with major-brand/private-brand differentials narrowed to 1¢ a gallon.' Oilgram, May 9, 1961. By the end of May the San Francisco battle ended on the same basis." This turned out to be not the end but only the beginning of the end.

one might expect, the price leader in the area, Standard Oil Company of California.[60] Such a concern, as a result of careful study of the situation, can be expected to make an intelligent judgment as to whether the restoration of prices will be effective in bringing the "war" to an end. One does not know how much communication there is among competitors in such instances, but one could reason a priori that because of the antitrust implications the leader company would avoid anything that might be interpreted as collusive. It is, of course, well established that one firm may lead others up without any communication among them.[61] It is equally well established that noncollusive leader-follower pricing is quite lawful.[62]

Consequences of the "War"

The retail price structure that prevails following the termination of hostilities may be quite different from that obtaining before the outbreak of a "war." This may be due to "casualties" among certain of the competitors,[63] or to a change in attitude of the vanquished,[64] or both. At the conclusion of the 1961 California gasoline "war," although the price level was restored, two of the independent group (Wilshire and Douglas, which are major-company controlled) found it advisable to move from 2 cents below to 1 cent below the major-station price level for regular-grade gasoline.[65]

Fifteen months after the end of the 1961 California gasoline price war, the major-station independent-station price differential was still 1 cent for house brand (i.e., regular-grade) gasoline. However, the price of regular-grade gasoline in major-company stations was 30.9 cents, or 1 cent higher than it was immediately following the "war." Moreover, the differential that existed between the regular-grade and the premium-grade product was wider in some major-company stations than before—while premium grade was only 3 cents higher in some companies' stations, high-octane gasoline was priced at as much as 5 cents higher than regular grade in others. Casual observation indicates that no such differentials obtained in independent retail operations. One can only guess about the degree of stability that can be maintained under the present price structure.

In considering the accomplishments of this "war," one might wonder whether, from the point of view of those in the industry, the results justified the costs involved. If we assume that an imbalance existed among supplier companies, the firms adversely affected certainly thought that

---

[60] See "Price War in L.A. May be Ended Soon," *The Oil Daily*, May 9, 1961, p. 1. But see "Price Wars Continuing in California Areas," *The Oil Daily*, June 15, 1961, p. 6; and "Price War Worsening," *The Oil Daily*, October 5, 1961, p. 14.

[61] See Ralph Cassady, Jr., *Price Making and Price Behavior in the Petroleum Industry* (New Haven: Yale University Press, 1954), pp. 86–90.

[62] *Ibid.*, pp. 105–8.

[63] See footnote 26, p. 363, and footnote 56, p. 374.

[64] They may be chastened and hence much less aggressive.

[65] See footnote 58, p. 375. See also "Independents to Raise Price of Gasoline," *Los Angeles Times*, April 18, 1961, Pt. III, p. 1.

correction was in order. They would not otherwise have made the initial move. The firms that first cut price must have known also that there was at least a chance that competitors would react as they did. From the point of view of the single-flag sellers, the initial price adjustment must have appeared unavoidable. Once this move was made, all subsequent actions followed from the fact that competitors found it necessary to protect their markets.

IV. CONCLUSIONS

In the preceding sections of this essay, an attempt has been made to analyze price warfare as a particular species of competitive dynamics. Price wars were isolated from other price behavior patterns and their various dimensions examined in considerable detail in order to provide as clear a picture as possible of the nature of this competitive phenomenon. Several aspects of the subject should be emphasized.

1. In discussing price warfare, it must be constantly kept in mind that we are considering a specific type of competitive behavior pattern typi-fied by a multilateral or bilateral price-cutting action. Price wars have been found by the author to occur mainly at the retail level in a score or more mercandise or service fields. In some of these fields, price warfare is a rare phenomenon; but in others, numerous wars have been waged over the years.

There is no question but that the gasoline field is unique as far as the prevalence of price warfare is concerned. In no other field is there nearly as much open price conflict. There appear to be several reasons for this: (a) gasoline is a joint product with periodic gluts that result from the need to refine large amounts of a complementary product (i.e., heating oil) in preparation for a high seasonal demand; (b) gasoline is a high-demand product with prices that are known to consumer-buyers and on which substantial savings can be effected on a repeat-purchase basis; [66] (c) the sale of gasoline at a lower price in certain areas by an independent fringe of competitors produces a shift in market shares over time and leads to corrective pricing on the part of those adversely affected; (d) con-sumer buyers generally recognize that the various motor fuels are close substitutes for one another; (e) consumers of this product are extremely mobile and can easily shift from one vendor to another; and (f) suppliers who become involved in price warfare subsidize their dealers and thus assume the major part of the consequences of uninhibited price behavior.

2. The causes of price wars are both basic and proximate. There may be a strong tendency toward a gasoline war because of sloppy supply conditions, yet a "war" may not occur until a potentially high volume station with a favorable supply contract but no initial sales volume in-

---

[66] It is an interesting fact that if all consumers were highly price conscious and purchased their product on a rational basis, then competition would force prices to uniform levels.

vades the field. Such a situation calls for penetration pricing that may adversely affect competitors who will move to protect themselves and thus precipitate price warfare. To bring a "war" to an end without correcting the underlying difficulty may simply result in a temporary truce. Consequently, the "war" may break out again at any time.

A question might be raised as to whether price warfare has become more or less prevalent over the years. If one were considering all kinds of price competitive patterns—including unilateral price action by industrial giants—one might conclude that there was less now than heretofore. Much of the predatory activity existing in earlier years, however, must be excluded, because it does not fall within the price war definition.[67] Given the specific nature of price warfare, it may well be that this type of pricing behavior is more common now than in past years. Such a conclusion should not be surprising in that the greater amount of present-day price warfare is found in the sale of gasoline, a commodity of relatively recent widespread use.

3. A key factor in assessing price wars is to consider what, if anything, they accomplish. To answer such a question, one must qualify it by asking, "Accomplish for whom?" If one considers the results from the point of view of the ultimate consumer, a certain set of conclusions might be reached. If his concern is with the accomplishment from the standpoint of competitors, different conclusions might be drawn. One's analysis of accomplishments would also depend upon which competitor is being considered—the victor or the vanquished. The matter might also be looked at from the point of view of society as a whole. When this is done, a distinction must be made between short-term and long-term results in order to come to anything even close to a definitive solution.

This type of analysis is even more involved than it at first appears, because we cannot choose between price warfare and absence of price warfare without introducing an extraneous factor—legislative circumscription—into the competitive arena. That is, one cannot provide restraints against abnormal competitive behavior without the danger of introducing restrictions upon normal competitive activities. Such legislative restrictions may well affect the vigor of the normal competitive process and by so doing adversely affect competition.

One might conclude that remedies for price warfare should never be utilized. On the other hand, when some vendor or group of vendors attempts to injure or eliminate a troublesome rival by use of the price weapon, circumscription would be in order. A government body, such as a state attorney general's office, might well keep its investigatory eye

---

[67] For an extensive discussion of predatory pricing activities in the earlier years, see Ralph Cassady, Jr., and William F. Brown, "Exclusionary Tactics in American Business Competition," *UCLA Law Review*, January, 1961, particularly pp. 90–108, and 129–34.

on price war situations for evidence of predatory intent.[68] If predatory activity were detected, appropriate action under state antitrust laws could be taken.[69] In the absence of such activity, price warfare might well remain unchecked, for it is evidence of ultravigorous competitive activity in an era in which competition is, if anything, too soft.

4. One of the most interesting aspects of a study of price wars is the absence of such "warfare" in millions of price-making situations that occur every year throughout the world. It is no wonder that we have price wars occasionally—the wonder is that we do not have more! This circumstance suggests that price makers practice self-restraint because they know that unrestrained price cutting may lead to "war."

At a recent meeting attended by this author, a world-renowned economic theorist remarked that while economic theory does not adequately deal with the presence of price warfare, existing theory explains normal competition, which is characterized by the absence of price warfare. Perhaps the present analysis will stimulate some business theorists to pick up where this essay leaves off and to develop a much needed definitive theory of price warfare.

---

[68] See, for example, State of California's Attorney General's *Report of Investigation of the Current Gasoline Price War in California*, April 17, 1961, mimeographed.

[69] See, for example, the provisions of the California State law relating to combinations and restraints in trade (the Cartwright Act), *Cal. Bus. and Profs. Code*, Secs., 16,700 to 16,758, including the recently amended sections 16,727, 16,750, 16,752, 16,754, and 16,754.5.

25. A PROBABILISTIC APPROACH TO CONSUMER BEHAVIOR

By Alfred A. Kuehn* and Ralph L. Day†

OBSERVERS of consumer behavior (whether business executives, marketing researchers, or academicians) are often frustrated and disappointed by what they consider to be inconsistent and irrational behavior on the part of consumers. The results of surveys and market tests often seem to be contradictory. Although the study of consumer behavior will never be an easy task, some of the difficulties of interpreting research findings and increasing our understanding of this topic can be overcome through the use of improved conceptual frameworks.

Until very recently, consumer behavior has been discussed almost exclusively in "exact" or nonprobabilistic terms. Consumers have been categorized in such terms as "buyers" and "nonbuyers" or as "heavy users" and "light users." The study of brand choice has been approached by dividing consumers into three or four categories according to their degree of "brand loyalty." Although such approaches to describing states or patterns of consumer behavior have been useful, they typically waste information, frequently lead to misunderstandings and generally are of limited value in developing dynamic models for purposes of analysis and forecasting. This essay discusses the alternative approach of expressing states of being or expected actions of consumers in probabilistic terms and illustrates how this approach can sharpen analysis and aid in the construction of better predictive models.

Are Consumers Inconsistent?

The results obtained in repeat paired comparison tests are frequently cited as evidence of the inconsistency of consumer behavior. In "blind" paired comparison testing, samples of two brands of a product are packaged in plain wrappers or containers so that no clues are given to the identities of the brands. The two samples are identified only by numbers

---

* Graduate School of Industrial Administration, Carnegie Institute of Technology.
† College of Business Administration, The Pennsylvania State University.

or letters which have been tested for psychological neutrality. After the housewives in a test group have used both samples of the product in their homes, they are asked to choose the one which they prefer. The distressing part for researchers occurs when such a test is repeated with the same housewives and the same brands under identical circumstances. Typically, a substantial number of the subjects who said that they preferred brand A over brand B on the first trial will say that they prefer brand B over brand A on the second trial.

Many marketing executives and researchers have been discouraged by such results and have been led to view consumers as so inconsistent and unpredictable that little can be gained from the study of their behavior. Are results such as those described above evidence that a substantial proportion of consumers behave in an inconsistent and unpredictable manner? Or, should one expect a substantial number of reversals on a repeat test even though each housewife really has some degree of preference for one of the brands over the other? The answer depends on the frame of reference used in thinking about consumer behavior. If one thinks only in terms of "right" or "wrong" responses to a particular choice situation, then consumers are frequently inconsistent. If a consumer reports that she prefers brand B on the first test, then the only "correct" response is for her to say she prefers B on the repeat test. The choice of brand A on the repeat test is inconsistent if consumer choice is considered an exact process.

Upon reflection, however, there are a number of plausible explanations for reversals in repeat paired comparison tests not implying fickleness or flighty behavior. Housewives are neither automatons nor laboratory technicians. Variations in the way they use the samples in the two tests might cause them to choose one of the brands on the first trial and the other on the second. If, for example, the product being tested is a liquid dishwashing detergent, the results obtained might be influenced by differences in water temperatures, variations in the quantities of the two samples used, differences in the types of food particles on the dishes, or many other factors. Some housewives may have been influenced more in their choice by the way they felt when they used the different samples than by actual differences in the product. If the housewife was in good spirits when using one sample and "out of sorts" when using the other, she is likely to have reported a preference for the sample tested under the more favorable conditions if the degree of actual product difference was not great.

When the many possible influences which might affect a consumer's evaluation of the samples on a repeat paired comparison test are considered, it seems clear that there is some chance that any housewife who does not have an unusually strong preference for either of the products will reverse herself. The weaker the true relative preference for one of the products, the more likely it is that a reversal will occur. If a housewife likes the two products equally well, then she is as likely to reverse herself on a repeat test as not.

Probability or Certainty?

If the expected behavior of the consumer is viewed in probabilistic terms rather than as an exact process, then occurrences such as reversals on a repeat paired comparison test are not evidences of inconsistent or irrational behavior. Suppose that a particular housewife prefers a high-sudsing detergent to a low-sudsing detergent. If she is given two samples of detergent which are identical except that one has a substantially higher sudsing level than the other, the chances are that she will choose the one with the higher sudsing level. However, it is not at all certain that she will choose the sample with the higher level of sudsing ability on any particular trial. In other words, the probability of choosing the preferred product is greater than .5 but less than 1. The probability level will vary between pure chance ($P = .5$) and certainty ($P = 1$), according to the degree of actual difference between the samples, the housewife's general ability to recognize differences, and the strength of her preferences.

For purposes of illustration, consider a homogeneous group of housewives with a relative preference for brand A such that each housewife has a probability of .7 of choosing A on a paired comparison test of A and B. Let us then suppose that a paired comparison test was run. Seventy percent of the housewives would be expected to report a preference for product A and 30 % would be expected to report a preference for product B. What should we anticipate the results to be on a repeat test? We would expect 70% of those choosing A on the first trial to choose A on the second, and would expect the other 30% to choose B. Of those choosing B on the first trial, we would also expect 70% to choose A on the second and 30% to choose B. Thus we would have 49% choosing A on both trials, 9% choosing B on both trials, 21% choosing A then B, and 21% choosing B then A (see Figure 1). Thus, 42% of the individuals in a test group could be expected to reverse themselves if each member had a .7 probability of choosing one of the two products.

FIGURE 1

EXPECTED RESULTS OF A REPEAT PAIR COMPARISON TEST WHEN $P_A = .7$
FOR ALL CONSUMERS TESTED

SECOND TRIAL

		A	B	
FIRST TRIAL	A	49	21	70%
	B	21	9	30%
		70%	30%	100%

Only in those cases where virtually all consumers have very strong preferences for one or the other of the two brands being compared will we find a small number of reversals on a repeat test. Many brands of competing products are not so differentiated in their attributes that the average consumer can distinguish between them with a high degree of precision. When consumer behavior is viewed in probabilistic terms, such occurrences as reversals in paired comparison tests do not signify either irrationality or inconsistency. By providing a more realistic frame of reference for considering the expected actions of consumers in either product tests or in the marketplace, the probabilistic approach permits us to view consumer behavior as generally consistent and predictable.

Probabilistic Models of Consumer Behavior

Probabilistic models of the individual consumer's choice of alternative brands can be very useful in understanding consumer behavior and predicting results in the marketplace. At the most basic level, the state of an individual who frequently buys a particular kind of product might be reflected by a set of probabilities related to his choice of a brand the next time he makes a purchase. Suppose that there are four brands of a product on the market and these are designated A, B, C, and D. Any particular consumer must choose among these brands when he makes a purchase. At a given point in time, the particular brand to be chosen on the next purchase occasion is not wholly predetermined but neither is it likely to be a matter of pure chance. Most consumers are predisposed to favor some particular brand or brands over others. These predispositions can be the result of recent experiences, custom or habit, reference group behavior, the influence of advertising, or a great variety of other factors. The actual likelihood of purchase will also be influenced by factors external to the individual such as the availability of favored products in the particular stores he patronizes. For the hypothesized four-brand case, a particular consumer might have the following probabilities of choosing the various brands on his next purchase: $P_A = .80$, $P_B = .10$, $P_C = .05$, $P_D = .05$. In other words, the chances are 4 out of 5 that he will buy A, 1 in 10 that he will buy B, 1 in 20 that he will buy C, and 1 in 20 that he will buy D.

A verbal interpretation of the above set of probabilities might be that the hypothetical consumer generally favors brand A but will use some other brand if his retailer is out of A, if an attractive deal is available, or perhaps just to obtain variety on some occasion. A particular consumer's set of probabilities can be expected to change over time.[1] Even if there are no specific events or occurrences which directly affect the consumer's probabilities, the mere passage of time will tend to modify purchase probabilities as circumstances change and memories fade. The probability of purchasing a highly favored brand will tend to decrease or "decay" with

---

[1] Alfred A. Kuehn, "Consumer Brand Choice as a Learning Process," *Journal of Advertising Research*, Vol. 2 (December, 1962), pp. 10–17.

the passage of time even if no significant "events" occur such as a repeat purchase of the brand, the purchase of a competing brand, or exposure to advertising. Figure 2 illustrates how the probability of the consumer's purchase of brand A in the above example might decay with time, in the absence of any significant events. One explanation of this decay might be that pleasant experiences or associations with the favorite brand and unpleasant experiences or associations with the less well-liked brands tend to be forgotten with time. Thus the probability of purchase of a favored brand tends to decline and there is a concurrent increase in the probability of purchase of other brands.

FIGURE 2

DECAY OF P_A OVER TIME (NO SIGNIFICANT EVENTS)

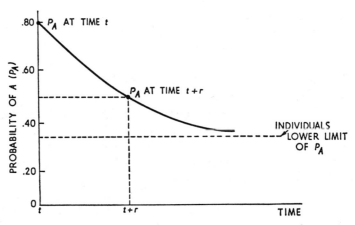

When the product is one which the individual consumer purchases frequently or if some or all of the brands are frequently advertised in media to which he is exposed, the consumer's experiences will tend to have more significance than will the mere passage of time. Each purchase of the product, whether it is of the most favored brand or of one of the others, will tend to modify the consumer's purchase probabilities. In general, the purchase of any particular brand tends to increase the probability of that brand's purchase on the next buying occasion and to decrease the probability of other brands being purchased at that time. If it is a "regular" purchase rather than one on a manufacturer's "deal" or a temporary retailer's "special," the influence of the purchase on future behavior will normally be greater.

Other occurrences, such as exposures to advertising, may also have significant effects on the consumer's purchase probabilities. Figure 3 illustrates how a series of events might influence the level of P_A in subsequent periods. The probability of purchasing A which existed in time period t declined as nothing of significance occurred in $t + 1$. A new purchase of brand A in $t + 2$ raised the probability of purchasing A in the next period back to about the same level as in time t. However, a "deal" purchase of brand B occurred in $t + 3$ and reduced P_A. In $t + 4$, a "regular" purchase of B lowered the probability of future purchases of A to a greater extent than did the "deal" purchase. In $t + 5$, the consumer's exposure to a television advertising campaign by brand C further lowered P_A slightly. A purchase of brand A in $t + 6$ raised P_A and an extensive print advertising campaign by brand A raised P_A again in $t + 7$. No events occurred in $t + 8$ and the probability of purchasing A on the next buying occasion declined.

FIGURE 3

CHANGES IN P_A OVER TIME

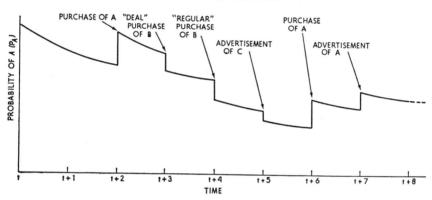

The simple probabilistic model of consumer behavior provides a useful means of presenting information about the likely behavior of an individual the next time he purchases a particular product. This information is presented in the form of a set of purchase probabilities related to the various available brands. When the consumer's probabilities of purchasing the various brands on the next purchase are combined with his probability of making a purchase in the next time period, a useful static model of the individual's purchase behavior is obtained. When a method is added for revising the set of purchase probabilities for the next time period $(t + 1)$ in the light of actual behavior during the immediate past period (t), a dynamic model of an individual consumer's purchase behavior is provided.

A model which has proved to be highly useful for providing revised purchase probabilities can be described as a generalized form of the Bush-Mosteller stochastic learning model.[2] The output of this model is determined by the four parameters of the model which are estimated from purchase histories. These parameters are the intercepts and slopes of the two lines referred to in Figure 4 as the Purchase Operator and the Rejec-

[2] Robert R. Bush and Frederick Mosteller, *Stochastic Models for Learning* (New York: John Wiley & Sons, Inc., 1955).

tion Operator. If the consumer purchases brand A on a given buying occasion (time t), his probability of again purchasing brand A if he buys at all during the next time period $(t + 1)$ is read from the Purchase Operator. If he chooses some other brand in time t, then his probability of purchasing brand A in $t + 1$ will be read off of the Rejection Operator. This latter instance is illustrated in Figure 4.[3]

By treating the purchase and rejection operators as functions of time and of various marketing variables, the model can be used to reflect the influence of many factors other than the observed past purchases of the various brands. This model has been useful in providing a conceptual framework for understanding individual consumer behavior and offers promise of improved theories of consumer choice. It should also contribute to the study of aggregate market behavior. The probabilistic approach thus lends itself to the construction of models at various levels of aggregation.

FIGURE 4

A MODEL FOR REVISING PURCHASE PROBABILITIES

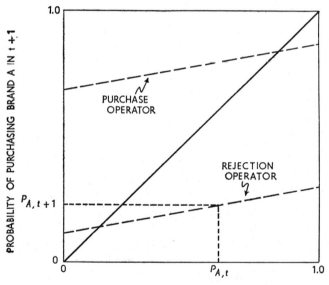

PROBABILITY OF PURCHASING BRAND A IN t

Probabilistic Models and Marketing Variables

Many parallels exist between the probabilistic approach to developing complex marketing models that reflect promotional efforts and yield predictions of marketing results and the methods of nuclear physicists. In estimating shielding requirements for nuclear reactors, physicists utilize probabilistic models of the behavior of nuclear particles. Through the

---

[3] For additional discussion and illustrations, see Kuehn, *op. cit.*

use of Monte Carlo techniques, they can make accurate predictions as to the number of escaping particles with various levels of shielding and are able to design efficient shielding systems for proposed reactors. The marketing model builder deals with his problems in much the same way. The prime differences are: the marketing scientist concerns himself with the purchasing behavior of individuals or households rather than with nuclear particles; the relevant events are "regular" purchases, "deal" purchases, and advertising exposures rather than collisions among particles; and the aggregate results are measured in numbers of purchases (sales) rather than the number of particles passing through the shielding.

Probabilistic models of consumer behavior are still at an early stage of development.[4] Emphasis so far has been on understanding the influence of marketing variables such as advertising, price changes, product changes, and special promotions rather than on forecasting future sales. If a particular probabilistic model seems to provide good predictions of some aspect of market behavior, the reasons why the model works are more important at the present stage of marketing science than the fact that it does work.

The basic structure of a probabilistic model of consumer brand choice behavior was outlined above and illustrated in Figure 4. This model has been thoroughly tested with consumer panel data for well-established, branded, nondurable consumer grocery and drug items. The model seems to be quite consistent with consumer behavior as regards these products. As the model would indicate, the purchase of a particular brand on one buying occasion seems to reinforce (increase) the probability of the purchase of that brand on the next buying occasion and its rejection (purchase of a competing brand) seems to reduce the probability of its purchase on the next buying occasion. Purchase probabilities tend to decay with time at different rates for different product classes. Because of the time decay of repurchase probability, consumers who frequently purchase a product tend to build up greater loyalties than do infrequent purchasers.

Recent applications of the brand choice model have been directed toward measuring the effects of various kinds of "deals" (coupons, price-off packs, merchandise packs, two for the price of one, etc.). In studies of the effects of deals utilizing consumer panel data, the regular purchases of each household was studied chronologically along with information on the deals which had been bought. The model provided an estimate of the probability that the household would choose any particular brand at the time each successive purchase was reported. It incorporated any effects that regular purchases, deals, and the passage of time might have had on

---

[4] For a brief discussion of some of the early efforts, see Alfred A. Kuehn and Ralph L. Day, "Simulation and Operational Gaming," in Wroe Alderson and Stanley J. Shapiro (eds.), *Marketing and the Computer* (Englewood Cliffs, N.J.: Prentice-Hall, Inc., 1963), p. 242.

altering the estimated purchase probabilities. The best estimates of each of these effects were taken to be those values which minimized in the aggregate the deviations between the estimated probabilities of purchase and the relative purchase frequencies actually recorded.

The relative attraction of each of the various types of deals for each brand was identified for households distributed over the range of "regular" purchase probabilities. This permitted one to distinguish between deal sales made in lieu of regular current and future sales to a customer who was "stocking up," and deal sales representing increased business. Similarly, the conversion effects associated with deal purchases were measured to provide an indication of the apparent effect on future sales resulting from the increased exposure of households to the product as a result of the deal merchandise. Estimates of the attraction and conversion effects of the various types of deals allow an evaluation of the economics of each type of deal.

Whether or not it is feasible to utilize panel data in empirical studies of the effects of advertising within the framework of the brand choice model is still uncertain.[5] A number of formidable obstacles must first be surmounted. Probably, the most serious question is whether or not the effects of advertising exposures are sufficiently large to permit meaningful estimates to be developed from existing panels. Another serious problem hinges on the development of techniques to estimate the effects of the larger number of variables in the system. Perhaps less serious is the problem of obtaining advertising exposure data from panel families. Such data could be collected in terms of "circulation" or "sets tuned" rather than actual exposure to the advertising carried by the various media. This would permit evaluation and projection of advertising effectiveness on a basis comparable to the most reliable aggregate media statistics.

Would controlled advertising schedules be required in order to study the effects of advertising? The answers appears to be no, although some planned variations in advertising schedules might be desirable. A pilot study of the distribution of household exposures to advertisements of competitors suggests that natural variations in frequency of exposure occur in large enough numbers to offer hope of estimating the influences of advertising even under rather stable overall market conditions. Some households become exposed to more advertisements of one brand than another in one period of time whereas the reverse may be true in the subsequent time period. Simultaneously, the frequencies of exposure of certain other families will be moving in roughly the opposite direction. This natural shifting of consumers in terms of their exposure to the advertising of competing brands can be examined in a framework similar to

---

[5] The brand choice model has proved to be of theoretical value in analyzing the effects of advertising. See Alfred A. Kuehn, "How Advertising Performance Depends on Other Marketing Factors," *Journal of Adveritsing Research*, Vol. 2 (March, 1962), pp. 2–10.

that used in studying the brand choice behavior of households. It provides a basis for measuring the changes in brand buying behavior associated with changes in exposure to competing advertisements.

Probabilistic Models of Consumer Preferences

A somewhat different approach from that utilized in the brand choice model has been taken in the design of probabilistic models of consumer behavior for the study of consumer preference distributions.[6] Models providing estimates of the distribution of consumer preferences over various levels of a product attribute and yielding a probabilistic measure of consumer's ability to recognize the level which he actually prefers have been developed.

This approach is applicable when some characteristic is clearly important in determining consumers' overall preferences for a product and that characteristic can be controlled at different levels in manufacture. A scale of values for the characteristic is established, ranging in equal steps from the lowest to the highest feasible value. One preference study utilizing this approach involved the amount of flavoring materials in chocolate ice cream. A "chocolatiness" scale was established with steps ranging from "very light" to "very dark chocolate." Carefully formulated test batches of ice cream were made up so that other factors such as the amount of sugar, the total amount of fats, and the total amount of solids were held constant in all batches. Each flavor level was tested against every other level in a series of pair comparison tests. The results were analyzed, and a distribution (weighting) of consumers over the various flavor levels was obtained. In addition, an estimate of the probability that a consumer would recognize the "chocolatiness" level he preferred was obtained.

This kind of information is likely to be of great value to a manufacturer. Drawing upon knowledge of the distribution of consumer preferences over various levels of a product characteristic and upon information on the current levels of competitor's products, the alert firm could obtain a definite advantage by producing a product more closely suited to the preferences of a sizeable segment of the market. Estimates of the abilities of consumers to recognize varying degrees of difference would have important implications for the exact level of product characteristic the manufacturer should offer.

Summary Statement

When consumer behavior is considered in "exact" terms rather than in probabilistic terms, there is considerable danger of oversimplification or of outright misunderstanding of observed behavior. There is often a tendency to dichotomize consumers with such terms as "buyers" and "nonbuyers" or to divide them into a small number of categories to cover wide

---

[6] Alfred A. Kuehn and Ralph L. Day, "Strategy of Product Quality," *Harvard Business Review*, November–December, 1962, pp. 100–110.

ranges of behavior as is done when all consumers are classified into three or four degrees of "brand loyalty." This essay has used the repeat paired comparison test to illustrate how the tendency to categorize consumers and make exact predictions has led many observers to conclude that consumers are inconsistent and unpredictable. A probabilitsic interpretation of the same data makes the test results appear both reasonable and consistent. Even though a housewife may truly prefer one product sample to another, she cannot be expected to be perfectly accurate in recognizing the one she prefers. Being neither an automaton nor a laboratory technician, she may be influenced in her choice by factors other than the actual differences between two samples. Thus it is reasonable to think of her ability to recognize the sample she prefers in probabilistic terms. If her preferences are strong and the differences in product are great, she will have a high probability of selecting the one she truly prefers. But if differences are slight and her preferences are weak, the probability that the housewife will recognize the item she prefers may be little better than .5. It was shown that when the results of repeat tests are interpreted in probabilistic terms, reversals are not necessarily evidence of inconsistency or unpredictability.

When the state of a consumer is reflected by a set of probabilities related to the brands which are available for purchase on his next buying occasion, the basis of a probabilistic model of brand choice behavior is provided. A model which provides a structure for revising this set of probabilities with the passage of time and the occurrence of significant events has been described. Successful applications of this model in studying sequences of purchases and the effects of special promotions were reported, and the possible future application of the brand choice model to the study of advertising effectiveness was outlined. A probabilistic model of consumer preference distributions was also discussed briefly.

Although probabilistic models of consumer behavior are still at an early stage of their development, considerable progress has already been made and the promise of future applications seems great. At present, the probabilistic approach provides a useful conceptual framework for evaluating consumer behavior and interpreting research results. In the future, this same approach can be expected to make a major contribution to the development of complex marketing models.

26. A REGIONAL SCIENCE APPROACH TO MARKET PROJECTIONS

Walter Isard and Gerald A. P. Carrothers

TECHNIQUES of regional analysis which may be expected to be useful in making projections of future markets for goods, services, labor, and other resources in the various regions of a nation or any other system of regions have developed rapidly in recent years. These techniques have been spelled out elsewhere in considerable detail.[1]

One of the purposes of this brief essay is to suggest the salient features of some of these techniques. Another, and more important, purpose is to outline a way in which the stronger elements of these techniques might be synthesized to yield more telling numerical forecasts of the size and composition of markets in the various regions of a nation such as the United States.

There are, of course, many ways in which these desirable features of the many techniques could be synthesized. The following paragraphs illustrate only one of the possibilities.[2] Chart 1 indicates certain of the basic techniques and steps involved in such an approach. The chart is basic to the discussion and should be referred to as the argument is developed.

Since projections of national output by industry are employed in this approach, the analysis may be said to begin with assumptions on birth rates, death rates, net migration, state of technology, consumer tastes and values. These assumptions, as well as others, underlie estimates of future national population, labor force, average productivity, and National Product. The estimates in turn lead to projections of national output by in-

---

[1] In particular, see W. Isard *et al., Methods of Regional Analysis: An Introduction to Regional Science* (New York: John Wiley & Sons, Inc., 1960); and the *Papers and Proceedings of the Regional Science Association,* Vol. 1 (1955) to 10 (1963). Also see Gerald A. P. Carrothers, "An Historical Review of the Gravity and Potential Concepts of Human Interaction," *Journal of the American Institute of Planners,* Vol. 22 (Spring, 1956), for the development of one "family" of such techniques.

[2] For other possibilities, see W. Isard *et al., op. cit.,* chaps. xii and xiii.

dustry through the use of national input-output and other techniques.[3] All these items are indicated at the extreme left of Chart 1.

The analysis essentially begins with the first of the three assumptions found in the *First Approximations* column of Chart 1. Each industry is assumed to grow in each region at the same rate as it grows in the nation. Projection of *Total Employment by Region* on the basis of this assumption is central to the industry composition method. Once total employment for each region is obtained, crude estimates for each region of population, income, and size of market can be made. These estimates again represent only first approximations and are required for the next step which involves basic location-cost analysis.

Three techniques are employed in the basic location-cost analysis: (1) comparative cost study, (2) industrial complex analysis, and (3) interregional linear programming. These three techniques are indicated in the circles in the center of Chart 1, immediately to the right of the *First Approximations* column. Research with these three techniques concentrates upon cost-sensitive industries. The noncost-sensitive, or "footloose," industries for which analysis may not be possible because of limited research funds can be handled by a simpler projection technique such as the industrial composition method.

Comparative Cost Study

The comparative cost approach typically proceeds for any given industry on the basis of (1) an established or anticipated pattern of markets and (2) a given geographic distribution of raw materials and other productive factors used in the industry.[4] Both existing and hypothetical production points for serving the market are considered in order to identify the production point that can produce and deliver output to the market at lowest cost. In the comparative cost approach, it is generally necessary to consider only those production and transport elements which give rise to significant interregional cost differences. Those production cost components and location factors which do not vary from region to region may be, for the most part, ignored at this point. Since many production costs do not exhibit systematic or significant regional variation, concentration on interregional differences leads to considerable savings in research time.

The comparative cost technique has already been successfully employed for the study of such industries as iron and steel, glass, aluminum, and other electro-processes.

---

[3] For further discussion of these points, see *ibid.*, chap. xii.

[4] See *ibid.*, p. 233. Further discussion and specific examples are contained in chap. vii.

CHART 1

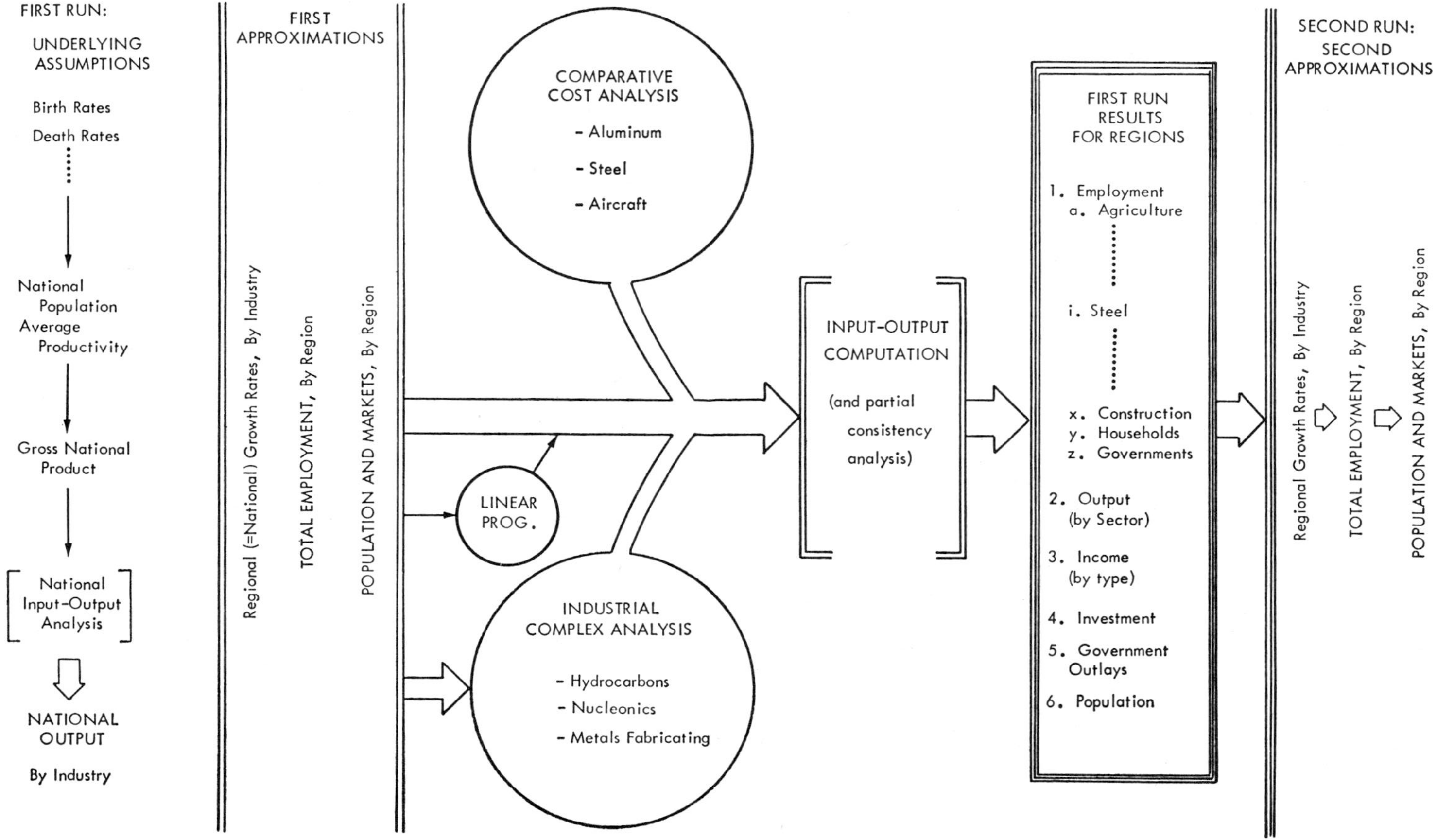

FIRST RUN:
UNDERLYING
ASSUMPTIONS

Birth Rates
Death Rates
. . . .
→ National
Population
Average
Productivity
→ Gross National
Product
→ [National
Input-Output
Analysis]
⇨ NATIONAL
OUTPUT

By Industry

FIRST
APPROXIMATIONS

Regional (=National) Growth Rates, By Industry

TOTAL EMPLOYMENT, By Region

POPULATION AND MARKETS, By Region

COMPARATIVE
COST ANALYSIS

- Aluminum
- Steel
- Aircraft

LINEAR
PROG.

INDUSTRIAL
COMPLEX ANALYSIS

- Hydrocarbons
- Nucleonics
- Metals Fabricating

INPUT-OUTPUT
COMPUTATION

(and partial
consistency
analysis)

FIRST RUN
RESULTS
FOR REGIONS

1. Employment
   a. Agriculture
   . . . .
   i. Steel
   . . . .
   x. Construction
   y. Households
   z. Governments
2. Output
   (by Sector)
3. Income
   (by type)
4. Investment
5. Government
   Outlays
6. Population

SECOND RUN:
SECOND
APPROXIMATIONS

Regional Growth Rates, By Industry

TOTAL EMPLOYMENT, By Region

POPULATION AND MARKETS, By Region

Industrial Complex Analysis

As shown in Chart 1, a second basic location-cost approach is the industrial complex technique. This approach recognizes that comparative cost analysis and other techniques which look at single activities or industries in isolation are not appropriate in certain situations. There are sets or subsystems of activities which, as a spatially connected group, are subject to important economies in production, marketing, and other interrelated operations. These economies may stem from the common use of a facility or pool of skilled labor, or from savings in transport and fuel cost, or from additional revenue resulting from the upgrading of each one's by-products, etc. Hence it becomes necessary to account for at least a major fraction of such spatial juxtaposition economies. The industrial complex technique is specifically designed to perform this task. It does so by setting down the input-output relations between the related activities and by linking the total magnitudes of input and outputs associated with any defined complex to markets by regions (as indicated in the *First Approximations* column) and to economies of scale and other pertinent economic functions. The industrial complex technique has already been employed in the analysis of the oil refining-petrochemical-synthetic materials complexes.

Interregional Linear Programming

A third approach which helps identify efficient spatial distribution of basic cost-sensitive industries is the interregional linear programming approach. The empirical aspects of this research technique have not been as fully developed on a multicommodity basis as the two other approaches previously discussed. However, it has considerable potential for projection purposes. Given the established markets for an industry, by region (*First Approximations* column of Chart 1), interregional linear programming reveals that spatial distribution of production which might be most efficient in terms of total production and delivery cost. The airline industry and coal mining are two examples of activities having location patterns which might be projected in this manner.

Input-Output Computation

The three location-cost techniques discussed above provide a first set of materials on the location patterns, by region, of the basic cost-sensitive industries in the United States economy. The next step is to form a basic set of activities for each region consolidating and synthesizing this material with information on the regional distribution of the footloose industries and other industries not previously investigated. The input-output computation is then applied to this basic set of activities for each region to make projections of output and employment in the remaining economic activities, which consist primarily of local service and market-oriented undertakings. Where regional coefficients are available or readily obtainable, they are utilized along with national coefficients. Either an inverse of a reduced input-output matrix, or a round-by-round computation is applicable, depending upon the circumstances.

The arrows in the center of Chart 1, stemming from the *Comparative Cost* circle, from the *Linear Programming* circle, from the *Industrial Complex* circle, and from the *First Approximations* column indicate the feeding of materials on the basic set of activities, by region, into the input-output computation (indicated by the large brackets). The input-output computation not only gives projections for activities already treated, but also helps introduce basic consistency checks upon both the materials fed into it and the results obtained.

Discrepancies in the Analysis

The input-output computation yields, for each region, first-run results on Employment (total and by sector), Output (total and by sector), Income (total and by type), Investment, Government Outlays, Population, Household Expenditures, Exports, Imports, etc. Many discrepancies and inconsistencies in these first-run results are to be expected. The discrepancies arise at several steps in the analysis, as discussed more fully elsewhere.[5]

After comparative cost, industrial complex, and interregional linear programming studies are completed, a pattern of output levels for the several basic cost-sensitive producing sectors of each region is obtained. This pattern, in all likelihood, will differ from the assumptions of output levels for the same sectors made at the beginning of the analysis. Also, the sum of payments to households generated by these sectors will, in all likelihood, differ from that total of household payments by these same sectors implicit in the first approximations of regional population and markets. Finally, the sum of payments to government generated by these sectors will, in all likelihood, differ from the comparable figures implicit in the regional government expenditures levels assumed in the first approximations.

Another set of discrepancies crops up after the input-output computations have been performed. As already discussed, this computation yields, for any given sector, the set of requirements for its outputs and services. The resulting total gross output may well differ from the level initially assumed in the first approximations.

For each region a third set of discrepancies arises because the total output level for any basic cost-sensitive sector (as required by the input-output computation) is not likely to be the same as the level derived by a comparative cost, industrial complex, or linear programming study.

As indicated elsewhere,[6] these discrepancies and internal inconsistencies

---

[5] *Ibid.*, pp. 593–96.
[6] *Ibid.*, pp. 596–601.

may be eliminated in part by reruns of the framework. The levels of total gross output by sector obtained from the first run of the framework may be used to provide the basic information on initial regional markets for a second run of the framework. Household income for each region may be estimated by summing payments over all sectors using the level of these sectors derived from the input-output computation and associated analysis. Similarly, the other final demand sectors for a region may be reestimated for second-run use on the basis of output levels and other results of the first-run computation. For the level of each sector (producing and final demand), input requirements consistent with the derived level may be calculated. When, for each region, the input requirements are summed over all its producing sectors and are added with the required deliveries to its final demand sectors, the set of initial markets to be employed in the second run is obtained.

Second-Run Analysis

Once the new sets of initial markets for all regions are obtained, the comparative cost, industrial complex, and linear programming studies are redone to establish a new (more consistent) level for each basic cost-sensitive sector in each region. Based on these new levels, the subsequent input-output steps are repeated. Most of the basic materials and analysis performed in the initial comparative cost and industrial complex studies will remain relevant for the second and all succeeding runs of the framework. Consequently, such runs can be performed with little additional expense.

Presumably, the results of the second run would contain fewer and smaller discrepancies and also differ less from the initial market assumptions than the results of the first run. Presumably, too, some of the remaining discrepancies can be ironed out by conducting a third run and even a fourth run of the framework. There is no rigorous proof either that the rerun procedures will lead to smaller and smaller discrepancies, or that the steps outlined will lead to the best possible results. However, no form of social science analysis embraces the entire set of forces at play, or even a large fraction of these forces. The sophisticated analyst brings judgment and experience to bear on his research. These qualities help him to reach results which are consistent with the interplay of those forces which he has tried to accommodate, yet which are not too greatly at variance with possible effects of other factors outside the scope of his analysis. This is especially true of the framework discussed in the preceding paragraphs. Comparative cost, industrial complex, linear programming, and input-output techniques can be judiciously used in combination with more standard techniques, such as industrial composition analysis, to yield increasingly reliable results only if judgment and experience are brought to bear upon the results obtained.

Conclusion

The above paragraphs have developed only one of many ways in which techniques of regional science may be synthesized for use in marketing analysis. This particular method is based primarily upon procedures of regional input-output analysis. Other approaches might center in large part around interregional linear programming, or potential and spatial interaction models, or some other specific analytic method. It is clear that no one way can be judged "best" in any general sense. The choice of those techniques to be combined must be oriented to the specific objectives of the given marketing research project, to the available personnel and financial resources, and even to the inclinations of the researcher himself. Whatever the surrounding circumstances, there are bound to be some techniques of regional science applicable to marketing research.

Index

INDEX

D

This book has been set on the Linotype in 10 point Janson, leaded 2 points and 9 point Janson, leaded 1 point. Chapter numbers and titles are in 18 point Garamont. The size of the type page is 27 by 47 picas.